Mark Antony Lower

A Compendious History of Sussex
Volume II

AF282000

Salzwasser

Mark Antony Lower

A Compendious History of Sussex
Volume II

1. Auflage | ISBN: 978-3-84604-738-5

Erscheinungsort: Frankfurt, Deutschland

Erscheinungsjahr: 2020

Salzwasser Verlag GmbH

Reprint of the original, first published in 1870.

Compendious History of Sussex.

A COMPENDIOUS

History of Sussex,

TOPOGRAPHICAL, ARCHÆOLOGICAL & ANECDOTICAL.

Containing an Index to the first Twenty Volumes of the
"Sussex Archæological Collections."

By Mark Antony Lower, M.A.,

FELLOW OF THE SOCIETIES OF ANTIQUARIES OF NORMANDY, AMERICA, NEWCASTLE-
UPON-TYNE, MEMBER OF THE ACADEMY OF SCIENCES OF CAEN, AND ONE
OF THE FOUNDERS OF THE SUSSEX ARCHÆOLOGICAL SOCIETY.

VOL. II.

LEWES:—GEO. P. BACON.
LONDON :—JOHN RUSSELL SMITH, 36, SOHO SQUARE.
BRIGHTON :—W. J. SMITH.

1870.

HISTORY OF SUSSEX.

JEVINGTON.

A parish in the Hundred of Willingdon; Rape of Pevensey; distant five miles south-west from Hailsham, and about the same distance from Eastbourne. Post-town, Eastbourne. Railway station, Polegate, distant about two miles. Union, Eastbourne. Population in 1811, 280; in 1861, 263. Benefice, a Rectory, valued at £400; Patron, the Duke of Devonshire; Incumbent, Rev. H. T. Grace, M.A., of Pembroke College, Cambridge. Date of earliest Parish Register, 1661. Acreage, 2,099.

This parish lies wholly on the South Downs, and the village, though in a valley, occupies a lofty site, the wells being almost 200 feet deep. Its aspect is highly romantic, and the Downs are seen in perfection. Harewick or Harrick Bottom (perhaps from the Anglo-Saxon *here* and *wic*—the stronghold of an army) has conspicuous marks of an ancient camp. The manor has been successively in the families of St. Clere, Parker, and Spencer, Earl of Wilmington. From the last-mentioned it has passed to the Duke of Devonshire. Jevington Rectory is also a manor. The manor-house has some marks of antiquity. Wannock was the seat of the family of Rochester, and at Filching there is a fine old timbered house. James Lambert, the well-known local artist, who so copiously illustrated the researches of Sir William Burrell, was born at Jevington in 1725. ("Sussex Worthies," p. 39.)

The church (St. Andrew) has a nave, with north aisle and chancel. A massive square tower at the west end has very ancient, and I think, pre-Norman, features. Affixed to the east wall of the tower, inside, is a very rude early carving, about two feet in height, representing our Saviour bruising the head of the serpent—probably Anglo-Saxon art. There are memorials for the names of Markwick, Eversfield, Rochester, Manningham, Collier, &c. One of the bells is inscribed to St. Katherine.

[S. A. C. Manor-rents, xiv, 263. Filching stream, xv, 157. Bells, xvi, 215.]

B

KEYMER.

Domesday, *Chemer;* vulgo, *Kymer;* a parish in the Hundred of Buttinghill; Rape of Lewes; distant ten miles north from Brighton. Post-
town, Hurst-Pierpoint. It has two stations of the Brighton and South
Coast railway, viz., Hassock's Gate and Burgess Hill. Union, Cuckfield. Population in 1811, 536; at present, upwards of 2,000. Benefice, a Perpetual Curacy annexed to the rectory of Clayton; Patron,
Brasenose College; Incumbent, the Ven. James Garbett, M.A.,
Archdeacon of Chichester. Date of earliest Parish Register, 1601;
Acreage, 3,538.

This formerly obscure little village has risen, in consequence of railway communication between London and Brighton,
to be a place of rising population and importance. The principal points are St. John's Common and Burgess-hill, formerly
by-words, but now the favourite retreats of the prosperous
traders of Brighton, who have handsome villa residences here.
The parish is long and narrow, and commands, from various
points, picturesque views of the South Down range of hills,
near whose foot it stands, and over the adjacent Wealden district.
At the date of Domesday, William de Wateville held Chemer.
The powerful and ubiquitous Azor had held it of the Confessor.
It contained fourteen hides, and the arable was twenty-five
plough lands. There were 36 villeins and eleven bondmen, a
church, three ministri, forty acres of meadow, two mills, and
seven houses in Lewes. Before the Conquest the manor was
estimated at £14, but at the time of the Survey at £12. It
passed like Clayton, from the De Warennes to the Fitz-Alans.
On the attainder of Richard, Earl of Arundel, in 1397, it was
forfeited to the Crown, but was restored to his family on the
accession of Henry VI. After many changes of proprietorship
of no historical interest, it passed to the family of Cook, and
was successively purchased by the Chatfields and Bayntuns. The
manor extends into the somewhat remote parishes of Balcombe,
Bolney, Worth, and Cuckfield. The manor courts were held
at Brookland, an old farm-house on Valebridge or Walbridge
Common. One of the Domesday mills which stood near the
source of the stream issuing from the chalk-hill, no longer
exists. Valebridge appears to represent the other mill, and
there is a large pond, formerly perhaps connected with iron-
works. About half a century ago the pond bay gave way, and
rushed through the mill-house, which stood at a lower level,
carrying everything before it, including a bed upon which a
woman was lying. Happily this singular voyage was impeded
by some great branches of trees, which stopped the vessel, and
the passenger escaped without detriment!

The manor of Ockley belonged, *temp.* Henry III., to Nicholas de Hogan, by the service of half a knight's fee and three barbed arrows, payable to the barony of Lewes. In the early part of the seventeenth century it was the property of George Luxford, Esq., whose descendants possessed it for several generations. Ultimately it passed to the ancient Sussex family of Wood, and is now the property of James Wood, Esq. The estate called Oldland was purchased in 34th Henry VIII., of the Michelbornes, by John Turner, whose descendants were connected, through many generations, with this parish and Ditchling, and are now somewhat widely dispersed through the county.

The church (the dedication of which I cannot ascertain) is thus described by Mr. Hussey (1852). It consists of " chancel, nave, south porch, and west tower. The chancel is apsidal, not merely rounded at the extremity, but the curve commences from the junction of the nave. The chancel arch is round, the piers being square blocks of masonry, with abaci at the spring of the arch. One small Norman window is visible, though closed ; the others are Decorated insertions. The tower, which, with the rest of the building, has been greatly patched and plastered, is in two stages, the lower Norman," and the upper, apparently of later date, yet early. The low shingled spire is a curious piece of work, as if one had been capped over by another. I have seen such instances in Normandy, but never elsewhere in England. So much for the building in 1852; but since that time nearly the whole edifice has been re-constructed, after the modern taste, with several additions and much ornamentation, concerning which one may say, "De gustibus," &c. However, it is a handsome little edifice, and reflects credit on the architect, Mr. E. E. Scott. There are inscriptions to the memory of the families of Luxford and Plumer. A new district church (St. John) was erected for the accommodation of the parishes of Clayton and Keymer, in 1863. The benefice is in the patronage of the rector, the Incumbent being the Rev. George Kirk Weston, M.A. From the name of St. John's Common in this parish, it is presumed that a chapel with that dedication formerly existed there. Gault prevails in this parish, and excellent bricks and pottery are made; and there is a large annual fair for sheep, &c., which is known in the vernacular as " St. Joneses fair."

[S. A. C. Domesday mills, v, 271. Encaustic tiles, xii, 10. xvi, 126. xviii, 189. Chapel of St. John, xiii, 46. Family of Turner of Oldland, xiii, 251. xvii, 111, 248. Michelborne family, xiii, 251. Church, xvi, 134. Bells, xvi, 215. St. John's Common, xvi, 251. River Adur, xvi, 251. Mural paintings, xvii, 249. Flint Celt, xviii, 64. Ockley manor, xx, 27. Knights Hospitallers, xx, 27.]

KINGSTON-JUXTA-LEWES.

A parish in the Hundred of Swanborough; Rape of Lewes; distant two miles south-west of Lewes, its Post-town and Railway station. Union, Newhaven. Population, in 1811, 149; in 1861, 137. Benefice, united with Iford. Date of earliest Parish Register, 1654. Acreage, 1,653. *Chief Landowner*, the Rev. John Goring, of Wiston.

It lies chiefly on the South Downs, from the highest point of which, in this range, is a magnificent view over the north-east portion of the county. Kingston, though traditionally deriving its name from the Saxon Kings, is not mentioned in Domesday. The church is named in a charter of Bishop Seffrid, about the year 1200; and in 1397 Richard II. granted the manor to Thomas, Duke of Norfolk, and it was afterwards held by the Priory of Lewes until the Dissolution. After the attainder of Thomas, Lord Cromwell, it was held by the Crown until about 28th Elizabeth, when it was in the hands of Sir Philip Sydney, who left it to his daughter, Elizabeth, Countess of Rutland. In the 17th century it belonged to the Vinalls, and at a later period to Robert Maitland, Esq., from whom it passed by sale to the Gorings of Wiston. The manor-house is ancient, apparently of the Early English period; but it has been much mutilated within the last few years.* The church, which belongs to the early part of the 14th century, and which was much injured by lightning in 1865, consists of a nave, chancel, and a very small square tower, with a tiled roof. It has three bells, two of which are ancient, and inscribed respectively to St. Mary and St. Anne. It contains memorials of the family of Vinall, and in the church-yard are others for those of Zouch,† Ade, Glover, Rogers, &c. In a lane leading from the village to Ashcombe there is a sand-pit, a habitat of the sand-martin, rare in this district; and near it is a kind of tumulus, called "Nan Kemp's grave." There is a tradition that this "Nan," whoever she was, murdered her infant, committed suicide, and was buried in this "crossways."

[S. A. C. Drinker acre, ix, 305. Goblin charcoal-spinner, xiii, 226. Cockshut stream, xv, 163. Alchorne of, xvi, 49. Bells, xvi, 215. Cade's insurrection, xviii, 29. Smythwick, xviii, 29. Vinall family, xviii, 39.]

KINGSTON (near Worthing).

A small parish, or rather fragment of one, containing 582 acres of land, and from 40 to 50 inhabitants. Mr. Hussey

* The present occupant of the house is my friend Mr. Joseph Cooper, F.S.A., who well appreciates and preserves the relics of this ancient abode.
† The last of this family, known as "Madam Zouch," was burnt to death in the hall of Kingston manor-house in the year 1730.

("Churches," p. 246) has given so excellent an account of this place, that I shall content myself with an abstract of his article :—" Great part of this parish, the church included, appears to have been absorbed by the sea. It is now, though nominally a rectory, annexed to the vicarage and parish of Ferring. The old register still exists, reaching from A.D. 1570 to 1660, after which date there is no further entry, whence we may conjecture that the church ceased to be used in 1661. The register is styled that of the *chapel* of Kingston. In the remaining portion of this parish near the sea, the Vicar of Ferring possesses about 1½ acre of glebe, which has been suggested as the possible site of the destroyed church ; but no foundations or vestiges of masonry are visible in the field. A map of the early part of the 17th century shows ' Kingston Chapel,' and a similar entry occurs in Hondius' map of 1610, and in Kip's and Camden's. A tradition of the country points out certain rocks in the sea, below high-water mark, as the site of the church. It is more probable that it stood in the neighbourhood of the field above-mentioned, where, on each side of the road, it is quite evident there were formerly several houses." Thus, as at Cudlow, Middleton, Selsey, and many other parishes, the sea, restrained within no fixed limits, has gradually eaten away our southern coast—

" And fishes swim where birds were wont to sing."

KINGSTON BOWSEY.

Domesday, *Chingestun ;* vulgo, *Kingston-by-Sea ;* a parish in the Half-Hundred of Fishersgate ; Rape of Bramber ; distant one mile east from Shoreham, which is its Post-town. It has a Railway station on the South Coast line. Union, Steyning. Population in 1811, 60 ; in 1861, 93. Benefice, a Rectory, valued at £280. Patron, Lord Leconfield ; Incumbent, Rev. W. Onions Purton, M.A. Date of earliest Parish Register, 1591. Acreage, 799. *Chief Landowner,* William Pennington Gorringe, Esq., who possesses nearly the whole parish, and resides at Kingston House.

The river Adur, after many changes of outlet, now debouches at Kingston Harbour, and this once unimportant parish has a considerable amount of trade in consequence of its being the station of the London, Brighton, and South Coast Railway for merchandise landed at the port of Shoreham. Bonding warehouses, ponds, quays, corn warehouses, malthouses, shipbuilding yards, coke-ovens, &c., have been constructed, and have rendered this small parish of more note than when it boasted of Saxon Kings as its owners. According to Domesday, it had been held by Azor of King Harold. Under the new dynasty, Ralph held the principal part of W. de Braose. A church then existed. From the 12th to the 14th century the Norman family of De Buci, or Bowsey, were lords, and gave their name as a suffix, which has been ignorantly corrupted to "by sea." Later possessors were Fyfhide and Sondes. From *temp.* Henry VII. to the middle of the 17th century it belonged to the Lewknors, then to Fagge and Norton, which last sold it in 1798 to William Gorringe, Esq. The manor-house has traces of *temp.* Henry VII. and VIII., and is supposed to have been originally much larger.

The church (St. Julian) has Norman and Early English features, with Decorated and Perpendicular insertions. In the north wall of the chancel is a recessed tomb of about 1500— probably of a Lewknor, whose arms occur in an adjoining window, and also on the rood-screen. The tower, which is vaulted, stands between the nave and the chancel, and a dilapidated north aisle was removed in the last century. There are many memorials for the family of Blaker, and for the names of Dawson, Mills, Monke, and Norton. The building is admirably kept, and forms a good study for the artist.

[S. A. C. William, parson of the church of St. Julian of Kyngeston, ix, 235. Smugglers, x, 81. Manor, and "Bullockers," xiii, 48. Bell, xvi, 215. Buci family, and river Adur, xvi, 255. Lewknor, xvii, 97. Civil marriages at Glynde, xix, 202.]

KIRDFORD.

Vulgo, *Kard-foord*, and *Kay-foord;* a parish in the Hundred of Rotherbridge; Rape of Arundel; distant five miles north-east of Petworth, its Post-town and Union. Railway station, Billingshurst, distant about six miles. Population in 1811, 1,452; in 1861, 1,784. Benefice, a Vicarage, valued at £500; Patron, Lord Leconfield; Incumbent, Rev. John Francis Cole, B.A., of Worcester College, Oxford. Date of earliest Parish Register, 1569. Acreage, more than 15,000. *Chief Landowners*, the Earl of Winterton, Lord Leconfield, representatives of the late Lady Newburgh, John Napper, Esq., William Peachey, Esq., Richard Hasler, Esq. *Seats*, Shillinglee Park, Earl of Winterton; Ifold, J. Napper, Esq.; Ebernowe, William Peachey, Esq.; Barkfold, Captain Barwell, &c.

This, as will be seen by the figures above, is a very large parish. It is also historically interesting and important. In 519 Cerdic, founder of the West-Saxon kingdom, fought a great battle with the Britons, at a place called in the Saxon Chronicle Cerdices-ford. Mr. Hussey (p. 247) thinks this conflict occurred here—*sed dubito*, as Charford in Hampshire seems to have a superior claim. The soil is generally a stiff clay, and there is much rough, heathy land, with coppice and timber. Sussex marble, a geological deposit of fresh water shells, imbedded in petrified mud, and called Petworth marble, Laughton marble, &c., is quarried in its best condition in this parish. It appears in many churches and mansions in Sussex, and is the finest stone, when properly polished, that the county can produce. The Archbishop's chair at Canterbury is composed of it. Some of the slabs of this beautiful material dug up in this parish have been three feet thick and seven feet long.

Kirdford does not occur in Domesday, *eo nomine;* but in the reign of Henry I., one of the sons of Roger de Montgomeri, Earl of Arundel and Chichester, endowed the abbey of Seez in Normandy with the church of *Kuerdford.*

The principal manor in the parish is Schullinglegh, or SHIL-LINGLEE, which was attached to the Honour of Arundel, and the Earls had a great park here. When Henry VIII. made forced exchanges with his subjects about 1542, the Crown-parker, Richard Bowyer, got possession, and Shillinglee was annexed to the Honour of Petworth; but it was afterwards re-annexed to the Arundel estate. In 1616, Thomas, Earl of Arundel, sold the manor to Gerard Gore, Alderman of London, for £4,587. His heiress, Sarah, married Sir Edward Turnour, Chief-baron of the Exchequer, of an ancient Suffolk family, dating from *temp.* Henry IV. The second son of this marriage established himself at Shillinglee, and ultimately the estate was transmitted through a female line to Edward Turnour Garth, Esq. In 1581 the park of Shillinglee is described as being six miles in compass within the pale, and a right is recognized that the farmer of the parsonage should have, in a "mast year" (*i.e.*, when acorns were plentiful), the right of feeding 30 hogs, or more, for seven weeks. The house and park of Shillinglee are situated in the northern part of the parish. The mansion was built in the early part of the 18th century, and in 1778 the first Earl of Winterton added a south front, with an elegant vestibule and several excellent rooms. The present Earl of Winterton, fourth in descent from the first peer, possesses a large portion of the great tithes. The house is surrounded by very picturesque forest scenery, and there is a lake of 70 acres. Including Ash Park, King's Park, &c., the ring fence comprises more than six thousand acres. Another considerable estate in Kirdford is PLEISTOW, or PLAY-STOW, parcel of the manor of Slyndon, once belonging to the see of Canterbury, and it is said that the Archbishops occasionally retired hither, and had a private oratory. (Dallaway.) This estate has descended in the same line as Slyndon. A large farm and estate at Playstow belonged for several generations to the families of Steere and Lee.

HIBERNOW, IBERNHOO, or EBERNOWE, a very ancient manor, was attached to the Honour of Arundel. Henry VIII., in one of his forced exchanges—that made with William, Earl of Arundel—seized this manor. The Crown retained it till 1592. It afterwards passed to John Brown, and from him to John Smyth, citizen of London. Another line of descent is given by other authorities, who state that it was appendant to the manor of Halnaker; that it was confirmed in 1542 to Thomas, Lord la Warr; in 1554 to Henry, Earl of Arundel; and in 1593 to Anthony, Viscount Montague. Both accounts agree that it was purchased in 1703 by William Peachey, Esq., and descended to his family. The parish contains the three manors of Pailingham, Bedeham, and Barkfold. In the early part of the present century, Edward Napper, Esq., of Ifold, built a commodious mansion. The Benefice was given to the Abbey of Seez, in Normandy. At the Dissolution, it passed to Henry, Earl of Arundel, and at a later date from Lord John Lumley to Sir Peter Bettesworth. From that family it descended to Sir Richard Worsley, Bart.

The church, dedicated to St. Mary, is spacious, with a lofty tower at the west end. There are monumental inscriptions to the families of Peachey, Winterton, &c. A few years since, during repairs, several mural paintings were brought to light. At the east end was the Crucifixion; and on other walls, St. Nicholas restoring to life two children who had been salted down in a tub; St. Catherine on her wheel; a king exhorted to good by a counsellor on one side, and to evil by a demon on the other; and (apparently) the Adoration of the Magi. These have mostly been plastered over, and the present incumbent had careful drawings of them. The chapel at PLAISTOW is dependent on Kirdford church. The old church, being in a state of dilapidation, was replaced by a new and larger one in 1856, dedicated to the Holy Trinity.

It appears that the manufacture of glass was carried on here in 1581, when "David, son of Mr. Barry, glassmaker, stranger, was baptized." The fact of glassmaking ever having been carried on in this county has been doubted. Charnock's "Breviary of Philosophy" has the following lines on the subject :—

> "As for glassmakers they be scant in this land,
> Yet one there is as I do understand,
> And in Sussex now is his habitation,
> At Chedingfold he works of his occupation."

Chiddingfold is within a short distance of Kirdford, although just within the county of Surrey.

[S. A. C. Iron-works, ii, 212. Church of, xii, 93. xix, 103. Osbornes of, xii, 93 Floats of, xii, 94. Pleistow chapel, xii, 94. Shillinglee, xiii, 313. xvi, 256. Queen Elizabeth at, xiii, 313. Pleistow in, xiii, 313.

Arundel, Earl of, residing here, xiv, 8. Bonvilles lands in, xv, 59. Bells of, xvi, 215. Pleistow bell, xvi, 220. Arun, river at, xvi, 256. Serf woman stolen by Poachers, xvii, 120. Kempes had lands, &c., in, xix, 119.]

LAMBERHURST.

(Anglo-Saxon *lambru* (lambs) and *hyrst*—a woody place, but suitable for the pasturage of lambs ?) The church and great part of the village street are in Kent, in the Lathe of Aylesford. The Sussex portion is in the Hundred of Loxfield-Camden. This lies at the north-east corner of Pevensey rape. The Tyse, a branch of the Medway, runs through the parish. The population does not exceed 1,700, and the area is, Kent, 3,590 ; Sussex, 1,700 acres. The principal residence is Court Lodge, the property of the Morland family.

The manor of Lamberhurst was held in ancient times by the Norman family of Crevecœur, and at later dates the names of Lenham, Chidcroft, and Kenith are connected with it. Nicholas de Kenith gave it to Robertsbridge Abbey. Henry VIII. granted it to Sir Henry Sydney. In 1607 it passed to the family of Porter, and after several changes it was purchased *temp.* George I. by William Morland, Esq. Hodleigh, another manor, belonged to the canons of Lingfield in Surrey, and at the Dissolution it was granted to the Cardens, and passed from them to the Filmers.

SCOTNEY CASTLE, in this parish, gave name to the family of De Scotney. The manor lies chiefly in the Sussex portion. The house is castellated, and surrounded by a moat; but of the original building few traces remain. The most conspicuous of the ancient proprietors was Walter de Scotney, who was tried and hanged at Winchester in 1259 for administering poison to Richard, Earl of Gloucester, and his brother William, from which the former died. After the extinction of this family, it passed, *temp.* Edward III., to the Ashburnhams, and by them was sold to Henry Chicheley, Archbishop of Canterbury, whose niece conveyed it by marriage to John Darrell, of Cale Hill, in Kent, Esq. In 1774 John Darrell, Esq., sold it to Mr. John Richards, of Robertsbridge, of whom it was purchased by Edward Hussey, Esq., grandfather of Edward Hussey, Esq., the present owner. BAYHAM ABBEY is partly in this parish. (See that article.)

Lamberhurst formerly possessed the largest iron-manufactory in Sussex. Gloucester Furnace, partly in this parish and partly in Wadhurst, was the greatest establishment in the south of England. Large cannons were cast here, and some, it is said, were smuggled to France, for the use of privateers acting against

England. Here is said to have been wrought the great balustrade round St. Paul's, which cost more than £11,000, though Mayfield disputes this. There seem to have been chapels in this parish called respectively Passeley and La Leake. The former may have been in Ticehurst.

[S. A. C. Iron-works, ii, 212. iii, 241. Scotneys of, viii, 153. xiii, 171. xvi, 272. Chapels, xiii, 47. Stannyndens of, xiii, 92. Grant of lands by Elizabeth, xiii, 110. An Ashburnham at Agincourt, xv, 125. River Tyse or Tees,xvi, 272. "Little Sussex" and Beaul-bourne, xvi, 272. London road to Rye, xix, 166.]

LANCING.

Domesday, *Lancings;* a parish in the Hundred of Brightford ; Rape of Bramber; distant two miles north-east from Worthing ; Post-town, Shoreham. It has a Railway station. Population in 1811, 519 ; in 1861, 901. Benefice, a Vicarage, valued at £151 ; Patron, Bishop of London ; Incumbent, Rev. Frederick Fisher Watson, M.A., of Caius College, Cambridge. Date of earliest Parish Register, 1580. Acreage, 2,524. *Chief Landowner*, Lieut.-Colonel Carr Lloyd, Manor-house.

Before the Conquest Lewin held Lancings of the Confessor; subsequently Robert held it of William de Braose, Lord of Bramber. Lewin was assessed at 16 hides and a roodland. Robert, his Norman successor, had 12 hides and 1½ rood. The arable was five plough-lands. There were in the demesne 13 villeins and 7 bondmen. There was a mill, and also 7 salt-pans. Two Knights possessed, besides, 2½ hides and 11 salt-pans. Two Ralphs are mentioned among the tenants, one of whom had five additional salt-pans. This proves that the manufacture of salt in this seaboard parish was formerly of considerable extent. The ante-Domesday rental was £9, and subsequently £7. The details of the survey of *Lancings* are particularly minute. About the end of the 13th century, Ranulf de Broc, and John de Gaddesden, held each two knights' fees in Lancing and the neighbourhood. The manors of South Lancing, North Lancing, Monks, and Lyons, originally very small, have long been united in the proprietorship of one lord. The manors of South Lancing and Lyons belonged to the great estate of Robert le Sauvage, and descended as Broadwater. Those of North Lancing, with Monks, after having been long in the possession of the families of Avenel and De Brok, came, perhaps by marriage, into that of Poynings. *Temp.* Henry VII. it was sold to Sir Reginald Bray, who transferred it to George, Lord Abergavenny. Subsequently it was in the Goring family, and so descended to the Biddulphs, as Burton. These formerly distinct, but now united manors, extend, according to Cartwright, from West sea-mills gate, in Broadwater, to a place where the Adur (before the new cut was made about 1760) debouched into the sea, and thence ascend the old course of the river in the middle of the stream beyond the bridge. There has long been a question of right of *foreshore* between the lords of Lancing and their eastern neighbour. If the river is to be taken as the limit of the two lordships, the boundary must have changed many times, as there has been a constant tendency of the Adur, as of nearly all our Sussex rivers, towards the east, caused by the dashing of the Atlantic wave, driven by the south-west winds, up the English Channel. Even now, as I write, the question of the boundary of Lancing manor is *sub lite*. The Adur first and naturally debouched at Shoreham, but at subsequent periods, by the force of Caurus, it was driven eastward to different points almost as far as Brighton, and has frequently found its outlet far from the present one of Kingston harbour, which is so fortified by human agency that it seems probable that it will remain there. In the meantime, who has right to the *foreshore* to the south of this bend of the Adur? Let lawyers decide by the law of *wrecca maris*.* In 1684, Sir William Goring embanked 600 acres of land in this parish, by which he made a valuable addition to his land called the "Salts-farm." The manors of North and South Lancing were sold, in 1827, by John Biddulph, Esq., to James Martin Lloyd, Esq., and they now belong to Colonel George Carr Lloyd. There are two other manors of small extent in the parish called Lancing and Grants; the latter named after the family of Le Graunt, who possessed it in 1309. It afterwards (1567) passed to the Boords. It ultimately became the property of the Lloyds. There is, besides, a small manor on the north side of the parish, called How in Domesday, and now How Court. At the date of Domesday William Fitz-Barnard held it of William de Warenne. It had been previously held by Earl Godwin at six hides. Six salt-pans are mentioned, showing that the manor extended either to the sea or the Adur, then, perhaps, an estuary. Before the Conquest it was valued at £4; afterwards at £6. This manor descended, by consanguinity or purchase, through the families of De Combes, Halsham, Shirley, and Caryll, to that of Lloyd. The manor, according to Cartwright, pays tithe of corn and hay of about 294 acres to the rector of West Grinstead, and of about 45 to the vicar of Henfield.

Mr Hussey thinks "it may be admitted a probable conjecture that this parish derives its name from *Wlencing*, one of the sons of Ælla, the founder of the South Saxon kingdom." Considerable

---

* This suit has just been decided against the lord of Lancing.

foundations of buildings, a bath, coins, interments, &c., were discovered on Lancing Down in 1828, but were destroyed by an ignorant proprietor. The coins range from Claudius to Gallienus, showing a long possession of the spot by the Romans. Full particulars of the discovery will be found in the scarce and extremely valuable " Collectanea Antiqua " of Mr. Charles Roach Smith, F.S.A., Vol. i, 92.

The great tithes, with the exceptions just mentioned, were given by Sir Michael de Poynings to the Friary of Motinden, in the parish of Headcorn in Kent. It is curious to note that the lands at this period (the time of Edward III.) were valued at threepence per acre. The priest, however, received £23 6s. 8d. per annum. At the dissolution of the monasteries it was exchanged for certain lands in the see of Lincoln. Afterwards it passed, by lease, through the family of Barttelot to that of Lloyd. Mention is made in the Nonæ rolls (1341) of lands and a watermill destroyed by the sea.

The church (St. James) is composed of tower, chancel, nave, and north and south aisles. The porch on the south side, and the west door, are described by Cartwright as Early Norman. There are additions and insertions of much later styles. The tower stands between the nave and chancel, and seems to have been much loftier than at present. It appears that in 1618 the upper part of the tower was taken down, and the present pyramidal cap added. In the chancel there is " an arch of the age of Edward III., under which was no doubt anciently an effigy." (Cartwright.) The following names are commemorated on monumental stones in this church ; Martin, Temple, Lloyd, Bartlett, Pyxe, Bury, Jones, Winton, Tanner, Hersee, Olliver, Nash, &c. In the parish register is the following curious entry :—" John Wolven, commonly called the honest man, buried June 13, 1691." In 1685 many persons died of an infectious distemper. It is singular that, from 1669 to 1673,the funerals at New Shoreham are registered here.

In this parish, on a commanding height, stands an extensive building, called St. Nicholas' College, founded for the purpose of educating boys of the middle classes in what are called "high church" principles. The edifice is handsome and commodious, and was erected chiefly through the exertions of the Rev. N. Woodard, D.C.L., who is styled provost, not only of this school, but of similar establishments at Hurst-Pierpoint, Shoreham, Ardingly, and elsewhere. The Rev. R. E. Sanderson, M.A., assisted by several other clergymen, has charge of this important school.

[S. A. C. Domesday watermill, v, 271. Church, xii, 107. De Broc, xv, 15. Rents to Boxgrove, v. 119. Bells, xvi, 215. How Court, xix, 68. Shirleys of, xix, 68.]

LANGNEY, vulgo LANGLEY.

Langney Point is an advanced tongue of shingle, situated about three miles south-west of Pevensey, at the extremity of Pevensey Bay. The shingle, driven hither by heavy south-west tides, is at one point upwards of a mile across, and is patched here and there with furze. Near it is a large lagoon called Crumble Pond. Langney is locally in the parish of Westham. It is now a farm, and was anciently a grange belonging to the Priory of Lewes. The lands were granted, or confirmed, by divers benefactors, William Malfield, his wife and two sons, Simon de Echingham, Peter of Savoy, and King Henry III. The De Echinghams, however, reserved certain rights over the monks of Lewes, such as meat, drink, and lodgment for themselves, their horses, palfreys, grooms, and hunting-dogs during three days per annum, and the instruction of their servitor in the duties of a cook in the monks' kitchen. This claim was found burdensome by the brethren, and so in 1308, Sir William de Echingham accepted £100 by way of commutation. It is curious to note that a powerful Baron, for such he was, should seek the assistance of "abstemious monks " in his *cuisine*. The house at Langney, though much modernized, retains several vestiges of its former state, including a beautiful chapel, which was nearly entire when I visited the spot some years since.

LAUGHTON.

Domesday, *Lestone;* a parish in the Hundred of Shiplake; Rape of Pevensey; distant six miles north-east from Lewes, its Railway station; Post-town, Hawkhurst; Union, Hailsham. Population in 1811, 612; in 1861, 742. Benefice, a Vicarage, valued at £256. Patron, the Earl of Chichester; Incumbent, Rev. Charles Dennis Charlton, M.A., of St. John's College, Cambridge. Date of earliest Parish Register, 1650. Acreage, 5,075. *Chief Landowner*, the Earl of Chichester, who 'possesses nearly the whole of the parish. *Seat*, Laughton Lodge, Sir James Duke, Bart., formerly Lord Mayor of London.

This is a parish of diversified soil and level, and of almost every variety of character, from a rich alluvial valley to woodlands and uplands of comparatively small value. The freshwater shelly concretion, called Sussex marble, is found in the south part of the parish, and is locally known as Laughton marble. The tributary of the Ouse, named the Ritch, flows through Laughton Level. The manor of Laughton, one of the most extensive in this part of Sussex, includes the greater part of the hundred of Shiplake, and has sub-infeudations both within and beyond that boundary. In Saxon times Earl Godwin held it, and after the Conquest it passed with the rape to the Earl of Moreton. There were 16 salt-pans on the estuary of the Ritch. During the Edwardian period the manor belonged successively to the great families of Badlesmere, Spenser, and De Vere. The next lords were the Pelhams, who have held it in continuity for the last five centuries, and the Earl of Chichester still has from it his second title, Baron Pelham of Laughton.

Laughton Place was the seat of the chivalrous Sir John Pelham, who, in 1356, at the battle of Poictiers, took prisoner John, King of France, and so won the far-famed Pelham badge of the *Buckle*, which is still to be seen on many a church tower in East Sussex. The house, which is moated, was rebuilt in 1534 by Sir William Pelham, and still presents some features of the fortalice of that date. It is built of brick, and contains some beautifully moulded ornaments, among which the Buckle is conspicuous. In the reign of Elizabeth the Pelhams removed their chief residence from this house to Halland, where they built a splendid mansion on the site of the seat of the Halle family. (See Ore.) This mansion was on the borders of Laughton and East Hothly, the boundary line of the parishes passing through the site. (See East Hothly.)

The church is composed of chancel, nave, and west tower, in styles varying from Early English to Decorated. The chancel, which serves as a mausoleum for the Pelham family, was rebuilt by the Duke of Newcastle in the last century. The vaults beneath contain the mortal remains of a long line of that illustrious race. In the spandrels of the doorway of the tower are the arms of Pelham and Colbrand, the latter family having formerly been owners of the estate called Colbrand's in this parish. There are inscriptions for the names of Pelham, Benge, Wenham, Courthope, &c.

Chamber's Court, in this parish, was the original seat of the ancient family of De la Chambre, afterwards of Litlington, Rodmell, Denton, East Bourne, and Chyngton. It is now a small farmhouse only.

[S. A. C. King Edward I. visits, i, 138. Laughton Place, vii, 64. xv, 163. xvi, 292. xvii, 249. Pelham family, iv, 125. x, 211. xiv, 234. xvi, 292, 296. xvii, 249. Duke of Newcastle, xi, 219. Shoosmith family, xii, 255. Land given by Queen Elizabeth, xiii, 48. Family of De la Chambre, xiii, 258. xiv, 213. Salt-pans, xiv, 211. Broomham, xiv, 213. Peckham, xiv, 221, 227. Ritch river, xv, 163. Bells, xvi, 215. Oratory at Laughton, xvii, 249. Jack Cade's adherents, xviii, 25. Park of, xix, 173.]

EAST LAVANT.

A Parish in the Hundred of Aldwick, Rape of Chichester; distant 2¼ miles north-west from Chichester, its Post-town and Railway station.

Union, West Hampnett. Population in 1811, 348; in 1861, with West Lavant, 421. Benefice, a Rectory, valued at £410; Patron, Lord Willoughby de Broke; Incumbent, Rev. Henry Legge, M.A., of Christ Church, Oxford. Date of earliest Parish Register, 1653. Acreage, 2,884. *Chief Landowner*, the Duke of Richmond.

Like the other two villages bearing this name, it derives its designation from the little river Lavant, which finds its outlet at Chichester Harbour. WEST LAVANT, a tything belonging to this parish, is separated from it by Mid Lavant, which intervenes. The Domesday manor of Loventune, or Levitone, by which this place is supposed to be meant, was held, in the time of the Confessor, by Godwin, a priest, and afterwards by Osborne, Bishop of Exeter. It was assessed at six hides, and was appropriated to the church of Bosham. It was afterwards transferred to the see of Canterbury, and subsequently came to the Crown. In 1560 Queen Elizabeth granted it to Sir Richard Baker, and in 1775 it was sold to Charles, third Duke of Richmond.

The church (St. Mary) has Norman features, and consists of an ancient nave, with a chancel of much later date. The floor, says Horsfield, has slabs of Sussex marble, ornamented with crosses, one of which bears, in Lombardic characters, the legend " Priez qui passez par ici, pur l'alme Luci de Mildebi." " All you that pass by, pray for the soul of Lucy de Mildebi." There are other inscriptions to the names of Cawse, Stockton, Henshaw, Heberden, and Compton.

[S. A. C. (Including Mid-Lavant.) May of Rawmere, v, 47. xix, 95. Roman road, x, 169. Church, xii, 74. xix, 169. Mid-Lavant Church, xii, 75. xix, 169. Bells, xvi, 216. River Lavant, xvi, 261. Henshawe, Bishop of Peterborough, xix, 92, Rawmere, v, 47. xix, 95, 167. London Road to Chichester, xix, 167. Oxford Road, xix, 169. Lavant, West, and Crowshall House of the Millers, Barts., xix, 169.]

MID-LAVANT.

A parish in the Hundred of Westbourne; Rape of Chichester; distant two miles north-west from Chichester, its Post-town and Railway station. Union, West Hampnett. Population in 1811, 215; in 1861, 257. Benefice, a Perpetual Curacy, valued at £50; Patron, the Duke of Richmond; Incumbent, Rev. Walter Hook, B.A. Date of earliest Parish Register, 1567. Acreage, 350. *Chief Landowner*, the Duke of Richmond.

The little river Lavant, which flows into Chichester Harbour, gives name to three villages on its banks, called respectively East, Mid, and West Lavant. In Domesday *Loventune* is mentioned, but to which, or whether to all the three places the record refers is uncertain. It is placed in the hundred of Sille-tone (Singleton). Before the Conquest it belonged to Earl God-win; afterwards Ivo held it of Roger, Earl of Montgomeri. It consisted of nine hides. In 1581 Richard May of Rawmere held the manor of Mid-Lavant, and it continued in his family almost two centuries. Thomas May Knight, Esq., sold it to Charles, third Duke of Richmond. The large mansion com-menced by Richard May towards the end of the reign of Eliza-beth, and finished by his son, *temp.* James I., was taken down by the Duke of Richmond many years since.

The church (St. Nicholas) was originally very small. The only ancient windows remaining are two lancets in the chancel, and a very small round-headed one in the nave. (Hussey.) Some mural paintings were discovered here about the year 1849. The modern church, consisting of nave and chancel, was erected by the family of May in the former part of the eighteenth century. There is a marble effigy of life size, of Dame Mary May, who died in 1681.

[S. A. C. See under East Lavant.]

LEOMINSTER.   (See Lyminster.)

LEWES.

Domesday, *Lewes;* a borough and market-town, and, for civil purposes, the County-town of Sussex. It is distant 50 miles south from London, and the meridian of Greenwich passes through its western extremity. It gives name to a Rape, an Archdeaconry, and a Union. It has a Post-office, and a station of the South Coast Rail-way, from which several lines radiate. Its population in 1811 was 6,664, and in 1861, 10,116. Including the suburbs of Southover, Cliffe, and, South Malling, it contains seven parishes, and for con-venience, these will be dealt with collectively.

Except Brighton it is the largest town on the South Down range. Lewes proper rises rather abruptly from the Ouse, its navigable river, upon a spur of the Downs, by one long thoroughfare called High Street, running in the direction of Brighton, and nearly a mile in length : the lateral streets are generally small and unimportant. The suburb called the Cliffe lies on the east side of the Ouse, in the Rape of Pevensey. South Malling is also in Pevensey Rape, and is a continuation of the Cliffe in two streets. Southover, as its first syllable im-plies, occupies a position south and south-west of the town.

Newhaven, six miles southward, is the port of Lewes, and, together with the railway, greatly assists the commerce of the town. For picturesqueness of situation few places can compare with Lewes. The keep of its Castle rises with much grandeur as the central object, a kind of Acropolis, and forms a noble object from every point of view. There is much irregular natural beauty everywhere, and to add to its attractions the late William Cobbett pronounced it to be " the town of clean windows and pretty faces!" The etymology of the name is very uncertain, and much truly ridiculous conjecture has been spent upon it. (See Dr. Charnock's "Local Etymology.") The town and its name are both unquestionably Celtic in origin, and the second syllable, es, doubtless means water, in allusion to the situation on what was once a considerable estuary of the English Channel.

Of the early history of the town little can be ascertained. Roman urns, coins, &c., have frequently been discovered, and Lewes has been supposed to be identical with the obscure station known as *Mutuantonis*. Earlier remains of the pre-historic period have also frequently been exhumed from the neighbouring downs. In Saxon times Lewes became more important, and previously to the reign of Athelstan had two mints which continued to issue a silver coinage down to the days of Harold. Specimens of Lewes pennies were discovered both in the "Alfriston find" and in the more remarkable one at Washington, in 1866. So early as the days of the Heptarchy, Malling had become a seat of Christianity, Ceadwalla, king of Wessex and Sussex having there founded a college, which he gave to the church of Canterbury. At the Conquest King William I. gave to William de Warenne, the husband of his daughter Gundrada, together with enormous possessions in Surrey, Yorkshire, Norfolk, &c., the town and rape of Lewes, that is to say a sixth part of the whole county. The account of the town in Domesday is very curious. Edward the Confessor had 127 burgesses in domain, who paid him in rent and toll, £6 13s. 1½d., and 20s. as a subsidy, when he sent an armament to guard the seas. The purchaser of a man paid 4d. toll ; a murderer could expiate his crime for 7s. 4d., an adulterer and a runaway singularly enough paid more, viz., 8s. 4d. each. The population is supposed at this period to have been less than 1900 persons.

William de Warenne, having made Lewes his chief residence and *caput baroniæ*, erected a magnificent Castle, probably on the site of an older fortress. In conjunction with his illustrious consort he also founded the great Priory of St. Pancras, in Southover. Their successors, the Earls of Warenne and Surrey, played an active part in field and council. John, seventh Earl, took part with Henry III., but deserted him in the hour of danger. When

Edward I. issued his commission to ascertain by what right the great feudal lords held their lands, the Earl drew a rusty old sword, exclaiming: " By this weapon did my ancestor win his lands, at Hastings, and with the same I will defend them ! " His grandson of the same name, eighth and last Lord of Lewes, of his name, died in 1347, when the Barony devolved upon his sister Alice, wife of Edmund Fitz-Alan, Earl of Arundel, in whose heirs general, the Earls of Abergavenny and De la Warr, and the Duke of Norfolk, the barony now jointly vests. From the early part of the fifteenth century the lords were non-resident, and Lewes lost its feudal importance.

In 1205, 1209, and 1213, King John paid hurried visits to the town, and in 1264 occurred on the Downs, close by, the memorable Battle of Lewes. The confederated Barons having taken arms under Simon de Montfort, the two hostile armies met in deadly strife on the 14th of May. Henry III. had lodged himself on the previous night at the Priory, while Prince Edward had made the Castle his head quarters. Simon de Montfort and his troops made a hasty march from London towards Lewes, and the battle took place to the north-westward of the town, the fury of the warfare having ranged, according to tradition, from Mount Harry (so named from the King?) to the Castle itself, and even beyond, into the marshy estuary of the Ouse. The result of this battle is well known. The Baronial party were victorious. Henry and Prince Edward were fain to take refuge at the Priory. Richard, titular King of the Romans, and brother of the King, was captured in a windmill near the site of the Black Horse Inn; and after the slaughter of thousands of men on each side, a *mise* or treaty was entered into between the belligerents, which eventually resulted in the establishment of a representative government, and it is not too much to assert that the " great Battle of the Constitution " was fought on Lewes hills. Such numerous details of the battle, its causes, and consequences, have been given in Mr. Blaauw's researchful work, " The Baron's War," that we have no need to enlarge on this grand historical event.

King Edward I. was several times at Lewes, between the years 1276 and 1305. In 1377 the French having made a hostile descent upon our coast at Rottingdean, John de Cariloco, Prior of St. Pancras, with some neighbouring gentlemen and a body of rustics, met them on the Downs between the two points. Though the little Lewes army succeeded in driving the enemy to their ships, the prior and two attendant knights were carried off as prisoners. At this period Lewes was a well-fortified town, and traces of the wall still remain. It had a prison and a market, a merchant-guild, and a staple of wool. It also contained three conventual establishments and fourteen parish churches, besides chapels and hospitals. Nothing of interest is recorded for several generations, but in 1537 the Priory was dissolved, and what had been the main stay of the repute and prosperity of the town disappeared. In 1545 the French again invaded Sussex, but a Lewes knight, Sir Nicholas Pelham, ancestor of the Earl of Chichester, repulsed them valiantly. In the reign of Queen Mary, Lewes, as the county town, was the scene of many of those *holocausts* which disgraced her times. Sixteen martyrs to the cause of the Reformation were burnt in the *forum* of Lewes—the local Smithfield, opposite the Star inn—between 1555 and 1557, the last "burnt-offering to a good conscience" being the well-known iron-master, Richard Woodman, and nine others, five of whom were women. At a later period most of the county gentry had town houses in Lewes, and a great portion of the High Street was occupied with these residences, many of which, with spacious gardens, remain. Daniel de Foe, in his "Tour," 1724, and Dr. Burton in his "Iter Sussexiense," some years later, give graphic accounts of the town. In the course of the French war, Lewes became a considerable military station, and extensive barracks were built at the western extremity of the town. During the gay career of the Prince Regent (George IV.) that personage annually visited Lewes for three days for the races. In 1830 King William and Queen Adelaide had a loyal reception; and Queen Victoria has also passed through the town *en route* for Buxted Park, the residence of her Lord Chamberlain, the late Earl of Liverpool.

Lewes Castle, as we have seen, was built by De Warenne soon after the Conquest. Its existing remains are the Keep, which occupies a commanding artificial mound, and dominates the town in a manner truly feudal; some walls of the *enciente*; and the Barbican or advanced work, a picturesque gateway of the fourteenth century, covering the simple Norman semi-circular perforation of the wall, which was the original gate. This once frowning stronghold included a base court more than 800 feet in its longest diameter, and had, besides the Keep proper, another elevation called the Brackmount, on which formerly stood a kind of second keep, or a strong tower. The precinct now contains two or three private residences, and an excellent bowling-green. In 1850 the Sussex Archæological Society hired the Castle of the Lords of the Borough, which they still occupy —the keep as a museum of local antiquities, and the barbican as a council-chamber. The leads of the keep command a noble and picturesque view, embracing the Weald, the site of the Battle, the port of Newhaven, and that remarkable geological "fault," the Combe, in the range called Cliff Hill.

The Priory, which lies in a meadow in the suburban parish
of Southover, was founded, as before stated, by William de
Warenne and Gundrada, about the year 1078, and dedicated
to St. Pancras, the martyr, to whose honour a small wooden
church had existed on the spot before the Conquest. It was
of the Cluniac order, a branch of the Benedictines, and the
first house of that denomination in England. Its endowments were enormous, and its prior being mitred, subsequently became a peer of the realm. The first prior was
Lanzo, a man of great piety and learning, and there were
few monasteries in this country which enjoyed so wide a
reputation. Among those who added to its endowments
and found sepulture in its church were the De Warennes,
Clares, De Veres, St. Johns, Fitz-Alans, De Lancasters, and
Nevilles. The vicissitudes of this great Priory have been set
forth in several notices by Mr. Blaauw in "Sussex Archæological
Collections." At the dissolution of the religious houses by
Henry VIII., in 1537, the revenues were estimated at £1,091
9s. 6d., equal to at least £10,000 at the present day. The Vicar
General, Cromwell, immediately ordered the work of demolition
to commence, and one Portinari, an Italian, speedily performed
the execrable deed of levelling with the ground, the great church,
equal in extent to most cathedrals, the chapter-house, cloisters,
&c., so that to-day we see in a few rude and unintelligible walls
all that remains of this once enormous group of buildings,
which occupied with its adjunct of "Calvary," garden, pigeon-
house, and stews for fish, a splendid area of forty acres. Cromwell himself got a grant of the Priory and all its possessions,
and after that favourite's deposition they were granted by Henry
to his repudiated queen, Anne of Cleves. Tradition assigns as
her residence the old porched house of the Pelhams, in the
High Street of Southover; but there is no proof: indeed poor
Anne seems to have had as many residences and places of death
as Oliver Cromwell had skulls. At a later date Thomas Sackville, the Elizabethan poet and statesman, had a house on the
site of the Priory, called the Lord's place, which was burnt
down. The manor of Southover subsequently passed to the
families of Tufton, Trayton, Durrant, and Verrall, William
Verrall, Esq., being the existing lord. The portion of the priory
demesne which contains the ruins belongs to Mrs. John Blaker.
A short distance to the north-east of the ruins is a remarkable
mound with a spiral pathway, obviously the ancient Calvary of
the monastery. The earth of which it is constructed was evidently taken from an adjacent depressed spot, called from its
shape the Dripping-pan, and now devoted to cricket matches
and other public amusements.

During the progress of the excavations necessary for the formation of the South-Coast Railway, which passes through the Priory grounds, occurred, in 1845, one of the most remarkable archæological discoveries of our times. This was no less than two small leaden coffers, less than three feet in length, containing respectively the bones of WILLELM' (de Warenne) and GUNDRADA, the founder and foundress of the Priory, who had died before the completion of the great church, and been buried in the ordinary manner. On the completion of that edifice their bones were doubtless exhumed and removed to the more honourable place of sepulture. The names of both these illustrious personages were inscribed on the lids of the coffers, which are preserved in Southover church. Many other objects of antiquarian interest were brought to light at the same time.

The other monastic institutions of Lewes were:—(1.) Malling Deanery, previously mentioned as having been founded in Saxon times, which was dissolved by Henry VIII., in 1545. It was originally built at Old Malling, and afterwards removed to South Malling, in the same parish. The assassins of Thomas à Becket took shelter here in their flight on the second night after the murder at Canterbury, and the notable miracle of the table in the great hall having tilted itself to throw off the blood-stained armour of the knights is known to the readers of Stanley's Memorials of Canterbury. (2.) The house of Grey Friars without the east gate of the town. Of its foundation nothing is known, and it possesses little history, except that two of the brethren mediated between Henry III. and the Barons in 1264. After the Dissolution it became a private residence, and was pulled down to make room for the railway station in 1845. (3.) The hospital of St. James, near the gate of the Priory, for thirteen poor brethren and sisters, whose duty was to pray for the founders and their heirs. The chapel, now much patched, is still standing. (4.) A miserable old thatched cottage in St. Anne's, called the Spital, represents the Hospital of St. Nicholas, a place of rest and entertainment for pilgrims to St. Pancras' Priory.

A brief topographical account of Lewes follows. *Southover Church*, dedicated to St. John the Baptist, stands in the southern suburb of the town. It is in various styles, from Early Norman to the non-descript of the 18th century—the brick tower being of the last-mentioned period. It stands just outside the ancient gateway of the Priory, and contains a very elegant sacellum, erected in 1867, in which are preserved the remains of the founder and foundress, previously mentioned. This church formerly had chapels dedicated to SS. Katherine and Erasmus, which have disappeared. There are many inscriptions to the Newton, Verrall, and other families. Near it is a curious and picturesque

old Elizabethan mansion, which was built with part of the
materials of the Priory, by William Newton, Esq., steward of
Lord Buckhurst, Earl of Dorset. It has quaint gables and window frames. The date on the mantel-piece of the dining-room
shows the year of its erection to be 1572. It was the residence
of the Newton family, until within the last few years; but now
belongs to Captain Wyndham. In the time of the late Colonel
Newton, George IV., when Prince-Regent, was a frequent visitor
here.

Leaving the west end of Southover at the point where the road
to Newhaven and Seaford commences, and passing along Win-
terbourne Lane (so-called from a pellucid stream which runs
only during the winter season), we reach the Spital, or hospital
of St. Nicholas, just mentioned. Close to this is the large county
gaol. Descending towards the town we see the church of St.
Anne, anciently St. Mary Westout. Outside the western walls
of Lewes there formerly stood two churches, St. Peter and St.
Mary. The houses of the former parish principally contained
in what was called Antioch Street (possibly a reminiscence of
the Crusades), were burnt down in the 16th century, and the two
parishes were united under the name of St. Anne. The church
thus designated is an Early English structure, and contains
some interesting features, especially a barrel-shaped font with
fretwork ornaments, probably of Saxon date. Near the church
is "Shelley's," so-called from its having long been the seat of a
branch of that eminent Sussex family. Dr. Johnson, on a visit
to the Thrales at Brighton, once spent a day at this mansion,
and a hitherto unrecorded anecdote may here be given. The
philosopher was walking in the garden with a little Miss Shelley,
two or three years old, in his hand, until at last, being tired of
her companionship, he deliberately placed her between the
branches of a cherry-tree, and there left her. At dinner time
there was a hue and cry after the child, and Johnson, recollect-
ing himself, said, "O, I left her in a tree!" The tree survived
this incident until within recent years, and was always known
as "Dr. Johnson's cherry-tree." Near this house is the grammar-school, founded about 1512, by Dame Agnes Morley; and,
still further down the street, there stood till lately a building
called St. Anne's House, long the pleasant abode of the writer
of these pages, but now replaced by a modern structure of the
metropolitan cut. That house had many historical remem-
brances, it having been the abode, in the time of James I., of
John Rowe, principal of Clifford's Inn, a great lawyer and an
eminent local antiquary; and subsequently, the property of Sir
Roger Newdigate, founder of the Newdigate prize for English
poetry at Oxford. The town was formerly fortified with walls,

the West-gate of which we next approach; the others being the
East-gate and the Water-gate; but the traces of all are now very
slight. *St. Michael's Church*, hard by, has a few ancient features,
but it was chiefly rebuilt in the worst taste of the 18th century.
Its round tower, however, remains, as well as two brasses;
one for a knight of the 15th century, and another for 𝔍𝔬𝔥𝔢𝔰
𝔅𝔯𝔞𝔭𝔡𝔣𝔬𝔯𝔡𝔢, rector, with the date 1457. There is also a mural
monument to Sir Nicholas Pelham, the gallant defender of Seaford, who died in 1559. The epitaph assures us that:—

> "What time the French sought to have sack't Sea-Foord,
> This *Pelham* did re*pel* 'em back aboord!"

In this parish are two other places deserving of notice; first,
the old "town house" of the Goring family, long since converted into a Presbyterian chapel, and an ancient dwelling re-
cognised by a singular carving of Pan at one corner, but more
noteworthy as the residence for some time of Tom Paine, the
atheistical writer of the "Age of Reason," who was then a local
exciseman. He wrote that execrable book in this house, and
the table on which he wrote it was, about fifty years since, in
the possession of the late William Lee of this town. In this
parish also resided the late Dr. Gideon Mantell, the celebrated
geologist, who collected the "Mantellian Museum," of Sussex
fossils, &c., now in the British Museum. A little lower in the
street is the County-hall, for courts of assize and other public
business; a building with a handsome *façade*. The original
town-hall stood, before the erection of this edifice, in the
middle of the High-street. Next come two ancient inns, the
White Hart (modernized) and the Star. The latter has some
historical celebrity, for in front of it the Protestants were
burnt during the Marian persecution. In this inn is a very
fine Jacobean staircase brought hither from Slaugham Place
in the last century. In the market-tower, close at hand, is the
great town bell called Gabriel, of the time of Henry VIII.
From this point we pass down School-hill, a steep declivity, towards the site of the ancient monastery of the Grey Friars, of
which no remains exist, the ground being partly occupied by a
very handsome building called the FitzRoy Memorial Library.
This edifice, which cost nearly £5,000, was presented by the
widow of the late Right Hon. Henry Fitzroy (M.P. for Lewes
for more than twenty years), to the town, and it contains a
valuable collection of books, a school of art, &c. Close by is
the bridge over the Ouse, and the suburb called the Cliffe is next
entered. It has a church dedicated to *St. Thomas à Becket*, formerly a chapel dependent on South Malling. This building,
though principally of the Perpendicular period, with some

modern churchwardenizations, contains traces of much earlier architecture. In the south aisle there was formerly a guild or fraternity of St. Thomas. Passing a sharp angle on the left, we proceed towards Malling, leaving on the right that remarkable chasm in the chalk formation called the "Coombe." Near at hand is "Jireh," one of the largest dissenting chapels in the county, in the little cemetery of which lie the remains of the well-known William Huntington, the Hyper-Calvinist, with the curious epitaph : "Here lies the Coalheaver, beloved of his God, but abhorred of men. The omniscient Judge, at the grand assize, shall ratify this to the confusion of many thousands, for England and its metropolis shall know that there hath been a prophet among them.—W. H., S.S." This was composed by the deceased himself, an arrogant but clever man, who having married the widow of a Lord Mayor, and looking, with a touch of envy perhaps, at the D.D.'s of the period, gave himself the title of "Sinner Saved" (S.S.). *Malling Church* is a simple fabric, consisting of a nave only, and stands at a considerable distance from the population. It was erected in 1628, under the will of John Stansfield, Esq., who endowed it as a perpetual curacy, and one of the foundation stones was laid by his afterwards eminent grandson, John Evelyn, author of "Sylva," &c., who records that circumstance in his "Diary." There are memorials to the names of Kempe, Spence, Grantham, Courthope, Cayley, Brodie, &c.; but the most striking inscription is that which records the death, in December, 1836, of eight persons who were killed in South Street, in this parish, by a very remarkable *avalanche*. A vast mass of drifted snow slipped from its position, on the crest of Cliffe-hill, overturned a range of cottages, and destroyed these poor people. Malling was one of the oldest seats of Christianity in the county, and I have already noticed it in this article. Few remains of it now exist, and, at some unknown date, the College was removed lower down the banks of the Ouse to what is called South Malling, near the present church, to the site of the mansion now possessed by E. C. Currey, Esq., where it remained until the Reformation. This house is still called Malling "Deanery," and was long the seat of the ancient family of Spence. Malling House belongs to the family of Crofts, the representative of which is Henry Crofts, Esq., of Sompting Abbots. Returning once more to Lewes proper, we must notice *St. John's Church*, a modern brick structure, which we cannot commend, as it is a kind of hybrid between a castle and a barn. It supersedes a very venerable structure, probably of the time of the Confessor, which was pulled down in 1838 to meet the necessities of an increased population. Some relics of the old edifice have been preserved and built into the walls of the new, including the mouldings of a Saxon doorway, and especially an ancient monument arranged in the form of an arch, with the following inscription cut on fifteen stones in two semi-circular lines :—

" CLAUDITUR HIO MILES, DANORUM REGIA PROLES ;
MANGNUS NOMEN EI, MANGNÆ NOTA PROGENEI :
DEPONENS MANGNUM, SE MORIBUS INDUIT AGNUM,
PREPETE PRO VITA, FIT PARVULUS ARNAOORITA."

" Here is immured a Soldier of the Royal Family of Denmark, whose name *Magnus* * bespeaks his distinguished lineage. Relinquishing his greatness, he assumes the deportment of a lamb, and exchanges a life of ambition for that of a lowly anchorite."

Of the history of this person and his connection with the Kings of Denmark nothing can be discovered. He appears to have been one of those fanatics who caused themselves to be shut up within the walls of churches in what were called *inclusoria*, and making a vow of silence for life. The inscription has been regarded as a mortuary epitaph, but it is not so, as the Rev. E. Turner in an able article, mentioned below, sufficiently proves. The tradition that he was a Danish marauder slain at the Wallands, hard by, in a conflict with the English, is totally unfounded, as the inscription is of the thirteenth century.

The church-yard of St. John occupies part of a very small camp considered to be Roman, part of the *vallum* of which is traceable. There are memorials to the names of Shore, Le Pla, Campion, Crofts, &c., and one to Thomas Blunt, an eminent *barber* of Lewes, who made several donations to the borough, including a silver-gilt loving-cup, still used on festive occasions. The inscription on his tomb is in Latin, and records his various bequests. The last couplet is to this effect :—

" These gifts he gave, this done, himself to death is given;
These gifts he gave, and thus received the gifts of heaven ! "

All Saints' Church is also a plain, inelegant building, erected in 1807, with the exception of the tower, which is in the Perpendicular style. There are memorials for the names of Trayton, Durrant, Isted, Blunt, Woollgar, and for John Stansfield, Gent., the founder of Malling church. There are traces of many churches now destroyed. Near the top of School-hill stood St. Nicholas, or the "broken church," the remembrance of which is retained in the name of St. Nicholas (*vulgo* Dolphin) lane. St. Mary's-lane, *vulgo* " Simmery-lane," was named after a now destroyed church, some remains of which are supposed to exist in the cellar of the house of Mr. Richards, nearly opposite the Star

* Misspelt Mangnus.

hotel. In what is called Campion's lane stood the church of St. Andrew; and near the office of the "Sussex Advertiser" was another church dedicated to St. Mary in Foro, as the market was in early times held near that spot. A few yards distant, St. Martin's-lane indicates a church under the invocation of that famous military saint, who shared his cloak with a poor frozen beggar. These churches all stood on the south side of the High-street. St. Swithin's-lane also probably indicates the existence of a church dedicated to that saint. Lewes abounds with dissenting chapels of nearly every denomination, and possesses a Roman Catholic chapel, lately erected.

The town was for a long time in a stationary position, and the population did not increase; but of late an impetus has been given to the building trade. Some excellent houses have sprung up, and it is believed that in a few years Lewes will be second to few towns near the South Coast, especially should Mr. W. E. Baxter's project for a new suburb, "Wallands Park," be carried out. The natural and artificial advantages of the town are very great indeed.

Among the eminent residents or natives of Lewes must be reckoned Sir Thomas Browne, author of "Religio Medici;" Richard Challenor, D.D., the celebrated Roman Catholic bishop and theologian, born 1691; Paul Dunvan, author of a "History of Lewes and Brighthelmstone" (1795); John Elliot, the antiquary, born 1725; John Evelyn, author of "Sylva," &c.; the Rev. T. W. Horsfield, the historian of Sussex, who died in 1837; Dr. Gideon Mantell, F.R.S., the renowned geologist; Richard Russell, M.D., the founder of Brighton, born 1687; John Tabor, M.D., the eminent physician and antiquary; Thomas Twyne, M.D., the great physician and classical scholar, who lies buried in St. Anne's church, with a very quaint inscription, dated 1613; James Lambert, a local self-taught artist of the last century, whose drawings of Sussex antiquities are in the Burrell Collections in the British Museum; John Dudeney, the philosophical shepherd and schoolmaster (ob. 1852); John Rowe, lawyer and antiquary (see *ante*). Edmund Dudley, the well-known minister of Henry VII., and the co-extortioner of Richard Empson, was the son of a travelling carpenter who settled at Lewes Priory, and there Edmund is said to have received his education.

The following is a list of the Benefices of Lewes :—

All Saints, Rectory.—Patron, C. Goring, Esq.; held by the Rev. Robt. Straffen, M.A.; value, £206. Population in 1861, 2,092.

St. Anne.—Patron, the Lord Chancellor; £190; Rector, Rev. Augustus J. Parsons, M.A., of Trinity College, Cambridge. Population, 980.

Southover, St. John the Baptist.—The same Patron and Incumbent; value, £97. Population, 1,344.

St. John-sub-Castro.—Patron, Rev. C. D. Crofts, M.A.; Rector, Rev.

Arthur Pearson Perfect, M.A.; value, £250. Population, 2,308. This parish has a considerable rural district, extending widely, and partly detached from the town. Within its limits lie Landport, a large farm, and Allington, where there was formerly a moated manor-house and a chapel. The intersecting parish is Hamsey.

St. Michael.—Patron, the Lord Chancellor ; Rector, the Rev. Frederick Woolley, B.C.L.; value, £116. Population, 1,076.

St. Thomas at Cliffe.—A peculiar ; Patron, the Archbishop ; Rector, the Rev. J. C. Russell, M.A., of St. Peter's College, Cambridge ; value, £130. Population, 1,568.

South Malling.—A Peculiar ; Patron, G. C. Courthope, Esq. ; Perpetual Curate or Vicar, Rev. John Warburton ; value, £117. Population, 716. In this parish is the *quasi* hamlet of Stoneham, formerly attached to the Deanery of Malling. It was anciently a Beadlewick, and now principally consists of two good farms. The acreage is 2,680.

The *Precinct of the Castle* (extra parochial), contains a population of 32.

[S. A. C. In consequence of the great antiquity and historical interest of Lewes, the number of references to that place in the " Sussex Archæological Collections" is necessarily large, and the paper by the late Mr. W. Figg, F.S.A., should be especially referred to.—Relics found at, i, 43. Priory, and its seals, ii, 7. Battle of, ii, 28. v, 274. xix, 164. Dudeney, John, ii, 252. Priory, iii, 185, 230. vi, 253. vii, 217. xviii, 58. xx, 141, 187. South Malling College, v, 127 *(Turner).* Seal, viii, 270. Archdeaconry seal, v, 199. British urn, *ibid.* Malling watermills, Domesday, v, 271. King John's visit, ii, 133. King Henry III., ii, 137. King Edward I., 138. Lantern in Priory *(Figg).* Dr. Burton's description of the town " Iter Sussex." Kidder family, ix, 128. Newton family *(Noyes),* ix, 312. xvi, 49. xvii, 258. Royal mint, ix, 369. xix, 164, 189. xx, 214 *(Lucas).* Star Hotel. Slaugham staircase, drawn by N. H. Lower, x, 163. Medieval pottery, x, 193. xviii, 190. The Castle a Prison? x, 213. Goring family, xi, 64. Woughton, Tortington Priory, had lands at (possibly Offham, in Hamsey), xi, 110. Magnus, or *Mangnus,* Prince and Hermit, at St. John's, and Hermitess of St. Mary, xii, 132, 134. Memorials of Old Lewes, xiii, 1 *(Figg).* Lord Goring's residence, xiii, 13. xix, 100. Lewes Priory, license to fortify, xiii, 112. Southover, Heneage family Prayer-book, xiii, 315. Newdigates and Bromfields, xiv, 229. Dr. Russell, the founder of Brighton, xiv, 266. Old Malling, earliest seat of Christianity in East Sussex, xv, 163. Burdett, of Southover, xx, 66. Sufferings of Lewes Quakers *(Figg),* xvi, 65. Rickman family, xvi, 72. Church bells, xvi, 205, 216. Rowe, John, xx, 85. Southover Free-school, xvii, 79. Colonel H. Morley, M.P., ironmaster, xviii, 14. Complicity of the Prior, constables, and people of Lewes and Southover, with Jack Cade, and their pardons, xviii, 25, *et seq.* Prior of, xviii, 44. Museum of Antiquities in the Castle *(Lower* and *Chapman),* xviii, 60. De Braose effigy at Southover, xviii, 62. Shirley family, xviii, 133. Castle, xviii, 176. Thomas Lucas, merchant, 1634, xviii, 176. Cliffe old Vicarage, xviii, 195. Giles, bell-founder, xix, 43. Whitfeld family, xix, 90 *(Lower).* Fitzherbert family, xix, 179. The " Friars," xix, 179. Stempe family, and Springett family, xx, 35. Heath family, xx, 62. Banns published in Market, xx, 83. Rev. R. Cecil, anecdote, xx, 133. Lewes Races, xx, 227.]

LINCH (or Lynch).

Domesday, *Lince;* a parish in the Hundred of Easebourne; Rape of Chichester; distant five miles north-west from Midhurst, its Post-town, Union, and Railway-station. Population in 1811, 84; in 1861, 111. Benefice, a Rectory, valued at £80; Patron, the Earl of Egmont; Incumbent, Rev. R. Cooke Bull, M.A., of Emmanuel College, Cambridge. Date of earliest Parish Register, 1701. Acreage, 1,220. *Chief Landowner*, The Earl of Egmont. *Seat*, Hollycombe, B. F. Pratt, Esq.

This parish is composed of "disjecta membra," of which about 700 acres lie at the northern foot of the South Downs (Linch Farm), and the remainder about six miles northward, in the romantic, but unproductive, neighbourhood of Farnhurst.

Lince was held before the Conquest of Edward the Confessor, by Ulric. It was rated at five hides. There were six ploughlands, a church, two ministri, and a wood of 10 hogs. In 1570 it was part of the estate of Thomas, Duke of Norfolk, and subsequently became the property of the Viscountess Montague. Hollycombe, the residence of Barlow Frederick Pratt, Esq., was built from a design by Nash, and was formerly inhabited by Sir Charles William Taylor, Bart.

The benefice anciently belonged to the Priory of Easebourne. The present church was erected about 1705.

[S. A. C. Ironworks, ii, 214. Chapel of, xii, 73. Church-bell, xvi, 217.]

LINCHMERE (or Lynchmere).

A parish in the Hundred of Easebourne; Rape of Chichester; distant about five miles from Midhurst; Post-town, Haslemere.; Union, Midhurst. Population in 1811, 258; in 1861, 283. Benefice, a Perpetual Curacy, valued at £60; Patron and Incumbent, Rev. W. Henry Parson, M.A., of Magdalen Hall, Oxford. Date of earliest Parish Register, 1560. Acreage, 2,101. *Chief Landowners*, The Earl of Egmont, the Rev. W. H. Parson, Hasler Hollist, Esq., and Mrs. Harriott.

This frontier parish abuts on the counties of Hampshire and Surrey, and its surface includes arable, pasture, woodland, and heath, while the subsoil yields peat. At an early period it was held by the Percys. It then became the property of the Fitz-Alans, and at a later date it belonged to Sir William Fitz William; and subsequently it descended as Cowdray. The church (St. Peter) is small and interesting, and was restored in 1856. The scenery is very picturesque.

For SHULBRED PRIORY, in this parish, see that article.

[S. A. C. Ironworks, ii, 213. Shulbred Priory, vii, 217. xviii, 195. Church, xii, 82. Church-bells, xvi, 217.]

LINDFIELD.

Vulgo, *Linvul;* a parish in the Hundred of Burleigh-Arches; Rape of
Pevensey; distant 3½ miles east from Cuckfield. It is a Post-town.
Railway station, Hayward's Heath, distant about 1½ mile. Union,
Cuckfield. Population in 1811, 1,237; in 1861, 1,917. Benefice,
a Perpetual Curacy, valued at £100; Patron, W. M. Kearnes, Esq.;
Incumbent, Rev. J. Milner, M.A. Date of earliest Parish Register,
1559. Acreage, 5,776. *Seats,* Pax-Hill Park, P. Northall Laurie,
Esq.; Buxshalls, W. D. Jollands, Esq.; Gravelye, Summer Hill,
Beadle Hill, Sunte House, Oat Hall, The Welkin, Milton House, and
Little Walsted.

Lindfield is situated in a most picturesque country, and its
broad village street, with its antique timbered houses, is exceedingly interesting. Any one tired of the bustle of this changeful
life might safely retire to Lindfield as one of the most peaceful
spots in Britain. Its name appears to be derived from the
Anglo-Saxon *linde,* a linden, or lime tree, and *feld,* a field.

The manor anciently belonged to the College of Malling near
Lewes, and was thence known as the manor of South-Mal-
ling-Lindfield. Tradition speaks of a convent in this parish,
but of its history and situation I can obtain no particulars.
There are several ancient residences. Pax-Hill is a stone mansion, built late in the reign of Elizabeth, on an elevated spot,
and surrounded with a deer park. It was long the residence of
a branch of the Boord or Board family, and the last male heir
of that line dying in 1787, left it to his three daughters and
co-heiresses, one of whom married Gibbs Crawfurd, Esq., whose
grand-daughter was wife of Arthur W. W. Smith, Esq. Albert
Smith, brother of the latter, the well-known comic lecturer and
writer, built a *châlet* near the park, and occasionally resided
there. Kenwardes, an ancient building, now occupied as a farm-
house, was long a seat of the old Sussex family of Chaloner, or
Challener, of whom was Major Chaloner, a partizan of Cromwell. He was an influential magistrate, and many *lay* marriages
were performed before him. East Maskalls formerly belonged
to a family of that name, and was owned, in the seventeenth century, by a branch of the Newtons, of the same family as the
Newtons of Southover, near Lewes, from whom it descended to
the family of Noyes. The mansion was constructed in the old
timber-framed style, and was long in a very ruinous condition,
and tenanted by cottagers. The arms of the Newtons, in painted
glass, were formerly in the windows. Sir Isaac Newton is supposed to have been a connection of an earlier line of this family.
Sunte belonged to the family of Hamlyn. John Hamlyn, Esq.,
who died in 1774 left two daughters and co-heiresses. Anne,

the elder, married John Borrer, Esq. of Henfield, and afterwards John Dennet, Esq., of Woodmancote: it is now the seat
of George Catt, Esq. Buxshalls, supposed to have been the
residence of a branch of the ancient family of Boxhulle of Robertsbridge, one of whom was K. G. in the reign of Edward III.,
is a pleasant modern erection on an ancient site. Paper works
were formerly carried on in this parish.

The church (St. John the Baptist), principally in the Perpendicular style, is a picturesque object. The tower seems to be
Early English, and has a shingled spire. The building is
cruciform, and on the south is a parvise, or small apartment
over the entrance. The north transept was rebuilt, during the
repairs which the building underwent some years ago. Those
repairs were carried out without the smallest regard to pro-
priety or respect for antiquity. Some of the most beautiful
fragments of fourteenth-century glass I ever saw were removed from one of the south windows, and a brass plate to the
memory of 𝕽𝖞𝖈𝖍𝖆𝖗𝖉 𝕮𝖍𝖆𝖑𝖑𝖊𝖓𝖊𝖗, which I remember *in situ*, on a
stone on the floor, now lies before me. It bears the date of 1501.
Beautiful wood carvings were also removed from the church; in
short, there was a general spoliation of nearly all that was
ancient. There are, or were, mortuary inscriptions to the names
of Allen, Board, Burrell, Wildbee, Spence, &c. A Perpendicular
altar-tomb has been removed, and the brasses of a slab representing a man, woman, and seven children have also been taken
away. All this spoliation, which grieves the antiquary's heart,
is owing to the singular ecclesiastical condition of the parish.
It was, at a very early date, one of the " peculiars" of the Archbishops of Canterbury, and as such was granted by Archbishop
Theobald, in 1150, to the College of Malling. On the dissolution of that establishment, in 1546, it was given to Sir Thomas
Palmer of Angmering, a gentleman of the Privy Chamber of
Henry VIII., an enormous acquirer of church property in Sussex,
and it remained in lay hands, the holder being bound to repair
the chancel and provide an " honest priest" for the services of
the church. This poor cleric got about £30 a year, and sometimes as little as £20, while the impropriator derived a large
sum from the parish in tithes, &c. This led to a very lax state
of things; the Archbishop declined to interfere, and not unfre-
quently no service was held. Even worse than this, the last
rites of the church could hardly be performed, and it is said
that within the nineteenth century bodies of deceased parishioners have remained in the church for several days for want
of an officiating priest ! A better state of things, however, now
prevails. A curious " Boke of Accompts" of the parish, dating
from 1580, came into the hands of the Sussex Archæological
Society some years since, but is now in proper custody. It is

full of interesting matter, and an abstract of it has been printed in vol. xix of the "Collections." It appears from this document that the inhabitants did all in their power to maintain the fabric of the church, and that they were particularly fond of bell ringing. There are at present five bells.

It may be mentioned that there is in the church a very unusual sepulchral effigy, impressed or incised on three glazed tiles, the entire size of the memorial being 45 inches by 15: the date is 1520. In 1848 a curious mural painting was disclosed on the east wall of the south transept. It represented the Archangel St. Michael and St. Margaret, with a dragon of many heads at their feet. The Archangel held a pair of scales, in which he was weighing the souls of the dead.

Altogether there are in Sussex few parishes of more interest than Lindfield, either for the antiquary or the artist. The well-known and respected Sussex family of Verral seem to have originated here, and the name was formerly written *Fairhall.*

[S. A. C. Mural paintings, ii, 129. Iron-works, ii, 214. xix, 41. Borde family, vi, 197. xix, 40, 43, 48. xx, 61. Newtons of East Mascalls, ix, 312. xvii, 259. xix, 40, 48, 49. Nunnery (?), x, 213. Paxhill and its neighbourhood (*Blencowe*), xi, i. East Mascalls, xi, i, 83. Trimmens Columbarium, xi, 5. Chaloners of, xi, 12. xiv, 149. xviii, 25, 39. xix, 37, 40, 49. Hamlyns of, xi, 81. xix, 48. Henslows of, xiv, 47. Vine, schoolmaster and antiquary of, xiv, 227. xix, 195. Combers of, xvi, 48. Giles of, xvi, 48. Bells of, xvi, 217. Men of, and Jack Cade, xviii, 25. Tuppens of, xviii, 162. Parochial Documents, xix, 36 (*Lower*). Granted to the College of Malling, *ibid.* Killingbeck, xix, 38. Roodloft in church, xix, 37. Finches in, xix, 40, 48. Scrase bridge in, xix, 41. Skaymes Hill in, xix, 41. Bedles Hill in, xix, 41. Sunt in, xix, 41, 48. Hour-glass in the church, xix, 43. Subscription to Cumberland churches, *ibid.* Books of Martyrs, &c., &c., belonged to the church, xix, 47. xx, 225. Church-marks at, xix, 48. Gravelygh in, xix, 48. Oate-Hall in, xix, 48. Boxhulles in, *ibid.* Pelling of Pellingbridge, xix, 49. Bartlott of, xix, 51.]

LITLINGTON.

Vulgo, *Lillinton;* a parish in the Hundred of Longbridge; Rape of Pevensey; distant about four miles from Seaford; Post-town, Lewes; Railway station, Berwick, distant about three miles. Union, Eastbourne. Population in 1811, 117; in 1861, 134. Benefice, a Rectory, valued at £105; Patrons, Representatives of Rev. Thomas Scutt; Incumbent, Rev. Richard White, B.A., of Durham University. Date of earliest Parish Register, 1695. Acreage, 893. *Chief Landowner*, T. S. Richardson, Esq. *Seat*, Clapham House, at present the residence of C. T. Latrobe, Esq., C.B., formerly Governor of Victoria.

A small South Down parish on the river Cuckmere. The

etymology is obvious. The manor is a sub-infeudation of Bishop-ston. *Temp.* Henry II. it was the property of the family of Husée, or Hosatus, who gave a rent from a mill here to Dureford Abbey in West Sussex. Since that time it has been held by Hunt, Rootes, Pelham, Mallory, Bean, and Scutt. Chambers Court, now destroyed, received its name from the ancient family of De la Chambre, originally of Chambers Court, in Laughton, and subsequently of Rodmill, Denton, and Seaford. One of the name was at Agincourt.

The church consists of a nave, chancel, and bell-turret, with a spire. Of the three bells one is inscribed to St. John. The chancel and other portions are Norman. The west end is Deco-rated or earlier. Two sedilia, a piscina, and traces of a rood-loft remain; also in the north wall of the chancel a Perpendicular tomb-arch. (Hussey.) On the floor was a fractured stone, marked with crosses, which was originally the altar. In the north-west angle of the nave is a very small newel staircase. The church has recently been restored, at an expense of £600. Here are ex-tensive nursery, fruit, and pleasure gardens, beautifully situated on rising ground near the river Cuckmere.

[S. A. C.   Marshall gifts to, xiii, 52. Chambers of, xiii, 258. xiv, 213. De la Chambre at Agincourt, xv, 131. Bells, xvi, 141, 217.]

LITTLEHAMPTON, or HAMPTON-PARVA.

Domesday, *Hantone;* a parish in the Hundred of Poling; Rape of Arundel; distant four miles from Arundel. It is a Post-town, and has a Railway station on the South Coast line. Union, East Preston. Population in 1811, 882 ; in 1861, 2,350. Benefice, a Vicarage, valued at £175 ; Patron, the Bishop of Chichester ; Incumbent, Rev. Charles Rum-ball, B.A., of Magdalen Hall, Oxford. Date of earliest Parish Re-gister, 1642. Acreage, 1,222.

Littlehampton is bounded on the south by the English Channel, and on the west by the Arun. It is the port of Arundel, and enjoys a considerable coasting trade, which has of late years added materially to the population. Before the Conquest, the Countess Goda, daughter of Ethelred II., had a hide in this manor. Afterwards it belonged to Earl Roger de Montgomeri. Before the confiscation of the alien priories, the French abbeys of Seez and Almanesche had lands here. At the Dissolution these lands came into the possession of the Crown, and the manor of Littlehampton, cum Tottington (in Lyminster), was sold in 1562, to John Palmer, Esq., of Angmering. Sir Thomas Palmer, his son, succeeded in 1571. In 1712 Thomas, Duke of Norfolk, purchased the lands which now belong to the present Duke of Norfolk. Baylies Court is an outlying portion of this parish, that of Climping intervening. As is usual with Sussex rivers, the Arun has been driven by the force of the south-west winds, which tend by the accumulation of shingle, to the east. By this alteration the outlet of the river is now in Climping. In 1734, an Act was passed for erecting piers and repairing Arundel Harbour in the parish of Littlehampton. In 1739 a small battery was constructed for the protection of the port, and a new one has been built on the west side of the river. Ship-building is carried on here to a considerable extent, and Little-hampton has lately become a watering-place of considerable attractions. It is quiet, and possesses the advantages of agree-able scenery, a pure air, and excellent sea-sands. Regattas and races are annually held.

The Empress Maude is said to have landed here in 1139, on a visit to Queen Adeliza at Arundel, after which she was besieged there by King Stephen.

The church (Our Lady) having been found too small for the population was taken down in 1826, and a larger one erected. In the new church the east window, a round-headed doorway, and the ancient font have been preserved. There is one bell. The ecclesiastical history of this parish is very curious. At the confiscation of the church lands by Henry V., on the dissolution of the alien priories before mentioned, a portion of them was granted to the Nunnery of Sion in Middlesex, and the other portion to the College of Arundel. The latter establishment found an officiating priest for the cure of souls, who was styled " Clericus conductitius," or removable curate. In the time of Henry VIII., Henry, Earl of Arundel, became possessed of the lands which had belonged to Arundel College, and his moiety was transferred by him to John Edmondes, Esq. The other moiety was retained by the Crown till 3rd Elizabeth, when, by an exchange, it passed to the see of Chichester, and the Bishop became impropriator, the vicarage being held under seques-tration.

Tanner mentions a Priory in Littlehampton called Athering-ton ; but this seems to rest upon the assumption that the monks of Seez had a cell here, whereas it appears that there was only a single monk resident, who acted as Bailiff, and hence the place acquired the name of Baylie's Court.

[S. A. C. Church, xii, 92. Baldwins, xii, 92. Edmondes, *ibid*. Holy-bread land, xiv, 155. Church bell, xvi, 217. Arun river, xvi, 259.]

LODSWORTH.

A Parish locally in the Hundred of Easebourne; Rape of Chichester; distant 3½ miles west from Petworth, its Post town and Railway station. Union, Midhurst. Population in 1811, 393; in 1861, 629. Benefice, a Perpetual Curacy, valued at £56. Patron, the Earl of Egmont; Incumbent, Rev. C. Leopold S. Clarke, M.A., of New College, Oxford. Date of earliest Parish Register, 1563. Acreage, 1,805. *Chief Landowners*, The Earl of Egmont, W. T. Mitford, J. Henry, and H. Hollist, Esquires. *Seats*, Lodsworth House, Hasler Hollist, Esq.; Blackdown House, James Henry, Esq. (see Lurgashall.)

This long and narrow parish is intersected in its southern portion by the Western Rother, which is here crossed by a bridge. The parish is famous for its growth of apples.

The *Liberty* of Lodsworth, which is co-extensive with the parish, possesses remarkable privileges, viz.—exemption from hundred-courts, from tolls in any fair or market, and from the jurisdiction of the sheriff—but the bailiff of the Bishop of London is to return all writs. A three-weeks' court may be held for recovery of debts by a jury of free suitors, with imprisonment for debt within the gaol belonging to the liberty. No inquisitions *post-mortem* are to be held for lands, &c. These immunities and privileges are set forth in an Inspeximus dated 3rd Henry VI., 1425. The parish was an early appendage to the see of London, and these peculiar rights were granted by one of the Bishops, but what the parish gained in temporal matters it lost in spiritual, for the cure of souls of the church of St. Peter devolved on a stipendiary priest, while the great tithes accrued to St. Paul's. This was literally "robbing Peter to pay Paul." The manor was granted by Henry VIII. to Sir Anthony Browne, who annexed it to Cowdray, with which it has ever since passed. Lodsworth House, the seat of Hasler Hollist, Esq., is a modern mansion with a tower, in a small but beautiful park. Mr. Hollist took the name in exchange from Capron, a family who held lands in Lodsworth in the thirteenth century.

The church (St. Peter) is sometimes described as a chapel to Easebourne. It consists of a nave, chancel, transepts, aisles, and a square tower, and has been almost entirely rebuilt within the last few years. It contains several memorials for the families of Hollist and Bridger. Of the old manor-house adjacent to the churchyard the following account was printed a few years since:—"It is now a farmhouse and much shorn of its former dimensions. Many of its rooms are much dilapidated. One or two heavy buttresses and a pointed window partly blocked up remain, and in the kitchen is a good fire back with the arms of the 1st Viscount Montague, with sixteen quarterings and supporters. There is a dungeon in the house." This may have been the "liberty prison" of Lodsworth. The site of the "liberty gallows" is pointed out at a place called Galley-hill.

[S. A. C. FitzHeriz lands belonging to priory of Hardham, xi, 114. Chapel, xii, 94. Rents to Boxgrove, xv, 119. Bells, xvi, 217. Liberty and gaol, xx, 31.]

LOXWOOD (or Loxwood End).

A hamlet and ancient chapelry of Wisborough Green. The chapel was erected by license of Bishop Robert Praty, in 1414. Three maiden sisters are said to have improved and endowed it about 1540. It consists of nave and chancel.

LULLINGTON.

Vulgo, *Linkun*, or Little Chapel, a Parish in the Hundred of Alciston; Rape of Pevensey; distant nine miles south-east from Lewes, which is its Post-town. Railway station, Berwick, distant about three miles. Union, Eastbourne. Population in 1811, 48; in 1861, 16! Benefice, a Vicarage, valued at £40; Patron, the Bishop of Chichester; Sequestrator, Rev. Henry Kelson, M.A., of Sidney-Sussex College, Cambridge. Date of earliest Parish Register, 1721. Acreage, 1,162.

This South Down parish has one of the smallest populations in the county; as also the smallest church, the interior of which measures only about 16 feet square. It is, however, only the chancel of the original Early English structure. This parish was originally a chapelry to Alciston.

About forty years since a gentleman attended morning service here, when the congregation amounted to twelve persons. The curate was a remarkably diminutive man: he preached from John xi, 35, and the offertory realized 18d.—upon which the stranger remarked that it was the smallest church, the smallest parson, the shortest text, and the smallest collection he had ever witnessed.

The manor was held 28th Elizabeth by Sir Philip Sydney. It afterwards passed to the Sackvilles, whose descendants still possess it. The Woodhams family have held the farm for many generations.

[S. A. C. Domesday watermill, v, 271. Marshall's legacy, xiii, 52. Bell, xvi, 217. Manor to Battle Abbey, xvii, 54. Stone of, xvii, 151. Woodhams family, xvii, 241. A Lullington man in Cade's rebellion, xviii, 27.]

LURGASHALL.

A parish in the Hundred of Rotherbridge; Rape of Arundel; distant five miles north-west from Petworth, its Post-town and Railway station. Union, Midhurst. Population in 1811, 549; in 1861, 727. Benefice, a Rectory, valued at £463; Patron, Lord Leconfield; Incumbent, Rev. Septimus Fairles, B.A., of St. John's College, Cambridge. Date of earliest Parish Register, 1559. Acreage, 4,850. *Chief Landowners*, Lord Leconfield, Lord Egmont, W. T. Mitford, Esq., and Hasler Hollist, Esq. *Seat*, Blackdown Cottage, General Yaldwin.

The ancient spellings Lodekersale, Lotegershale, &c., justify the derivation of the name of this parish from Leodgarius (corruptly Leger), whose *aula* or hall it probably was, in Saxon times. The situation is truly romantic, and from Blackdown Hill views certainly unequalled in Sussex for grandeur and variety can be obtained. This hill, which is of triangular form, lies half in this parish—the rest in Lodsworth and Farnhurst. It is a remarkable cropping up of the greensand formation, and rises towards Lurgashall to a bold promontory 800 feet above the level of the sea. It is covered with furze, holly, and timber, and from its grand and sombre appearance well deserves its name. Blackdown House, just over the border of the parish, in Lodsworth, is one of the most romantically situated mansions in West Sussex. It was partly built in 1640, by William Yaldwin, Esq., who was High Sheriff of the county in 1656, and a partisan of Cromwell; and from this circumstance tradition has intimately associated Blackdown with that personage. The estate belonged for eight generations to the Yaldwins, from William Yaldwin, who died in 1590, to the present William Henry Yaldwyn, Esq., who has recently sold it to James Henry, Esq. The manors in the parish are Diddlesfold and River. About half the great stag park of Petworth is in Lurgashall, and the lords of Petworth have until lately paid a modus of a fat buck and doe to the parson, who at present receives £10 in lieu thereof. The church (St. Lawrence) consists of a nave and chancel, with a tower and shingled spire on the south side. The chancel (Early English) was rebuilt some years since, and the tower is of the Perpendicular period. Adjoining the south porch, to the west, is an open cloister of timber frame, which is said to have been built for the accommodation of remote parishioners who therein ate their dinner between matins and evensong. The nave, in 1866, 7, underwent thorough *preservation*, and in the course of removing the plaster from both sides of the walls, very ancient herringbone masonry, and a north door (I think unquestionably Saxon) were discovered. On the plaster inside were disclosed three rude coats of arms, probably of the 14th century. I. Ten annulets, 4, 3, 2, 1; II. Five fusils—Dawtry of Petworth. III. Chequy—the arms of Lewes Priory. The last coat is accounted for by the fact that Seffrid II., Bishop of Chichester, 1180-1204, granted this church to the Priory of Lewes, which held it until the Dissolution. The building, which is full of interesting features, contains many memorials for the Yaldwyns of Blackdown. The parish reckons among its rectors a William Cobden, James Bramston, author of "The Art of Politics," and Nicholas Turner, brother of Charlotte Smith. (See "Worthies of Sussex," pp. 58 and 15.) In this parish and that of Chiddingfold, just over the Surrey border, are to be found various members of the supposed Saxon family of Enticknapp, now in plebeian condition, and called by their neighbours and themselves *Emlet*.

[S. A. C. Shelvestrode family, xii, 29. Church, xii, 74. James Bramston, xiv, 8. Bells, xvi, 217. River Rother, xvi, 260.]

LYMINSTER, or LEOMINSTER.

Vulgo, *Limster;* a parish in the Hundred of Poling ; Rape of Arundel; near its Post-town, Arundel. Union, East Preston. Population in 1811, 554 ; in 1861, 801. Benefice, a Vicarage, valued at £350 ; Patron, the Bishop of London ; Incumbent, Rev. Matthew Enraght, M.A., of Trinity College, Dublin. Date of earliest Parish Register, 1556. Acreage, 3,230. There are several excellent mansions and residences in the parish, and in its tything Warningcamp.

The etymology of this name is " Leonis monasterium," the convent of St. Leo. It is found in records as Lolinminster, and sometimes Nonneminster, from a nunnery which existed here in ancient times. About half the parish is meadow and brook land, in the valley of the Arun. The earliest mention of the place is in the will of King Alfred, who bequeaths it to his nephew Osferd. Whether this place or the town in Hereford-shire is the place from which Suane, son of Earl Godwin, in-veigled the Abbess, is uncertain. (See Pevensey.) From Domesday it appears that it was held in demesne by the Confessor, and after the Conquest by Earl Roger. It then contained twenty hides never taxed. There were forty-four ploughlands, sixty-eight villeins, and forty-three cottagers, a church, a mill, and two salt-pans, and wood for thirty swine. Its value was £50. Robert held a small estate, which, *temp.* Confessor, had belonged to Azor, and was worth 10s.

The manor followed the descent of the earldom of Arundel,

until it was transferred by sale, *temp.* Elizabeth, to Richard Knight, of Chawton, co. Hants. In 1679 it devolved by the wife of Sir Richard Knight to Richard Martin, son of Michael Martin, by Frances, daughter and co-heiress of Sir Christopher Lewknor, after a circuitous descent through female heirs, whose husbands successively took the name of Knight. In 1786, T. May Knight, Esq., sold the manor to Charles Goring, Esq., of Wiston, with whose representative it remains.

COURTWICK, formerly called "Powers in Wyke," was granted by Henry III. to Stephen le Power, and it descended in the female line to the Apsleys and Bellinghams. At the Reformation it belonged to the monastery of Tewkesbury, and was granted by Henry VIII. to Robert Palmer, of Parham. By his descendant it was conveyed in 1722 to James Colebrook, whose son sold it in 1772 to Richard Bagnall, by whom it was sold in 1774 to Richard Wyatt, Esq., and his great grandson, Hugh Wyatt, Esq., LL.D., is the present owner.

Tottington is mentioned in Domesday as a distinct manor, though held like Lyminster by Azor and by Robert. Totentune was rated at four hides; before the Conquest it was rated at 60s., afterwards at 70s. It is now a hamlet lying in the southeast part of the parish adjacent to Little-Hampton. It belongs to the Duke of Norfolk.

WARNINGCAMP is a district or tything comprising about a third part of the parish, and is bounded by the Arun. Turgod held "Warnecha" of the Confessor, and after the Conquest Nigellus held it. This also was rated at four hides. *Temp.* Confessoris it was worth 60s., afterwards 20s., then 50s., so that some calamity probably befel it at the Norman invasion. The manor of Blakehurst, which contains the whole of Warningcamp, has been possessed by Morley, Geere, Cheale, Whitbread, and Margesson. It is now annexed to the demesne of Arundel Castle. The area is 919 acres, and the population in 1861 was 107. Warningcamp was anciently a distinct parish, but it seems to have been ecclesiastically united with Lyminster before 1292. It is mentioned as a chapelry in 1492. The church or chapel was on the hill to the north-west of the hamlet, but the last vestiges were removed in 1847, when a cottage was erected on the site. Batworth Park is an ancient appendage to Arundel Castle. It is loftily situated, and commands a fine view of the Castle. Cavalry barracks were built here in 1800, but have been removed.

THE NUNNERY of Lyminster was of the Benedictine order, founded on the basis of the Saxon establishment by an early member of the De Montgomeri family, soon after the Conquest. The church and demesnes were then given to the nuns of Almanesche in Normandy, also founded by Roger de Montgomeri, and it continued to be a cell. The convent consisted of a prioress and four nuns. *Temp.* Henry V. the possessions were confiscated, and later the impropriate tythes were granted as part of the foundation of Eton College. It is now held by lessees. The site of the nunnery has been built upon, and no trace of the ancient walls is left. The Chart farm, formerly part of the monastic estate, passed through a succession of owners to the widely-spread and numerous West Sussex family of Duke.

The church (St. Mary Magdalen) comprises west tower, nave, with north aisle and porch, and an unusually long chancel. The tower is Transition Norman, but the greater part of the building is Early English, with Perpendicular insertions. There is a musical peal of six bells. The chancel arch is of peculiar construction, and very lofty. I have not seen this building, but from Mr. Hussey's account of it, it has many points of interest, though Dallaway describes it as of "the coarse parochial architecture," whatever that may mean. It contains monuments for the families of Blake, Groome, Wyatt, &c. In ancient times there were in this small church altars dedicated respectively to Our Lady and SSS. Stephen, John, and Catherine.*

The Priory of PYNEHAM or DE CALCETO, like Warningcamp, has long been annexed to this parish. See Pyneham.

[S.A.C. Domesday watermills, v, 271. Manor of Courtwick, x, 213. Calceto Priory, xi, 89. xviii, 56. Warningcamp (and its vineyard), xi, 102-3. Blakehurst belonged to Tortington Priory, xi, 110. Church, xi, 118. xii, 94. Hobgens of, *ibid.* Warningcamp chapel, *ibid.* Ropers of, *ibid.* Wyatts of Courtwick, xiii, 303. Lands given to Boxgrove, xv, 97. Madgwick of, xvi, 50. Bells, xvi, 216. River Arun at, xvi, 258. Knucker-hole and its legend, xviii, 180 *(Evershed).*]

MADEHURST.

A parish in the Hundred of Avisford; Rape of Arundel; distant three miles north-west from Arundel, its Post-town and Railway station. Union, West Hampnett. Population in 1811, 132; in 1861, 208. Benefice, a Vicarage, valued at £100; Patron, John Charles Fletcher, Esq.; Incumbent, Rev. Henry Nicholls, M.A., of Wadham College, Oxford. Date of earliest Parish Register 1639. Acreage, 1,908. J. C. Fletcher, Esq., of Dale Park, is owner of the entire parish.

Dallaway supposes this parish to have formed, originally, part of Arundel forest. From *temp.* Edward I. to 1593, or later, it belonged to the Arundel estate. In the reign of James

* Mr. Gibbon mentions from ancient wills, "the Good Cross of Lyminster," and two or three curious bequests.

I. the manor passed to Sir Garret Kempe of Slyndon, and James-Anthony, Earl of Newburgh, sold it to Sir George Thomas, Bart., who died in 1815. That gentleman enclosed the lands now known as Dale Park, and erected the large and splendid mansion, from the designs of Bonomi, in 1784. His son aliened it to Thomas Read Kemp, Esq., M.P., who re-sold it to John Smith, Esq., M.P. It is now the property and seat of John Charles Fletcher, Esq.

The church (St. Mary Magdalen), described by Dallaway as "of the plainest architecture," was repaired in 1864, when a north aisle and a new chancel were added, chiefly at the charge of the patron.

[S. A. C. Hoskyn, xii, 69. Church, xii, 95. Page, xvi, 50. Bells, xvi, 218. Kempes had lands in, xix, 119.]

EAST MARDEN.

A parish in the Hundred of Westbourne; Rape of Chichester; distant eight miles north-west from Chichester; Post-town, Petersfield. Union, Westbourne. Population in 1811, 52; in 1861, 63. Benefice, a Vicarage, valued at £162; Patron, the Bishop of Chichester; Incumbent, Rev. Charles Philip Lyne, M.A., of Queen's College, Oxford. Date of earliest Parish Register, 1691. Acreage, 968.

See under *Upmarden*. The prebend of East Marden in Chichester Cathedral was founded in the reign of Henry I., probably by the family of Aguillon, when the manor, which is co-extensive with the parish, was annexed to it. The prebendary has usually leased the site and lands for three lives, and thus the families of Juxon, Brereton, Longcroft, Barwell, and Woods, have been lessees. It is now in the hands of W. Leyland Woods, Esq.

The church (St. Peter) is described by Dallaway as having "a nave or pace only, and remarkable for great antiquity, from that circumstance." A recent account describes it as a handsome Early English structure.

[S. A. C. Church xii, 74. Bell, xvi, 218.]

NORTH MARDEN.

A parish in the Hundred of Westbourne; Rape of Chichester; distant nine miles north from Chichester. Post-town, Petersfield. Union, Westbourne. Population in 1811, 23; in 1861, 28. Benefice, a

Rectory, valued at £70; Patron, the Lord of the Manor; Incumbent, Rev. Andrew Vogan. Date of earliest Parish Register, 1813. Acreage, 682.

See under *Upmarden*. In 1475 the manor was held by Sir George Browne, of Betchworth Castle, who was beheaded by Richard III. in 1483. It remained in the Crown until it was granted, by Queen Elizabeth, to William Grenefield. In later times it belong to the Jenmans and Peckhams, and from the latter it has descended to Admiral Sir Phipps Hornby.

"The church," says Horsfield, "has nothing requiring remark." It certainly deserves notice for the apsidal termination of the chancel, which marks it of the Early Norman period. There are not more than four or five other instances of the apsis in the parish churches of Sussex. The rest of the building appears to be Early English.

[S. A. C. Church, xvi, 134. Bell, xvi, 218.]

MARESFIELD.

Vulgo, *Maresfull;* a parish in the Hundred of Rushmonden; Rape of Pevensey; distant two miles north from Uckfield, its Post-town and Railway station. Union, Uckfield. Population in 1811, 1,117; in 1861, 1,911. Benefice, a Rectory valued at £645; Patron, Charles Salisbury Butler, Esq.; Incumbent, Rev. Edward Turner, M.A., of Balliol College, Oxford. Date of earliest Parish Register, 1538. Acreage, 7,750. *Chief Landowners*, The Representatives of the late Sir John Shelley, Bart.

The history of this parish has been fully written in the " Sussex Collections," by the Rev. Edward Turner, Rector. The soil varies from a stiff loam to a light sand, while Ashdown Forest, a large portion of which lies in the parish, belongs to the iron-sand formation, and is very barren. Its want of fertility is, in some measure, compensated by scenic beauty. The shape of the parish is irregular; its length from south east to north west being fully seven miles, while its average breadth is two only. A nearly isolated part, called Stumbletts, bordering on West Hothly and East Grinstead, lies in a deep forest dell, and not far from their parish churches. Here dwell about forty of the Maresfield folk at a distance of 6½ miles from the parish church. This hamlet and Pippingford warren are both alluded to by Horace Smith, in " Brambletye." Of the origin of the name of Maresfield we can only guess. In ancient documents it is spelt Marrysfeld, and Marysfield. As Mr. Turner conjectures, the district may formerly have been dedicated to St. Mary, though the church has now another invocation.

The church (St. Bartholomew), which, with the village, stands near the southern limit of the parish, is of the Perpendicular style, but has clearly been engrafted on a much earlier building, portions of the chancel and the east window being Decorated. It consists of a chancel, nave, and west embattled tower. The architecture is very simple, but the interior, the walls of which were originally covered with paintings in distemper, is much encumbered by a heavy gallery, and the Shelley pew. In the chancel are a piscina, and three iron grave-slabs, one of which is dated 1667. There are more recent records of the names of Michell, Kidder, &c. The tower contains six modern bells. The north porch, removed some years since from its original position, has some bold oak carving.

The seats in the parish are of no great antiquity. The principal is Maresfield Park. The house, which was called "The Cross," was the residence of the Newnham family, from whom it came to Sir John Shelley, father of the late Sir John Villiers Shelley, Bart., formerly M.P. for Westminster. Sir John Shelley having inherited the estate through his mother, Wilhelmina, daughter and heiress of John Newnham, Esq., added to the old house, and made it a competent residence. It includes a library, sixty feet in length. The family of De Newenham is of great antiquity in the district, as appears from documents of *temp*. Edward III., and earlier. Another house, upon a larger scale, is Twyford Lodge, near Stumbletts, before mentioned. It was built by the late General Sewell, who inherited the estate from his uncle, William Sewell, Esq., one of the six Clerks in Chancery. In the 17th century, William Newnham, Esq., purchased a large tract of Ashdown Forest, called Pippingford, which he enclosed and partially planted. It subsequently passed, by sale, first to William Bradford, Esq., and then to Henry Shirley, Esq. The latter made large additions to the house, which was burnt down in 1836. The estate subsequently became the property of John Mortimer, Esq., who built a spacious house, which commands extensive views over the adjacent wild and romantic scenery. Forest Lodge is another modern house, the residence of Captain William Noble; and Twyford Abbey is that of Robert Trotter, Esq. The only two houses of considerable antiquity are, 1st, "The Park," now a farm house, with few ancient features. This was the residence in the 16th and 17th centuries of the family of Rootes, or Rutes, a name of frequent occurrence in this district. Originally it possessed a well-timbered park. The present Maresfield Park, then, is a modern substitution for "The Cross." The lands, with the advowson of the church, formed part of the estate of Viscount Gage, until 1850, when they were purchased by Sir J. V. Shelley. 2nd, "Marshalls." The property, doubtless, belonged originally to a branch of the ancient Sussex family of Marescal or Marshall, some of whose members served the office of Sheriff as early as *temp.* Richard I. and John. In much later times it would seem to have belonged to the Relfes, and it afterwards came to the Nutts, a branch of the family settled at Mays, in Selmeston, in the 17th century. By one of the Nutts the present stone mansion was built during the Stuart period. From the last of that family it passed to the Holfords, and it afterwards came by purchase to Sir John V. Shelley, Bart. A large house, built in the last century by Mr. William Newnham, was called Street House. It stood opposite the church, but was pulled down by the late Sir J. V. Shelley, when the entrance gate to his grounds, a building in the medieval taste, was erected. The family of Kidder were of long standing in the parish. They were here, according to Mr. Turner, *temp.* Edward II., and one at least of them was Bailiff of Ashdown. They sent off branches to East Grinstead, Lewes, and many other places; one branch went to the United States. Richard Kidder, Bishop of Bath and Wells, was of this stock. The Manor of Duddleswell, partly in Maresfield, belongs to the Earl de la Warr, and there are copious records respecting it among the Burrell MSS. On a commanding site at Duddleswell stands the elegant residence of Elphinstone Barchard, Esq. In this parish are two excellent nursery gardens, belonging respectively to Mr. Wood and Mr. Mitchell. The latter is widely renowned for its roses, and for the finest specimens of the Araucaria imbricata known in England.

There were three considerable iron-works in Maresfield; at Old Land; at the Old Forge, near Lampool; and at the Forge, at the south extremity of the parish, on the site now occupied by gunpowder works. At Old Land the scoriæ, or refuse of the smelted iron, known as "cinders," cover many acres of land, in beds varying from three to six feet in thickness. That the works were carried on here by the Romans at a very early period of their dominion in Britain, I have fully shown in vol. ii. of the "Sussex Collections." Remains of that people in coins, fibulæ, Samian, and other pottery, were found in these cinder-beds in and before the year 1844, when the cinders were much employed in the repair of roads in the neighbourhood. At the "Old Forge" cannon were cast, and balls have frequently been found in the neighbouring proof-bank.

Among the learned rectors of Maresfield was the Rev. Henry Michell, who held the living for fifty years, and the vicarage of Brighton for forty-five. He was instituted to the benefice in 1739. His great erudition is well known, and his friend Clarke, of Buxted, characterized him as a man of great taste and sound judgment, who "read Greek in the country." (See Memoir in

"Worthies of Sussex," p. 230.) The rectory of Maresfield, at the time of the Nonæ Return in 1342, had considerable rights in the chase of Ashdown, including pasturage for twenty head of cattle, and pannage for twenty-four hogs, so that we may conclude that the parson had a well-stored larder. There are many other matters of interest in Mr. Turner's paper, to which I beg to refer the reader.

[S. A. C., including the references to *Ashdown* and *Nutley*. Iron works, ii, 171, 214. iii, 243, 245. xviii, 16, 62, 68. Extracts from Parish Register, iv, 244. Kings Edward II. and Edward III. at, vi, 54. ix, 154. xiv, 45. John of Gaunt at, xiv, 45. Royal hunting seat, viii, 32. xvii, 121. John Wickliffe at, ix, 42. Free chapels of Nutley and Dudeney, ix, 41, 43. xiv, 43. xx, 230. Kidders of, ix, 125. Nutts of Marshalls, xi, 49. xiv, 147. Marshalls of, xi, 83. xiv ,146. xv, 213. Coins, Roman, Saxon, &c., ii, 169. xiv, 38. xiv, 36. xviii, 67. xvii. 252. Church, xii, 17. Shelleys of, xiii, 140. Ashdown Forest, xiv, 34. Cade's insurrection, xviii, 28. Earl of Dorset at Duddleswell Lodge,xiv, 51. The last deer of Ashdown, xiv, 62. Parochial History (*Turner*), xiv, 138. Michelborne of, xiv, 150. Rootes of, xiv, 237. Keymer of, xiv, 237. Bells, xvi, 218, 219. Pilt-down, xvii, 252. Twyford Lodge, xix, 37. Mill, xix, 206. Church of John Pettyt, ix, 43. xiv, 46. Levetts of, xix, 94.]

MAYFIELD.

Vulgo, *Maŏvul*; a town and parish in the Hundred of Loxfield-Pelham; Rape of Pevensey; distant 8½ miles from Tunbridge Wells; Post-town, Hawkhurst; Railway station, Jarvis Brook, distant about 2 miles; Union, Uckfield. Population in 1811, 2,079; in 1861, 2,688. Benefice, a Vicarage, valued at £834; Patron and Incumbent, Rev. H. T. M. Kirby, M.A., of St. John's College, Cambridge. Date of earliest Parish Register, 1,572. Acreage, 13,604. *Chief Landowners*, The Marquis Camden, Right Hon. H. Brand, M.P., Sir F. Sykes, Bart., John Hoskins, Esq. *Seats, &c.*, Lower House, Walter Sprott, Esq.; Tidebrook, T. W. Adams, Esq.; Skipper's Hill, S. Hughes Esq.; Sunny Bank, Donald Barclay, Esq.; Summer Hill, W. Taylor, Esq.; The Vicarage, Rev. H. T. M. Kirby, &c.

Of Mayfield, Mr. Durrant Cooper remarks:—"This is the ground of Sussex miracles and wonders. The very name of Loxfield reminds us of the evil spirit; whilst here it was that St. Dunstan, finding the orientation of his first wooden church rather defective, placed his shoulder to the corner, according to Eadmer, and left it due East and West; and here, too, whilst at work at the forge, turning a horse-shoe, he perceived the 'old gentleman' (in the guise of a beautiful lady) at his anvil, and seizing him by the nose made him vanish."* The legend goes

* S. A. C. Vol. xxi., p. 1.

on to state that when the Saint had the foul fiend well in the grasp of his tongs the latter flew away with him, and he, with the pertinacity which always distinguished him, hung on to the demon for the distance of three miles, and at length descended at a place still called Dunstan's Bridge. The pincers, anvil, and hammer of the Saint are yet preserved in the ante-chapel of the Palace, and they were formerly regarded as irrefragable evidence of the truth of the legend!

St. Dunstan certainly had a *mansio* or resting-place at May-field, and he was doubtless founder of the original church previously to the year 988, the date of his death. Subsequent Archbishops of Canterbury enlarged Dunstan's palace until it became one of the stateliest edifices in the South of England, and was able to give reception to royalty. King Edward I. visited it on several occasions, 1297, 1305. Simon de Meopham, Archbishop, and his successor both died here, and it was here that, in 1332, a Council* for the regulation of Saints' days was held. Numerous deeds, ranging from 1294, to the date of the Reformation, prove that Mayfield (Magafelda) was a favourite residence of the Primates, who held it until Cranmer surrendered it together with the manor, park, and good lands, to Henry VIII. About the year 1350 Archbishop Islip erected the magnificent hall, and many of the other buildings still remaining. The hall itself is 70 feet by 39, and 60 feet high to the apex of the roof. Some parts of the Palace are in the Perpendicular style of the early part of the 16th century. The *ensemble* before the date of the Reformation must have been very grand. Besides the great hall there was a quadrangle at the east end, with projections in the form of square towers. To the south of the Palace the gate-house still remains; it is of the 15th century, and has a lofty pointed arch, now partly blocked up. To return to the hall, it was stripped of its roof towards the end of the last century, and for many years the three grand supporting arches open to the weather remained, one of the finest specimens of the noble and picturesque in Gothic architecture. The character of the building has been well described in Vol. ii. of the "Sussex Archæological Collections," and in Vol. xxiii. of the "Journal of the British Archæological Asssociation," and to them I must refer for many exceedingly interesting details. A short time since, when the Palace was partially restored for the purpose of using it as a Convent, the roof was reinstated, and what was for ages the banqueting-hall of the Archbishops was refitted as a chapel for the Roman-Catholic Sisterhood. Another principal apartment of the Palace bears the name of Queen Elizabeth's room, from

* This was called *Concilium Maghfeldense.*

the tradition that that sovereign occupied it during a temporary
visit to Mayfield. Another feature of the building is a remarkably strong and massive staircase of stone, leading from the
ground floor to the upper apartments. No traces of the true
original chapel remain.

After the alienation of the Palace by Cramner, in 1545, Sir
John Gresham purchased it, and members of his family held it,
and occasionally resided here. Among the number was Sir
Thomas Gresham, the founder of the Royal Exchange, whose
crest, the grasshopper, appears with the date 1571, in "Queen
Elizabeth's room." In 1579 the Palace and estate were devised
to Sir Henry Neville, who appears to have resided at Mayfield,
but in 1597 he sold the palace and manor to Thomas May, Esq.,
of the Franchise in Burwash, whose wife and son sold them in 1617
to John Baker, Esq., in whose descendants they long vested. In
1863 the Duchess of Leeds bought the Palace for conventual
purposes, and the adaptation of the buildings to that use was
entrusted to Mr. Pugin. The hundred and manor were separated
from the Palace, and passed from the Bakers through the Pelhams to the Marquis Camden in 1790.

The park, called Frankham, for the archiepiscopal venison,
was upwards of 400 acres in extent, while the fishponds, measuring 9 acres, attested, as Mr. Cooper observes, "the care for the
welfare of the most reverend prelates on fast days."

Mayfield parish is divided into four districts, called quarters,
namely, Town, Moushill, Five-ash, and Bibleham. The last-named
was formerly called Bivelham, and was the seat of iron-works
when this and the neighbouring parishes were largely engaged
in that industry. To the iron trade succeeded hop-growing, and
in 1837 no less than 614 acres of hop-gardens existed.

The name of Cade prevailed in this parish for many generations,
John being the favourite prænomen.* This goes far to confirm
the statement that Jack Cade, the rebel, who was slain in the
adjacent parish of Heathfield in 1450, was an East Sussex man,
and not an Irishman, as some of our chroniclers assert. Thomas
May, the poet, and historian of the Long Parliament, son of the
purchaser of the estate from Sir H. Neville, lived in his early
days at Mayfield, and Sir Thomas Jenner, the celebrated lawyer
and judge, first saw the light in this parish in 1638.

Mayfield parish contains, besides the manor of its own name,
those of *Isenhurst*, which was formerly part of the possessions
of Michelham Priory, and at later dates the property of the
families of Baker, Kirby, and Treherne; and *Bibleham*, long in
the possession of the Pelhams, but now belonging to the Right
Hon. Henry Brand, M.P. In the last generation the three princi-

* See Mr. W. D. Cooper, in "Sussex Archæological Collections," vol. xxi.

pal residences were known as 1st, Upper House, the Palace; 2nd, Middle House, built in 1575 by William Houghton—this is one of the most curious timber houses in Sussex, and is a picturesque study for the artist; 3rd, Lower House, belonged, in the time of Henry VI., to the family of Aynscombe, and bore the name of Aylwins, probably from some earlier proprietor.

Besides the visit of Queen Elizabeth to Mayfield (1573) to see the great merchant-prince, Sir Thomas Gresham, this old town has had the honour of entertaining royalty in our own times. In 1833 Queen (then Princess) Victoria spent a few hours in surveying the principal objects of this ancient place.

The church, dedicated to St. Dunstan, together with a large part of the town, was burnt down in 1389. The nave, aisles, and choir, and also a chantry, dedicated to St. Alban, were destroyed, but the tower, which is now crowned with a shingled spire, retains traces of Early English architecture. The rebuilding of the fabric took place early in the 15th century, and has some very interesting features, including two piscinæ and a hagioscope. The central window, which escaped the fire, is in the *flamboyant* style. Among the vicars may be named (1.) John de Wickliffe, appointed 1361, and who has been mistaken for the great Reformer. (2.) George Carleton, afterwards Bishop of Llandaff, from whence he was translated to Chichester. (3.) John Maynard, of an old family of Rotherfield. One of his ancestors, William Maynard, was burnt at Lewes for Protestantism in 1557.* This vicar, who was appointed one of the Assembly of Divines, lies buried in the church-yard, and his epitaph assures us that "he shone for 40 years the light and glory of this church of Mayfield." Within the church are numerous inscriptions to the names of Baker, extending over many generations, while other names occurring on the various monuments are Cole, Roberts, Farnden, Houghton, Grant, Aynscombe, Godfrey, Rivers, etc. There are six bells. In the church-yard there formerly stood, it is said, a tombstone with this remarkable effusion :—

" O, reader, if that thou *canst* read,
    Look down upon this stone,
    Death is the man, do what you can,
    That never spareth none !"

The church has lately undergone extensive repairs and restorations.

HADLOW DOWN, in this parish, is a distinct ecclesiastical

---

* Two Protestant martyrs were burnt in the town of Mayfield itself in 1556, viz., John Hart, shoemaker, and Thomas Ravendale, currier. (Foxe.)

district, and FIVE ASHES is a scattered hamlet, about 2½ miles
south-west of the town.   There are several considerable man-
sions in the parish.   Gatehouse, at the south-west corner of
Mayfield, has been owned in succession by the families of
Fuller, Apsley, Dalrymple, and Thomas (Treherne).   Hadlow
House, long the residence of the family of Day, is now that of
John Hoskins, Esq.   At Isenhurst resides Sir Frederic Sykes,
Bart., and there are several other houses in the rural portion
of the parish, some of which are particularized above.

[S. A. C. Ironworks, ii, 214. iii, 241. xviii, 15. Palace of (*Hoare*), ii,
221. Parish register extracts, iv, 256. May family, v, 47. John Baker,
sheriff, v, 60. Baker family, xiii, 96. Morley family, ironworks here, ii,
214. v, 91. Queen Elizabeth at, v, 190. Seal of Friars of Cologne, v, 200.
King Edward I. visits Mayfield, ii, 142. Walter Gale, the schoolmaster,
his Journal, ix, 182. John Wilmshurst, xiii, 58. St. Dunstan's legend,
xiii, 221. *Ibid*, 227. John Edwards, Esq., of Herrings, and his javelin
escort, xiii, 230. Edwards family, xvi, 48. xix, 88. Isted of Morehouse,
xiv, 102. Weston and Day, xvi, 49. Church bells, xvi, 218. Relfes of,
xviii, 14. Ironworks at Bibleham and Hawksden, xviii, 16. Adherents of
Jack Cade, xviii, 23. *Ibid*, 30. Antique sword found at, xviii, 64. Over-
seers' accompts, xviii, 196. Civil marriages at Glynde, xix, 202.]

MERSTON.

Domesday, *Mersitone*; a parish in the Hundred of Box and Stockbridge;
Rape of Chichester ; distant three miles south east from Chichester,
its Post-town. Railway station, Drayton, distant about two miles
north. Union, West Hampnett. Population in 1811, 84; in 1861,
79. Benefice, a Rectory valued at £265; Patron, the Lord Chancellor; Incumbent, Rev. R. F. Chambers, of Trinity College, Dublin.
Date of earliest Parish Register, 1751. Acreage, 710. *Chief Landowner*, J. Godman, Esq., lord of the manor.

A small flat parish.   Before the Conquest, Gort held it of
King Edward, afterwards one Oismelin was tenant of Earl
Roger.   It descended like Hunston to Robert de Monte Alto,
and later to John Bonville.   Afterwards the Carylls had it till
1777.   The Right Hon. Thomas Steele sold it to an ancestor of
the present proprietor and lord of the manor.   The church, of
which an etching is given in Nibbs's churches, consists of nave,
chancel, north aisle, and dovecot steeple.   It is Early English,
with Decorated insertions. The situation is pleasing and picturesque.   A trout stream, which runs through the parish, had
three mills at the date of Domesday.

[S. A. C. Domesday mills, v, 271. Bell of, xvi. 218.]

MICHELHAM PRIORY.

This house of Augustinian canons, dedicated to the Holy Trinity, was founded in the parish of Arlington shortly before the year 1229, by Gilbert de Aquila, whose ancestor, Engenulf de l'Aigle, came over with the Conqueror, and, "with shield slung at his neck, and gallantly handling his spear, struck down many of the English." (Roman de Rou.) The De Aquilas were for several generations lords of Pevensey Castle and its Rape. This place is supposed to have derived its name from Gislebertus Magnus (Anglo-Saxon *micel*) and *ham*, abode or home. The foundation charter confers on the canons his lordship of Michelham, with its park, villeins, and rents; and lands in Hailsham, Willingdon, the Dicker, the Broyle, and other woods in Sussex, with pastures for sixty beasts, and pannage for a hundred hogs, as also the manor of Chyngton in Seaford, where the brethren had afterwards a grange and chapel. A full account of the charters, royal confirmations, &c., relating to this priory is given in Vol. vi. of the "Sussex Collections," by the Rev. G. Miles Cooper. To this new foundation many knightly and gentle families afterwards became benefactors, giving lands in "la Knocke" (retained in Knock-hatch, one of the ancient entrances to Michelham Park), Kelle, Jevington, Brighthelmston (whence the manor of Brighthelmston-Michelham), Ditton in Westham, Willingdon, Isinghurst in Mayfield, Horsted-Keynes, Hartfield, and Cowden. The churches of Laughton and Hailsham were also attached to the foundation. In 1398 the conventual buildings appear to have been in bad condition, consequent upon inundations of the sea on their lands, and as a means of assistance the churches of Alfriston and Fletching were appropriated to the establishment. Thenceforward the priory appears to have possessed a competent revenue, and the prior had forest rights with herbage and pannage in Wilmington, Clavregge in Waldron, Hawkehurste in East Hothly, the Dicker, the Broyle, Waldron, Bromeknoll in Ashdown Forest, and Laughton. There is but little history attached to this monastery, except occasional lawsuits. In 1302, Edward I., on one of his southern progresses, passed a night at the priory. At or just before the dissolution the brethren were eight in number. That event occurred in 1537, when the income was valued at £191 19s. 3d.

The priory was erected on a rich alluvial soil, in the valley of the river Cuckmere, which was here made a spacious square moat with upwards of five acres of water, enclosing an area of eight acres. The situation is extremely picturesque, and the remains of the conventual buildings are still considerable. The gateway continues entire, and is one of the most interesting objects in Sussex. It is an embattled tower about 50 feet in height, with four square-headed windows, and a wide entrance, with a depressed arch, apparently of the fifteenth century. The house itself, having always been inhabited, retains many ancient features. The south side presents a handsome elevation of great length, and on the north side are the remains of the chapel of good Early English work, though much mutilated. The crypt remains unchanged with its groining ribs almost intact. There is a small narrow passage with Early English ribs, and connected with it is a curious recess called "Isaac's Hole," which is conjectured to have been a penitentiary. After the dissolution Michelham became a private residence and was occupied by the families of Marshall, Pelham, &c. It eventually became the property of the Sackvilles, in whose representatives it is still vested. To the lover of the picturesque and the antiquary, Michelham offers a treat rarely to be met with in the south of England.

MIDDLETON.

Domesday, *Middeltone;* a parish in the Hundred of Avisford; Rape of Arundel; distant three miles east from Bognor, its Post-town. Railway station, Yapton, distant about three miles north. Union, West Hampnett. Population in 1811, 50; in 1861, 89. Benefice, a Rectory valued at £180; Patron, G. Hartwell Roe, Esq.; Incumbent, Rev. Alfred Conder, M.A., of Queen's College, Cambridge. Date of earliest Parish Register, 1560. Acreage, 362. *Seat,* Middleton House, Harry Whieldon, Esq.

This parish has suffered greatly from the encroachments of the sea. Between 1292 and the date of the Nonæ roll, 1341, forty acres of arable land had disappeared. Since then much greater ravages have occurred. Altogether it is estimated that since the Conquest more than half the parish has been absorbed. The church (St. Nicholas), which originally stood in the centre of the parish, is mentioned by Cartwright in 1832 as a small, low building. "The south aisle, tower, and half the chancel," he says, "with the whole south side of the churchyard, have been absorbed, and are now covered with shingle." Since that time the building has entirely disappeared, and a new church was erected in 1849. Charlotte Smith's sonnet on Middleton church has often been quoted. A reef of rocks, called Middleton ledge, projecting more than a mile from the shore, points out the former sea margin.

Before the Conquest five free men held Middeltone, and afterwards William held it of Earl Roger. A church is mentioned.

In 1319, John la Warr was mesne lord, and it has since vested in the families of St. John, Poynings, West, Bridger, Thompson, and Coote. The small tything of ELMER gave name to a family *temp*. Henry III.

[S. A. C. Norton of, xii, 90. Church, xii, 95. xviii, 94, 100.]

MIDHURST.

Vulgo, *Medhust;* a parish, borough, and market-town, in the Hundred of Easebourne; Rape of Chichester; distant twelve miles north from Chichester, and six west from Petworth. It has a Railway-station on the Mid-Sussex line. Union, Midhurst. Population in 1811, 1,256; in 1861, 1,340. Benefice, a Perpetual Curacy, valued at £170; Patron, the Earl of Egmont; Incumbent, Rev. William Haydon, M.A., of University College, Oxford. Date of earliest Parish Register, 1565. Acreage, 671.

Midhurst is one of the many interesting spots with which West Sussex abounds, and, though not rich in historical associations, possesses much picturesque beauty, and a most salubrious climate. The notion that it represents a Roman station called Miba or Mida is utterly groundless. The name is Saxon, from *middan* and *hirst*, and signifies a place in the midst of woody ground. The town, which lies on the south bank of the Rother, consists principally of North Street, the rising ground known as Rumbold's Hill, and West Street. Midhurst is not mentioned in Domesday, as at that period it was probably included, both manorially and ecclesiastically, in Easebourne. In the reign of Henry I., Savaric de Bohun obtained 4¼ knights' fees, and held of the honour of Arundel. By that monarch it was erected into a minor barony or lordship, and was held of the King. *Temp*. Edward I., Walter, Lord Beke of Eresby, was in possession, with remainder to the De Bohuns.* John de Bohun was summoned to Parliament as Baron of Midhurst, probably in reward of his services in Flanders and at Cressy, but after his death, in 1367, this peerage seems to have discontinued. His descendant, John de Bohun, died without male issue, and his estates here and elsewhere passed, *temp*. Henry VII., to his two daughters and co-heiresses, Mary, wife of Sir David Owen, natural son of Owen Tudor, grandfather of Henry VII., and Ursula, wife of Robert Southwell, of Suffolk. Upon a hill rising above the Rother stood the baronial castle of the De Bohuns, with its chapel of St. Anne, the site being now overgrown with

* In 1278 the demesne is described as containing a messuage, two parks, and two mills.

stately trees. From the dedication of the chapel, the place supposed to have been deserted as early as the reign of Edward III., is still called St. Anne's-hill, *vulgo,* "Tan Hill." King Edward I. visited Midhurst in 1286, 1299, and 1305. In the last-mentioned year his son, the first Prince of Wales, stayed here four days in order to overtake his father, whom he had offended. The names of Butler and Hoad, still retained at Midhurst, seem to represent those of Le Botiler and Ode, who are mentioned in the records relating to the visit of the "long-shanked king."

Midhurst is a borough by prescription. It sent two members to Parliament from *temp.* Edward II.; but in 1832 it was limited to one, and even to secure that one, it was necessary to annex several adjacent parishes. Two or three personages well known to fame have represented the borough, including Charles James Fox, and, more recently, Samuel Warren, Q.C., author of "Ten Thousand a Year," &c. The patronage of the borough has passed through the families of Fagg, Peachey, Knight, and the Lords Montague, to that of Smith, J. Abel Smith, M.P., being the present owner. There were formerly about 120 burgage tenements, which entitled their respective owners to vote. One of the Lords Montague pulled some of them down that he might enlarge Cowdray Park, but had stones inscribed "a Burgage" put into the wall to indicate their sites, whereupon a noble duke remarked that "so low had the elective franchise fallen, that at Midhurst the very stones appeared as voters for members of Parliament!" The Knights of St. John of Jerusalem had a Commandery here, probably as successors to the Knights-Templars, when the latter order was dissolved by King Edward II. They had jurisdiction over a district still known as the Liberty of St. John, which is independent of both the borough and manor of Midhurst. After the Reformation it was granted in 1542 to Sir William Fitz-William, K.G. The liberty extends into several neighbouring parishes.

The church, dedicated, according to ancient wills, to St. Mary Magdalen, but popularly ascribed to St. Denis, is a chapel-of-ease to Easebourne. The building, which is neither very ancient nor imposing, is principally of the Perpendicular style of *temp.* Henry VI. It consists of nave, chancel, and two small aisles on the south side separated by a tower, the lower part of which appears to be either Norman or very Early English. The west aisle or chapel, built by the executors of William, Earl of Southampton, contained a costly monument to the first Lord Montague and his two wives, but this has been removed. In 1422 Henry Bageley or Baggele founded in this church a brotherhood and a chantry for his soul. Mr. Cooper informs us that he became a Lollard, and was burnt in Smithfield in 1431. There is now little of interest within the building, and the existing monuments are for the families of Mellish, Cresswell, Bailey, Fisher, Shirley, Bridgman, Morrison, Golding, Robson, Upperton, &c. The tower contains six bells. A grammar-school was founded here in 1672 by Mr. Gilbert Hannam, a coverlet-maker, for " 12 poore men's sonnes," who must be neither Romanists nor Dissenters. The school arose upon this foundation to be one of the best in the county. Three Bailys (all D.D.'s) were in succession head-masters; and in the time of the first Dr. Baily the private scholars numbered 70. Richard Cobden and Sir Charles Lyell were boys here. The building was enlarged by successive masters, but of late, by reason of internal mismanagement, the school has been disused, and, when I last visited the schoolhouse, nearly every window of it had been broken by stonethrowers. There are several excellent residences within and about the town. At Todham formerly stood a mansion, containing a chapel, built in the reign of Queen Elizabeth, by George Denis. It contained the arms of Denis, Rose, Pelham, &c.

W. D. Cooper, Esq., has written an account of " Midhurst: its Lords and its inhabitants," in Vol. xx. of the " Sussex Collections," which, though very interesting, is too long for even an outline here.

[S. A. C. Free chapel, iii, 23. xx, 28. Bohuns, v, 178. vii, 22. Visit of the Society to, xx. Report, ix. Midhurst, its lords, landowners, &c. (Cooper), xx, 1—33. Owens of, v, 178. Fitz-Williams, v, 179. Montagues, v, 179. xx, 204. Poyntz of, v, 179. xv, 136. Domesday watermill at Todham (Qy. Coster's mill), v, 272. King Edward I. at, i, 138. xx, 8. ii, 85, 138, 143, 152. The storm of 1703, xii, 55. xx, 204. Church, xii, 74. xx, 24. Bells, xvi, 218. Hearth-tax, xv, 71. Grammar school, xv, 73. xx, 26, 203. Parish charities, xvi, 61. River Rother, xvi, 259. Aylwins of, xvii, 254. xix, 93. London road to Chichester, xix, 167. St. Anne's Hill, xx, 175. Castle of, xx, Report. Belonged to Arundel, xx, 1. Families of Boteler, Puffere, Hosey, Lundenisse, Chedingfold,- Horne, and Tanner, xx, 7. Exton of, xx, 11. Brotherhood of, xx, 15, 24. Denis of Todham, xx, 15. Families of Turner, Lewknor, and Napper, xx, 19. Families of Taylor and Woodecote, xx, 7. Baggele, Lollard and martyr, xx, 24. Torton Priory lands, xx, 25. Incumbents, ibid. Liberty of St. John, xx, 27. Cobdens of, xvi, 51. xx, 29. Hollis of, xx, 29. Races at, xx, 227.]

MILLAND. (See Trotton.)

MILTON STREET.

A hamlet of Arlington, close to Wilmington, whither the inhabitants repair for divine worship, &c., on account of the

remoteness of their parish church. Milton Court, the ancient
manor house, has been for the last two centuries in the tenancy
of the very old Sussex family of Ade. There were before the
erection of the present house, remains of the old manorial
chapel. The late Mr. Charles Ade, the well-known archæologist and numismatist, was father of the present tenant, Mr. J.
S. Ade.

MOUNTFIELD.

Domesday, *Montifelle;* vulgo, *Muntful;* a parish in the Hundred of
Netherfield; Rape of Hastings; distant four miles north from
Battle. Post-town, Hawkhurst. Railway station, Robertsbridge,
distant about 2½ miles. Union, Battle. Population in 1811, 581; in
1861, 585. Benefice, a Vicarage, valued at £180. Patron, Earl De
la Warr; Incumbent, Rev. William Margesson, M.A., of Christ
Church, Oxon. Date of earliest Parish Register, 1558. Acreage,
3,841. *Seats,* Court Lodge (*now* Mountfield Court), Edward Christopher Egerton, Esq., M.P.; and Rushton Park, Wm. Rushton
Adamson, Esq.

A well-wooded and pleasingly undulated parish. The
manor is an infeudation of Echingham. Gode held it of the
Confessor, but after the great Survey, Reinbert held Montifelle
of the Earl of Eu. *Temp.* Henry III., and probably earlier, it
belonged to the family of Sokeners. In that reign William,
son and heir of Roger Sokeners, granted to Benedict, son of
Robert de Hokestepe, the lands of Westdune and Loleland in
this manor. The Hokestepe family (whose name is now corrupted to Huckstepp) are of great antiquity in these parts. In
23rd Edward I. William de Echingham was lord, and the manor
continued with his descendants until 1468. From the Tyrwhitts,
who inherited from that baronial race, it passed to the family
of English, who about the year 1660 sold it to that of Nicholl,
in whose possession it remained until within the last few years.
The manor of Farne or Vinehall, anciently Fynhawe, gave name
to the family of De Fynhawe, who ultimately wrote themselves
Vinall, settled at Kingston near Lewes, and became extinct about
the end of the 17th century. It afterwards belonged to the family
of Dunk, and then to that of Davis. It has lately passed by
sale from Mr. Tilden Smith to W. R. Adamson, Esq., by whom
it has been re-named Rushton Park, and the mansion possesses
every appliance of luxury, including gas made on the spot, and
commands a fine view. Glattingham is another reputed manor.
In a wood upon it, called the Castle Wood, remains of an ancient
moated mansion were traceable not long since. The site, with a

few acres of land, though locally in Mountfield, belongs to the parish of Echingham. The property called Walters belonged successively to the families of Hickes, Dunmoll, Mercer, and Durrant.

In 1863 a remarkable discovery was made in an enclosure called Barn Field, in this parish. It consisted of torques, pen-annular rings, &c., of solid gold, which may have formed the personal ornaments of a King or Druid of the Celtic period. This treasure-trove, estimated to weigh nearly thirteen pounds, and worth £650 sterling, was discovered by a ploughman, and sold by him as old brass for 6d. per pound. The purchasers, who knew the value, sold their nefarious prize to a refiner in London, who consigned it to the melting pot! This is one of the most serious losses that Sussex archæology ever sustained; but it is satisfactory to state that after an inquest made by the coroner of the district, and criminal proceedings taken at Lewes Assizes, the guilty parties, Thomas and Willet, were imprisoned in the county gaol until payment of the value of their plunder (assessed at £530) should be paid. The refiner himself ought, perhaps, to have gone through the fiery trial of a prosecution for such barbarous destruction of historical remains. Sixteen yeomen and labourers of this parish were concerned in Jack Cade's rising, 1450.

The church (All Saints) was restored some years since, chiefly at the cost of Earl de la Warr. It consists of a chancel, nave, and bell-turret, with an ancient bell inscribed to St. Augustine. The style is Early English. On a window in the nave are the arms of Echingham, and on the font is a shield with three escallops (2 and 1), a coat which occurs at Dallington, Roberts-bridge, &c. There is a monument for the Hicks family.

[S. A. C. Ironworks, iii, 245. Weekes of, iron-masters, xi, 82. Church, xiii, 136. Gold ornaments found *(Combe)*, xv. vii, 238. xvi, 310. River Brede, xv, 154. Bell, xvi, 218. Tithes to Battle, xvii, 24. Cade's adherents, xviii, 26.]

NORTH MUNDHAM.

Domesday, *Mundreham;* a parish in the Hundred of Box and Stockbridge; Rape of Chichester; distant two miles south-east from Chichester, its Post-town ; Railway station, Drayton, distant about 2½ miles. Union, West Hampnett. Population in 1811, 430 ; in 1861, 426. Benefice, a Vicarage, with Hunston annexed, value £645. Patron, Representatives of the late J. B. Fletcher, Esq.; Incumbent, Rev. Charles Dudding Holland, B.A., of Caius College, Cambridge. Date of earliest Parish Register, 1558. Acreage, 1,882. *Chief Landowners,* Miss Merricks and J. Bayton, Esq. *Seats,* Runcton House, Miss Merricks; Mundham House, Mrs. Hollingdale.

A pleasant sequestered village on a fertile soil. Goda, the mother of Harold, held the manor of Edward the Confessor. After the Conquest it was part of the barony of Earl Roger de Montgomeri. It had a church and 2½ mills. At a later date it was possessed by Robert de Monte Alto, and descended to the St. Johns. In more recent times the Lords La Warr, the Bowyers, Coverts, Balletts, and Breretons held it. Rochintone, presumed to be the same as Runcton, is also mentioned in Domesday. At the Dissolution, Mundham and Runcton were purchased by Thomas Bowyer, an eminent citizen of London, whose family had been connected with Sussex from the time of Henry IV. It has been for three generations in the family of Merricks. It formerly had a chapel. Leythorne, in this parish, was one of the manors of Bishop Sherburne, who bequeathed it to the Dean and Chapter of Chichester. Sir Thomas Bowyer, a great Royalist, rebuilt the house in stately fashion. It was destroyed in 1798. A younger branch of the Bowyers had the estate of Vinitrow in this parish. Brimfast, another small estate, was part of the grant of Ceadwalla to Bishop Wilfred; and Fishers belonged to the family of Merlot.

The church (St. Stephen) consists of nave, chancel, north and south aisles under one roof span, and embattled west tower. It is a rude, picturesque building, with Norman, Early English, and later features. Dallaway says that the chapel of St. Mary Magdalene was founded by a member of the St. John family of Halnaker, before 1348, at the end of the north aisle. There are several curious monuments and inscriptions for the families of Bowyer, Cassey, Byrch, Evans, Woodyer, Covert, Newland, and Bigs.

[S. A. C. Bowyer of Leythorne, v, 47. xvi, 50. Domesday watermills, v, 271. Bonvilles, lords of, xv, 59. Lands, &c., to Boxgrove Priory, and church rebuilt, xv, 91, 92. Bells, xvi, 219. Topography of, xviii, 94.]

MUNTHAM.

A considerable estate, extending into the parishes of Findon, Sullington, and Washington. It belonged from early times (46th Edward III.) to a family of the same name, whose original *habitat* appears to have been in the parish of Itchingfield, this being an outlying portion of their manor. In 12th Henry VI. John Apsley was owner; and in 1st Edward VI. it belonged to his descendant, Nicholas Apsley, whose son sold it to the Shelley family.   Later it was owned by the families of Crowe, Middleton, and Montague.   In 1765 it became the property of William Frankland, Esq., of the baronet family of Thirkleby, co. York, and a descendant, through female lines, of Oliver Cromwell. The house, which lies in a deep dell, was built by Anthony, Viscount Montague, as a hunting-box.   Mr. Frankland (who had been, for those days, an adventurous spirit, having for some time resided at Bengal, returned, in the character of a tatar or messenger, and visited Bagdad, Jerusalem, the site of, Babylon, Palmyra, and many other places) greatly enlarged the house.   There he employed himself in mechanical pursuits, and made his habitation a kind of museum for organs, turning lathes, looms, &c., at the cost of more than £20,000.   He pursued his favourite tastes at Muntham for 40 years of his life, and died in 1805, more than 84 years of age.   He had a good collection of pictures illustrative of his descent from Cromwell.

NETHERFIELD.

A hamlet in the parish of Battle, giving name to a hundred. The qualifying *nether* I could never understand, as the place is seated on high ground, and from it the coast of France may be clearly discerned.   A memorial church (St. John the Baptist), with parsonage-house and schools, was erected here about 1860, by Sarah Lady Webster, for her husband, Sir Godfrey Webster, Bart., of Battle Abbey.   This is a great accommodation for many of the outlying inhabitants of Battle.   The patron is the Bishop of Chichester, and the present Incumbent is the Rev. Thomas Partington, M.A.

NEWHAVEN (otherwise MEECHING).

A parish in the Hundred of Holmstrow; Rape of Lewes; distant 6½ miles south of Lewes, its Post-town. It has two railway stations on a branch of the South Coast line; and gives name to a Union. Population in 1811, 755; in 1861, 1,886.   Benefice, a Rectory, valued at £186 ; Patron and Incumbent, Rev. Ebenezer P. Southwood, M.A., of Trinity College, Cambridge. Date of earliest Parish Register, 1553. Acreage, 1,217.

What was, three hundred years since, the village of Meeching has, both previously and since, undergone considerable vicissitudes—greater perhaps than any other place on the Sussex coast.   The natural embouchure of the estuary of the Ouse was here in early times, and during the days of Roman occupation it was of sufficient importance to be defended by massive

earthworks, the remains of which we see on the western side of
the present port, and known as Castle Hill. The inroads of the
sea greatly altered the contour of the coast at this point,
and for centuries the ancient bed of the river was driven, by the
accumulation of shingle, three miles eastward, to Seaford, which
thus became an important haven. In the 16th century, by the
application of art, the Ouse was made to debouch at or near its
ancient point, and at New-Haven it has become more recently
one of the principal harbours on our coast. Some antiquaries
have fixed here the commencement of the great Roman *via*,
known as the Ermin Street. At the present time it is one of
the principal ports for communication between London and
Paris, on by far the most direct route. Powerful steamers daily
ply between it and Dieppe, and it has a considerable coasting
traffic. With a further outlay of money and engineering skill,
its advantages might be greatly increased, and some sanguine
minds have fixed here " the Liverpool of the South." Government authority has been brought to bear, and a fort of enormous
strength to mount 42 guns is in course of construction on the
Castle Hill; the total cost, including accommodation for 300
men, is estimated at £150,000. During the necessary excavations
attention has been drawn to the existence of an extensive
" kitchen-midden " or dust heap of a Roman camp, containing
broken pottery, animal remains, and other relics of the past.
The geological features of the cliff at Newhaven are very remarkable. It was at Newhaven that Louis-Philippe and his Queen
landed on their escape from France in 1848.

The town of Newhaven proper consists principally of one hilly
street to the west of the Ouse; another portion lies to the east
of the river, and is in the parish of Denton.

The manor of Meeching is not named in Domesday. It belonged
to the De Warennes in the 14th century. Much later it was
vested in the Gibbons, relatives of the historian. From him it
passed to his friend, the Earl of Sheffield, father of the present
noble proprietor.

The church (St. Michael) stands on a hill to the west of the
town. The western portion is recent and of no interest, but the
tower, placed near the east end of the building, with a semi-
circular apse is remarkable, and bears a striking resemblance to
that of Yainville, near Jumièges in Normandy. It is probably
one of the earliest Norman erections in England. On the north
side of the church-yard is an obelisk commemorating 105 men,
the Captain and crew of the Brazen, sloop of war, wrecked on
the Ave rocks in this parish, in 1800.

[S. A. C. Roman remains, v, 263. Humphrey's Inventory, vi, 190
Church, ix, 89 (*Lower*). xvi, 134. Smugglers, x, 81. Battery, xi, 151.

"Tipper" Ale, xi, 214. Drayton Polyolb., xv, 164. Quakers' xvi, 87.
Bell, xvi, 219. Jack Cade, xviii, 24. "Kitchen-Midden," xviii, 165-169
(*Lower*). Road to London, xix, 155, 163. Slate shipped from West-
moreland, xx, 78.]

NEWICK.

A parish in the Hundred of Barcombe; Rape of Lewes; distant 4½ miles
west from Uckfield, its Post-town and nearest Railway station. Union,
Chailey. Population in 1811, 452; in 1861, 991. Benefice, a Rec-
tory, valued at £387. Incumbent, Rev. William Powell, M.A., of
Oriel College, Oxford. Date of earliest Parish Register, 1559.
Acreage, 1,966. *Seats*, Newick Park, James H. Sclater, Esq.;
Beechland, Thomas St. Leger Blaauw, Esq.; Newick Lodge, M. T.
Archer, Esq., &c.

The surface of this parish is somewhat undulating, and has
agreeably diversified scenery. There are several mineral springs
near the Ouse, which runs through the parish. Newick Place
or Park was formerly the seat of the Hon. George Vernon, lord
of the manor. It is finely situated, and commands views of a
well-wooded and fertile country. Beechland, the residence of
the late William Henry Blaauw, Esq., M.A., F.S.A., the accomplished Sussex Antiquary, is an elegant mansion. The Rectory
is a delightful residence. All these houses are approached by
avenues.

Newick (*novus vicus*) does not seem to be of great antiquity.
It is not mentioned in Domesday, but it may have been included
in the manor of Barcombe, then Bercham. In 9th Edward I. it
was held by John, Earl of Warenne, Ralph de Camoys, Simon
de Petroponte, and the Prior of Lewes. In 28th Henry VI. the
Prior of Lewes solely held Newyke. In 12th Elizabeth, it seems
to have been a subinfeudation of the manor of Westmeston, as
it is mentionened in the Burrell MSS. that "the tenants of this
manor have long time used to do their suit to the Lords of the
manor of Westmeston, being six miles distant, which affirme
their custumes to be in all things as in Westmeston." In 24th
Elizabeth, Gregory Fynes, Lord Dacre, and Lady Anne his wife,
conveyed this manor with other lands to George Goring, Esq.,
of Lewes. Among subsequent lords have been the Boords of
Cuckfield, Longley of London, Relfe, the Lords Mansell, and the
Vernon family. Lord Vernon in 1791 had it for life. It was
afterwards sold to Sir Elijah Impey, from whom it passed to
James Powell, Esq. It is now the property of James Henry
Sclater, Esq. Other manors extend into the parish.

The church (St. Mary) consists of a chancel, nave with north

aisle, (added about the year 1836). The south porch is in the
Decorated style, as is also the west tower, which contains three
bells. The chancel, is Early English, having Decorated windows
under earlier arches. There are a piscina, and two sedilia, all
rich. In the nave were formerly four small Norman windows, of
which two and a Norman door were obliterated in erecting the
aisle; one window still appears in the south wall. (Hussey.)
The church contains memorials for members of the families
of Vernon, Mansell, and others. The view from the leads of the
tower over the Wealden district, especially towards the east, is
remarkably fine.

[S. A. C. Ironworks, ii, 215. Seal of William de la Chapel, ii, 303·
Prior of Lewes, iii, 41. Parish Register extracts, iv, 255. Buddesslyde,
xiii, 48. Bells, xvi, 219. Cade's insurrection, xviii, 29. Robert Payne's
school at East Grinstead, xx, 143.]

NEWTIMBER.

Domesday, *Nivembre;* a parish in the Hundred of Poynings; Rape of
Lewes; distant four miles south-west from Hassock's Gate station.
Post-town, Hurst-Pierpoint. Union, Cuckfield. Population in 1811,
173; in 1861, 162. Benefice, a Rectory; Patron, Arthur Pitman
Gordon, Esq.; Incumbent, Rev. A. Pitman Gordon, M.A., of Christ
Church, Oxford. Date of earliest Parish Register, 1558. Acreage,
1,663. *Chief Landowners,* Ch. H. Wm. Gordon, Esq., and Lord
Leconfield. *Seat,* Newtimber Place, C. H. W. Gordon, Esq.

This parish lies at the northern foot of the South Downs.
The scenery is bold and romantic, and there are many agreeable
undulations of surface. The principal house is Newtimber Place,
a brick building with remains of a moat. It has passed in
modern times through the families of Osborne and Newnham,
to that of Gordon, the present owners. Domesday Book informs
us that Nivembre belonged to William de Warenne. Previously
it had been the fee of Alfech (Elphick?) an allodial tenant. It
was rated at ten hides. There were fourteen villeins, seven
bondmen, a mill yielding 20d., and a wood for three hogs.
Walter de Dunstanville gave Niewtymbre to his wife Dionysia.
Alan de Dunstanville gave it to the monks of Lewes Priory to
pray for the soul of his wife, but it would appear that a descendant
of De Warenne claimed it by inheritance. Later it came to the
great family of De Bohun. At the dissolution of the monasteries it was the property of Lewes Priory, and Henry VIII.
granted it first to the vicar-general Cromwell, and afterwards
to Anne of Cleves. In 15th Elizabeth, Edward Darell appears
to have died seised of the manor. From the Darells it came

to the family of Bellingham, then very influential in this district. Subsequent owners have been Woodcock, Cust, Osborne, Newnham, and Gordon, the present possessors. The paramount lord of Newtimber is the Duke of Norfolk, in virtue of his descent from the De Warennes, the ancient lords of the Rape of Lewes. Another manor in this parish is Saddlescombe, for which see a separate article. Interments of an ancient date—apparently warriors, each with a weapon by his side—were discovered near the earthwork called Wolstonbury, in 1765.

The church (St. John the Evangelist) is small (probably of Early English date) and consists of a nave, chancel, and a square flint tower (date 1839) of rather good aspect, which boasts of one bell only. The building contained some years since, a few remains of painted glass, as also a cross, the arms of De Bohun ; but not having visited this church I cannot say whether they still exist. There are inscriptions to the families of Osborne, Newnham, &c. The Countess de Priseche, who, with her husband the Count, had, after the French Revolution, been guests of G. L. Newnham, Esq., was buried in this church in 1793, and her coronet was suspended over her grave.

[S. A. C. Parish register, iv, 275. Domesday mill, v, 271. Saddlescombe, Knights-Templars of, ix, 227. Byne family, xii, 111. Roman road, xiv, 178. Church bell, xvi, 219. Washbrook stream, xvi, 252.]

NINFIELD.

A parish in the Hundred of its own name; Rape of Hastings ; distant ten miles north-west from Hastings. Post-town, Battle. Railway station, Battle, distant about five miles. Union, Hailsham. Population in 1811, 505 ; in 1861, 587. Benefice, a Vicarage, valued at £451 ; Patrons, Dean and Chapter of Canterbury; Incumbent, Rev. George Rainier, B.A., of Brasenose College, Oxford. Date of earliest Parish Register, 1663. Acreage, 2,554.

This parish is seated on an eminence, and commands an interesting view, including Battle Abbey, part of Hastings, Ashburnham, Crowhurst Park, part of the range of the South Downs, and, in the distance, Pevensey bay and Eastbourne. The highest elevation in the parish is Standard Hill, on which stands an old house with gables, and an inscription in raised letters on the front, as follows :—

" God's providence is my inheritance. Except the Lord build the house, they labour in vain that build it. Here we have (1659) no abidence."

" The origin of this inscription is supposed to be, that a former proprietor was displeased with his heir, and determined to disinherit him, but the heir unexpectedly recovering possession of his inheritance, inscribed these words on his dwelling for a memorial." (Hastings Past and Present.)

In a subsidy roll of 1327 for the parish occurs the name of Stephen atte Standard.

The Domesday account of this place is by no means clear, and it is impossible to ascertain whether it or the adjacent vill of Netherfield is intended. The manor belonged to the Earls of Eu, during the ascendancy of that family in the Rape; but after their forfeiture it passed to the family of Hastings. In 1295 the families of Cherche and Brun appear as the principal land-owners.

The church (St. Mary) comprises chancel and nave, and a large wooden bell-turret over the west end of the latter. It contains only one bell, dedicated to St. Martin, with an Old English inscription. The architecture is partly Early English and partly Decorated. There is little of interest in the church. There are memorials to the names of Luxford of Moorhall, in this parish, Dunk, Bowyer, Clark, and Fuller. At the south-east corner of the church-yard is a grand old yew tree.

The parish register contains the following rather curious entry : "Anno Domini, 1669, June 23, was buried Joseph Tysehurst, a boy (son of the late William Tysehurst) who on Witsunday morning fell from climbing a magpy's nest, and was smothered in a pond of mud, his heels sticking upright."

More-hall was for several generations the estate of a branch of the ancient family of Wenham of Wenham Hall, in Suffolk, who continued to hold it down to the latter half of the seventeenth century.

[S. A. C. Chapel of, xiii, 135, 144. Weekes of, xiv, 116. Asten stream, xv, 156. Bell, xvi, 219. Lands to Battle Abbey, xvii, 43. Notes of and its registers (*Sharpe's MSS.*), xvii, 57. Families of Brown, Milward, and Ingram, xvii, 58, 59. Inundation, xvii, 59. Estons of, xvii, 130.]

NORTHEYE   (See with HIDNEY).

NORTHIAM.

Vulgo, *Norgem;* a parish in the Hundred of Staple, bounded on the north by the river Rother, which separates it from Kent; Rape of Hastings; distant eight miles north-west from Rye; Post-town, Staplehurst. Union, Rye. Population in 1811, 1,114; in 1861, 1,260.

Benefice, a Rectory, valued at £800. The patronage has long been
in the family of Lord; Incumbent, Rev. John Octavius Lord, M.A.
Date of earliest Parish Register, 1558. Acreage, 3,486. *Seat*,
Brickwall, Thomas Frewen, Esq.

> " O rare Norgem ! thou dost far exceed
> Beckley, Peasmarsh, Udimore, and Brede."

This ancient distich has relation to the superior importance
of this parish to some of its neighbours. Without detracting
from the merits of the other four, we may certainly accord high
praise to this, for its truly rural and delightful aspect, with its
pleasing admixture of arable, pasture, meadows, woods, and
hop-gardens. In Domesday the manor is called simply Hiham,
the prefix *North* having probably been applied in order to distinguish it from the neighbouring places called Higham, in
Salehurst, and Petit Higham, the site of New Winchelsea. The
manor belonged, in Saxon times, to Earl Godwin, and afterwards to the Earl of Eu in person. It contained two hides,
and was valued at £6. "It had been devastated"—probably by
an overflow of the Rother, which is its northern boundary. In
24th Edward III. William Fiennes was lord, and in 9th Edward
IV. Richard F., Lord Dacre, held it with Ewhurst, late the possessions of John Brenchley and Thomas Ashburnham, and before
of Henry Sharnden and Richard Codyng, by the service of 1½
knight's fee. The next recorded holder of the manor is Nicholas
Tufton, who died in 1539, and by his will directed his body to
be buried in the church of Northiam, before the altar of St.
Nicholas, with a tombstone, and his picture, and a writing
thereon. The direction was obeyed, but the brass has been torn
off in modern times, though it is engraved in Grose, vol. i.
His son, John Tufton, succeeded him in the manor. The manor
of Tufton, or Toketon, gave name to the important family of
De Toketon, who resided in Northiam for several centuries, and
became ancestors of the Tuftons, Earls of Thanet. Their abode,
called Tufton Place, is now represented by a farm-house. Among
the Brickwall evidences is a deed executed at Northiam in
1362, to which Simon de Toketon was a witness. About the
end of the last century the then Lord Thanet sold it to the
late Edward Jeremiah Curteis, Esq., whose grandson, Herbert
Mascall Curteis, Esq., sold it, a few years since, to Lord Harry
Vane, now Duke of Cleveland. The family of Tufton ceased to
be resident here from the sixteenth century, when they removed
to Hothfield, in Kent. Dixter, another manor, which has long
been in the Springett family, gave name to the De Dixternes at
an early date. Adam and William De Dixterne are mentioned
in a deed of 1296, and John Dykesterne was vicar of Rye in

1306.[*] The manor seems to have passed to the widely-spread Sussex family of Tregoz, for in 1330 the King granted to Thomas Tregoz license to fortify his manse here with a wall of stone and lime, and to crenelate the same. To this family it would appear that that of Elrington succeeded, as in 1479 John Elryngton, Knight, obtained a similar license for Dixtherne and Udeymere. This Sir John Elryngton was Keeper of the Wardrobe to Edward IV., Treasurer of the Household to Edward V., and Constable of Windsor Castle. He married Margaret, daughter and co-heiress of Thomas Echingham. Some remains of the ancient manor-house exist. It was a timber-framed edifice; one half only is now standing. The architectural details are strictly medieval, and the hall contains some rudely carved armorials on the trusses which support the roof, but they have not been critically examined. An antique house hard by bears the date of 1583, and another at Hole farm has some curious details. Well-house, on the Frewen estate, is another timbered building of considerable antiquity, with a hall open to the roof. A picturesque farm-house, called Carriers, on the Brickwall estate, is also ancient, and is, according to tradition, the birth-place of Archbishop Frewen (See post). On the village-green, near the church-yard, is a hollow tree, 24 feet in circumference, called Queen Elizabeth's Oak, from the circumstance that on August 11, 1573, the maiden queen, en route from Mr. Guldeford's, at Hempstead, to the town of Rye, dined under this tree, the viands being furnished by Mr. George Bishopp, who dwelt opposite the oak in the antique timbered house still existing, which was the abode of his family for many generations. During the repast her Majesty changed her shoes, and the pair she took off, having been begged from her attendants, are still preserved at Brickwall. The tradition of the Queen's having dined at Northiam is fully confirmed by the book of the Comptroller of Her Majesty's household of the date, which also states that she again dined at Northiam on her return journey on the 14th August following.

Brickwall House ranks amongst the most interesting mansions of East Sussex. It was originally the residence of the Whites, a family long connected with Rye and Winchelsea. John White purchased the estate in 1492. Towards the end of Elizabeth, William White succeeded, and married Mary, sister of Sir Thomas Sackville, K.B., of Sedlescombe. He put a new three-gabled front to the mansion. At his death the property was sold for the benefit of three daughters and co-heiresses. The purchaser (in 1666) was Stephen Frewen, Alderman of London.

[*] The family of *Dexter* still exists in East Sussex.

The family of Frewen, doubtless of Saxon origin, were long established in Worcestershire. Richard Frewen, of Earl's Croome in that county, purchased the advowson of Northiam, and presented his son John to the living in 1583. John Frewen was a learned and pious Puritan divine of high standing, and author of several theological works. He continued Rector here till his death in 1628. He was father of Accepted Frewen, the well-known Archbishop of York; Thankful, Secretary to Lord-Keeper Coventry; and Stephen, Alderman of London, who died at Brickwall in 1679. His estates passed to his son, Thomas Frewen, M.P. for Rye, from 1679 to 1699. Brickwall descended, after the death of his widow, to Sir Edward Frewen, his son by his first wife. About 1685, having travelled on the Continent, he returned hither, and built the banqueting-room at Brickwall in the Louis-Quatorze style, and employed French artists to execute the ceilings of this, and the grand staircase, at an outlay of £800. The hall was intended for the entertainment of the Corporation of Rye, of which borough the family held the patronage. After Sir Edward's grandson's death, the mansion was neglected by the family, who preferred living at their seats in Yorkshire or Leicestershire; but the present owner, who came to reside in 1830, restored it to nearly its former state. There is a valuable collection of pictures, including works by C. Jansen, Holbein, Lely, &c. Among the Frewen portraits are John Frewen, the Puritan, by Mark Gerard, 1627, very quaint and characteristic, Archbishop Frewen, Alderman Frewen, Accepted Frewen, Archbishop of York, and numerous others by eminent painters. The gardens are preserved in the old Dutch taste. A fine avenue of oaks, said to have been planted from acorns from the Queen's Oak, is now represented by a single fine tree. The north front is a good specimen of the timbered house, but the other three sides were cased with brick by Sir Edward Frewen.

The church (of which Hussey gives a view) forms a striking pile. The old portions consist of nave with aisles, and square battlemented tower, more than half of which is Norman, with small stone spire, unique in this district. There are traces of Early English, Decorated and Perpendicular in the building. The old chancel, which contained three sedilia and a piscina, was removed to make way for a larger one in 1837, 8, and an addition was also made on the north side. In 1846, Thomas Frewen, Esq., erected a handsome Mausoleum * over the vaults containing the remains of his ancestors. It is in the Tudor style, from designs by Smirke. On each wall are nine shields,

* By a special "faculty" this Mausoleum is exempt from all ecclesiastical jurisdiction.

with impalements and quarterings, shewing the Frewen alliances. The armorial window and the roof decorations are by Willement, and the carvings both in wood and stone were wrought by a self-taught artist of Rye. The Frewen monuments, formerly in the chancel, were removed into this mausoleum, and soon after its erection a beautiful memorial, with a bust by Behnes, was erected for Anne, wife of Thomas Frewen, Esq., who died in 1844. The other memorials in the church are principally to the memory of members of the Frewen family, four of whom were rectors here. The only brass now remaining (see that of Nicholas Tufton, *ante*) is a priest in canonicals, 𝕽𝕺𝖇𝖊𝖗𝖙 𝕭𝖊𝖚𝖋𝖔𝖗𝖉, "sumtyme person of this churche," 1518. In the church-yard there is a yew-tree, probably older than any part of the church. The "Church-house," near the building, is supposed to be of the date of Henry VIII., and is in the form of the letter H. Here lived and died the Puritan, John Frewen, who had purchased it in 1592, and several of his successors, previously to their removal to Brickwall. For memoirs of John Frewen, and several members of his remarkable family, see "Worthies of Sussex."

Considering the numerous points of interest which this parish possesses, we may well repeat the apostrophe—

O, rare Norgem !

[S. A. C. Frewens, iv, 24. xiv, xii, xvi, 302. Visit of Queen Elizabeth, v, 190. Tradesmen's Tokens, x, 208. Weekes of, xi, 82. Dixter or Dixthern, xiii, 112, 117, 270. Tregoz of, xiii, 112. Horner in, xiii, 140. Tufton family, xiii, 140. xiv, 100. xx, 65. White family, xvi, 43. Church bells, xvi, 219. Brickwall, xvi, 302. xix, 166. Iron-works, xviii, 15. Cade's insurrection, xviii, 27. London-road, xix, 166. Springett of, xx, 46.]

NORTH-CHAPEL.

A parish in the Hundred of Rotherbridge; Rape of Arundel; distant five miles from Petworth, its Post-town and Railway station. Union, Midhurst. Population in 1811, 634 ; in 1861, 785 ; Benefice, a Rectory, valued at £284 ; Patron, Lord Leconfield ; Incumbent, Rev. Robert Witherby, M.A., of St. John's College, Cambridge. Date of earliest Parish Register, 1716. Acreage, 3,854. *Chief Landowners*, Lord Leconfield, and George Baker, Esq.

North-Chapel was dismembered from Petworth by Act of Parliament, in 1693. The village is on the old road from London to Petworth, and, as its name implies, it was formerly a chapelry only of Petworth, whence its name.

The manor was originally a portion of the Honour of Petworth. The land belongs, principally, to Lord Leconfield.

The church stands on an elevation, and is dedicated, according to Mr. Gibbon, to St. John Baptist, though others say to St. Michael. The building formerly had a nave or pace only, with a tower at the west end with a shingled covering, and the whole structure is described by Dallaway, as of "coarse ancient architecture," but additions have been subsequently made. The Rev. Colin Milne, LL.D., held the rectory in the last century. He was author of a Botanical Dictionary published in 1770, and other works. There are three bells of modern date. Ironworks formerly existed here.

[S. A. C. Ironworks, ii, 215. iii, 245. xviii, 16. Bells, xvi, 205. River Arun, xvi, 256, London road to Chichester, xix, 167.]

NUTBOURNE (See Pulborough).

NUTHURST.

A parish in the Hundred of Singlecross; Rape of Bramber; distant four miles south from Horsham station; Post-town and Union, Horsham. Population in 1811, 539; in 1861, 767. Benefice, a Rectory, valued at £480; Patron, the Bishop of London; Incumbent, Rev. John Ommaney McCarogher, M.A., of Magdalen College, Oxford. Date of earliest Parish Register, 1562. Acreage, 3,260. *Chief Landowners*, J. T. Nelthorpe, Esq., Walter Burrell, Esq., and Major John Aldridge. *Seats*, Nuthurst Lodge, J. Tuder Nelthorpe, Esq.; Swallowfield, S. H. Bigg, Esq.

This parish, which lies to the west of St. Leonard's Forest, is picturesque and well-wooded. Mr. Nelthorpe's residence, Nuthurst Lodge, commands a very extensive view over the Weald, reaching to the South Downs; and the sea is occasionally visible. Highurst, containing about 100 acres, is part of this parish, though it is insulated within the neighbouring parish of Cowfold. The manors of Shortsfield and Nutham extend over the greater part of the parish.

The patronage of the church formerly belonged to the abbey of Fécamp in Normandy. About the year 1230, a dispute arose between the Bishop of Chichester and the monastery of Fécamp, respecting the jurisdiction of the former over the canons and clerks of Steyning, and an award was made that Steyning should be free from the ordinary jurisdiction of the Bishop; but in order that the church of Chichester might not suffer detriment, all rights of advowson, &c., which had belonged to Fécamp abbey in Notehurst, Bury, and Slynfold, should be handed over to the bishop and his successors.

The church (St. Andrew), consists of tower, nave, and chancel, the last of which has in its windows some remains of ancient painted glass. The style is Decorated, and the tower is described by Cartwright as a low one, "at the west end of the building, formed of large blocks of timber like the tower at Itchingfield." It has a shingled spire. The porch is interesting for its ornamented spandrels. There are three bells. The building has memorials for the names of Nelthorpe, Tuder, Aldridge, &c. A brass was discovered about the year 1856. It consisted of a plate embedded in Sussex marble, and there were indents of a chalice and paten. It commemorates 𝕿𝖍𝖔𝖒𝖆𝖘 𝕵𝖗𝖊𝖓𝖘𝖍𝖊, rector of the church, who died 1486.

George Edgeley, rector of this church, was made D.D. in 1643. He is described in the Chancellor's letter as a prebendary of Chichester and rector of Nuthurst, a Senior of the University of Cambridge, a grave and orthodox divine—a "person that hath expressed his loyalty by his active services and passive sufferings for the defence of his Majesty's person, religion, and laws." (See Walker's "Sufferings of the Clergy.")

[S. A. C. Brass in church, ix, 370. Church, xii, 108. Patching of, xvi, 49. Sedgwick Lodge, xvi, 70. George Foxe and the Sussex Quakers, xvi, 70, 71. Church bells, xvi, 219. Mille of, xvii, 112. Alewyne of, xvii, 254. Jack Cade's adherents here, xviii, 23, 38. Pierce of, xix, 95.]

NUTLEY.

A pleasant hamlet of the parish of Maresfield, three miles north of the parish church. It is a small village and ecclesiastical district. A small church (St. James), in the Early English style, was built in 1848, and consists of a chancel and nave, with bell-turret. The living is a Perpetual curacy, value £125, in the gift of the Rector of Maresfield. Incumbent the Rev. William Albert Smallpiece, M.A. The name is derived from the Anglo-Saxon *hnut*, a nut, and *leag*, indicating a part of the forest of Ashdown comparatively open, but abounding with hazel. When the forest possessed a hunting-seat, under the earlier Edwards and John of Gaunt, Nutley appears to have been a small vill, then called Notley or Notlye. It possessed a chapel known as the free chapel of Maresfield or Notley. The great Reformer Wycliffe is said to have performed divine offices here, when under the patronage of John of Gaunt. Before 1541 the chapel was disused. The site was about half a mile west of the present village, near a wood still called chapel wood. The font was rescued, by the Rev. E. Turner, from a cow-yard, and is in his possession.

[S. A. C. For references, see under *Maresfield*.]

OFFHAM.

A considerable hamlet of Hamsey, about two miles from Lewes, on the ancient Ermin Street and the old London road. A great portion of the population of the parish reside here; and by the beneficence of the late Sir Henry Shiffner, Bart. of Coombe, and other members of his family, a church (St. Peter) was erected, to replace the old edifice, which is rather remote and inconvenient of access. It is built in a style somewhat French, and consists of a nave, tower, with shingled spire, eastward, and an apsidal chancel beyond. It is beautifully situated on a rising ground, and forms from every point of view an elegant adjunct to the landscape. This hamlet is popularly supposed to derive its name from its being an "off," or outlying place; but the old orthographies, Wougham, Woffam, Okeham, &c., do not support that etymology. Offham chalk-pits afford a good study for the geologist; and it is worth recording that the first railway constructed in Sussex connects these pits with a branch of the river Ouse for the conveyance of chalk and lime. It is a very steep *incline*, and was planned about the beginning of this century by Mr. Cater Rand, a schoolmaster of Lewes.

OFFHAM.

A hamlet of South Stoke near Arundel.

ORE.

A parish in the Hundred of Baldslow; Rape of Hastings; distant nearly two miles north from Hastings, its Post-town and Railway station. Union, Hastings. Population in 1811, 331; in 1861, 1,636. Benefice, a Rectory, valued at £575; Incumbent, Rev. William Twiss Turner, M.A., of Trinity College, Cambridge. Date of earliest Parish Register, 1558. Acreage, 2,150. *Seats,* Ore Place, Thomas Spalding, Esq.; Coghurst, C. Hay Frewen, Esq., M.P.; Woodlands, Thomas Frewen, Esq.; and many elegant villa residences.

This parish, which may now be considered a fashionable suburb of Hastings, is remarkable for its bold undulations, steep roads, commanding scenery—overlooking the town and the English Channel—and a charming mixture of woodland and pasture. In the reign of Henry III., the manor was possessed by a family of the same name, and at a later period Richard Hallé, or Hawley, originally of Halland, in East Hothly, married the heiress, Anne, daughter of John Ore. Their descendants possessed it for about six generations, when it passed to the family of Crispe. From 1686 to 1768 it belonged to the Carylls; afterwards, successively, to General Murray, the hero of Quebec, to W. Lucas Shadwell (1821), and to Sir Howard Elphinstone, Bart. The mansion of Ore Place is modern. There seems no reasonable ground for the tradition that it stands on the site of a house built by John of Gaunt, which afterwards became a monastic establishment. Indeed the continuous occupation, by the Ores and Hawleys, from the 13th to the 17th century, almost precludes the possibility of such erection and subsequent use.

Coghurst Hall is a commodious mansion in a fine well-wooded park, the seat of Charles Hay Frewen, Esq., M.P. It belonged, in 1712, to the family of Fletcher, whose heiress conveyed it in marriage to the Dynes of Westfield. Mary Fletcher Dyne, their heiress, married in the 18th century Musgrave Brisco, Esq., of Wakefield and Ripon, and so carried this, and other good lands, to that family. The Hastings union-house and public cemetery are both in this parish.

The church (St. Helen) is an unpretending edifice of nave, chancel, south aisle, added in 1821, and low square tower. In the nave are, or lately were, several gravestones, including a brass for a man and his wife (arms and inscription removed), the indent of another brass (probably of the Ore or Hawley family), and two inscriptions for the Crispe family, with their arms. There are also monuments for General Murray (1794) and his relatives, and for members of the Whitears, Cowells, Norths, and others. For the use of the parishioners living on the borders of Fairlight, a handsome church, called Christ Church, was erected in 1859.

[S. A. C. Relfe of, xiv, 85. Crispe of, xvi, 47. Bell, xvi, 219. Tithes to Battle Abbey, xvii, 55. Encaustic tiles, xviii, 66. Sir Richard de Ore, Knight, xix, 53. Worked flints, xix, 53 (*Smart*). Hays of, xx, 65.]

OTHAM ABBEY.

This ancient monastic establishment was founded in the parish of Hailsham for monks of the Premonstratensian order, by Ralph de Dene, a member of a Norman family resident at West Dean *orientalis*, in the latter half of the 12th century. From the charter of foundation, it appears that a chapel had previously existed here, and had been served by certain monks of the order. The abbey of Otteham or Hotteham was dedicated to St. Laurence, and was endowed with lands and tenements in Sussex. Among the subsequent benefactors to the house were the families of De Aquila, De Brode (of the ' Broad ' in Hellingly), De Herst, De la Water, De St. Leger, &c. The place chosen for the monastery was an unfortunate one—the soil was damp and unproductive; wherefore the brethren ("propter magnas et intolerabiles inedias loci de Otteham") besought Ela de Sackville, the founder's daughter, to translate them to a more salubrious spot, which was done, and Bayham was the place fixed on. (See Bayham.) Previously one of the De Brodes had invited the monks to settle at his church of Hellingly, of which Hailsham was then a chapel. From the time of the transfer to Bayham, Otteham remained as a grange, with its chapel and a ministering brother or two, with a lamp burning night and day before St. Laurence's altar. Mention is made of an image of that saint in gold, silver, and wax, and tithes were payable from many lands for the sustentation of the chapel. A paper by the Rev. G. Miles Cooper, in Vol. v. of the "Sussex Collections," gives many interesting particulars of the benefactors to the establishment, and the presumed sites of its possessions.

Very little remains to attest the existence of Otteham Abbey, except the ancient and much dilapidated chapel, which has features of the 13th century, and still possesses a battered sedile and piscina. It is adjacent to Otham farm-house, and used as a stable. What a falling off from St. Laurence in silver, gold, and wax, to a home for cart-horses!

This district of Hailsham is called Otham Quarter.

OVING. •

Vulgo, *Ooving;* a parish in the Hundred of Box and Stockbridge; Rape of Chichester; distant three miles east from Chichester, its Post-town. Railway station, Drayton. Union, West Hampnett. Population in 1811, 476; in 1861, 949. Benefice, a Vicarage, valued at £350; Patron, the Bishop of Chichester; Incumbent, Rev. Alex. Peters Birrell, M.A., of Sidney-Sussex College, Cambridge. Date of earliest Parish Register, 1561. Acreage, 2,946. *Chief Landowners,* Rev. George Henry Woods, of Shopwyke, and Lord Leconfield.

This parish is very flat and fertile, being chiefly good arable land. Shopwyke House, the residence of the Rev. G. H. Woods, is one of the most elegant mansions in West Sussex. Shopwyke, though not strictly a tything or hamlet, is a very interesting place. The manor is presumed to have been a part of the manor of Aldingbourne, which belonged to the see of Selsey, and a prebend was here formed for Chichester Cathedral. The manor-house and the *corpus* of the prebend belong to the Precentor of Chichester. The Prebendal-house was formerly the residence of the old family of Elson, who possessed consider-able property in this district. Shopwyke, or Shopwyke-Eagle, is an ancient manor in this parish, and Colworth and Woodhorne are prebendal manors. Groves and Drayton formerly be-longed to the Priory of Boxgrove. After the Dissolution, Drayton came into the possession of the Chatfields of Ditchling and Treyford. The Chatfields were succeeded by the Elsons before mentioned.

The church appears to have been originally Early English, but there are insertions of a much later date, and transepts have been added. There are inscriptions to the names of Woodyer, Elson, Walter, Teness, and Green.*

The Rev. Thomas Agar Holland, formerly vicar of Oving, having in his mind the name of his parish and that of Shopwyke, which is reasonably derived from the Anglo-Saxon *sceap* and *wic*, "the village of sheep," wrote the following elegant epigram:—

IN OVINIAM.

"Pasce meas pecudas, ter, Petro dixit Iesus,
Quo velut in scopulo, condidit Ipse Domum :
Sic mihi, (num sperem ?) præbetur Ovinia curæ,
In cœlos, agni, quin ut agantur oves."
"T. A. H., minister of Oving, 1828."

[S. A. C. Church, xii, 75. Groves belonged to Boxgrove Priory, xv, 119. Bells, xvi, 219.]

OVINGDEAN.

Domesday, *Hovingedene;* a parish in the Hundred of Younsmere; Rape of Lewes; distant three miles from Brighton, its Post-town and Rail-way station. Union, Newhaven. Population in 1811, 75 ; in 1861, 121. Benefice, a Rectory, valued at £335; Incumbent, Rev. Alfred Stead, M.A., of Caius College, Cambridge, who is also Patron. Date of earliest Parish Register, 1700. Acreage, 1,618. *Chief Land-owner,* Representatives of the late Charles Beard, Esq. *Seat,* Oving-dean House, E. Macnaughton, Esq.

This parish lies wholly on the South Downs, and the village is a secluded spot. Alnod held the manor of the Confessor, as allodial tenant; after the Conquest, Godfrey held it of De Warenne. The Lady Eddeva also held three hides of Edward. The Domesday account is particularly circumstantial. There were a small church and four dependents. Walter de Pierpoint appears to have been the lord *temp.* Henry VI., and George Goring *temp.* Edward VI. About the end of the sixteenth cen-

---

* Mrs. Susannah Green gave £2,000 for the support of three poor widows. This charitable lady's monument is placed in the north transept.

tury the manor belonged to the family of Geere, from whom it descended to Elizabeth Newton, wife of the late W. C. Mabbott, Esq., of Southover. The manor house, now much modernized, was occupied in 1651 by Mr. Maunsell, and an unfounded tradition asserts that Charles II., after his flight from the battle of Worcester, took shelter here while awaiting the means of escape to France. This presumed incident is the conspicuous feature of Mr. Harrison Ainsworth's pleasant novel called "Ovingdean Grange." The Rev. Mr. Morgan, in a letter addressed to Sir William Burrell, in 1780, describes the village as consisting of one farm-house, three cottages, and a mean, thatched parsonage-house. He adds, that "when the Geeres lived at Ovingdean farm, Charles II. lay concealed here till he had an opportunity of embarking at Brighton for France. His appearance had such an effect upon the good woman of the house that her next child (a very fine boy) was said to be the picture of the King!" (Burrell MS., 5684.) How this myth of the "mutton-eating king" having visited Ovingdean arose, it is impossible to say, for he certainly came no nearer the village than Brighton, nearly three miles distant. There would appear, however, to be some slight association of the Geere family with the King's escape, as their descendants possessed, a few years since, some relics, which were always understood to have been presented by the King. Ovingdean House was formerly the seat of the Kemp family.

The church has chancel, nave, and west tower, with features of the Norman, Early English, and Decorated styles. (Hussey.) Some more recent authorities consider a few of the features unquestionably of Saxon date. Mr. Gordon M. Hills speaks of it as an "almost perfect Saxon church." (Journal of the British Archæological Association, 1867, p. 8.) There are memorials for the names of Cooper of Lewes, Lane, Kemp, Marshall, Palliser, &c.

[S. A. C. Pierpoint, xi, 55. Goring, xi, 66. Quaint account of Ovingdean, xiii, 307. Bell, xvi, 219.]

PAGHAM.

A parish in the Hundred of Aldwick ; Rape of Chichester; distant four miles south-west from Bognor ; Post-town, Chichester ; Union, West Hampnett. Population in 1811, 847 ; in 1861, 988. Benefice, a Vicarage, valued at £300 ; Patron, Archbishop of Canterbury ; Incumbent, Rev. Ralph Barker, B.A., of St. Peter's College, Cambridge. Date of earliest Parish Register, 1707. Acreage, 4,376.

This sea-coast parish is very fertile, and produces abundance

of wheat. Its village proper is close to the little inlet of the
Channel called Pagham Harbour, an estuary said to have been
formed by a sudden irruption of the sea about the beginning of
the fourteenth century, which, according to the Nonæ Roll, devastated 2,700 acres of land. Only small craft can enter this
little port. Pagham Creek is a famous resort for wild fowl,
several of great rarity, and in severe winters, as Mr. A. E. Knox
informs us, flocks of wild swans are always to be seen and heard
here. The manor was granted by Ceadwalla, King of the South
Saxons, to St. Wilfred, and continued, with the advowson, in
episcopal possession through many centuries. It was a very
important estate, and was held, both before and after the Con-
• quest, by the Archbishops of Canterbury, who made it their
occasional residence, and constituted it a Deanery, including all
the "Peculiars" in West Sussex. In the reign of the Confessor
the manor was rated at 50 hides, and afterwards at 34. A
curious custom existed as to pig breeding. For herbage every
seventh pig was payable to the lord, and the Record adds "that
this custom was established throughout the whole county of
Sussex," but I have not found an instance of it anywhere else.
A mill, perhaps on the site of what is now the large tide-mill at
Sidlesham, is mentioned, as also a church, together with another
church at Chichester, which must be that of All Saints in the
Pallant in that city, still in the gift of the Archbishop. The
parish is subdivided into five tythings—Nytimber-with-Pagham,
Crimsham, South Mundham, Aldwicke, and Seven-households.
Aldwicke was a valuable possession, and gave name to the sur-
rounding hundred. In this hamlet a miniature watering-place
has sprung up. It contains several excellent residences, particularly Aldwick House, the property of B. Bond Cabbell, Esq.,
F.S.A. A small chapel-of-ease was built here a few years since
by the Rev. Edward Houghton Johnson, M.A.

The parish church (said to be St. Thomas à Becket) is good
Early English, though much injured by modern repairs. It was
probably built by an archbishop soon after Thomas's canoniza-
tion. It had an altar of St. Nycolas, and three brotherhoods
of St. Andrew, St. Matthew, and the Holyrood. It consists of
chancel, nave, with aisles, a transept, and tower, with a low,
shingled spire. There are five bells. At the east end of the
north aisle was a chantry, founded in 1383 by John Bowrere (the
modern Borrer) and Alice, his wife. Richard Hede, the last
incumbent, received a pension of £5. In Pope Nicholas' taxation, 1291, the church of Pagham "cum capella" is mentioned.
This chapel was dedicated to St. Andrew, and some remains of
it are mentioned by Dallaway as existing in his time. On a
slab in the chancel of the church there are remains of a Lombardic

inscription for **Symon.** . . . "Templi Rector fuit hujus." The relics of the body of this ancient priest, in his canonicals, in a stone coffin, were brought to light some years ago on the removal of the slab. There are other memorials for the names of Barfoote, Darling, Pechell (of the baronet's family), Peachey, and Godman, and one for Edmunde Darell, Esquior, " Clerke of the Caterie" to Queen Elizabeth, 1579. The Darells were a branch of the Calehill and Scotney family, and were of Bowley, or Boley, in this parish. Remains of the archiepiscopal palace are visible to the south-east of the church.

Dixon gives many interesting particulars as to the geology of this and the adjacent parishes. Messrs. Dixon, C. Roach Smith, and other numismatical writers have printed notices of the British and Roman coins found on this part of the Sussex coast.

[S. A. C. Coins, Roman and British, i, 29. v, 206. Domesday mill, v, 271. Visit of King John, i, 134. Bowrers of, xi, 80. Atte-Mores of Chilvercroft, xii, 37. Church, xii, 75. Humphrey the Hermit, xii, 134. Queen Elizabeth patroness of living, xiii, 48. Merchant guild, xv, 176. Bells, xvi, 219 Harbour, xvi, 260. Landing of the Saxons, xviii, 182. Slindon, xix, 126.]

PARHAM.

Domesday, *Perham ;* a parish in the Hundred of West Easewrith ; Rape of Arundel ; distant five miles south-west from Pulborough station, ten miles south-east from Petworth, and six north-east from Arundel. Post-town, Hurst-Pierpoint. Union, Thakeham. Population in 1811, 58 ; in 1861, 71. Benefice, a Rectory, valued at £100, in the gift of Lord de la Zouch ; Incumbent, Rev. James Beck, M.A., of Corpus Christi College, Cambridge. Date of earliest Parish Register, 1538. Acreage, 1,264.

This is a small parish in form approaching to a square, and consists of arable, pasture, wood, and down, in nearly equal portions. The soils vary from sand to chalk and marl. There is no proper village, and the only house of importance is the noble mansion of Lord de la Zouch, shortly to be described. The manor of Perham was held before the Conquest by Tovi, a free man, and afterwards of Earl Roger de Montgomeri by Robert I., was rated at three hides, and had two villeins, a cottar, and a mill. The value was £3 per annum. Early in the reign of Edward III. it had passed to the influential family of Tregoz, who had inherited from that of St. John. In 1399 Edward Tregoz was lord. It afterwards appears to have vested in the Crown. In 1550 Robert Palmer, third son of Thomas Palmer, of Angmering, was seised of it, and his son Sir Thomas Palmer completed the present manor-house, and enclosed a park. Sir Thomas Palmer, his grandson, sold the estate to Sir Thomas Bisshopp, of Henfield, in 1597, who was created a baronet in 1620. Sir Cecil Bisshopp, the eighth who held that title, was summoned to Parliament by writ in 1815, as Baron Zouche of Haryngworth, which title had been in abeyance since 1625. This ancient barony by writ dates from 2nd Edward II., 1308. Parham came by the marriage of Harriet-Anne, daughter of Sir Cecil Bisshopp, to the Honourable Robert Curzon, third son of Ashton Viscount Curzon. Their son, the present Lord de la Zouche, on the death of his mother in 1870, succeeded to the title and estates.

The Abbey of St. Peter of Westminster held lands in Parham from the time of the Confessor, which were rated in his time at seven hides, though in Domesday at only three. There were eight villeins and five cottars. These lands, with the advowson of the church, appear to have vested in the Abbey till the dissolution. They now form a principal portion of the manorial estate.

Parham House was built early in the 16th century, on a very grand scale, but has received subsequent additions. Like many other mansions of the same character in the county, it lies at the foot of the South Downs in a fine park full of picturesque beauty, abounding with venerable oaks, and well stocked with fallow deer, together with a famous heronry. There are several noble apartments, particularly the hall, 51 feet by 26, and 24 in height, and the picture gallery, 158 feet long, which contains numerous fine portraits of the builder of Parham House, of the Bisshopp family and their connections, of Queen Elizabeth, and of various officers of state and other noble and gentle personages. The dining and drawing-rooms, with other apartments, also possess many excellent paintings. Parham is one grand museum of ancient and modern art and literary rarities. Many of the objects have been collected by the antiquarian skill and industry of the present noble possessor, the author of "Monasteries of the Levant," and other works. The library contains about 100 writings on tablets of stone and wood ; Egyptian papyri, a large number of ancient MSS., chiefly on vellum, some being of the fourth century, and several in the Greek, Coptic, and Syriac languages, written before the year 1000, some beautifully illuminated ; early printed books, including several Caxtons and Wynkyn de Wordes, first printed editions of Homer and Virgil, early Bibles, the five folio editions of Shakspeare, a copy of the "World of Wonders," containing an autograph of the great bard himself. Then there is a superb collection of ancient gold and silver plate, enamels, and ivory carvings, most beautiful to behold, and most precious to possess. A considerable number of these objects are ecclesiastical. In the hall are the arms of Queen Elizabeth, over the spot on which that illustrious lady is said to have dined in 1592. This apartment is graced with "armoires," containing an important collection of armour of all countries and ages, of which the greater part, belonging to the 15th century, was collected by the noble and accomplished owner of Parham ("fortunate puer") from the deserted church of St. Irene at Constantinople. What adds to their interest is the fact that these steel vestments once clad the gallant defenders of the last of the imperial Paleologi against the Turks on the fall of the Eastern Empire before Mahomet II. in 1452. Lord de la Zouche drew up the particulars of his priceless purchase, and his account of these articles and the other objects in the hall, lies on the great table for the inspection of the privileged visitor. Well did a living worthy remark of the grand collection in this mansion :—

> " In any house who can *compare* 'em,
> Those precious things that lie at *Par*-ham ?"

The church (St. Peter?) is a small building of nave and south aisle, probably of early date, but much modernized, with the addition of a tower in 1800, at the expense of the Bisshopp family. It has a small spire and one bell. The font is of lead, impressed with the arms of Andrew Peverell, knight of the shire in 1351, and inscribed IHS. NAZAR. (Jesus of Nazareth.) There are slabs in the chancel to the memory of some of the Bisshopp family.

[S. A. C. Domesday watermill, v, 271. Visit of Queen Elizabeth, v, 197. Barrows at, ix, 116. Palmer at Agincourt, xv, 130. Bell, xvi, 220. Bisshopp of, xvii, 82. xix, 107, 158. Chalk used in building Parham House, xx, 187.]

PATCHAM, *alias* Pecham.

Domesday, *Piceam;* a South Down parish, constituting the Hundred of Dean; Rape of Lewes; distant three miles north from Brighton, its Post-town and Railway station. Union, Steyning. Population in 1811, 331; in 1861, 638. Benefice, a Vicarage, valued at £110; Patron, the Lord Chancellor; Incumbent, Rev. John Allen, M.A. Date of earliest Parish Register, 1717. Acreage, 4,398. *Chief Landowners*, the Earl of Abergavenny, Colonel Paine, Lady Ogle, and — Tillstone, Esq. *Seats*, Patcham Place, Colonel Paine; Withdean Court, Lady Ogle; Moulscombe, E. S. Tillstone, Esq.; Withdean Hall, H. C. Lacy, Esq.; &c.

Patcham was, in Saxon times, an important manor, and belonged to Earl Harold, who derived from it the very large sum of one hundred pounds per annum. The tenantry consisted of 143 villeins and 45 bondmen, having 82 ploughs. Connected with the church there were 16 dependents, and there was pannage for 100 hogs. Twenty six houses in Lewes also appertained to the manor. It afterwards formed part of the barony of Lewes. At present the Earl of Abergavenny is lord, and Lady Ogle, daughter and heiress of the late Thomas William Roe, Esq., possesses the manors of Withdean Court and Withdean Cayliffe. Withdean Court, recently partly rebuilt by Lady Ogle, is traditionally one of the residences of Anne of Cleves, who had a grant of the manor in 1541. *Withdean*, a considerable hamlet, was written in the 16th century Wyghtdeane, and is commonly pronounced Whiting. Moulscombe belonged, from the 15th to the 19th century and, traditionally, from the time of the Conquest, to the family of Webb. Patcham Place was one of the seats of the Lords La Warr. A branch of the great family of Shelley afterwards possessed it for several generations, until their removal to Southover and Lewes. Subsequently the baronet family of Stapley had it for two or three descents, and Sir John Stapley sold it, with the impropriation, to John Lilly, gentleman, whose nephew aliened it in 1719, to George, Lord Abergavenny. In 1764, a good estate here was purchased by John Paine, Esq., ancestor of the present owner. The house, which is partly of the date of Queen Elizabeth, is situated on the Downs, with beautiful adjuncts of wood and lawn.

In my "Worthies of Sussex," p. 285, I have adduced my reasons for believing that John Peckham, Archbishop of Canterbury, ob. 1294, was a native of this parish. A family of De Pecham resided here, *temp.* Edward I. Another family of great antiquity in Sussex, the Farncombes, derived their name from the lands called Varncombe in this parish, in or before the reign of Edward III.

The church (All Saints) consists of chancel, nave, and west tower, with battlements. Hussey describes it as containing features of Transition-Norman, Decorated, and Perpendicular architecture. Besides more recent monuments, the church and church-yard have memorials for Shelley, 1594; Stapley (17th century), Paine, Farncombe, Roe, and Jones.

Hollingbury hill or " castle " is a castrametation in the southeast quarter of this parish. Armillæ, celts, and other British remains have been found near this spot. Let us hope that the contemplated "ploughing up " of this ancient fort will not be ignorantly persisted in.

[S. A. C. Colonel Anthony Stapley, v, 66. King Edward I. at, ii, 153. Smugglers, ix, 195. Church to Lewes Priory, xiii, 244. Stapley family, ii, 117. xiii, 252. Bells, xvi, 220. Wellesbourne stream, and rhymes, by Mr. J. Ellis, xvi, 247. Shelley family, xix, 175.]

PATCHING.

Domesday, *Patchings;* a parish in the Hundred of its own name, which is co-extensive with it; Rape of Arundel; distant five miles north-west from Worthing; Post-town, Arundel; Railway station, Ang-mering, distant about 2½ miles. Union, Sutton. Population in 1811, 183; in 1861, 275. Benefice, a Rectory (a peculiar of Canter-bury), valued at £218; Patron, the Archbishop of Canterbury; In-cumbent, Rev. Edmund Tew, M.A., of Magdalen Hall, Oxford. Date of earliest Parish Register, 1598. Acreage, 1,748.

In 948 Patching was given, by Wlfric, to Christ Church, Canterbury, and in Domesday it is included in the territory of the Archbishop. According to that record, it was appropriated to the monks for their clothing. Godfrey de Mealing was ten-ant in 1155. From *temp.* Edward I., to 1446, or later, it was held by the knightly family of Le Waleys. From 33rd Henry VIII. it was held by the Shelleys with Michelgrove, until 1800, when it was bought by Richard Walker, Esq., whose son, R. W. Walker, sold it in 1828 to Bernard-Edward, Duke of Norfolk.

A church is mentioned in Domesday. It was dependent on the mother-church of Tarring until 1282, when it was made a separate Rectory. The existing building "is of larger dimen-sions than the generality of parish churches in this neighbour-hood, and the plan is rather uncommon. The nave had origin-ally an aisle on the north side, at the east end of which aisle the tower, which about 1790 had a shingled spire, was placed; the chancel had also an aisle or chapel attached to the north side, which has been taken down. The west end of the nave has been reduced in length." (Cartwright, 1830.) The building was renovated about 1856 by Sir John Kirkland, then resident here. Mr. Hussey considers the tower Transition-Norman. There are memorials for Delany, Jordan, Symmons, Bushby, &c. The villagers have a tradition that "some Archbishop" was buried at Patching.

For an account of the plot concocted by William Shelley and others in Patcham copse, 25th Elizabeth, in favour of Mary, Queen of Scots, see "Worthies of Sussex," p. 130. In the beechwoods of this parish the truffle (*Lycoperdon tuber*) is found. A man named William Leech, from the West Indies, settled here about the end of the last century, and with the aid of dogs carried on the business of a truffle-hunter till his death.

[S. A. C. Bell, xvi, 220. Patching pond subsidiary to the Arun, xvi, 258. Butlers, xvii, 222. Fortescue, Lord of the Manor, xx, 59.]

PEASMARSH.

Vulgo, *Peasmesh;* a parish in the Hundred of Goldspur; Rape of Hastings; distant three miles north-west from Rye, its Railway station. Post-town, Staplehurst. Union, Rye. Population in 1811, 781; in 1861, 906. Benefice, a Vicarage, valued at £261; Patron, Sidney Sussex College (through the gift of — Giles, Vicar of Peasmarsh, who died 1569); Incumbent, Rev. William Richard Ick, B.D., of that College. Date of earliest Parish Register, 1569. Acreage, 3,718. *Seats,* Peasmarsh Place, H. Mascall Curteis, Esq.; Woodside, T. Smith Pix, Esq.

It is a well-wooded parish, bounded on the north by the Rother. It gave name to a family, of whom James, son and heir of Sir John Pesemarsh, was party to a deed in 1482. ("Battle Abbey Deeds," p. 124.) In 3rd Edward II. Stephen Burghersh had free warren, and in 7th Henry IV. Elizabeth, wife of Nicholas Vurrell, held the manor. In 3rd and 4th Philip and Mary Anthony, Viscount Montague, sold to Robert Sheppard the glebe of the parsonage or prebend of Pesemershe, and his descendants were connected with the parish for several generations. In 1719 the manor continued in the heirs of Edward Sheppard, Esq. In 1743 the Mascalls were in possession, and so continued until 1821, when Caroline, co-heiress of Robert Mascall, Esq., conveyed it by marriage to Herbert Barrett Curteis, Esq., father of the present proprietor.

The church (St. Peter and St. Paul), which has lately been restored, is principally in the Early English style, though the chancel arch is Norman. It consists of chancel, nave, with aisles, and tower with spire. " In the south wall are four small arches, one of which is a piscina." There are tablets and inscriptions for the names of Mascall, Delves, Shephard, Parr, Smith, Holt, Webber, Lettice, &c.

William Pattison, a poet of the last century, was the son of a farmer in this parish. He was born in 1706, and studied partly at Appleby school, co. Westmorland. He entered Sidney Sussex College, Cambridge, but recklessly left the University and commenced the career of a literary adventurer in London, where, after a course of vice and misery, he died at the early age of 21. His impure works, printed by the profligate Curll, are now seldom heard of. (See " Worthies of Sussex," 172-175.)

[S. A. C. Weekes of, xi, 82. Pearson and Shepherd, xiii, 57. Church, xiii, 137. Lands submerged by sea, xiii, 176. Morley manor in, xiv, 112. Bells, xvi, 220. Richard Oxenbridge of Peasmarsh, Constable of Goldspur, in Cade's rising, xviii, 25, 39.]

PECULIARS of the ARCHBISHOP of CANTERBURY.

Ceadwalla, King of the South Saxons, who died in 688, granted to the Archbishop of Canterbury various manors, extending from Lewes into the Primate's own diocese, so that he could travel from the archiepiscopal see to the county town of Sussex without quitting his own territory. These manors are circumstantially mentioned in Domesday. The Bishops of Chichester had no jurisdiction in the churches of these manors, and as "Peculiars" of the see of Canterbury, and in the gift of the successive Archbishops, the latter have, until within late years, held their periodical Visitations. Recent legislation, however, has thrown the benefices into the diocese of Chichester, though the Archbishop still holds the patronage. These remarks apply principally to the East Sussex Peculiars, but there are others in the Archdeaconry of Chichester which have been placed under the same ecclesiastical regulations. The Peculiars are as follows :—

East Sussex (locally within the Archdeaconry of Lewes and Deanery of South Malling)—Mayfield, Buxted, with Uckfield annexed, Isfield, Edburton, Stanmer, Framfield, Glynde, St. Thomas-at-Cliffe, Ringmer, and Wadhurst.

In West Sussex there are, in the Archdeaconry of Chichester and in the Deanery of Pagham—Pagham church with its chapel, Lavant, Tangmere, Slyndon, and All Saints, Chichester; and, in the Deanery of Tarring—Tarring and Patcham.

In several of these places the Archbishops had *mansiones*, or resting-places, specially Mayfield Palace, Tarble Down in Framfield, Broyle in Ringmer, South Malling, West Tarring, Pagham, and Slyndon. All these places were occasionally occupied by the Primate in his periodical journeys and visitations.

PENHURST.

A parish in the Hundred of Netherfield; Rape of Hastings; distant four miles north-west from Battle, its Post-town and Railway station. Union, Battle. Population in 1811, 67; in 1861, 105. Benefice, a Rectory, united with Ashburnham (which see). Date of earliest Parish Register, 1692. Acreage, 1,462. *Chief Landowner*, the Earl of Ashburnham.

An undulating and well-wooded parish, as its latter syllable implies. In early times it gave name to the family of De Penherst, who held under the lords of Bodiam so late as 9th Edward IV. In 8th James I. the Michelbornes of Clayton, and subsequently Joan Busbridge, widow, held it under the same infeudation, by the yearly rent of 24s. for every leap-year, and 18s. for every other year! The manor has long been added to the Ashburnham estate.

The church is small, consisting of a nave, chancel, and low square tower, in the "later style of English architecture." (Horsfield.) There are some remains of antiquity which were more perfect when the church was visited by Sir William Burrell. He mentions, among the painted glass in the east window, figures, architectural designs, the arms of Pelham, and those of Penhurst. (Sa. a mullet of 6 points, arg.) Some traces of the rood-loft also existed, and upon the beam "Ecce Homo" between the sentences (right) "Venite benedicti in regnum Patris mei," and (left) "Ite maledicti in ignem eternum." The four windows of the nave had also quarries of painted glass. An iron slab in the chancel commemorates Peter Gower, 1703. Towards the end of the last century the Rev. Joseph Wise, an author of some repute, held this benefice.

[S. A. C. Iron-works, ii, 215. Bell, xvi, 220. Lands belonging to Battle Abbey, xvii, 33. Arms of Penhurst, vi, 76.]

PETT.

A parish in the Hundred of Guestling; Rape of Hastings; distant 4½ miles north-east from Hastings, its Post-town. Union, Hastings. Population in 1811, 233; in 1861, 320. Benefice, a Rectory, valued at £512; Patron, Henry Young, Esq.; Incumbent, Rev. Frederick Young, M.A., of Balliol College, Oxon. Date of earliest Parish Register, 1675. Acreage, 2,350.

The manor of Pett, which lies chiefly in this parish and Guestling, is said to be identical with the devastated manor of *Luet*, mentioned in Domesday, but I think Fairlight has a better claim to that designation. It belonged in 1368 to Henry Halle, of Ore, from whose family it appears to have passed to the Levetts. In 1574 John Fletcher died seised of the manor and advowson. In the 18th century it belonged to the Medleys, and passed as Buxted to the late Earl of Liverpool.

Part of the parish is flat, and known as Pett Level, but other portions are undulating and agreeable. From one point the coast of France is discernible in clear weather. The village is pleasantly situated nearly midway between Winchelsea and Hastings. Its seabord is defended (?) by eight Martello towers. The church (St. Mary and St. Peter) was rebuilt in 1864, and contains monuments for the Wynch family; also one by Westmacott to Cordelia Sayer, 1820, and a brass plate to George Theobald, 1641, " He gave a bell freely to grace the new steeple

—Ring out his prayse therefore, ye good people." The military
canal extends from Cliff-end in this parish to Hythe, a distance
of 23 miles. The geological changes on this part of the coast
are shown by the remains of a submerged forest, visible on the
sands at low water during spring tides.

[S. A. C. Military canal, xv, 155. Church bell, xvi, 220. Crouche,
benefactor to church, xvii, 125. Piseing John, xix, 95.]

PETWORTH.

Domesday *Peteorde*; vulgo, *Pettuth*; a market-town and parish in the
Hundred of Rotherbridge; Rape of Arundel; distant 14 miles north-
east from Chichester. It is a Post-town, and has a railway station,
distant from the town 1½ miles. Union, Petworth. Population in
1811, 2,459 ; in 1861, 3,368. Benefice, a Rectory, valued at £850.
It was formerly of very great extent, and included the now detached
chapelries of Duncton and Northchapel. Patron, Lord Leconfield ;
Incumbent, Rev. Charles Holland, M.A., of University College,
Oxon. Date of earliest Parish Register, 1559. Acreage, 5,982.
Chief Landowner, Lord Leconfield. *Seats*, Petworth House, Lord
Leconfield; Hilliers, Colonel Willm. Barttelot, M.P. ; Newgrove, J.
H. Robinson, Esq., &c.

This fine old town is surpassed in interest by very few in
the county. Besides the notices of it in Dallaway, Horsfield,
&c., it has had its historians in Dr. Roger Turner, (S. A. C.)
xiv, and, more recently, in a monograph by the Rev. F. H. Arnold,
1864. Mr. Arnold remarks that " while Petworth is characterized
by the beauty of its scenery, the magnificence of its park, the
number of its charitable institutions, and more recently by
the treasures of art collected in Petworth House, the history
of the place itself possesses, at least, as much interest as usually
attaches to other towns, with which it may be fitly compared."
It has been connected for many centuries, in an undisturbed line
of succession, with one of the greatest of our historical races,
and " Percy-honoured " is an epithet which it may properly
claim and bear.

The etymology of Petworth seems to be " the *worth* or estate
of *Peta*," though the compilers of Domesday thought proper to
spell it Peteorde. No more than modern Frenchmen, could they
get over our Saxon *theta.* See the analogous instance of Ordinges
for Worthing. Petworth was held as a free manor of Edward
the Confessor by a Saxon lady called Eddeva. Roger, Earl of
Chichester and Arundel, granted it to his Norman friend and
vassal, Robert de Belesme, whose son, " Robert the Cruel," succeeded. On his forfeiture Henry I. bequeathed it to his second

wife Adeliza, who re-married William de Albini, Earl of Arundel ; but Petworth was conveyed by gift from the queen to her brother Joceline de Louvaine (1140) as an infeudation of Arundel, by the service of being Castellan there. Josceline took the name of Percy on his marriage with Agnes, daughter of William de Percy, 3rd in descent from a companion of the Conqueror. He was succeeded by his son Henry, whose brother Richard was one of the Magna-Charta barons. The next conspicuous personages of this great line were, Henry the 4th lord, who was taken prisoner by the Barons at the battle of Lewes in 1264, and his successor Henry, who was at Dunbar and Bannockburn. Henry son of the latter, and his son Henry, the seventh lord, figure largely in war and public affairs in the 14th century. Henry, the 8th lord of Petworth was created Earl of Northumberland by Richard II., and from that date, as Mr. Arnold remarks, a series of catastrophes ensue. The duke, who was also Earl-Marshal, took the side of Wickliffe against Courtenay, Bishop of London, in 1337, and had a narrow escape of his life. His son was the widely-renowned Hotspur, whose history is so well known as the opponent of Henry IV., and for his subsequent turbulent career. His history belongs to England rather than to Alnwick and Petworth. His sword is among the treasures of Petworth House. Hotspur's son, the 2nd Earl, is supposed to be one of the heroes of Chevy Chase, though he could not have fallen there at the hand of the Scotch knight, since that fate was reserved for him at the battle of St. Albans. Henry, the 3rd Earl, was born at Leconfield, co. York, another of the great Percy estates, in 1421. Like his father he adhered to the Lancastrian cause, and commanded and fell at the sanguinary battle of Towton. Henry, 4th Earl, was assassinated at his house at Cocksedge, near Thirsk. Henry, 5th Earl, was a conspicuous personage in the court of Henry VIII., and was present at the Battle of the Spurs. From the celebrated "Northumberland Household Book" it appears that his ordinary establishment consisted of 223 persons. Henry Algernon, the 6th Earl, was in the retinue of Wolsey, and a lover of Anna Boleyn, and it is a lucky circumstance that he did not lose his head as well as his heart. He afterwards married the Lady Mary Talbot, but left no issue. His brother Thomas was beheaded for treason in Aske's rebellion, but he left a son of his own name who succeeded his uncle as the 7th Earl of Northumberland, he having previously been created by Queen Mary, in 1557, Baron Percy, of Cockermouth and Petworth. He was a zealous Romanist, and taking up arms against Elizabeth, fled to Scotland, where he was beheaded at the command of the Earl of Morton. His brother Henry, 8th Earl, became a Protestant, and long enjoyed the favour of Elizabeth, but at length, on suspicion of

complicity with Thockmorton and Paget for the liberation of
the Queen of Scots, he was committed to the Tower, where he
committed suicide with a "dag" or pistol in 1585. Henry, 9th
Earl, laboured under the unjust suspicion of having been concerned in the Gunpowder Plot (in which his relative Thomas
Percy took part) and was imprisoned in the Tower for more than
15 years, where he solaced himself in the pursuits of science. He
paid a fine of £20,000 and was discharged on his parole that he
would not go more than 30 miles from Petworth House. He
was a great patron of science. An admirable portrait of him by
Vandyke is preserved at Petworth. His son Algernon, 10th
Earl, and K.G., was Lord High-Admiral of England. He sided
with the Parliament at first, but was averse to the execution
of Charles I. The care of the monarch's children was entrusted
to him, and he treated them with the utmost kindness. During
the Commonwealth he lived in retirement at Petworth, delight-
ing in rural occupations. He assisted Monk in the restoration of Charles II., and became a Privy Councillor. His first
wife was the Lady Anne Cecil, and as a memorial of the marriage
an oak tree was planted in Petworth Park, which still maintains
a vigorous existence. By his second wife, the Lady Elizabeth
Howard, he was father of Josceline, the eleventh and last Earl
of Northumberland, who died in 1670, leaving a daughter Elizabeth, Baroness Percy, in whom vested the ancestral honours and
the vast estates of the Percys. She had many suitors, and was
"three times a wife before she was 16." Her 3rd husband was
Charles Seymour, the "proud," and 6th Duke of Somerset, by
whom she had 13 children, but only three daughters and one
son survived. He lived in almost regal state, and exacted the
utmost servility from his children and dependents, but although
he declined to take the name of Percy as he had covenanted to
do, he always treated his duchess with the greatest devotion
and respect. He possessed many noble qualities, and was a
firm adherent to the reformed religion. He gave his services to
the Prince of Orange, and on the death of Queen Anne was
active in promoting the interests of George I. He died in 1748,
when his only son, Algernon, succeeded him as the 7th Duke of
Somerset, and owner of Petworth, having previously been created
Earl of Northumberland by George II., with remainder, in default
of heirs male, to Sir Hugh Smythson, Bart., the husband of his
only daughter Elizabeth. The Duke was subsequently created
Baron Cockermouth and Earl of Egremont, with ultimate
remainder to Sir Charles Wyndham, eldest son of his sister,
Lady Catherine Seymour, who had married the celebrated statesman, Sir William Wyndham—

> "Wyndham, just to freedom and the throne,
> The master of our passions and his own."

Duke Algernon died in 1750, when Sir H. Smythson became Earl of Northumberland, and Sir Charles Wyndham, Earl of Egremont and lord of the honour of Petworth. The latter died in 1763, and was succeeded by his son, then only 12 years old.

This was George O'Brien Wyndham, third Earl of Egremont, who during the greater part of his long life resided at Petworth, and from his liberal patronage of the arts and sciences became widely known as the Mæcenas of his age. He died in 1837, aged 85 (see "Sussex Worthies," p. 90), leaving his vast possessions to his eldest natural son, the present proprietor, George Wyndham, who was created Baron Leconfield, of Leconfield, co. York, in 1859.

Petworth House has always been one of the principal seats in the county. In 1309 Henry de Percy had license to fortify his manors of Petworth and Leconfield. A representation of the old house, which stood on nearly the present site, is given in Vol. xiv, of the "Sussex Collections." It shows in the foreground a large quadrangle with a gateway, and behind it another half-finished quadrangle. Fuller says, "Petworth, the house of the Earls of Northumberland, is most famous for a stately stable, the best of any subject's in Christendon, as it affords stabling in state for three score horses." What is now a park of two thousand acres was, in the days of the early Percies, a great forest; but partly from the ravages of the iron-works, and partly for æsthetic reasons, Petworth Park, with its ten miles of stone ring fence, has become one of the most celebrated in England for its magnitude, and for its graceful admixture of wood, water, and undulating lawn. Petworth received royal visits from Edward II. and Edward VI. Whether Elizabeth came hither is undecided. George IV. (Prince Regent) was here in 1814, and Queen Victoria in 1846.

On the Duke of Somerset's coming into possession he began to pull down the old Percy house and to build the present palatial mansion, which is 322 feet in length, and 62 feet high to the parapet. Its aspect is not pleasing, as, from its monotonous façade, without any considerable projections or recesses, it more resembles a portion of some great city street than one of the most important baronial mansions in the kingdom. The only part of the old edifice retained is the chapel—a gloomy apartment decorated with the arms and devices of the Percies and their alliances.

Adequately to describe the *interior* of Petworth House would require from a critical pen a volume much larger than the present. Its marbles, its pictures, more than 600 in number, executed by more than 200 artists, and its wondrous wood carvings, deserve a special historian. Here are glorious Claudes, and genuine Holbeins and Vandykes, with productions of nearly every other master both ancient and modern, including several of Turner, marked by the usual exaggerations of that great artist. Many of the portraits are, of course, those of the Percies, Somersets, and Wyndhams, and of Sovereigns contemporaneous with them. For descriptions the reader is referred to "Murray's Handbook of Sussex," "Waagen's Art Treasures of Great Britain," and to a catalogue by A. E. Knox, Esq. The wood-carvings by Grinling Gibbons are truly marvellous, and so indeed are those of Ritson, a northern protegé of Lord Egremont, who was employed to complete some of the decorations. The sculptures, which form a large collection, were chiefly purchased at Rome for Charles, Earl of Egremont, who ordered many of them to be supplied with the limbs of which time or violence had deprived them. Hence an ill-natured wag once characterized the collection as a "hospital for decayed statues." It will probably be found, however, that when adverse criticism has done its worst, common candour will allow that few collections of art in Europe amassed by a private family, can vie with the glories of "Princely Petworth."

The church, dedicated to our Lady of Pity or of the Assumption, contains a chapel of St. Thomas à Becket, and is supposed originally to have belonged to the family of De Alta Ripa, or Dawtrey, formerly influential here. Petworth had a church in Saxon times, and has probably never wanted one since; but modern repairs have so obliterated or concealed ancient features, that a few traces only of Early Decorated and Perpendicular work are to be seen. Indeed, the late Earl of Egremont almost entirely rebuilt the church at a cost of £15,000, about 1827, from designs by Barry, with a spire reaching the altitude of 180 feet. Many Percies lie entombed in Becket's chapel with brass plates and other memorials. There are also a fine statue of Lord Egremont in a sitting posture, by Bailey, and two tombs of the Dawtreys. In the nave and chancel are some interesting memorials to the Rectors and others, one of them to Dr. Wickens, an early work by Flaxman. As a great church prize, Petworth has had many eminent incumbents. Parson Acon, according to Leland, "builded the spire of the faire steeple." King, the poetical Bishop of Chichester, was supplanted in Puritan times by the fanatical Dr. Cheynell, the antagonist of Chillingworth. The rectory-house was built by Montague and Duppa, successively Bishops of Chichester, predecessors of King in that see. Dr. John Price was chaplain to General Monk, and aided in the Restoration of Charles II. Charles Dunster, the translator of Aristophanes, was also rector here. Indeed, for a long series of years the rectors of Petworth have been in some way or other distinguished. Notices of some of them will be found in the

"Worthies of Sussex," viz., John Edmund, p. 326; Richard
Montague, p. 116; Brian Duppa, p. 116; King, p. 117; Cheynell,
p. 309; Dunster, p. 343.

A fair was formerly kept here for nine consecutive days, but
was suspended in the year 1666 in consequence of the plague.
Petworth gives name to a beautiful marble composed of univalve
freshwater shells, which is found in this and other parts of Sussex.
Iron-works were carried on at Petworth, and glass was manufactured between the town and Kirdford, in Glass-house-lane.
Petworth has numerous and munificent charities, particularly
those founded by Mr. Thompson in 1624, by the Duke of Somerset
in 1740, Taylor's 1753, and the Earl of Egremont's school, 1816.
The town consists of a few irregular streets with several excellent houses.   One of these, near the church, was the *town*
residence of the ancient family of Dawtrey, or De Alta Ripa,
connections of the Percys, whose "chiefest house, according to
Leland, is in Petworth paroche, caullid the More, half a mile
from Petworth toune." Moore House was dismantled in 1763,
and the remains became a farmstead, which still possesses traces
of former importance and heraldric display.   The Crescent, the
Percy badge, is found on several old houses; an inn here bears
that sign (the Half-Moon), and it is noteworthy that several
public-houses between Petworth and London, on the old route
of the Percies to court, are also "Half-Moons." Newgrove
was the seat of another ancient family, that of De Aula or Hall,
whose heiress married William Peachey in the 17th century.
His descendant, Sir Henry Peachey, was created a baronet in
1736, as "of New Grove." It now belongs to Lord Leconfield.
According to Mr. Arnold bull-baiting and cock-fighting were
practiced at Petworth late in the last century.

The Town-hall and market-house, a stone structure, was
built in 1793 by the late Earl of Egremont.   On one end is a
bust of William III., "in all the glories of his flowing wig."
In this Hall are held the Epiphany and Easter Sessions for the
Western division of Sussex. There is a large prison for the division, an elaborate account of which is given by Dallaway in his
preliminary History of the Rape of Arundel, up to the year
1819.

[S. A. C.   Iron-works, ii, 215. iii, 242. Queen Elizabeth, v, 197.
Domesday watermill, v, 271. King Edward 1. at, ii, 143. Edward II. at,
vi, 49. Church, xii, 95. Tredcroft family, *ibid.* Egremont, Earl of, xii,
96. Petworth House, xiii, viii, xiii, 109. Grinling Gibbons, and Ritson's,
wood carvings, xiii, xiii, xiv, 10. License to fortify, xiii, 109. De Percy
family, xiv, 2, 3. Thompson's hospital, xiii, 305. Petworth, a paper (*Rog.
Turner, M.D.*), xiv. 1-24. Charles, King of Spain at, xiv, 14. The
"Cecil oak," xiv, 16. Dawtrey or De Alta Ripa family, of Moore House,

PEVENSEY.

Domesday, *Pevenesel*; vulgo, *Pemsey*; a parish and Railway station (though the latter is locally in the parish of Westham) in the Hundred and Rape of its own name; distant ten miles west from Hastings. Union and Post-town, Eastbourne. Population in 1811, 254; in 1861, 385. Benefice, a Vicarage, valued at £1,100; Patron, the Bishop of Chichester; Incumbent, Rev. Henry Browne, M.A., of, Corpus Christi College, Cambridge. Date of earliest Parish Register, 1566. Acreage, 4,856.

No place of the same small population and minor importance in the South of England can vie in interest with Pevensey. Though now only a simple village street, it represents a great Roman station and fortress, and a very considerable stronghold of medieval days; and was the scene of many exciting historical events extending over centuries. It gives name to a hundred, a rape, a rich marsh, and that beautiful expanse of ocean, Pevensey Bay. It also possesses a separate jurisdiction, the "Lowey" or liberty, comprising the parishes of Pevensey and Westham, with portions of Hailsham and Bexhill, and is one of the principal limbs or members of the Cinque Ports.

The great and fertile plain stretching along the Sussex coast from the eastward of Beachy-head in the direction of Hastings, and inland towards Wartling, Hurst-Monceux, and Hailsham, now studded with great and fat beeves, was at some remote era covered by the sea, and what are known as "eyes" or elevations above the surrounding level—such as Chilleye, Northeye, Horseye, Rickney, &c., must have been islands, forming a miniature archipelago. As these are all of Saxon meaning, it may be presumed that, at the time of Saxon colonization, they were frequently or constantly insulated. It is almost certain that within the last thousand years, the waters approached very closely the town and castle of Pevensey, and even so lately as the year 1317, Edward II. granted to one Robert de Sassy, by the annual service of presenting a pair of gilt spurs, certain lands in the marsh of Pevensey and in the tenure of no man, because over-flowed by the sea. Like Hastings, Winchelsea, and Seaford, this place has, by the caprices of Father Neptune, lost the *port* which it once enjoyed, and it now requires almost a stretch of the imagination to believe that royal navies once rode in Pev-ensey harbour. Such, however, we have evidence in many an-cient records was once the case.

What gave importance to the place in the days of the Roman rule in Britain, was the erection of a large fortification or *cas-trum*, which has been undeniably proved to be the station called ANDERIDA, a word latinized from the British name Andrads-wald. The Britons appear to have had a settlement here in earlier times, both from the occasional discovery of British coins, and from the retention of Celtic words as names of places. The Castle of Pevensey, as we now behold it, exhibits two periods ; the one undoubtedly Roman, the other a medieval building, en-grafted upon the original structure. The date of the Roman building is inferred to have been of about the commencement of the Lower Empire. In the excavations which, in connection with Mr. C. Roach Smith, F.S.A., I carried on on the spot, we found coins of Gallienus, Postumus, Maximinian, Constantine, the Constantine family, and Magnentius. Other coins of cor-responding dates had been previously found on the spot, and they still frequently turn up.* It was long a matter of archæo-logical discussion whether Pevensey was the true site of Ande-rida. Seven other places have set up their claims to the hon-our, but the names of Petrie, Arthur Hussey, Roach Smith, and Thomas Wright are arrayed on this side. The arguments are too lengthened for even a *précis* here; nor is it necessary, as the site is now fixed here by common consent.

After the withdrawment of the Romans from Britain, some of the native Britons took up their residence in and around this stronghold, from which they were expelled by Ælla, the Saxon invader, and first king of the South Saxons. After the utter subjugation of the former, the Saxons gave to this place the name of *Andredes-ceaster*. The siege and subsequent slaughter of the poor inhabitants are described by ancient chroniclers as dreadful in the extreme. It is not until the year 792 that Pev-ensey appears under its modern appellation. It was then given, together with Hastings and Rotherfield, by the Saxon Duke Bertwald, to the abbey of St. Denis near Paris, in return for a

---

* The most remarkable coins ever found here are those of some of the Bactrian Kings, Radpluses, Menander, and Apollodotus, who flourished about 200 years B. C. How these relics of a dynasty founded by one of the Generals of Alexander the Great came hither, it is difficult to judge. Discredit has been cast on their discovery, but that they were found beneath the walls of Pevensey Castle is proved by undoubted evidence. See my *Chronicles of Pevensey*, 2nd edition, p. 4.

miraculous cure wrought on him by the bones of St. Denis himself, and those of others in that holy place. Here occurs another hiatus until A. D. 1042, but from that date a pretty connected history of Pevensey exists. In that year Swane, Earl of Oxford, a son of Godwin Earl of Kent, who had been compelled to fly into Denmark for attempting an illegal marriage with Edgiva, Abbess of Leominster, returning to England with eight ships, landed at the port of Pevensey. In 1049, Earl Godwin and his son entered the port and took away many ships.

The crowning event in the history of Pevensey was the landing there of William, Duke of Normandy, 28th September, 1066, a few days previously to his victory over Harold at the Battle of Hastings. The particulars of the chain of events connected with the Norman Conquest belong rather to general than local history; but several papers and notes in " Sussex Archæological Collections" serve for illustration. The celebrated piece of needlework, known as the Bayeux Tapestry, contains a representation of the landing AD PEVENESAE, the drawing up of the ships, the disembarkation of the horses and men, and several horsemen galloping towards Hastings in search of food for the army.

On the partition of the conquered lands, William bestowed the Rape of Pevensey (more than a sixth part of the county of Sussex) on his half-brother, Robert, Earl of Mortaigne, or Moreton, besides many others in other counties, amounting altogether to nearly 800 manors, of which 54 were in Sussex. He doubtless restored the outer walls of the Roman Castle, long a partial ruin, and added the little, or medieval castle, within the *enceinte* of the older fortification, making it at the same time the *caput baroniæ* of his Sussex estate.

In 1067 William returned to Normandy to receive the congratulations of his ancient subjects, taking with him as hostages Edgar Atheling, Archbishop Stigand, and others. He determined to sail from the same port at which he had landed, and accordingly embarked from Pevensey in the spring of the year.

Domesday contains a detailed account of Pevensey in 1086. It was in the territory of the Earl of Mortaigne. In the reign of the Confessor that king held 24 burgesses in domain, the toll producing 20s., port-dues 35s., and the pasturage 7s. 3d. rent. The Bishop of Chichester had five burgesses, and three priests had amongst them 23—total of burgesses in domain 52. At the time of the Earl's succession to the manor there were but 27, but twenty years later, at the making of the Record, the number arose to 109, and the toll produced £4. Thus it would appear that the Normans improved the condition of Pevensey in the early days of their rule. The town had a *mint*, which is mentioned. In the remarkable discovery of 26,500 coins at Beaworth, Hants, some years since, there were some struck at this place, with the name of the moneyer—JELFHEN-PEFNS.

In 1088, on the death of the Conqueror, the Earl of Moreton espoused the cause of Robert, against the usurpation of Rufus. Odo, Bishop of Bayeux, " a great tamer of the English," espoused the former side, held Pevensey Castle against Rufus, and sustained a six weeks' siege, but the Earl was at length compelled to succumb to the government of the usurper. He survived him, however, and after his death in the New Forest was favoured with a remarkable vision. According to Dugdale, " at the very hour that the King received the fatal wound, De Mortaigne, hunting in a lonely wood, in a place remote from the scene of the accident, was met by a very black goat, carrying the body of the King, ' all black and naked, and wounded through the midst of his breast.' The Earl adjuring the goat by the Holy Trinity to tell him what it was he so carried, the goat replied, ' I am carrying your king to judgment, yea, that tyrant William Rufus; for I am an evil spirit, and the revenger of the malice which he bore to the Church of God !' " The Earl was succeeded by his son William, who being opposed to the interests of Henry I. was taken prisoner at the battle of Tenerchebrai, at the same time as Duke Robert, and like that unfortunate prince lost his liberty, his eyes, and his patrimony. The last was, in 1104, conferred by Henry upon Gilbert de Aquila, grandson of a Norman knight of the same name who fell at Hastings. From him the barony of Pevensey received the designation of " The Honour of the Eagle," which it retained long after the extinction of the family. De Aquila was a personal friend of Henry I., and lost three children in the shipwreck of the " Blanche Nef," off Barfleur, in which the King's son and heir likewise perished on their voyage from Normandy. He was succeeded in 1118 by his son Richard de Aquila, a turbulent spirit, engaged in war with the English monarch, and had his English estate confiscated. He was also in arms against the King of France, who retaliated by burning his town and castle of Aquila in Normandy. King Henry condoned the offence against himself, but in 1127 he was again in open rebellion, and passed over to Normandy without the royal license, when his broad lands were again taken from him, and the Honour of the Eagle was granted by the King to his grandson Fitz-Empress, subsequently Henry II. The annals of Pevensey during these troublous times form a kind of epitome of English history, its successive lords having been mixed up with nearly every great event. In 1144, during the struggle between Stephen and the son of Maude, its castle was besieged by Stephen in person, who, finding it impregnable by force, reduced it by famine. The fortress at this time was under the command of Gilbert de Clare. In the treaty which followed between Stephen and Henry, it was stipulated that Pevensey and the other possessions of the outlaw, Richard de Aquila, should be settled upon William, son of King Stephen, who held them till Henry II.'s accession in 1254. This sovereign with great generosity reinstated Richard de Aquila in the honour of Pevensey, and the old rebel, growing penitent, gave to the Abbey of Grestein his manor of Willingdon, the herbage in his forest of Pevensey (Ashdown), and the tithes of Pevensey. In 1176 another Gilbert de Aquila succeeded to the Honour of the Eagle. He appears to have been of a more tranquil nature, the only mention of him being that he paid £21 17s. 6d. towards the fund collected for the redemption of Richard Cœur-de-Lion out of the hands of his Austrian captors. In 1195 that monarch granted to John de Palerne the custody of the castle gate of Pevensey. In 1205 a third Gilbert de Aquila, son of the preceding lord, succeeded, but being guilty of many excesses, and having gone over to Normandy without royal license, he forfeited all his estates, which were never restored to the family. He founded Michelham Priory, in the parish of Arlington, *temp.* Henry III.

In 1208 King John granted to the barons (freemen) of Pevensey, on payment of 40 marks into the Exchequer, license to build a new town between Pevensey and Langney, but there is no evidence of the design having been carried out. In 1216 William, sixth Earl of Warenne, was in temporary possession of the castle, but having sided with the Dauphin of France against King John, the latter sent him a precept to deliver it up to Matthew Fitz-Herbert, who was commanded to demolish it, but happily that order was not fulfilled. In 1235 Henry III. granted the lordship, on conditions, to Gilbert Marshal, Earl of Pembroke, but he was deprived 24th Henry III., and in the following year he lost his life in a tournament. In 1241 the same king granted it to Peter of Savoy, his Queen's uncle, for life. In 1264 John, Earl of Warenne, having deserted Henry at the battle of Lewes, fled to this castle, which had been committed to his charge, and embarked the next day for France. The following year De Savoy's troops held out here for the King, and Simon de Montfort, son of the Earl of Leicester, besieged it, but was compelled to retire. In 1269 the honour and castle were settled upon Prince Edward (afterwards Edward I.), and they continued in the Crown till *temp.* Edward III. Among the custodians of the fortress during that period we find the names of Palerne, Bode, De la Gare, Sassy, and Newente, most of

whom belonged to Sussex families. In 44th Edward III. that
monarch settled Pevensey and its dependencies upon John of
Gaunt, " time-honoured Lancaster," and from that time the
Honour of the Eagle became part of the Duchy of Lancaster.
The duke granted the office of constable for life to Sir John Pelham in 1394, and on the usurpation of the Crown by Henry,
Duke of Lancaster (Henry IV.) Pelham adhered to the son of
his old master, and landed with him in Yorkshire to oppose his
cousin Richard. The Yorkist party attacked Pevensey Castle,
which was gallantly held out on behalf of her husband and the
King, 1399, by Lady Pelham, the wife of Sir John. She was
besieged by many of the forces of Sussex, Surrey, and Kent.
During the siege she wrote a letter to her husband, stating the
dangers by which she was beset, and the difficulty she had in
obtaining provisions. This epistle, which is of great interest,
has been several times printed, and it is supposed by Hallam to
be the earliest specimen of epistolary correspondence by a lady
in the English language.

"Strange eventful history" all this: but there is more yet to
come. In reward of his eminent services to the Lancastrian
cause, Henry IV. granted to Pelham and his heirs the office of
Constable of Pevensey Castle, with the Honour of the Eagle
and all lands and rights thereto appurtenant. This was in
1400; in 1405, Edward, Duke of York, being charged with
abetting the escape of the Earl of March and his brother from
Windsor, the king committed him to the custody of Sir John,
who held him prisoner here. The unfortunate prince seems
to have received great kindness from Thomas Playsted, his
gentleman-keeper, in the fortress, for in his will dated 1415,
is this item : " I bequeath to Thomas Pleistede £20 for the kindness which he showed me when I was in ward at Pevensey."
Again, in 1419 we have the record of a still more illustrious
prisoner. Queen Joan of Navarre, the last wife of Henry IV.,
and step-mother of the reigning king, being accused, with her
confessor, of the practice of necromancy and sorcery, with intent
to take away the monarch's life, she was committed to the
charge of Sir John Pelham, son of the Sir John before-men-
tioned. Here she remained prisoner for nine years, until the
second year of Henry VI., when she was restored to her dower.
In 1461 Sir William Fynes (who was afterwards slain at Barnet
fight) was appointed Constable for life ; and in 1478, 9 the Castle
and its appendages were settled on Elizabeth, queen-consort of
Edward IV., for life.

From this date the records are very scanty: the office of
Constable was still existing in 1553, when Richard Oxenbridge
held it. In 1587 a survey of the Sussex coast was made with a

view to its defence against the threatened invasion of the Spaniards. In this document, (just published by Mr. Baxter, of Lewes) the haven of Pevensey is shown running in a direction nearly due east of the Castle. At this point orders are made to construct two rampiers, one on each side. Other directions are given, including one which was happily not carried out; namely that, "The Castle of Pemsey is to be re-edified *or utterly rased!*" In 1650 a survey was made, by the Parliamentary commissioners. The manor is described as "the manor of Pevensey, alias Pemsey, sometimes styled the honour of Aquila, in the parishes of Pevensey, Westham, Haylsham, Bexhill, &c. The *materials* of the old castle are valued at £40." Thanks to John Warr, of Westminster, the purchaser, who did not pull down these venerable walls! In 1660 Pevensey was settled upon Henrietta, the queen-dowager. It was held as royal property until William III. granted it to the Bentincks, who sold it to the Right Honourable Spencer Compton, Earl of Wilmington and Viscount Pevensey. In 1755 it descended to his son Charles, Earl of Northampton, whose daughter marrying in 1782 Lord George Augustus Cavendish, Earl of Burlington, conveyed it into the family of the present noble owner, the Duke of Devonshire, who, among his numerous styles and titles, may write himself "Dominus Aquilæ."

For the last two or three centuries the history of the Castle has been an eventless one of desolation and gradual decay, though its sturdy walls will doubtless remain for centuries to delight the artistic eye, and furnish matter for the retrospective philosopher and antiquary. It is worthy of remark that in 1846, the Sussex Archæological Society held their first general meeting within the walls of this, the most ancient building in the county. On that occasion I read a paper which comprised most of the main facts mentioned above, which became the basis of my little work called the "Chronicles of Pevensey." Some years later Mr. Roach Smith, F.S.A., and myself conducted excavations here, and the results of our discoveries were published in Vol. vi. of the "Sussex Archæological Collections," but much more fully, in 1858, in a monograph by Mr. Smith, whose acquaintance with Roman remains is so widely known, under the title of "Report on Excavations made on the site of the Roman Castrum at Pevensey." To this able production reference must be made for minute architectural details, but a brief description is given below.

"Of all the Roman walled *Castra* in England," observes the learned author, "that of Pevensey presents the highest claims to our admiration. It is among the largest in extent; it is the best preserved; and approached either from the east or west its appearance is grand and imposing. The dilapidations not being seen, the visitor views it in much the same condition as it presented itself to the eyes of the Romans themselves." . . . . yet " fifteen centuries stand between himself and the builders. But this long space of time has passed; thirty (fifty?) generations of men have gone to dust, while the walls and towers before him seem yet only in their maturity, or, at the worst, in a vigorous old age. Let him tear aside the ivy that clings to the facing of the wall, and he will find the course of the mason's trowel marked as freshly as if the tool had smoothed the mortar only a few months since!"*

The Castle lies westward of the town of Pevensey, between it and the pleasant village street of ·Westham. In shape it approximates to an oval, having its longest diameter nearly east and west. The outward enclosure (the walls of the ancient Anderida), now a pasture-field, contains about 8½ acres. The inner fortification or medieval castle, about 1½ acres. The external walls are nearly entire, the greatest *hiatus* being on the south, through which there is a fine view of the Bay. The principal entrance is at the east end of Westham-street, and is flanked with two towers of nearly horse-shoe form. There are six other towers of similar shape on the north side, more or less ruinated, but still in remarkable preservation. The medieval castle is an irregular pentagon, and its gateway is flanked by two round towers much dilapidated; three more towers are still standing, and the remains of others are traceable. Part of the moat remains. The outer or Roman walls are upwards of twenty feet high and of vast thickness, and exhibit, in various parts, strata of Roman tiles. The Normans evidently added to the height of the walls in some places, and one of the towers has a remarkable superposition of a Norman structure upon it, which was evidently designed as a watch-tower, as it commands a view land-ward over a great tract of country; but as just intimated I cannot enter into the many architectural details of this most venerable ruin. I must, however, say a few words respecting the researches which Mr. Roach Smith and myself made in 1852. We commenced operations in July, and continued them throughout the year. It was proved that the massive flanking towers of the gateway, 28 feet apart, had originally been flanked by a wall, and that in it was the true *porta* or grand gate of the fortress. Fragments of *imbrices* or roof tiles from the original roof of the gateway were found, with a third-brass coin of Constantine, and at a higher level a penny of Canute. We next opened out a postern or minor gateway passing obliquely through

* Report, p. 12.

the northern wall, and to this the name of " Roach Smith's gate" was subsequently given. On the south side, where the wall had long since disappeared, we discovered by deep excavations that such a defence had originally existed, with a very small postern, though it had been a prevalent notion that water in that part had been a sufficient safeguard. In Roman times the sea must have reached almost as far as the wall. A landslip at this point is the probable cause of the disappearance of the fortifications. In the "little" or medieval castle, we discovered the foundations of the free chapel of Pevensey Castle, which is frequently mentioned in ancient records. It must have consisted of nave, north aisle and chancel, with walls thirty inches thick. Below the level of the floor of the chancel were found several skeletons, one of which having the arm-bones crossed over the chest, is presumed to be that of a priest. At the west end of the church a font of circular cup-shaped form was found *in situ*, though much fractured, and at the east end the basin or head of a pillar piscina of Early English character. A short time previously the well of the fortress had been discovered near the chapel. It is seven feet in diameter, and steined with solid ashlar. From the depth of about fifty feet, many skulls, said to have been those of *wolves*, were brought up, as well as several large round balls of sandstone, which were doubtless the projectiles discharged in old warfare by the catapult.

The parish church of St. Nicholas, the patron saint of Pevensey and of mariners, consists of nave, chancel, and north and south aisles, with a tower on the north side of the north aisle. The latter is very low, and supports a shingled spire. The prevailing style of the building is Early English. The columns of the nave are alternately octagonal and clustered. The chancel arch is lofty and acutely pointed. The capitals are beautifully foliated. The chancel is very long, with three lancet windows at the east end. There are brass plates in the south aisle for Edward Millward, 1619, and Elinor his wife, 1614. On the north wall of the chancel is an elaborate monument with the marble effigies of John Wheatley, gent., 1616, his wife Elizabeth, and Katherine, "their only davghter and heire."

The Corporation of Pevensey is a member of the Cinque-port of Hastings, and is governed by a bailiff, jurats, and commonalty. It comprises the parishes of Pevensey, Westham, and the south portion of Hailsham; originally portions of Bexhill and Wartling were included, thus making the liberty, leuga, or *lowey*, as it is sometimes called, almost co-extensive with the Marsh. The prison, with a court-house over it, resembles an old cottage. There are many peculiar customs and privileges. The corporation seal is a very curious piece of antiquity, exhibiting on the obverse an antique ship, and on the reverse two ships in full sail. It is probably of the 13th century.

The decline of Pevensey from its ancient importance to the condition of a small village of less than 400 inhabitants, has rendered its little municipality the butt of local satire, and many anecdotes reflecting upon the assumed ignorance of the natives are in existence; one especially, that the grand jury once found a prisoner guilty of manslaughter for stealing a pair of leather breeches, is a standing jest. These stories, or some of them, probably originated with Andrew Borde, once resident here, one of the most singular personages of the 16th century, and said to have been the prototype of Merry Andrews. He was in turn a Carthusian Friar, physician to Henry VIII., a quack-doctor at country fairs, a traveller in many lands, an author on various subjects, a court favourite, and a political spy. He finished his career as a prisoner in the Fleet in the year 1549. See " Worthies of Sussex," p. 27.

[S. A. C. Corporate seal, i, 21. Custumal of, iv, 209. xviii, 42. Blos seal of, found here, v, 205. Watermill in Domesday, v, 271. Henry I. at, v, 282. King Stephen at, i, 132. Edward II. at, vi, 46. Andredesceaster on, vi, 90. xi, 223. xix, 4. Wise Men of Gotham, vi, 207. xviii, 69, 72, 142. Excavations there by Messrs. Roach Smith and Lower, vi. 265 *(Lower)*. Royal Mint, ix, 369. Smugglers, x, 83. Old Cannons, xi, 152. Andrew Borde, notices of, xiii, 262. xix, 7. Pevensey Castle and Forest, xiv, 41. Muleward (Milward) at Agincourt, xv, 131. Church bells, xvi, 220. The Lowey, or Leuga, xvii, 6, 55. xviii, 42. Battle Abbey lands, xvii, 55. Pelham family, xvii, 249. Oratory at, xvii, 249. Bailiff of and Jack Cade, xviii, 18, 27. Statutes of Pevensey Marsh, xviii, 42. The Port, xviii, 42. xix, 1. Hospital of St. John the Baptist, xviii, 43. Catapult balls, xviii, 72. Horseye, Mankseye, Northeye, Hydneye, xix, 1, 3, 4. Swegen (Sweyn) and Beorn at Pevensey, xix, 79. The Sussex Thane who saw the approach of the Norman Armada, xix, 79. Alured gave East Grinstead to Lewes Priory, xx, 145.]

PIDDINGHOE.

Vulgo, *Pid'nhoo;* a parish in the Hundred of Holmstrow; Rape of Lewes, on the Ouse; one mile north from Newhaven. Post-town, Lewes. Railway station, Newhaven, distant about one mile. Union, Newhaven. Population in 1861, 208; in 1851, 243. Benefice, a vicarage, valued at £170; Patron and Incumbent, Rev. James Hutchins, M.A., of St. John's College, Oxford. Date of earliest Parish Register, 1540. Acreage, 2,658. *Chief Landowners,* The Earl of Chichester, and William Waterman, Esq.

The Anglo-Saxon *hó* signifies a heel-shaped projection into the water (Leo) and this name may be Peada-inga-hó, the ' hó ' of the sons of Peada, a well-known Saxon appellative. The geographical position of the village justifies the use of the last syllable. Piddinghoe belonged *temp.* Edward II. to the De Warennes; otherwise its history is obscure. The three manors of Plumpton-Piddinghoe, Horcome, and Harpingden are partly in the parish. The church now comprises a chancel, nave, north aisle, and a round tower, with an octagonal shingled spire. The south aisle and the north and south chapels of the chancel have been removed. The interior contains several interesting details, the prevailing character being Early English, though portions are of late Norman character. The round tower is one of the three of that form in the county, all of which stand near the west bank of the Ouse. Its material is flint, with small window openings, some of which are round-headed. For speculations on the reason for this form of tower see Hussey, p. 267. There are inscriptions for the families of Faulconer and Waterman. Deans in this parish was the seat of the family of Heath in the 16th and 17th centuries. On the road-side near the village is a chalk pit, interesting to geological observers. Piddinghoe produces bricks and pottery. A local witticism runs that the inhabitants " shoe their magpies !"

[S. A. C. Magpies shod here! xiii, 210. Bells, xvi, 220. Cade's insurrection, xviii, 24. Ancient relic, xviii, 70.]

PLAYDEN.

Domesday, *Pleidenham;* a parish on the Rother, in the Hundred of Goldspur; Rape of Hastings; distant ¾ of a mile north from Rye, its Post-town, Railway-station, and Union. Population in 1811, 223 ; in 1861, 305. Benefice, a Rectory, annexed to East Guldeford ; Patron, Rev. C. Shrubb; Incumbent, Rev. Charles Meade Ramus, M.A., of Trinity College, Cambridge. Date of earliest Parish Register, 1714. Acreage, 1,308.

The surface has pleasing undulations, and towards East Guldeford there is a promontory of rock, caused by the ancient washing of the Rother, and called Playden Cliff. Sandrock Hill commands a good coast view. The village has the singular *alias* of *Sauket,* or *Salt-cot,* Street, with reference, it is said, to the fisheries of Rye; but this I much doubt, as similar names are found in various parts of the world, remote from sea and from salt. The word is probably derived from Sanscrit roots; *e. g.,* there is a military station at the foot of the Himalayas called Sealcote. Before the Conquest, Playden was held of the Confessor by one Siulf, and here another probability crops up; may not the name be rendered " Siulf's cote," or habitation ?

After the Conquest the Earl of Eu held it in person, and there was a church. Portions of the manors of Playden-Mascall and Playden-Porter lie in the parish. The ancient family of De Guldeford and the Abbey of Robertsbridge had lands here.

The charitable establishment called the Hospital of St. Bartholomew of Rye is close outside that town, but in this parish. It belonged to the Norman abbey of Fécamp. It was originally founded for leprous persons, but when that disease died out, it became an almshouse for the poor. In 1379, an inquisition shows that one Robert Burton, master of the hospital, had cut down timber and sold crops from the lands of the establishment for his own behoof, and to the detriment of the poor inmates, who were obliged daily to beg their bread in Rye. After the Dissolution the site was granted to Andrew, Lord Windsor. A list of the wardens of the house, from 1343 to 1478, is given by Mr. Slade Butler in "Sussex Collections," xii, 136. A free chapel here is said to have been given by Henry VII. towards the building of the Chapel of the Virgin in Westminster Abbey.

The church (St. Michael) includes a nave with aisles, central tower with shingled spire, and chancel. The columns of the arcades which divide the nave from the aisles are alternately round and octagonal. There are memorials for the names of Legg, Clerk, and others; and an incised slab commemorates a Flemish brewer of the fifteenth century, with barrels, mash-stick, and fork. 𝕳𝔦𝔢𝔯 𝔦𝔰 𝔟𝔢𝔤𝔯𝔞𝔟𝔢' 𝕮𝔬𝔯𝔫𝔢𝔩𝔦𝔰 𝖅𝔬𝔠𝔱𝔪𝔞𝔫𝔫𝔰, 𝔟𝔦𝔡𝔱 𝔟𝔬𝔢𝔯 𝔡𝔢 𝔷𝔦𝔢𝔩𝔢.— "Here is interred Cornelius Zoctmanns. Pray for the soul." Near the church-yard is an ancient hollow oak, on the top of which a tar barrel sometimes served for a beacon. Extensive barracks existed at Playden during the French war.

[S. A. C. Chapel, xiii, 137, 143. Flemish brewer, viii, 337. xiii, 180. Idlers apprenticed, xvi, 26. Three church bells, xvi, 220. Hospital, xvii, 134. Salcote, xix, 167.]

PLAISTOW. (See Kirdford.)

PLUMPTON.

A parish in the Hundred of Street; Rape of Lewes; distant about five miles north-west of Lewes; Post-town, Hurst-Pierpoint. It has a Railway station. Union, Chailey. Population in 1811, 233; in 1861, 404. Benefice, a Rectory, valued at £380; in the gift of Trinity College, Cambridge; Incumbent, Rev. W. Woodward, B.A., of that College. Date of earliest Parish Register, 1558. Acreage, 2,423. *Chief Landowner*, the Earl of Chichester.

The parish lies principally on the northern side of the

South Downs, the escarpment of which is here very steep and lofty. Above it is a kind of "table land" unusual on these hills, called Plumpton Plain, where, according to tradition, some incidents of the battle of Lewes occurred. On the escarpment is a very large cross-patée incised in the turf, and visible at times from a great distance. Originally it was bared to the chalk, like the celebrated White Horse, and our Wilmington Giant of yore, but it is now overgrown with turf. Its origin and purpose are alike unknown.

The manor belonged to Earl Godwin, and after the Conquest to the Earls of Warenne. In later times it was held by the great Norman family of Bardolf (many particulars of whom are given in Stapleton's "Liber de Antiq. Leg."), and from them descended successively to William, Phelip Lord Bardolf, Viscount Beaumont, and Lord Hastings. On the attainder of this race for their adherence to the Lancastrian cause, it was forfeited to the Crown. It was afterwards granted to Sir John Fagg, but in 1522 it was vested in the ancient proprietors, who had been restored in blood, and then belonged to Elizabeth, wife of John, Earl of Oxford, widow of William, Viscount Beaumont, Lord Bardolf. Queen Elizabeth granted it to Sir Nicholas Carew, who died possessed of it in 1590. In 1627 Sir Henry Delves was lord, and in 1663 Anthony Springett. In the latter family it continued until 1763, when it passed by purchase to that of Pelham, its present owners. Among the Crown tenants of the manor were the Mascalls, who resided at Plumpton Place. One of this family, Leonard Mascall, wrote several books on rural pursuits, and he is said to have first introduced carp into England, placing them in the moat which surrounded his mansion.* He was also a grower of pippins, and a breeder of cattle, sheep, dogs, &c. He flourished in the sixteenth century, but the date of his death is unknown. (See "Worthies of Sussex," p. 53.) Plumpton Place still retains its moat and its carp, but the venerable mansion, shorn of its original importance, is now only the habitation of cottagers.

The church consists of a chancel, nave, with south porch and west tower, with shingled spire, and has features of Transition-Norman, Early English, and Perpendicular work. (Hussey.) Within are memorials for the families of Springett, Walker, Woodward, and Hampton. The last-named family, now represented by the families of Weekes and Borrer, held the advowson 200 years. John Dudeney, the philosophic shepherd and school-

---

* This, however, may well be doubted, as Dame Juliana Berners mentions the fish in her "Boke of St. Alban's," in the previous century. She describes it as a "daynteous fysshe, but there ben but few in Englonde, and therefore I wryte the lesse of hym."

master, was a native of this parish. ("Worthies of Sussex,"
p. 343.) Some curious mural paintings have lately been discovered in the church.

[S. A. C. Two watermills in Domesday, v, 271. Mascall, xiv, 222.
Plumpton Place, xv, 162. Bell, xvi, 220. Celt from, xviii, 66. Homewood
of, participator in Cade's insurrection, xviii, 29, 40. Church [and altar
tombs, xviii, 40. Mural paintings, xx, 198. Flint celt, xviii, 64. Tapestry
at Plumpton Place, xviii, 73. Springett family, xx, 36, 46.]

POLING.

A parish in the Hundred of its own name; Rape of Arundel; distant
three miles south-east from Arundel, its Post-town; Railway station,
Angmering, distant about 1½ mile. Union, East Preston. Population in 1811, 148; in 1861, 203. Benefice, a Vicarage, valued at
£158; Patron, the Bishop of Chichester; Incumbent, Rev. T.Trough-
ton Leete, M.A., of Caius College, Cambridge. Date of earliest
Parish Register, 1558. Acreage, 923.

As no mention of Poling is found in Domesday, Dallaway
thinks it was carved out of Angmering, and made a distinct
hundred at a later date. On the partition of the earldom of
Arundel in 1244 the hundred and manor of Poling were allotted
to John Fitz-Alan. In 1381 they were settled upon the newly
founded college of Arundel. In 1568 Sir John Caryll was lord.
It was afterwards incorporated with the Michelgrove estate.
From the Walker family, who held that property, it passed by
sale, in 1828, to Bernard-Edward, Duke of Norfolk. A small
Commandery of Knights-Templars was established here, probably on the endowment of one of the Fitz-Alan family. It
afterwards passed to the Knights-Hospitallers. A chapel, with
chambers for three knights, remained, having been used as a
farmhouse, until about 1830, when it was fitted up as a private
residence. A view, as it stood in 1780, is preserved among the
Burrell MSS.

The impropriation was given to the Abbey of Almenesche, in
Normandy, and was transferred in the thirteenth century to the
nunnery of Lyminster. The vicar is endowed with the whole
tythes. The church (St. Nicholas) appears to have been partly
rebuilt about the beginning of the fifteenth century, and comprises chancel, nave, south aisle, and west tower. There are
Transition-Norman features. The passage to the rood-loft is
still open. There is a half-length brass to Walter Baby, vicar
in the fifteenth century, and an inscription to Robert Dyneham,
vicar, 1707. For a notice of Richard Carpenter, the versatile
Vicar of Poling, who changed from Romanism to Protestantism

repeatedly, and was accounted " a theological mountebank," see " Worthies of Sussex," p. 326.

[S. A. C. Lands belonging to Calceto Priory—Tayller of, Fitz-Osmond of—Commandery of, xi, 101. John de Palenges xi, 103. Church and manor to Lyminster nunnery, xi, 118. Church, xii, 96. Bells, xvi, 220. Arun, tributary of, xvi, 259. Poling church, &c., xviii, 101. Gold British coin, found at, xviii, 69.]

PORTSLADE.

Domesday, *Portslade;* a parish in the Hundred of Fishersgate ; Rape of Lewes ; distant from Shoreham, its Post-town, three miles. It has a Railway station on the South-Coast line. Union, Steyning. Population in 1811, 358 ; in 1861, 1,103. Benefice, a Vicarage, united with Hangleton, valued for the Rectorial Tithes at £260, and Vicarial £142 ; Patron, the Earl de la Warr; Incumbent, Rev. Frederick George Holbrook, M.A. Date of earliest Parish Register, 1666. Acreage, 2,006. *Chief Landowners*, Rev. Wm. Hall, and Edw. Blaker, Esq.

This sea-side parish, though only on an average a mile in breadth, is four miles long. I have before remarked that in the majority of Sussex parishes these oblong dimensions are found, and that their general direction is north and south. The village occupies a pleasant declivity of the South Downs, and commands excellent land and sea-views. The parish contains several mansions and residences, particularly the Manor-House, belonging to the Borrer family, Portslade House to the Rev. W. Hall, East Hill to Edward Blaker, Esq., and Portslade Lodge to Miss Borrer. In Domesday, Portslade is stated to have been held by Osward, who also possessed it before the Conquest. It was exempt from land-tax, and the owner could change his residence at pleasure, and sell his property if he would—a noble instance of the liberality of Norman times ! In 2nd Henry III., the celebrated Hubert de Burgh, Earl of Kent,* who had married Beatrice de Warenne, became possessed of the manor in dower, and in 13th Henry III., Margaret, his daughter, by Margaret his wife, sister of Alexander, King of Scotland, was owner. From this period the manor frequently changed hands, and it has belonged to the families of De Grelly, De la Warr, Pelham, Snelling, Edwards, Fawkenor, Westbrook, Andrew, Foley, Watson, Davies, Lamb, Phillips, and Borrer. Near the church-yard are the ruins of the ancient manor-house, described by Mr. Hussey as "still exhibiting two tolerably perfect double-light round-headed windows.

* This eminent personage is said to have been the greatest subject in Europe. He was Chief Justiciary of England and Ireland, Governor of the Tower, and Castellan of Windsor. For a full notice of him see " Burke's Extinct Peerage," p. 97.

Of one the dividing mullion has a decidedly Norman capital. One fragment of wall is three feet three inches thick, and seems to have been overthrown by violence." Mr. Hussey considers that the latest date that can be assigned to this ruin is the Early English period. I should regard it as a fragment of Norman work. The church (St. Nicholas) consists of a chancel, nave, south aisle, and west tower. The chancel is Early English, with three sedilia and a piscina under trefoiled arches. Other portions of the building are in different styles, ranging from Transition-Norman to Perpendicular. In 1847 some mural paintings were discovered in this church, the subject being the Day of Judgment. The tower contains three bells, but not of very ancient date. There are mortuary inscriptions to the names of Clutton, Edwards, Cooke, Woodcock, Carpenter, Blaker, Borrer, and others.

It would appear that this parish anciently gave name to a family called De Portslade, as a Ralph de Portslade was accused, in 1303, of an offence against the Abbot of Bayham. Curious details of the transaction are given in Vol. xi. of the " Sussex Collections."

Like many other places on the Sussex Coast, Portslade has suffered much from the encroachments of the sea. The claim of this village to have been the *Portus Adurni* of Roman times, is not well supported, as it has been pretty well established that Bramber is the site of that station. Many Roman remains have, however, been found in the parish. COPPERAS GAP is a hamlet of this parish. It is on the road from Brighton to Shoreham. The population and houses have greatly increased in consequence of the formation of a canal towards Brighton, with a view to the supply of that town with coals and other commodities. A new district church (St. Andrew) has been erected for the population. Patron, the Bishop of Chichester.

[S. A. C. Mural paintings in church, i, 161. Ralph de Portslade, xi, 124. Church-house and Fuller family, xiii, 47. Roman road, xiv, 177. Church bells, xvi, 221. Edwards family, xix, 88. Blaker family, xix, 200.]

POYNINGS.

Domesday, *Poninges;* vulgo, *Punnins* and *Punnuns;* a parish in the Hundred of its own name ; Rape of Lewes ; distant six miles north-west from Brighton ; Post-town, Hurst-Pierpoint. Railway-station, Hassocks Gate, distant about 4½ miles. Union, Steyning. Population in 1811, 181 ; in 1861, 261. Benefice a Rectory, valued at £273, with 19 acres of Glebe and 70 acres in the parish of Pyecombe ; Incumbent, Rev. Thomas Agar Holland, M.A., of Worcester College, Oxford. Date of earliest Parish Register, 1558. Acreage, 1,643.

An elaborate account of this parish by the Rector opens

the 15th volume of the "Sussex Collections." The parish gives
name to a hundred, and is situated partly upon, and partly at
the base of, the South Down range. It is full of romantic
beauty. In a charter of King Eádgar, the name is written
Puningas; the termination *ingas* means here, as in numerous
other cases, offspring or descendants; hence this place must
have been colonized, in early Saxon days, by some member of
that race. Whether some such word as *Pun* or *Puna* existed as
a personal name, does not appear. According to Domesday,
William Fitz-Rainald held Poninges of William de Warenne.
Earl Godwin had previously presented it to Cola. It was assessed under both at eight hides, but paid no land-tax. The
arable was thirteen plough-lands; there were two ploughs in
the demesne and twenty-five villeins, and eight bondmen having fifteen ploughs. There were a church, two ministri, two
mills, fifty acres of meadow, and a wood of forty hogs. In the
time of the Confessor it was valued at £12, and was, at the date
of the Survey, worth but £10. This description clearly refers
to a much larger area than that comprised within the limits of
the modern Poynings. Fitz-Rainald was son of Rainald, second
brother of Robert de Pierpoint, Lord of Hurst-Pierpoint. *Temp.*
Stephen, its possessors took the name of De Ponynges, and the
family, afterwards ennobled, held the manor during nearly three
centuries, and for eleven generations in the male line. The
first of the family ennobled was Sir Michael, who was summoned to Parliament in 1294 as Baron de Ponynges. His
son Thomas was summoned to Parliament by King Edward
III. in 1337. In 1339 he perished in a great sea-fight with
the French near Sluys. His son followed the standard of
the same monarch in all his foreign wars from 1339 to 1355.
He was created a Knight-Banneret at Cressy, and was present
at the surrender of Calais, and also at the battle of Poictiers. He died in 1369, having jointly with his wife founded
the existing church of Poynings. In his will, proved in 1369, is
the following noticeable bequest: " I demise to him who may
be my heir, a ruby ring, which is *the charter of my heritage of
Poynings,* together with the helmet and armour which my
father demised to me." Thomas, 4th Baron Poynings, who was
born at Slaugham, where the family appear to have possessed
an estate, carried out the rebuilding of the church in accordance
with the wish of his parents. He died without issue, and his
brother Richard succeeded. The latter was summoned to Parliament 1382-5; attended the Black Prince in his campaign in
Spain; and died of disease at Villalpando in Leon. His son
Robert, born in 1380, succeeded to the barony. He served in
France under Richard II., with 30 men-at-arms and 60 archers,

and later, under Henry IV., V., VI., with 60 men-at-arms, and 180 archers, and was indeed, both in war and diplomacy, one of the greatest men of his time. He died in 1446. His eldest son, knight of the shire for Sussex, died before his father, in 1430. He had a son and a daughter; the son predeceased him, and the latter, Eleanor, on the death of her grandfather, the last Baron, became his heir. She married Sir Henry Percy, son and heir of Henry, 2nd Earl of Northumberland, thus conveying a very extensive estate into that illustrious house. The successive Barons de Poynings formed alliances with numerous important families, but now the name became extinct in the elder male line. The barony of Poynings merged in the superior dignity, and has ever since formed one of the subordinate titles of the Earls and Dukes of Northumberland. Sir Henry was summoned to Parliament in his wife's barony, and so continued until 1455, when he succeeded to the paternal Earldom. He espoused the Lancastrian cause, and fell while commanding its forces, at Towton fight in 1461. Thenceforward the Poynings blood was lost in the still more illustrious name of Percy. There were other persons of historical distinction collaterally descended from this ancient race. Sir Edward Poynings, K.G., who flourished under Kings Henry VII. and VIII., was grandson of Robert, the 6th Baron. He was Lord-Deputy of Ireland, and caused a series of laws of a highly beneficial kind to be enacted in the Irish Parliament of 1494, 5, assimilating the Irish laws to the English. His code was long known as "Poynings' Law," and was only repealed at the close of the last century. He was a great warrior and a thoughtful statesman. Lloyd, in his "State Worthies," says of him: "A serious and plodding brow bespoke this noble knight's deep prudence, and a smart look his resolved valour; who was a man vastly different in his publick capacity from what he was in private employment—

'Quemquam posse putas mores narrare futuros?
Dic mihi, si fias tu leo, qualis eris.'"

He held important trusts at Boulogne, Tournay, and in the Cinque Ports, and was much connected with state employments in the court of Henry VIII. His illegitimate son, Sir Thomas Poynings, also distinguished himself in military affairs, and was successively Marshal of Calais and Governor of Boulogne. In 1545 a second barony of Poynings was created in his favour, but he died shortly afterwards without issue, and the title expired with him.

In 1535 Algernon, 6th Earl of Northumberland, sold this estate to Henry VIII., who granted it in exchange for other manors, to his favourite, Sir Anthony Browne, K.G., ancestor of the Viscounts Montague, and in that family it continued until its extinction, and it is now vested in the Crown, under the Commissioners of Woods and Forests.

Mr. Holland gives in his paper a full ecclesiastical history of the parish. The church (Holy Trinity) was in the patronage of the Earls of Warenne, who gave it to Lewes Priory. A chantry of ancient foundation, dedicated to St. Mary, was long associated with the rectory. Its founder, doubtless one of the Lords Poynings, cannot be identified; but the 70 acres of land in Pyecombe, still attached to the rectory, and called the chantry, no doubt supplied the revenue of that foundation. The church is a cruciform building of beautiful and striking aspect—very superior in the *ensemble* to most of the churches of the district. Its large embattled tower, with its spacious nave, chancel and transepts, form altogether a cathedral-like group, very pleasant to behold. It is constructed of chalk and rubble, and cased with dressed flints. The dressings are chiefly of the yellow sandstone still dug in the district, and the original roofing was of Horsham stone. The interior is grand in its proportions. Four noble arches support the tower, and the east window is a striking object. The north transept is known as the Montague Chapel, and the south as the Poynings Chapel. The latter was long walled off, and in fact consigned to almost utter darkness, damp, and decay, as if the last resting place of a long line of chivalrous and pious lords of Poynings were a thing of nought! Thanks, however, to the late Dr. Holland, rector, and Hugh, 3rd Duke of Northumberland, this state of things was changed in 1842. Old monumental stones were replaced near their original sites, but they cannot be identified with any of the particular personages whose remains they covered. There are traces of brasses, and embossed crosses on some of them, but the only one whereof the inscription can be read has on it a memorial in Lombardic characters to the " 𝔇𝔞𝔪𝔢𝔱𝔱𝔢 𝔡𝔢 𝔅𝔦𝔰𝔰𝔢𝔩, de la Bor. ·." It had a floriated cross and shield, but these, with the brass letters which formerly passed round the verge of the stone, have been torn away by sacrilegious hands. Of the connection of this " Damette " (or unmarried lady) with the baronial family nothing is known. Over the chancel window, outside and over the porch, are the arms of Poynings. Some of the few encaustic tiles remaining have the arms of Richard, king of the Romans, brother of Henry III. In the chancel are three sedilia and a piscina under ogee arches, with a hood moulding. In a window of the north transept is a representation in ancient glass of the Annunciation. The font is octagonal, with ogee panels, and coeval with the church.

Of Poynings Place, the old baronial mansion, few remains

exist. It was probably deserted on the extinction of the family, and the Percys and Montagues had greater houses elsewhere. A drawing by Grimm in 1780, in the Burrell Collections, represents a lofty tower, a relic of the original edifice, and traces of terraces and avenues may still be noticed by the antiquarian eye. In 1727, a great part of the then existing remains was destroyed by fire, and in 1824 what remained of the tower fell down, so that it may now be said of this once noble fabric—

"Etiam periere ruinæ."

In this parish is the remarkable chasm of the South Downs, known as the *Devil's Dyke,* which looks almost like a work of art. So accurately are its sloping sides shaped, that we might imagine that some gigantic power had been employed to cut a cleft or gorge through the solid hill. Connected with it is an earthwork called the "Poor-man's wall," evidently a corruption of other words. The entrenchment is oval, and nearly a mile in circumference. The fact of a few Roman coins having been found here does not disprove a much higher antiquity. From the summit of the Dyke Hill there is a view hardly equalled in the South of England. It is said to embrace, under favourable lights, portions of six counties. Certainly the grand Weald is no where seen to greater advantage, while southward there is an extensive seaboard view, including Brighton, Shoreham, Worthing, and, occasionally, the Isle of Wight. On this height is an inn called the Dyke-House, which is the constant resort of pleasure parties from Brighton. The great geological chasm is popularly ascribed to the agency of Satan. Let our Sussex-loving antiquary, the late Mr. William Hamper, F.S.A., tell the story; for, although "decies repetita, placebit."—

"Five hundred years ago or more, or if you please in days of yore,
That wicked wight 'yclept Old Nick, renowned for many a wanton trick,
With envy, from the Downs beheld, the studded Churches of the Weald ;
Here, Poynings cruciform, and there, Hurst, Albourne, Bolney, Newtimber,
Cuckfield and more, with towering crest ; *Quæ nunc præscribere longum est ;*
Oft heard the undulating chime, proclaim around twas service time.
' Can I, with common patience see, these churches, and not one for me?
Shall I be cheated of my due, by such a sanctimonious crew ?'
He muttered twenty things beside, and swore *that* night the foaming tide,
Led through a vast and wondrous trench, should give these pious souls a drench!
Adown the West the Steeds of Day hasted merrily away.
And night in solemn pomp came on, Her lamp a star—a cloud her throne.
The lightsome Moon she was not there, but deck'd the other hemisphere.
Now with a fit capacious spade, so large, it was on purpose made,
Old Nick began, with much ado, to cut the lofty Downs in two ;
At every lift his spade threw out a thousand waggon loads, no doubt !
Oh ! had he laboured till the morrow, His envious work had wrought much
    sorrow.
The Weald, with verdant beauty graced, o'erwhelmed, a sad and watery waste !
But so it chanced, a good old dame, whose deed has long outlived her name,

Waked by the cramp at midnight hour, or just escaped the night-mare's power,
Rose from her humble bed, when lo! she heard Nick's *terrible ado!*
And by the starlight faintly spied this wicked wight, and Dyke so wide!
She knew him by his mighty size, his tail, his horns, his saucer eyes ;
And while with wonderment amazed, at workman and at work she gazed,
Swift cross her mind a thought there flew, that she by strategem, might do
A deed which luckily should save her country from a watery grave ;
By his own weapons fairly beating the father of all lies and cheating!
Forth from her casement in a minute, a sieve, with flaming candle in it,
She held to view :—and simple Nick, who ne'er suspecting such a trick,
(All rogues are fools) when first his sight a full orb'd luminary bright
Beheld—he fled—his work undone—scared at the sight of a *new Sun*,
And muttering curses that the day should drive him from his work away!
Night after night, this knowing dame watched—but again Nick never came!
Who now dares call the action evil, *To hold a candle to the Devil?*"

[S. A. C. Encaustic tile, iii, 239. Parish register extracts, iv, 279.
Domesday watermills, v, 271. xv, 53. De Poynings family, xi, 58. xiv,
182. xv, 5. Roman road, &c., xiv, 178. Parochial history (*Holland*), xv,
1. An ancient Andrew de Borde, xv, 6. xv, 24. Percy family, xv, 11.
Earls of Northumberland, *ibid.* Church, xv, 22, 236. xvi, 311. Inscriptions in church-yard, xv, 231. Earthworks and Devil's Dyke, iii, 173. xv,
55. Bells, xvi, 221, 311. Beard, Rev. George, xv, 231. xviii, 161.

PRESTON EPISCOPI.

Domesday, *Prestetone ;* vulgo, *Press'n ;* a parish in the Hundred of its
own name ; Rape of Lewes ; a mile north of Brighton, of which it
may be considered a suburb. Union, Steyning. Population in 1811 ;
429 ; in 1861, 1,044. Benefice, a Vicarage, with Hove annexed,
valued at £300 ; Patron, the Bishop of Chichester ; Incumbent,
Rev. Walter Kelly, M.A., of Caius College, Cambridge. Date of
earliest Parish Register, 1556. Acreage, 1,286.

It is beautifully situated in a dale ¯near the north-east outskirts of Brighton, and contains, besides Preston Place (the
manor-house), many excellent residences. The Brighton cavalry
barracks and water-works are in the parish. At no distant
date the village will become, like Hove, part and parcel of the
great town of Brighton. A new building scheme has been ab-
surdly called Preston*ville!* The origin of the name is obviously
Priests' *ton* or habitation, and as it formerly belonged to the
bishops of Chichester, it was for distinction's sake called Preston Episcopi. Prestetone is assessed, in Domesday, at 20 hides,
the arable, 12 plough-lands ; 30 villeins with 20 bondmen had
12 ploughs. There was a church, with 15 acres of meadow and
a wood of 2 hogs. The manor extends into several parishes,
contiguous and remote. The descent of the manor is obscure.
In 26th Henry VIII, the demesne lands were demised to Edward
Elderton, gentleman. In 34th Elizabeth, Sir Thomas Shirley, of
the Wiston family, became seised, and in that family it long re-

mained. Sir Richard Shirley, Bart., who died in 1705, demised it to his three daughters and co-heiresses. Ultimately Thomas Western, who had married one of them, became sole proprietor. His grandson, Charles Callis Western, Esq., in 1794, sold the estate for £17,600, to William Stanford, Esq., in whose representatives it now vests.

The church (St. Peter) is small, and though, as Mr. Hussey remarks, it has only chancel, nave, and small western tower, and possesses little ornament "it is an interesting building, being entirely in one style—the Early English, without the admixture of any other." The east end has three lancet windows within a large arch. In the north wall of the chancel is a sepulchral monument, the brasses of which are lost, with a Perpendicular altar-tomb, for one of the Shirley family, richly carved. In the south wall are a piscina, and three sedilia of different grades, all under trefoiled arches. In "Archæologia," Vol. xxiii, the Rev. Charles Townsend describes some mural paintings in this church, which are still visible. The principal subject is the murder of Thomas à Becket, and from the costume, &c., the date of this rude art is the time of Edward I. There are also figures of the Saviour, and several saints. In this church lie buried the remains of Francis Cheynell, D.D., the great Presbyterian controversialist, and the foe of Chillingworth; (see "Worthies of Sussex," p. 309), and in the church-yard is the tomb of the Rev. James Douglas, author of "Nenia Britannica" and various other works. He died in 1819, one of the ablest antiquaries of his time.

[S. A. C. Shirley family, xiv, 114, 232. xix, 63, 161. Church bells, xvi, 221. Church, xix, 63. Elrington family, xix, 64.]

PULBOROUGH.

Domesday, *Poleberge;* vulgo, *Pulber;* a parish in the Hundred of West Easwrith; Rape of Arundel; distant six miles from Petworth. Posttown, Petworth. It has a Railway station on the Mid-Sussex line of the Brighton Railway. Union, Thakeham. Population in 1811, 1,613; in 1861, 1,852. Benefice, a Rectory, valued at £1,750; Patron, Lord Leconfield; Incumbent, Rev. William Sinclair, M.A., of St. Mary Hall, Oxford. Date of earliest Parish Register, 1595. Acreage, 6,398. It is a market town.

Few names of places have a clearer etymology than this. It is Anglo-Saxon, *pul,* a pool, and *byrig,* an encampment, and applies well to the position of the parish. The village is a long street on the banks of the Arun, and contains a considerable population. That portion which is near the church is considerably elevated, and commands an excellent prospect. The ancient wooden bridge which formerly crossed the Arun, was replaced nearly eighty years since by the present structure of stone. Domesday informs us that in the time of the Confessor, Uluric held the manor, while, at the making of the Record, Robert held it of Earl Roger de Montgomeri. The land was 16 hides, and there were 35 villeins, 15 cottars, and 9 serfs. There were two churches, two mills, and two fisheries. *Temp.* Edward Conf. it was estimated at £16; afterwards at £22. With this important manor were connected those of "Nordborne," and "Nitinbreham," which extended into the Weald. John de Gatesden held two knights' fees in Pulberg of the Honour of Arundel. In 1290 Henry Hoese or Hussé, having married Joan, daughter of Alard le Fleming, of Newbridge in Pulborough, succeeded to part of the estate, while Walter de Lisle having married Florence, another co-heiress of Alard, obtained from the King free warren in their manor of Pulborough, with a fair to last three days at Newbridge. The Hussés and Lisles held the manor in joint tenure till 30th Henry VI., when Edmund atte Milne or Mille succeeded to one moiety. Nicholas Apsley, of the Thakeham family, succeeded through the heiress of Mille. In 1594 Anthony Oneley possessed one third part of the manor, which passed to the Shelleys, and the last John Apsley of Pulborough sold the other two-thirds to Henry Shelley, Esq., of Lewes, about 1732, and in that family it remained until the extinction of the Lewes Shelleys a few years since.

NORDBORNE or NUTBORNE, another manor and tything, lies partly in this parish and partly in West Chiltington. Two freemen held it of the Confessor, and after the Conquest Robert held it of Earl Roger, and Warin of him. It was an important manor, as it was rated at six hides, had two mills, 20 villeins, 4 cottars, and a wood of 12 swine. It was valued at £7. The family of La Zouche held it down to the year 1400. In 1545, Henry VIII. granted it to Henry, Earl of Arundel. Its 48 customary tenants now hold it under the Earl of Abergavenny. (Cartwright.) "Nitinbreham" was held before the Conquest by Lewin, "who might go whither he would." Afterwards Roger held it of the Earl, and Alward of him. There were 16 villeins, 3 cottars, and a wood for 10 swine.

Pulborough formerly contained several ancient seats, the principal of which Cartwright enumerates thus :—1, Mille Place, the seat of the Milles—site unknown; 2, Combe-lands, the abode of a family of that name, who preceded Mille; 3, Lodge Hill, in Pulborough Park, the residence of the Le Flemings,* and after-

* Edward II. permitted Alard le Fleming to rebuild his house in Pulborough Park, destroyed by fire, but not to embattle it.

wards the property of the Husseys and Lisles; 4, Old Place,
which belonged successively to the Apsleys, Moses, and Cole-
brookes—there are some picturesque remains of this mansion;
5, New Place, belonged successively to the Apsleys, Peacheys,
and Barttelots. The barn belonging to this house has Early
English windows, and is supposed to be of the time of
Edward I. Pulborough is an ancient site, and many traces of
Celtic and Roman possession have been brought to light. Mr.
P. J. Martin, in Vol. ix. of the "Sussex Collections," gives a
notice of a British settlement discovered by himself on Nutbourne Common, now enclosed, about the year 1819. On an
elevated part of the Common there were two depressed circular
barrows, measuring respectively 80 and 90 feet, which, on examination by Messrs. Martin and Cartwright, were not found to
contain any interments. There were circular depressions in the
centre, and the exterior rim of the circle exhibited the peculiarity of foundations of a wall of stone four feet thick. Several
relics of undoubted British manufacture were discovered; and
the conclusion arrived at by Mr. Martin is, that these barrows
were the dwelling-places of human beings—perhaps the pri-
meval hunters, who sought their game in what must then have
been a well-wooded country.

Many Roman remains have been discovered here. The Stane-
street, which ran from Regnum, (Chichester) to London, passes in
a straight line 3½ miles through this parish, and has never ceased,
since Roman times, to be the common highway. Its course
through Pulborough commences at what was the old ford of the
river Arun, and runs to Hadfoldsherne in the neighbouring
parish of Billingshurst. There were probably several military
stations on or near this *via*, and some indicia of considerable
interest have been discovered within the present century, but
before particularizing these, I should mention that there is, at
no great distance from the village on the west, a circular mound
of earth, mostly artificial. It is surrounded by a vallation, and
there are slight traces of a building. Other remains were found
here, but as they have not been preserved, nothing which could
indicate the date of this little fort or castellum is ascertained.
As it commands the ford of the river, and a wide view of the
surrounding country, it was probably a watch-tower. The late
eminent West Sussex geologist, Mr. P. J. Martin, F.G.S.,*
minutely examined the Stane-street in its passage through this
and other parishes, and the following notes are from his paper
in the "Sussex Collections." At Homestreet, a short distance
to the north of the east end of Pulborough street, are considerable indications of a remarkable township, or assemblage of

* See *ante.*

Roman buildings. The most notable of these is a circular mausoleum, situated on a slight elevation in a field called Huddlestone. The area is forty feet, and it is surrounded by a wall 11½ feet thick. Part of these walls has been grubbed up for the sake of the stones. When the plan of this mausoleum was laid bare it was declared that there were few equal to it out of Italy. At a short distance from this, at Broomer's Hill, four pigs of Roman lead were discovered just below the surface. They are stamped with the inscription ICLTRPVTBREXARG, which has been interpreted to mean *Tiberius Claudius, Tribunitiæ Potestatis Britanniæ Rex.* Some distance to the north is Borough farm, where very extensive buildings have been traced out, with considerable fragments of tesselated pavement and coloured stucco. Near at hand is a quarry, from which the stone of Pulborough church is said to have been taken, and from which there is little doubt the Romans drew materials for Bignor, and for the sarcophagi found at Avisford and elsewhere. In digging for foundations close to the village of Pulborough, fragments of Roman tile are turned up, as also Roman coins which have passed current both here and at Billingshurst as halfpence. All these discoveries tend to prove that, although not strictly a Roman station, Pulborough must have been rather thickly peopled with "the conquerors of the world."

The church (Our Lady of Assumption) is beautifully situated on a hill of sandstone, and has a picturesque appearance. It has an arcade with clerestory windows, forming two aisles, and these, as well as the tower, Cartwright believes to have been built *temp.* Henry IV. or Henry VI. There is a square embattled tower at the west end, of the same date. The chancel is of much earlier date, being the surviving portion of the original edifice. It contains three sedilia of equal height, and two slabs of Sussex marble despoiled of their brasses. The whole interior is particularly neat and appropriate. At the south-west of the church-yard there formerly stood a sepulchral chapel (Our Lady) belonging to the family of Mille. Towards the end of the last century it was taken down, when the slabs and brasses were placed in the chancel. A lych-gate has been erected at the entrance of the church-yard from the street, and has a pleasing appearance. The brasses removed from the chapel were figures of Edmund Mille, Gentilman, 1452, and Matilda his wife, and a plate for Richard Mille, their son and heir, 1478. There is a beautiful brass of an ecclesiastic in the habit of a canon of Chichester, surmounted by a canopy for Thos. Harlyng, rector of Ringwode and Polberg, 1423. There are other memorials for the families and names of Apsley, Coles, Legg, Spragg, Marriott,

Onely, Cobb, Tredcroft, &c. There are five bells, one of which is dedicated to St. Catherine.

At Newbridge there was a chapel which has long since been destroyed. It was dedicated to St. Helen.

[S. A. C. Four watermills, v, 271. Visit of Edward II., vi, 49. British settlement, ix, 109. Roman stone quarries, xi, 130, 143. xix, 130. Roman mausoleum, xi, 141. Roman road, xi, 139, Roman pigs of lead, remains of tesselated pavement, and remains at Nutbourne, xi, 143. Ancient fort, xi, 144. De L'Isle, xii, 35. Newbridge fair (1279) and Newbridge Wm. of, xii, 35. The Bridge there, xix, 158. Newbridge chapel, xii, 85. Newbridge House, and Alard le Fleming, xiii, 106. Church, xii, 96. Martin Peter J., xiv, 11. xvi, 52. Parish charity, xvi, 37. Apsley of, xvi, 50, 291. xix, 93. Church bells, xvi, 221. Old Place, xvi, 291. Nutbourne stream, rivers Arun and Rother and the Bridge, xvi, 257. Mille family, xvii, 110. Mille place, xvii, 111. Bookers of, xix, 94. Road to London, xix, 157. Mulseys in, xix, 158. Pulboro' common and Wickford Bridge, xix, 158.]

PYECOMBE.

A South-Down parish in the Hundred of Poynings; Rape of Lewes; distant six miles north from Brighton; Post-town, Hurst-Pierpoint; Railway station, Hassock's Gate, distant about 2½ miles. Union, Cuckfield. Population in 1811, 175; in 1861, 283. Benefice, a Rectory, valued at £345; Patron, the Lord Chancellor; Incumbent, Rev. John Morgan, M.A. Date of earliest Parish Register, 1561. Acreage, 2,249.

The village occupies one of the numerous valleys of the South Downs, whence the last syllable of the name. The parish is boldly undulated, and has in some places copses of underwood. It includes the conspicuous promontory called Wolstonbury, a Saxon designation signifying the " stronghold of Wulstan." From this elevation not only the Weald of Sussex, but the Surrey hills, and even a portion of Kent, can be clearly seen. Pyecombe is not mentioned in Domesday, but Pangdean is found under the orthography of Pinhedene. In 40th Edward III. this manor was held of the barony of Lewes by the service of keeping in repair the pales of Cuckfield park. It was included in the De Warenne grant to Edward II., yet Alice, sister of John, last Earl de Warenne, conveyed it in marriage to Edmund, Earl of Arundel, and his descendant, the Duke of Norfolk, is still lord paramount. In 1593 Sir Anthony Browne, Viscount Montague, died seised of it, and on the extinction of the male line of that family in the last century it lapsed to the Crown, and it is still held under a Crown lease.

Pyecombe, which from its chalky soil and good position should be a very healthy spot, has at different periods suffered severely from pestilence. It was visited by the plague in 1603, 1638, and 1678, and in the last great visitation of cholera several of the inhabitants died.

The church is a small ancient building of chancel, nave, and small low tile-capped tower at the west end. Its single bell is inscribed to St. Katherine. Hussey thinks the tower of Transition-Norman date, and the font is very curious and ancient, perhaps pre-Norman. The building has been much disguised by ill-applied " restorations." There are memorials for the names and families of Scrase (seventeenth century) and Barrett, Bysshe, and Beaumont (rectors). Sir Lewis Beaumont, Bart., was rector from 1702 to 1738. There are also two coffin-shaped slabs with crosses for earlier rectors. In the church-yard is a rudely constructed altar-tomb, with the date 1603. It is traditionally said to be to the memory of Mr. Hollingdale, tenant of Pangdean Farm. During the prevalence of the plague he betook himself to a cave, which he had excavated in the Way Down, a mile distant, but returning too soon to his home he took the infection, died, and was buried under this memorial.

[S. A. C. Parish registers and plague, iv, 276. Arrow-head found, viii, 268. Bysshe family, xiii, 252. Pangdean, xv, 20. Bell, xvi, 220.]

RACTON.

Domesday, *Rachitone;* a parish in the Hundred of Westbourne; Rape of Chichester; distant seven miles north-west from Chichester; Post-town, Emsworth. Union, Westbourne. Population in 1811, 102; in 1861, 95. Benefice, a Rectory, with the Chapelry of Lordington annexed, valued at £225; in the gift of the Dean and Chapter of Chichester; Incumbent, Rev. Frederick Henry Arnold, B.A. Date of earliest Parish Register, 1680. Acreage, 1,180.

This is a small parish of irregular outline, and borders on the west the county of Hants. The soil is that of the South Downs, chalk and marl. It is supposed to derive its name from Racon, a little " lavant," or intermittent stream, which flows through it. The village is unimportant. Fulco held the manor of the Confessor, and Ivo of Earl Roger. It was rated at five hides, and had eight villeins with 13 bondmen, and a wood of four hogs. Its Domesday value was £4. In 1284 Hugh Zanzaver was lord, and in the sixteenth century it came into the possession of the family of Gounter, or Gunter, from Gilleston, in Wales. It passed from that family in 1754, by an heiress, to William Legge, second Earl of Dartmouth.

LORDINGTON, the Hurditone of Domesday, is an ancient hamlet and chapelry in this parish. It is described as in the hundred of Guidenetroi, was rated at four hides, and had eight villeins, seven bordars, and a wood of three hogs. After the Conquest it was granted to Earl Roger de Montgomeri, and one of the two knights' fees passed in succession through the families of De Albini, Tatteshale, Romaine, De Lisle, and Bramshott. Towards the end of the fifteenth century, Lordington became the property of Sir Richard Pole, K.G., a cousin of Henry VII., who is supposed to have built Lordington House. The mansion was reconstructed on the old site in the seventeenth century, and retains some of the original features, particularly an ancient staircase. From the illustrious and historical house of Pole it passed in succession to the families of Lumley, Jermyn, Peckham, and Phipps.

The church contains a mural monument to a member of the Gunter family, who, with his wife and four sons and two daughters, are represented in a kneeling posture, St. John the Baptist standing in the centre. There is another monument to the Gunter family, with two kneeling figures, and a third has a bust of Sir Charles Gunter Nichol, K.B. Several slabs in the Gunter chapel are to the memory of members of the same family. There are two bells.

Racton was the residence of Colonel George Gunter, a faithful adherent to the cause of Charles II., who had the honour, after the battle of Worcester, of conducting the King across the country to Brighthelmston, whence the latter escaped safely to Fécamp, in Normandy.

[S. A. C. Gunters of, v. 48. xvi, 129, 265. xviii, 115. Lordington House (*Arnold*), v, 180. xvi, 265. Domesday mills, v, 271. Church, xii. 75. Bells, xvi, 221. Ems, or Emille river, xvi, 265. xviii, 185. Racon river, xviii, 185]

RINGMER.

A parish in the Hundred of its own name; Rape of Pevensey; distant three miles north-east from Lewes, its Post-town and Railway station. Union, Chailey. Population in 1811, 1,055; in 1861, 1,522. Benefice, a Vicarage, valued at £400; Patron, the Archbishop of Canterbury, it being one of his Peculiars; Incumbent, Rev. Edward Symonds, B.A., of Worcester College, Oxford. Date of earliest Parish Register, 1560. Acreage, 5,626. *Residences*, Middleham, Mrs. Constable; Delves House, the property of Sir Charles R. Blunt, Bart.; The Elms, Major Harwood; Park Gate, W. Alexander, Esq.; Wellingham, Miss Rickman.

The hundred to which this parish gives name is one of the

oldest on record in the county, being mentioned in very early documents of Saxon times. About the time of King John, when the College of South Malling was remodelled, the manor was divided into three beadlewicks, viz., Ranscombe, Framfield, and Ringmer, and these beadlewicks, in the time of Henry VIII., became distinct manors. In 3rd James I. the manor of Ringmer (Broyle Park excepted) was granted by the King to Edward, Earl of Worcester, and Sir Robert Johnson, by whom it was sold to Sir John Sidley and Sir George Rivers for £8,440. The same year it was sold for a similar sum to Thomas, Earl of Dorset, in whose heirs it still vests.

Broyle Park, deriving its name from the low Latin *bruillium,* a heathy plain, was long a park belonging to the Archbishops of Canterbury, who had a *mansio* or resting-place here when on their pastoral visits into Sussex. It was of great extent, probably of 2,000 acres, about 500 of which were in Framfield parish, and had a splendid herd of deer. *Temp.* Elizabeth it was taken possession of by the Crown. At a later date the Broyle was in the hands of the family of Springett, who dwelt at Broyle Place from the earlier part of the seventeenth century, and were afterwards baronets. Sir William Springett took an active part in the Civil Wars on the side of the Parliament, and was in command at Arundel in 1643, where he died. For a most interesting account of his death, written by his wife, see " Sussex Archæological Collections," vol. xx, p. 34. Broyle Place was a large rambling mansion of many gables, but it is now shorn down to the proportions of a farm house. The park has long been converted into arable land, and no traces of its timber and underwood remain. Near its ancient pale is a wayside inn, called the " Green Man," which was kept about a century since by a person who had been a *parker,* and the sign, which I remember, represented a stalwart man in his forester's suit of green. The Broyle is now a favourite spot for steeple chases, which are held annually. The surface of the parish of Ringmer is remarkably flat and unpicturesque, although the village itself is neat and interesting, surrounding an open space called Ringmer Green. Close adjoining is an old residence known as Delves House, which was, in the last century, a favourite resort of Gilbert White of Selborne, from whence he dated many of the letters of his charming book. The old pine grove, whither crossbills and others of the feathered nation did resort, still exists near the church yard. The soil of the parish, especially on the Broyle, is gault—excellent for the brickmaker—and it is worth notice that specimens of copper ore have been dug up here. This is " not geologically right," but it is true, as I can prove.*

* I am also prepared to prove that rich copper ore has been found in a *chalk* cutting close to Lewes. Impossible, says Geology : truth, say I.

The roads in this parish were formerly so intolerably bad that it is said that the Springetts of Broyle Place were formerly drawn to church in their carriage by a team of eight oxen. There were formerly artillery barracks in this parish. Ringmer Park, now disparked, was, in the fifteenth and sixteenth centuries, the seat of the family of Thatcher, who intermarried with the Challenors, Lewknors, Pelhams, Gages, &c, and were afterwards of Priest-hawes, in Westham.

The church (St. Mary) consists of chancel, nave, north and south aisles, with a modern wooden bell-turret over the west end. On each side of the chancel there is a manorial chapel, the appropriaton of which I cannot discover—probably the Broyle, and Ringmer park. Each contains a piscina. The prevailing style is Perpendicular. This church is very rich in mortuary memorials for the names and families of Springett, Whalley, Campion, Wynne, Tyro (a painfull preacher), Sadler, Snooke (second daughter of Rev. Gilbert White, of Selborne), whose husband Henry, "post vitam difficilem hic quiescit," Shadwell, Plumer, Jefferay, Crunden, Howell, and Elliott. The most interesting monuments are those of Mr. Jefferay and Sir William Springett, both of the 17th century. Altogether this is a very interesting parish.

[S. A. C. Parish register extracts, iv, 286. Springett of Broyle, v, 67. xiv, 161. xviii, 175. xix, 160. xx, 34 (*Lower*). Ancient ring, ix, 373. Barcary lands, xiii, 46. Jefferay family, xiv, 222. Thatcher family, xv, 162. xviii, 23, 38. Broyle park, xv, 162. River Ritch, xv, 163. Church bells, xvi, 221. Jack Cade, xviii, 25. Going to church with oxen, xix, 160. Fitzherbert family, xix, 175. Whalley family, xx, 45. Civil marriages at Glynde, xix, 202. Charities of, xx, 84. New family, xx, 88.]

RIPE or RYPE, *alias* ECKINGTON.

(A portion of the parish was known, within a few years, as "Eckington Corner.")

Domesday, *Rype;* a parish in the Hundred of Shiplake; Rape of Pevensey; distant three miles from Berwick station, and seven east of Lewes; Post-town, Hawkhurst. Union, West Firle. Population, in 1811, 331; in 1861, 361. Benefice, a Rectory, valued at £431; Patron, Exeter College, Oxford; Incumbent, Rev. R. Shuttleworth Sutton, M.A., formerly of that College. Date of earliest Parish Register, 1520 and 1538. Acreage, 1,120. *Chief Landowners*, Sir James Duke, Bart., and W. D. Weeden, Esq., of Hall Court.

This is a flat alluvial parish near a branch of the Ouse and probably received its name from its being on the *ripa* or bank of a river, once much more important than now, when the Ouse was a great estuary. There is a strong mineral spring in the parish called the Red ditch. There is a tradition of a village near the south-west boundary. In the Domesday survey Rype is mentioned as being in Edluestone hundred, which partly coincided with the modern hundred of Shiplake. Before that time it was one of the very numerous manors held by Harold, and was assessed at 23 hides, 8 of which were detached, and lay in the rape of Hastings. There were 10 plough-lands, 16 villeins, and 8 bondmen, with 8 salt-pans. *Temp. Confessoris* it was worth £12, afterwards only £8. After many changes of possession the manor came into the possession of Reginald West, Lord de la Warr, of whom a memorial still exists in the window of a small house in the parish, in the shape of the " chape " of a sword—a badge won at Poictiers, for the capture, under the Black Prince, of King John of France. *Temp.* Philip and Mary, the Earl of Rutland sold the manor to Sir John Gage.

The rectory anciently belonged to Lewes Priory. The church (St. John the Baptist) is a remarkably good and symmetrical building of no great size, and principally in the Decorated style. It consists of nave and chancel, with a square western tower, over the west door of which is the badge of the Pelham Buckle, so familiar in this district. The windows—the eastern one is particularly handsome—were formerly filled with painted glass; and emblems of the Evangelists, or portions of them, still exist. There are inscriptions to the names of Williamson, Acton, and Plumer. The family of Acton were resident here for at least three centuries; and at Hall Court the family of Lulham were very ancient. In close proximity to the modern residence are traces of the ancient abode of the Lulham family. At Mark-Cross in this parish, in the direction of Laughton, formerly stood a wayside cross dedicated to St. Mark, and in the latter parish, at a spot not far distant, was another called Stone Cross.

Opposed to the theory of geologists that copper ore should not appear in any stratum of this county, that metal has been found in the *gault* formation on Mr. Weeden's land, as also in the neighbouring parish of Ringmer, and I have even found it in the chalk formation close to Lewes.

[S. A. C. Ancient name, xiv, 211. xv, 163. Eckington manor, xiv, 211. Salt-pans, xiv, 211. xv, 163. Lulham family, xiv, 213. xviii, 25, 39. Jefferay and Martin families, xiv, 219, 232. Our Lady of Pity, xiv, 219. xv, 65. The river Ritch, xv, 163. Church bells, xvi, 223. Jack Cade's adherents, xviii, 25, 39. Hall Court, xviii, 39. Bronze relic, xviii, 69. Civil marriages at Glynde, xix, 202. Benefice belonged to Lewes Priory, xx, 141.]

ROBERTSBRIDGE.

A hamlet and small town in Salehurst, containing a large proportion of the population of that parish. It formerly possessed a chapel, dedicated to St. Catharine, and a holy well under the same invocation. In the old "coaching" times, this town was well known to travellers. At present it contains little of interest, except the ruins of its ancient Abbey, which lie somewhat to the east.

From the fact that Robertsbridge stands on the river Rother, here crossed by several bridges, it has been erroneously conjectured that the original name of the place was Rotherbridge. But the real etymology is *Pons Roberti*, "the bridge of Robert" (de St. Martin), the founder of the Abbey.

The history of this establishment has been well investigated by the Rev. George Miles Cooper, M.A., assisted by the previous researches of the Rev. E. Venables, M.A., and by a remarkable discovery at Penshurst Castle (the seat of Lord de Lisle,) of nearly 200 documents relating to the monastery, by the Rev. G. R. Bossier. ("Sussex Archæological Collections," Vol. viii.) The manner in which his lordship acquired them will be found in the sequel. The Abbey was of the Cistercian order, and dedicated to St. Mary. There is little doubt that Robert de St. Martin was the founder in 1176, though that honour has been claimed for his descendant, Alured de St. Martin, who, with the benefactions of Alicia his wife, seems to have so enlarged the establishment as to have become the reputed founder. Certain it is that the earliest seal of the house hitherto discovered has the legend, "de *Ponte Roberti;*" and it is worth noting that the counter-seal contains a representation of the Abbey-church, with a *bridge* of three arches close by.

The original endowment consisted of all the lands, tenements, tenants, and services, which the founder held of Geoffry de St. Martin and his heirs in the Rape of Hastings. Subsequent benefactors gave, or the monks themselves purchased, other manors and lands in the adjacent parishes of Pett, Guestling, Icklesham, Playden, and Iden. One of the earliest benefactors was Alicia, Countess of Eu, daughter of Adeliza, Queen of Henry I. Other members of this noble family conferred lands in Snargate, Worth, and Coombden, adjoining the Forest of Brightling, Sedlescombe, and Ewhurst, together with a prebend in the church of St. Mary of Hastings. Other lands were subsequently acquired in Fairlight, Promhill, Catsfield, Dallington, Burwash, Ivychurch, Echingham, Sutton (now in Seaford), Hellingly, Chiddingly, Waldron, Beckley, Mountfield, Bexhill, and many other places. Among the benefactors, besides the De St. Martins and the Earls of Eu, were the families of St. Leger, De Socknerse (in Brightling—a branch of the St. Legers), Lunsford, De Possingworth, De Herst, De Scotney, Alard, and De Abrincis. The multitudinous deeds, &c., above referred to, contain records of many law-suits in which the convent was concerned during several centuries. The rights of the monks as to lands were much infringed by neighbours with whose interests those of the former clashed. Even (as Mr. Cooper thinks) their very books were not safe, as there is in the Bodleian Library a MS. bearing this inscription:—" This book belongs to St. Mary of Robertsbridge: whosoever shall steal it, or sell it, or in any way alienate it from this house, let him be anathema maranatha." John, Bishop of Exeter, into whose hands the book fell, asserts that he acquired it in a lawful way, and states that he does not know "where the aforesaid house is !" For further interesting particulars respecting the Abbey I must refer to Mr. Cooper's elaborate paper; but one or two facts deserve special mention. Kings Edward I. and II. paid hasty visits to this monastery in their journeys in the South.

In 1192, when it was understood that Richard Cœur de Lion had been imprisoned on his return from Palestine, the Abbots of Robertsbridge and Boxley were sent as lords-justices to ascertain the place of his detention. They travelled over great part of Germany, and at last found him at large at Oxfer, in Bavaria.

This foundation suffered the common fate of religious houses in 30th Henry VIII., when its revenues amounted to more than £270—a large sum at the period, and probably representing about £2,600 at the present value of money. Two years later the site was granted to Sir William Sydney.* His successor, Sir Henry Sydney, Knight of the Garter, and Lord-Deputy of Ireland, was father of Sir Philip Sydney, the illustrious soldier and scholar, author of the "Arcadia," and of Mary, who married Henry, Earl of Pembroke, the eminent lady immortalized in the noble epitaph of Ben. Jonson, which cannot be too often quoted :—

> "Underneath this marble hearse,
> Lies the subject of all verse ;
> Sydney's sister, Pembroke's mother ;
> Death ! 'ere thou hast slain another
> Learned and fair, and good as she,
> Time shall throw a dart at thee."

I have in my possession a MS. entitled "Rental of Lands, appointed for the jointure of Mary, Countess of Pembroke, wife of Henry, Earl of Pembroke, and daughter of the Right Honourable Sir Henry Sydney, Knight of the Garter," &c. These

---

* Tanner (*Notitia*) says that at the Dissolution the convent consisted of twelve monks ; other authorities say that there were but nine, including the Abbot.

lands are mostly in the west of England, and in Wales; but as the MS. is bound up as the prefix of a much larger rental relating to Robertsbridge and other places in Sussex, Kent, and Hampshire, I conceive that a portion, at least, of the possessions of our abbey, became the property of the learned and beautiful lady aforesaid. They were possessed by the Sydneys, Earls of Leicester, until 1720, and in 1725 the property passed by purchase to Sir Thomas Webster, of Battle Abbey, at the cost of £28,000. At a later period it belonged to the family of Allfrey; but of the exact descent I have no particulars.

Of the few remains of this ancient Abbey, as now existing, the principal architectural features are the crumbling walls of the church in the farm-yard, and a kind of cottage farm-house, beneath which is a crypt in good preservation, and a portion of the refectory. In the church some members of the ancient families of De Bodiam, Dalyngruge, Pelham, and others had sepulture under stately tombs; but these, alas! have disappeared. The utilitarian age which succeeded the Reformation consigned them to viler uses, and the few relics which survive to our age are but the meagre *débris* of good medieval art. The mutilated effigy of the once potent founder of Bodiam Castle, Sir Edward Dalyngruge, dug up in 1823, is now in the Museum at Lewes Castle. When, about the year 1830, I first visited this venerable site, I found, and preserved sketches of, several mutilated carved stones, with crosses, &c., together with an inscription to William Bodiam, of very early date, probably of the 13th century; the arms and "buckle" of the family of Pelham, and several other heraldric remains. On my next visit, a few years later, I found that most of these had been broken up for the mending of neighbouring roads!

The Robertsbridge estate during the proprietorship of the Sydneys possessed several iron and steel works; and furnace ponds and forge ponds are mentioned in the MS. above referred to.

[S. A. C. Iron works, iii, 241, 246. xviii, 15. Visit of Edward I., ii, 141. Ditto of Edward II., vi, 44. The Abbey, viii, 141. xvii, 55. xviii, 71. xix, 13. The Abbot in Germany in search of Cœur de Lion ; Hay family, xiv, 100. xv, 84. xx, 65. River Rother, xv, 152. Jack Cade's adherents, xviii, 25. Glaziers' iron works, xviii, 16. Dalyngruge effigy, xii, 223. xviii, 71. London road to Rye, xix, 166.]

RODMELL.

Domesday, *Ramelle;* a parish on the Ouse, in the Hundred of Holmstrow ; Rape of Lewes ; distant 3½ miles south from Lewes, which is its Post-town and Railway station. Union, Newhaven. Population in 1811, 291; in 1861, 292. Benefice, a Rectory, valued at £375; Patron, the Bishop of Chichester; Incumbent, Rev. Peter de Putron, M.A., of Pembroke College, Oxford. Date of earliest Parish Register, 1704. Acreage, 1,924. *Chief Landowner*, the Earl of Abergavenny, who possesses nearly the entire parish.

The first syllable was formerly spelt *Rád*, and doubtless had reference to the military road, "Ermin-street," which passed through it. Domesday informs us that Harold held the manor, and that after the Conquest William de Warenne had it in domain, and was assessed for 64 hides. There were a church, 11 salt-pans (probably on the estuary of the Ouse), and a wood of 23 hogs. Forty-four houses in Lewes belonged to the manor, which extended much beyond the boundaries of the modern parish. It was granted by John de Warenne to Edward II., and subsequently belonged to a family who called themselves from it, De Radmeld. Sir Ralph Radmeld married, early in the fifteenth century, Margaret, co-heiress of her brother Hugh, second Lord Camoys, of Broadwater. His grandson, Sir William Radmyld, died without issue, when the property reverted to his two aunts, Elizabeth and Margaret. The latter married John Goring, Esq., of Burton, who died in 1495. After nine generations this, the elder line of Goring, terminated in Anne Goring, who married Richard Biddulph, Esq., of Biddulph Castle, co. Stafford, whose elder line became extinct by the death of John Biddulph, Esq., of Burton, in 1835. On his decease Thomas Stonor, Esq., of Stonor, co. Oxon, claimed as the heir of his great grandmother, Mary Biddulph, the barony of Camoys, which he obtained in 1839, after it had been in abeyance 413 years. In 27th Henry VIII. George, Lord Abergavenny, died possessed of Rodmell, which still belongs to his descendant, the Earl of Abergavenny. Northease, another manor, also belonged to the De Warennes, and has, probably in the same line, passed like Rodmell to the Earl of Abergavenny. It had a chapel of chancel and nave, 55 feet in length, some of the masonry of which, with mural paintings and carved oak, remained in the early part of the last century. The ancient lords of Rodmell had a park, of which the name now only exists. Hall Place, or Rodmell Place, was bought, in 1586, of Edward Deeds by John de la Chambre, Esq., of the Litlington family, whose descendants were in possession in 1690. The house, which had traces of considerable magnificence, was probably built by John de la Chambre, whose arms were to be seen before its demolition, some 30 years since, over the entrance of the porch. It afterwards passed to the families of Montague and Toghill, and of the latter it was purchased by the Saxbys, who resold it to the Earl of Abergavenny.

On a beautiful slope of the Downs, southward of the village, are evident traces of a pre-historic hamlet or village of some kind, with several small barrows.

The church (St. Peter) is a small building, of chancel, nave, with south aisle, west tower, and quadrangular shingled spire. On the south side of the high chancel is another, which was formerly attached to the manor of Rodmell. The building has Transition-Norman features, especially in its "diamond fretté" chancel arch, and in a curious hagioscope. Additions have been made in the Early English and Perpendicular styles, and the whole building has been restored by the present Rector. There are memorials for individuals of the families of Scottowe, Grundy, Griffiths, Gabbitas (rectors), Alchorne, Montague, &c. There is also a brass plate for a benefactress to the church, Agatha Broke, wife of John Broke, and daughter of John de Rademelde, date 1433. The other side of the plate has an inscription for John de la Chambre, Esq., 1673. For a notice of Henry Godman, ejected from the rectory of this church, *temp.* Charles II., see "Worthies of Sussex," p. 328.

[S. A. C. John Newman, clerk, a delinquent, v, 39. De la Chambre family, xiii, 258. Roswell, xiv, 254. Manor rents, xiv, 263. Bells, xvi, 221. Jack Cade's insurrection, xviii, 176. Burials in woollen, xviii, 190-193. Brookside, xviii, 191. Shingles on church roof, xix, 42. Gorings had lands here, xix, 100. London road to Newhaven, xix, 164, Northease, xix, 164. Grovers of Northease, xx, 90.]

ROGATE.

A long, straggling parish, in the Hundred of Dumpford; Rape of Chichester; distant four miles east from Petersfield, its Post-town and Railway station. Union, Midhurst. Population in 1811, 595; in 1861, 990. Benefice, a Vicarage, valued at £212; Patron, the Lord Chancellor; Incumbent, Rev. John Simeon Barrow, M.A. Date of earliest Parish Register, 1558. Acreage, 4,873. *Seats*, Rogate Lodge, Mrs. Wyndham; Fairoak, Hon. J. Jervis Carnegie; and Fyning House, J. W. Whitelock, Esq.

This parish, which joins Hampshire on the west, lies on the Western Rother, which is crossed by Habenbridge, a structure of five arches. It is full of varied and picturesque scenery of almost every kind, particularly the spot called Harting Combe, the western termination of the Weald, behind which the chalk hills of Surrey meet the western range of the South Downs, and form a kind of amphitheatre of wonderful beauty. Rogate, at the time of the Domesday survey, was part of the great lordship of Harting, and it is probable that a fourth hamlet or parish formerly existed here, called *North* Harting, in contradistinction to South, East, and West Harting. This idea is supported by the tradition that a church formerly stood here. *Temp.* Edward II. the manor belonged to the great family of Camoys, from whom it descended to the Radmylds, and to the Lewknors. Henry VIII. granted it to William, Earl of Southampton. After many changes it came, in the earlier part of the present century, to Lewis Buckle, Esq., of the Westmorland family. Fyning was possessed in the 16th century by Peter Bettesworth, and remained with his descendants for six generations, who also held Milland in Trotton, and Chithurst. On an eminence above the Rother are some vestiges of a fortified residence within a fosse, but of its origin nothing seems to be known. At Rake, in this parish, built into the front of a small house, is a large armorial stone, with the shield and supporters of the Lords Grey of Werke, which was brought from Up-park.

The church (St. Bartholomew) is small and ancient, with traces of Norman work. John Bonville of Halnaker, 9th Henry VII., gave to the Brotherhood of St. Katherine and St. Blaise in this church, 13s. 4d., to buy two kine to secure the prayers of the guild for ever.

In this parish is DUREFORD ABBEY, an account of which is given in another article.

[S. A. C. Church, xii, 76. Ancient Brotherhood, xv, 61. Bells, xvi, 221. River Rother, xvi, 259. Rogate, xviii, 94. Fyning House, xix, 169. Road from Midhurst to Winchester, xix, 169.]

ROTHERFIELD.

Vulgo, *Rudderful;* a parish in the Hundred of its own name ; Rape of Pevensey ; distant seven miles south from Tunbridge Wells, its Post-town. There is a Railway station in the parish, at Jarvis Brook. Union, Uckfield. Population in 1811, 2,122 ; in 1861, 3,413. Benefice, a Rectory, valued at £1,354 ; Patron, the Earl of Abergavenny; Incumbent, Rev. Alfred Child, M.A., of Exeter College, Oxford. Date of earliest Parish Register, 1539. Acreage, 14,733. *Chief Landowners*, Earl of Abergavenny, R. B. Fry, Esq., J. Scott, Esq., and the Goldsmiths' Company of London.

This very extensive and important parish, historically and picturesquely interesting, respectively to the archæologist and the artist, occupies an elevated district, Crowborough, within its limits, being one of the loftiest spots in the county, and possessing some historical associations. (See CROWBOROUGH.) In Saxon times it was known as Ritheramfeld and Redrefeld, from the circumstance that the river Rother rises here. Rotherfield is, perhaps, the principal *watershed* in this part of England, for,

from a commanding spot, it sends its waters to three rivers, the
Rother, debouching at Rye; the Ouse, which has its outlet at
Newhaven; and the Medway, which, joining the Thames, flows
into the German Ocean. The first-named river rises in the cellar
of the residence called Rother-House. When the Ouse joined
the English Channel at Seaford, before the formation of the
" New-Haven " at the village previously known as Meeching,
that river bore the *alias* of *Saforda*, and Rotherfield, although
contributing only a small stream to it, is described as " upon the
river Saforda " *(Super fluvium Saforda)* in very early documents.
Riderfeld was at an early period the possession of a Saxon Dux,
or chieftain, called Bertoaldus, who falling sick, and being in-
curable by neighbouring physicians, went to the great monastery
of St. Denis and St. Elutherius, near Paris, whose bones were
working mighty marvels for diseased persons. Here being fully
restored to health, he procured a few of their holy relics, brought
them to Rotherfield and dedicated a church to St. Denis, in 792,
which dedication still remains, and the older inhabitants of
Rotherfield remember the legend of their patron:—

> " Saint Denis had his head cut off ;
> He did not care for that ;
> He took it up and carried it
> Two miles without a hat !"

Among the "folk-lore" of the district is the notion that the
women of this parish, being often taller than those of the neighbourhood, possess an additional pair of ribs! Such witticisms
abound in this part of Sussex, but to return to sober history,
the vill of Ritherhamfeld was bequeathed by King Alfred to
his kinsman Osforth. The next mention we have of it is in
Domesday, where we learn that Earl Godwin was lord, and that
it was taxed for only three hides, the remainder having probably
been (as it long afterwards was) in the condition of unprofitable
forest land. There were, however, 26 ploughlands, and in demesne four more, with 14 villeins, with 6 borderers owning
14 ploughs. There were a park (See FRANT), and a wood of 40
hogs. In the time of Edward the Confessor it was worth £16,
but afterwise realized £30. From 18th Edward I. to 8th Edward
II. the manor was held by the noble family of De Clare. Afterwards it was in the possession of the Le Despencers, from whom
it passed to the Beauchamps, Earls of Warwick, and so to the
Nevilles, with whom it has remained, in the same line as Eridge,
the Earl of Abergavenny being the present lord. Rotherfield
rectory is another manor, and is sometimes called Dowlands.*

---

* William Dowland, several centuries since, is said to have endowed the church
with this manor, the demesne of which was 366 acres. The glebe is now estimated
at 110 acres, but the rector is charged with £100 per annum for the newly-formed
district of Eridge-Green.

Alchorne, a third manor, gave name to a family, formerly of considerable importance in Sussex. They resided at Rotherfield *temp*. King John, and their descendants, now chiefly in humble life, are still numerous in the county, under the name of All*corn* and All*chin!* The heraldic visitation of 1634 mentions the existence of the ancient coat of the Alchornes in the church. A gentle family named Luck were connected with the parish during the 16th and two following centuries. The family of Fermor, originally from Picardy, in the reign of Edward III., were among the principal inhabitants, and dwelt at Welches or Walshes for more than two hundred years. The manor derived its name from the family of Walsh, who were afterwards of Horeham in Waldron. The original house was on a different site from the present, and a moated enclosure remains. The present house was built by Alexander Fermor, and Elizabeth Fowle, his wife, in the 16th century. Over the hall door, when J last visited it, were their initials, Ax. F. and E. F., with the date 1551. The names of Luck and Fowle are still existing in East Sussex, but in a lower social position. For the Fermors, Baronets, see art. CROWBOROUGH. Walshes was some time in the family of Moon, and Mr. Robert Burgess Fry was lately proprietor. Mr. Fry had a minor manor within the precincts of Ashdown Forest, or Lancaster Great Park, which he held of the Duchy of Lancaster by fealty, and the payment of two roses, emblematical, perhaps, of the Lancastrian badge. A few years since, and perhaps still, the representative of the Duchy made a periodical visit to the old farm or manor-house, and snipped off two roses from a tree in front of the building, which he put into a button-hole of his coat, and walked away.

The history of Rotherfield church is interesting: it dates, as we have seen, from A. D. 792. When the Dux Bertoald founded it, he made a charter (see Monasticon) describing it as "the church which I have constructed on my estate in the vill called Ridrefelda, which I have inherited from my ancestors;" and he adds that, if any one shall attempt to seize, diminish, or usurp, anything from the monks (of St. Denis) he will have to answer to Almighty God, the King of Ages, when He shall come in His majesty and that of His holy angels, and when the wicked will go into everlasting punishment, &c. From the Monasticon (vi, 1053) it appears that the French monks founded a small convent as a cell to their house in connection with this church, or rather with Frant, which was then dependent on the mother church of Rotherfield. (Hussey's "Churches," 276.) This establishment, however, appears to have been of no importance, and, apparently, it did not survive the Norman Conquest; for either *temp*. William I. or II., Earl Gilbert de Clare gave this church to Rochester cathedral. The present building, occupying a commanding height, is a beautiful object in the scenery of the district. It has, what is very unusual in Sussex, an embattled tower surmounted by a shingled spire, which is light and of elegant proportions. It is of rather large size, with Early English and later features, and contains five bells, the tenor of which is supposed to weigh 36 cwt.; two of the others have inscriptions in Old English characters. There are memorials to the names of Fowle, Threele, Vintner, Luxford, Wickham, Fermor, &c. The chancel contains sedilia and a piscina, and on the north side of it is a chapel which formerly belonged to the noble family of Neville, with their arms and cognizances. The walls were anciently painted, and a representation of the martyrdom of St. Lawrence is now visible. There are interesting churchwardens' accounts dating from the reign of Henry VIII.

[S. A. C. Iron-works at, ii, 215. Domesday watermill, v, 271. Fowle family, ii, 54. xi, 12. xiv, 228. xvi, 30. Cheese, xiii, 229, note. King Alfred's will, xiii, 241. Early incumbents, xiii, 306. Source of the river Rother, and of a branch of the Ouse, xv, 151. xvi, 272. xv, 161. Moon of Walshes, xvi, 48. Church bells, xvi, 141, 221, 206. Four of the Cat family steal the Archbishop's deer, xvii, 120. Shingles on church, xix, 42.]

ROTTINGDEAN.

Domesday, *Rotingedene;* a parish in the Hundred of Younsmere; Rape of Lewes; distant four miles east from Brighton, its Post-town. The Railway stations of Brighton and Falmer are each distant about four miles. Union, Newhaven. Population in 1811, 559; in 1861, 1,016; Benefice, a Vicarage, valued at £332; Patron, the Earl of Abergavenny; Incumbent, Rev. Arthur Thomas, M.A., of Trinity College, Cambridge. Date of earliest Parish Register, 1558. Acreage, 3,630. *Seats,* Wottondean, Mrs. Strangways. The late Charles Beard, Esq., owner of much land in the district, also resided here.

The parish lies entirely upon the South Downs, and has a cliff frontage on the English Channel. It takes its final syllable from one of the numerous *denes* or valleys, which afford so graceful a variety to the Downs. The village is in the dene, and contains several agreeable residences. Many sea-side visitors frequent it in summer. The sea encroaches considerably, and within the memory of man it has been necessary to form three roads in the direction of Brighton, each previous one having given way to these incursions of the ocean. An indent or "gap," in the cliff which terminates the dene, once afforded the French facilities for landing here. This was in 1377, and Capgrave, the old chronicler, gives the following account of the event:—"In the same yere they londed in Southsex fast by a town cleped Rotyngdene, and ageyn him went the Prior of Lewes (John de Cherlieu), and there he was taken, and with him two knytes, Sir Jon Fallisle (Fawseley of Hamsey), and Sir Thomas Cheyne, and a sqwyere, Jon Brocas (of Sherrington)." This little battle, which Lord Berners calls "a sore scrimysshe," took place on the Downs in the direction of Lewes, that town being the object which the invaders had in view. A hundred Englishmen lost their lives, but the vigorous efforts of the Lewes army repulsed the Frenchmen, who gained no other booty than the Prior, the two knights, and the squire, from whom however they probably extorted heavy ransoms.

At the epoch of Domesday, Rottingdean was held by one Hugh of William de Warenne; it had previously been in the possession of Earl Godwin. The manor was included in the great grant of the Earl of Warenne to Edward II. Since 1738 it has belonged to the Earls of Abergavenny. Balsdean, another manor, was part of the estates of Lewes Priory. In 1st of Elizabeth Thomas Gratwicke was lord, and it was subsequently in the hands of the Shirleys and Burrells: it now belongs to the Beard family. This family is one of the oldest in the South Down district, and the name has been associated with Rottingdean for some centuries. The old manorial chapel of Balsdean has long been desecrated, and is now used as a stable. It has slight Norman and Decorated features. Pebbles of chalcedony and agate from the sea shore of this parish are turned to account by the lapidary.

The church (St. Margaret), though Early English, seems to stand on Norman foundations. At present the building consists of nave, chancel, and central tower with pyramidal cap, and a south aisle, lately rebuilt; the church was restored in 1855. There are memorials for the names of Beard, Pelling, Savage, &c. A mural monument commemorates the Rev. Thomas Redman Hooker, D.D., who was vicar here for many years, and prepared for the Universities many young men, who became in the lapse of time eminent for their learning and abilities. Among them may be named the late Duke of Wellington and Archbishop Manning.

[S. A. C. Enamelled copper found at, v, 105. Church, ix, 67. Pendrell of, x, 189. French invasion, xii, 42. xiii, 233. Beard family, xiii, 126. xvi, 79. Tumulus at, xv, 243. Bell, xvi, 222. Goring of, xix, 100. Newhaven to Shoreham, xix, 164.]

RUDGEWICK ; sometimes written RUDGWICK.

Vulgo, *Ridgick;* a parish in the Hundred of West Easwrith ; Rape of
Arundel ; distant seven miles north-west from Horsham, its Post-
town; it has a Railway station on the Horsham and Guildford
branch. Union, Petworth. Population in 1811, 837; in 1861, 1,068.
Benefice, a Vicarage, valued at £260; Patron, the Bishop of Chi-
chester; Incumbent, Rev. B. J. Drury, B.A., of Lincoln College,
Oxford. Date of earliest Parish Register, 1539. Acreage, 5,830.
Chief Landowners, the Duke of Norfolk, John King, Esq., Captain
Bunny, and John Napper, Esq.

The name of this considerable parish, as Dallaway observes,
is taken from the elevated position of its village, the Anglo-
Saxon *Rig-wic.* The subsoil is sandstone, and in some parts
there are beds of Horsham stone. The parish includes a considerable amount of woodland. The village stands upon a
pleasant eminence with an extensive prospect. Several houses
near the churchyard are within the manor of Polingfold, in
Ewhurst, Surrey. (Dallaway.) The manor of Dedisham, in
Slinfold, extends over a large part of the parish. Belonging to
this manorial estate there was anciently a large iron foundry
(with a hammer-pond), which according to tradition was destroyed after the taking of Arundel Castle by Sir William Waller,
who dispatched a party of soldiers for that purpose, when the
iron-master and several others were killed. (Dallaway.) A
similar destruction of iron-works by Waller's troops is said to
have taken place in St. Leonard's Forest. The manor of Hope,
which included the estates of Ockenden and Howick, was
granted by Henry VIII. to the family of Caryll, and passed
through the families of Shelley and Goring to the present owner.
King Henry III., in the 44th year of his reign, granted a charter
to Alard le Fleming to hold a fair in Rudgewick on the eve,
feast, and morrow of the Holy Trinity, to whom the church is
dedicated. The principal estate in Rudgewick was for many
generations possessed by the old Sussex family of Naldrett, and
is called Naldrett Place. The estate ultimately descended, in
the last century, after several lawsuits, to the family of Piggott.
The church was in ancient times endowed with 63 acres of
arable and woodland, and the impropriator has an ecclesiastical
manor. In the fifteenth century Edmund Mille, Esq., founded
a chantry of St. Christopher, called for some reason the *Salmon
Chantry,* in Arundel Church, the revenues of which were principally derived from this impropriation. The following is the
description given of the church of Rudgewick in 1832 :—" The
church is situated upon the ridge, and is of a better construction
than most others in this division of the county. It consists of

a nave, divided from a north aisle by a pointed arcade, with labelled windows, in which remains of richly stained glass are still seen. The tower at the west end is large, and likewise the chancel, which has demonstrations of an earlier era. In it are three stone stalls, or sedilia, with plain, round arches and an embattled top; and likewise a table tomb, at this time illegible." (Rape of Arundel, p. 388.) The building is dedicated to the Holy · Trinity, and there are six modern bells.

[S. A. C. Church of, xii, 98. Naldrett, xvi, 50. River Arun, xvi, 256. Honey-lane and Rowhook, xix, 158.]

ROUGHEY. (See Horsham, of which it is a small hamlet.)

RUMBOLDSWYKE.

Domesday, *Wiche;* vulgo, *Week;* a small parish in the Hundred of Box and Stockbridge; Rape of Chichester; distant one mile from Chichester, its Post-town and Railway station. Union, West Hampnett. Population in 1811, 269; in 1861, 582. Benefice, a Vicarage, valued at £246; Patrons, Dean and Chapter of Chichester; Incumbent, Rev. Stenning Johnson, B.A., of Merton College, Oxford. Date of earliest Parish Register, 1669. Acreage, 645.

This parish, rather populous for its area, includes the " Hornet," a suburb of Chichester. It was part of the earldom of Roger de Montgomeri, and passed to the De Albini family, and from them to the Fitz-Alans. In much later times John, Lord Lumley, possessed it, and it passed, as Stanstead, to Lewis Way, Esq. Another manor was held by the Knights-Hospitallers. Henry VIII. granted this to Sir Thomas White. In 23rd Elizabeth, Francis Bowyer held it of the Crown, and since that date it has belonged successively to Cawley, Farrington, Barwell, Dally, and Padwick.

The church is said to be dedicated to St. Rumbold, and there are two Rumwolds in the Roman calendar; but I think this ascription rests only upon a presumption founded on the name of the parish. Rumbold is much likelier to have been the Saxon proprietor than the patron saint. The building is small, consisting of chancel and nave, with bell-turret at the west end. This church is one of the Dean's Peculiars. In 1866 the building was enlarged by the addition of an aisle; and during the repairs traces of Roman tiles, probably from Regnum (Chichester), and herringbone work, were disclosed. The original church was in all probability pre-Norman.

[S. A. C. Bell, xvi, 222. Roman urns found at, xvii, 255. Knights Hospitallers' lands, xx, 27.]

RUSHLAKE-GREEN.

A hamlet of Warbleton.

RUSPER.

A parish in the Hundred of Singlecross; Rape of Bramber; distant five miles north-east from Horsham, its Post-town. Railway station, Faygate, distant about three miles. Union, Horsham. Population in 1811, 450; in 1861, 590. Benefice, a Rectory, valued at £202; Patroness, Mrs. Greene; Incumbent, Rev. Henry James Gore, M A., of Merton College, Oxford. Date of earliest Parish Register, 1560. Acreage, 3,126. *Chief Landowners*, Robert Henry Hurst, Esq., M.P., and Messrs. Broadwood. *Seat*, Nunnery, G. Gossett Hill, Esq.

This is a well-wooded parish on the Forest Ridge, the village street forming the watershed of tributaries of the Mole and the Arun. The farms are small, and some of the yeomanry are of considerable antiquity. According to tradition the family of Mutton have possessed the lands called Normans from the Conquest. A gentry family named Gardiner resided here in the 16th and 17th centuries. Lands bearing their name now belong to what is called Dog Smith's charity.

. A NUNNERY dedicated to St. Mary Magdalene existed in this parish. It was founded in or before the 12th century, as Mr. Way supposes, by one of the De Braose family, among whose vast possessions Rusper was included. It was of the Benedictine rule, and the constituents were called Moniales Nigrae. Seffrid II., Bishop of Chichester (1180-1204), confirmed to the sisterhood the churches of Rusper, Warnham, Ifield, and Selham. About 1231, John de Braose augmented the possessions by the gift of the church of Horsham. No other endowments appear to have been made, and the establishment fell into poverty and decay. In 1484 it is described as in a state of ruin, though this was not literally the case, as the revenues amounted at the Dissolution in 1535 to £39 14s. 6d. What remained of the conventual buildings was soon after destroyed. Queen Elizabeth granted the site to John Cowper, and it was subsequently the property of a family of Stone, one of whom in 1717 sold it to Sir Isaac Shard, a person so proverbially avaricious, that Hogarth introduced his portrait into his picture, "The Miser's Feast." His son, a young man of spirit, called on the painter, and drawing his sword cut a hole in the canvas. "Nunnery" was held by this family until William Shard, Esq., aliened it in 1791. After passing through several hands it was purchased by Thomas Sanctuary, Esq., High Sheriff, in 1830. Many interesting documents relating to this establishment have been printed by Mr. Way, S. A. C., Vol. v. The house built on the site of the Nunnery was a timbered structure, and a view of it, by Grimm, is given in S. A. C. v., 250. The present house is modern. In 1840 a beautiful enamelled chalice of the 12th or 13th century was discovered with human remains, presumed to be those of a Prioress, within the ambit of the Nunnery.

In 1450 the commons of Rowesparre, under Thomas Walter, and John Styles, and Thomas Bartelot, "gentilmen," rose in favour of Jack Cade.

The church (St. Mary), principally of the 14th century, consists of nave, aisles, chancel, and massive embattled tower. The body of the edifice was rebuilt in 1855, at the expense of the Broadwood family. In the nave are two brasses—the first for 𝔍𝔬𝔥𝔫 𝔡𝔢 𝔎𝔶𝔤𝔤𝔢𝔰𝔣𝔬𝔩𝔡, and 𝔄𝔤𝔫𝔢𝔰 his wife, with small half-length figures (14th century)—the other for 𝔗𝔥𝔬. 𝔆𝔥𝔞𝔩𝔩𝔬𝔫𝔢𝔯, and 𝔐𝔞𝔯𝔤𝔞𝔯𝔢𝔱, his wife (1532). Mr. Challoner is mentioned among the tenants of the Prioress. There are later memorials for the families of Wood, Broadwood, Priaulx, Chandler, Gardiner, Wallis, Stone, Ede, &c.

[S. A. C. Priory of, v, 244 (*Way*). Enamelled chalice, ix, 303 (*Way*), Borers, xi, 80. Church, xii, 108. Matthew, Stanbridge, and Steer. Quakers, xvi, 69. Bells, xvi, 222. River Mole, xvi, 269. Urrey of, xvii, 21. Jack Cade's rising abetted by four "gentilmen" of Rusper, xviii, 29. Cross found at, xviii, 209.

RUNTINGTON.

A small hamlet in Heathfield.

RUSTINGTON.

A parish in the Hundred of Poling; Rape of Arundel; distant 1½ mile east from Littlehampton, its Post-town. Its Railway station is Angmering, close by. Union, East Preston. Population in 1811, 292; in 1861, 340. Benefice, a Vicarage, valued at £159. Patron, the Bishop of Chichester; Incumbent, Rev. Henry John Rush, M.A., of Worcester College, Oxford. Date of earliest Parish Register, 1568. Acreage, 1,287. *Chief Landowners*, Mrs. Gratwicke, Mrs. Penfold, and Thomas Bushby, Esq.

It is a fertile agricultural parish, and contains several excellent private residences. The manor is mentioned in Domesday under (West) Prestetune. It was a constituent part of the barony of Midhurst, and as such belonged to the great family of De Bohun. From them it passed by heirs female to the Lesleys,

Barfords; and Cookes, down to about the beginning of the 16th century, and was divided into Eastcourt and Westcourt. After a great variety of changes of ownership it became the property of Charles, Duke of Norfolk, who in 1790 sold it to William Gratwicke, Esq., of Ham, in whose representatives it still vests. Prestetune itself belonged, before the Conquest, to a freewoman named Ulveva. It was subsequently held by Bohun, Tregoz, Lewknor, and Dawtrey, and in 1560 Thomas Baker, the maternal grandfather of the illustrious John Selden, was possessor. Later proprietors have been Alderton, Willes, Dawtrey, and Bushby of Arundel. Another estate passed through the families of Upperton, Barwick, Gratwicke, and Campion, and was purchased in 1810 by E. G. Penfold, Esq.

The church (St. Peter and St. Paul) is described by Hussey as " a *good church*, of chancel, north and south aisles (an addition to the east end of the former making a kind of transept), a heavy western tower, and north and west porches." He indicates Transition-Norman, Early English, and Perpendicular features. There are several details which deserve the notice of the ecclesiologist. The edifice had fallen into disrepair, but the zeal and benevolence of the present incumbent and some friends, have recently brought about a judicious restoration, and put the whole parish into " good repair."

[S. A. C. Encaustic tile, iii, 238. Arms of Cooke, ix, 365. Church to Nunnery of Lyminster, xi, 118. Church, xii, 98. Holy-bread lands, xiv, 156—for the meaning of this term see vol. vi, p. 244. Bell, xvi, 222. Belonged to the Lords of Arundel and the Bohuns, xx, 1, 2.]

RYE.

A borough, market-town, and parish in the Hundred of Goldspur; Rape of Hastings; distant nine miles north-east from Hastings, having a Railway station on the South Eastern line. Union, Rye. Population in 1811, 2,681; in 1861, 4,228. Benefice, a Vicarage, valued at £410; Patron, the Duke of Devonshire; Incumbent, Rev. Barrington S. Wright, M.A. Date of earliest Parish Register, 1538. Acreage, 2,313. *Seats,* Leasham-house, Major Edward Barrett Curteis ; Mountsfield, J. F. Plomley, Esq.

Rye is in many respects one of the most interesting towns in East Sussex. The name is probably derived from the old Norman *rive*, Latin *ripa*, a bank, which well describes its geographical character. It is near the eastern extremity of Sussex, and its situation near the mouth of the Eastern Rother has always given it some degree of commercial importance. It was not originally one of the Cinque-Ports, but in the early Norman period it was added, with its sister-town of Winchelsea, to that ancient league, the two being designated "nobiliora membra Quinque Portuum," and ranking next in order to the five original ports. In every other respect it has for centuries been regarded as equal to the original five ports. As an *actual* port for commerce it is the best of the series, most of which, be it said, are no longer ports at all. Some topographers have, without foundation, made it the Portus Novus of Ptolemy. The position of the town is somewhat grand and romantic, and from some points of view its fine old church becomes a kind of Acropolis. On entering Rye, the visitor is struck with its medieval appearance; narrow streets, paved with small boulders like "petrified kidneys," and antique gabled houses being its chief characteristics. That it was originally insulated appears pretty clear, as the surrounding alluvial soil must have been deposited by salt and fresh water. Of the antiquity of the town we can only guess from inferences, but as it was seated on the Rother, more anciently known as the Limene, and having its outfall much farther to the east, in the neighbourhood of Hythe in Kent, it must have been of some importance for shipmen as early at least as the time of the first Norsemen and Danes. We are told in the Saxon Chronicle, under the year 893, that 250 Danish ships entered the Limene, and in the year 1822 a discovery was made at Northiam, at a place not far from the present navigable river Rother, which helps to illustrate this point. A ship, presumed to have been one of this fleet, was discovered deeply imbedded in ten feet of mud and sand. She was 65 feet long and 14 feet wide, with cabin and forecastle, and on board of her were found a human skull, a pair of goat's horns, a poinard, the bricks of a fire-hearth, several square ornamental glazed tiles, some pottery, several pairs of shoes or sandals, and many other relics. For speculations on the ancient condition of Rye and its port, see Dugdale's "History of Imbanking," and the late Mr. William Holloway's "History of Rye." The hundred or manor of which the town formed part, is called in Domesday Staneings, and like Winchelsea and several other places in Sussex, was given by the Confessor to the Norman abbey of Fécamp, and so continued till 1267, when Henry III. resumed possession, giving the monks in exchange the manor of Cheltenham in the county of Gloucester, and other lands. Rye, like most of our southern ports, has been honoured by several royal visits. King John was there; so were Edward III., Henry VII., Henry VIII., and Elizabeth. The virgin queen was received with so much loyalty that she called the town "Rye Royal," on the same occasion that she re-christened Winchelsea as "Little London." This was in 1573, and, on her entrance to the town, being thirsty, she stopped at a little way-side well, and drank. The place is still existing, and is called Queen Elizabeth's spring. A quaint old stone commemorates the event. Charles II. was there too, and so were the two first Georges, all detained by stress of weather. The rooms occupied by George II. were in a house at the south-west corner of Middle-street. John Fletcher, the celebrated coadjutor of Beaumont the dramatist, was son of Richard Fletcher, vicar of Rye, afterwards Bishop of Bristol, and was born here in 1579. The town was fortified with a stone wall, at an early period; and need enough,* for it was several times attacked by the French, particularly in the reigns of Richard II. and Henry VI. In the former reign, 1377, the enemy landed with five vessels, and after having plundered the town, set it on fire. With his customary exaggeration, the chronicler Stowe, asserts that "within five hours they brought it wholly into ashes, with the church, that then was there of a wonderful beauty, conveying away foure of the richest of that towne prisoners, and slaying sixty-six, left not above eyght in the towne"—total population 78! Among other spoils they carried off 42 hogsheads of wine. It is matter of congratulation, however, that the church, though some of its masonry has marks of fire, was but slightly injured. In 1447, on the second irruption, the town records are supposed to have been burnt. In the reign of Edward VI., 37 hoys are said to have left the haven at one tide, "and never an Englishman among them." Rye suffered greatly in the 16th and 17th centuries from visitations of the plague and small-pox, which destroyed many hundreds of the inhabitants. In 1562, on the breaking out of the war in France between the Romanists and Huguenots, when Elizabeth sent out a large armament to support the latter, 600 soldiers sailed from Rye. The history of this war is so well known as to require here no further reference. Rye afterwards became a place of refuge for the harassed Huguenots, and no less than 500 were soon collected here, so that provision could hardly be made for the support of this sudden accession to the population. After the massacre of St. Bartholomew, 641 refugees entered the port, many remaining here, who had separate religious services, it is supposed in the old chapel of the Augustine Friars, under a Huguenot ministry. Some of the settlers were Flemings and Walloons. Jeake says that in 1582 there were 1,534 French refugees, though only a few of these can have settled here. In 1682 the Huguenots were permitted to have separate services in the parish church. At length, in 1685, came the Revocation of the Edict of Nantes, and Rye again received many additional refugees. The parish register contains very

---

* The royal license for fortifying "La Rye" was dated 3rd March, 1369. -

numerous entries of their births and burials. Many of the descendants remain in and about Rye, but with names so translated, misspelt, and Anglicized, that it is difficult to identify them. The names, however, of the Hamons, Taylors, Dansays, Guerins, Jewins, Valloys, Mercers, Sivyers, Michells, Lyons, Neves, Marrows, Tournays, Saverys, Reynoldses, Espinettes, Meryons, Gastons, Bournes, Paines, and several others, have long been denizened, in their corrupted orthography, in this part of Sussex. The flagon used by the French congregation was presented in 1860, by the venerable historian of Rye, the late Mr. W. Holloway, and his wife Sarah, née *Meryon*, to the vicar and churchwardens, and though only of lead, is still preserved among the utensils of the Holy Communion in the parish church. For these and many other details of the foreign Protestants of Rye, as a " city of refuge," I am indebted to the very researchful paper of Mr. W. Durrant Cooper, F.S.A., in the xiii. Vol. of the " Sussex Collections."

Besides the grand parish church, Horsfield mentions three small ecclesiastical establishments in Rye; the chapel of St. Clare; the chantry of St. Nicholas, both afterwards used for the deposit of ammunition,* and the house of the Friars Eremites of St. Augustine, the chapel of which was also applied to secular uses. Of the last we have little history. The parish church deserves careful examination, as being among the largest and most interesting in Sussex. The earliest portions are the central tower, the transepts, and the plain semi-circular arches opening into them from the aisles of the nave. These are early Norman. In both transepts are fragments of a Norman arcade, with the zig-zag moulding. The nave is Transition-Norman. The chancel has a chapel or a subsidary chancel on each side. The east window is rich Perpendicular, filled with what Murray's " Handbook of Kent and Sussex, p. 249," styles " Harlequin glass." A common tradition makes the communion table one of the spoils of the Spanish Armada, but it is certainly not older than *temp*. William III. The north or St. Clare's chapel is Early English, and it must have originally been very striking. The authority just quoted complains that " it is impossible to speak too severely of the present state of this beautiful chapel, desecrated, neglected, damp, and filled with ladders and fire-engines." It might be added that lately (when I last saw it) it was also the receptacle of a pillory and a " cucking-stool," which latter shows that the " good wives " of Rye of yore were rather addicted to scolding, and sometimes required a " ducking " in the river. The south, or St. Nicholas' chapel, was long used as a schoolroom for the poor. The church clock, the bells of which are

---

* These were doubtless adjuncts to the parochial church.

struck by a pair of fat gilt cherubs, is said, like the communion-table, to have been the gift of Queen Elizabeth, a statement open to much doubt, though Mr. Octavius Morgan thinks it is the most ancient clock in England still actually doing its work. The big pendulum swinging below attracts the notice of the stranger, as it seems as if intended to beat time to the services of the sanctuary. Near the communion-table is a brass to a civilian, **Thos. Hamon**, six times mayor of Rye, and thrice M.P. for the borough, whose " courage, justice, and gravitie " are duly noted. Within this church, too, lies my old tried friend, Charles Hicks, who was also six times mayor, and whose straightforwardness of character was not inferior to that of Hamon. The church contains several good mural monuments, notably one for John Wollett, Esq., with allegorical figures. Other records of the dead relate to the families of Lamb, Slade, *a quo* the local antiquary, George Slade Butler, Esq., F.S.A., Dansays, Haddock Lawrence, Collett, Hay, Prosser, Davis, Dawes, Procter, Threele, of Lewisham (now called Leasham), Miller, Pinkerton, Watson, Brazier, Morris, Glazier, Francis, Barham, Hounsell, Butler, Haffenden, Chatterton, Backhurst, Odiarne, Carleton, Durrant, Hope, Norton, Kennett, Grebbell, and many others "long to rehearse," but see Mr. G. S. Butler, in Vol. xiii. of the " Sussex Collections," where all the inscriptions in the church and churchyard are painstakingly recorded. In St. Clare's chancel is a monument to Allen Grebble, Esq., a member of one of the refugee families, and ten years mayor, who was assassinated in the church-yard in 1742, by a "sanguinary butcher" named Breeds, who slew him in mistake for his brother-in-law, Mr. Thomas Lamb, against whom he had a grudge. Breeds was hung in chains near the west end of the town, and the so-called "chains," an iron frame-work, are still preserved as a relic. The church contains eight bells, dated 1775, with quaint rhymed inscriptions.

Besides the church there are two ancient buildings in Rye. The Land-gate, on the north-east of the town, is of noble proportions, and forms a picturesque object. When the town was fortified, *temp.* Edward III., there were two other approaches called Ypres-gate, and Strand-gate, and a small postern at the bottom of Conduit-hill, but these have all disappeared within somewhat recent times, unless, indeed, the first-mentioned was identical with the castellated building still standing on the southeast of the town, on a rocky eminence, overlooking the harbour, and called *Ypres Tower*. It is a prevalent, but I believe unfounded, notion that this tower was named after William de Ypres, Earl of Kent, *temp.* King Stephen. This is quite improbable, since that noble is not known to have had any possessions in Rye, and, secondly, the architecture is of much later date. It seems more likely to have received its name from a family of Ypres who were inhabitants of Rye in the 14th and 15th centuries. The building, which is a strong square pile, with a round tower at each angle, having been repaired, is now used as the borough prison. Rye has returned members to Parliament,.as a borough by prescription, since 1369, and perhaps from an earlier date. By the Reform Act of 1832, the number was reduced from two members to one, and in order to return that one it was necessary to bring several of the adjacent parishes within the borough limit. Among more recent representatives have been, besides numerous members of county families, Sir Arthur Wellesley, afterwards Duke of Wellington, and another well-known soldier, Sir De Lacy Evans.

The history of the harbour has been given at large by Horsfield and Holloway, from the time when Rye was an insulated rock, until our own days, when the port is two miles from the town. Besides the main river Rother, two unimportant streams called the Brede and Tillingham-water, now reach the sea through the harbour. Considerable fisheries exist here, and in the last age smugglers carried on a profitable traffic. From hence, during the French war, newspapers and correspondence were clandestinely conveyed to the Emperor Napoleon.

Among other noteworthy inhabitants of Rye, were Samuel Jeake, sen., and his son and grandson of the same names. The former, born 1623, was a lawyer of eminence and learning, and as I have elsewhere had occasion to say, " He was in politics a roundhead, in religion a nonconformist, and in science almost encyclopædic." He was author of several works, including a huge volume of arithmetic, of almost 700 folio pages, with the learned title of " Logistikelogia," published under the auspices of the Royal Society; but the book by which he will be best remembered is his very valuable " Charters of the Cinque-Ports," translated with notes in 1678, but not published until 1728. It is the text-book of the customs and liberties of the Ports, and is very scarce. Mr. Jeake was a preacher, and was much persecuted for his religious sentiments. To modern notions it seems incompatible that this truly Christian man should have addicted himself to Astrology and Alchemy; but so it was, and though he had full faith in what we now deem orthodoxy, he like many others believed in these occult sciences, and produced many horoscopes, which are still preserved. He died in 1690. His only surviving child, the second Samuel Jeake, was born in 1652, and at the age of 19 was acquainted with all his father's studies, and even more. Less wise and more superstitious was he than his father. He was, however, a kindly Christian man, and full of schemes. One of these was to marry Elizabeth, the accomplished daughter of Mr. Richard Hartshorne, ex-master of the grammar-school of Rye, when she had reached the mature age of 13½ years! By this marriage he had several children, one of whom, the third Samuel Jeake, likewise dabbled in astrology, and was known by the vulgar as the " conjuror," but by the more cultivated as " Counsellor Jeake." He was also a mechanical genius, and invented an apparatus to enable him to fly. His failure, however, was as great as that of Icarus, though without the same unlucky result. See notices of the Jeake family, in " Sussex Worthies," and Holloway's " History of Rye." Bryan Twyne, the eminent scholar, was appointed vicar of Rye in 1613, but was chiefly resident at Oxford, of which university he was the champion. See " Sussex Worthies," p. 185.

[S. A. C. Town seals, i, 18. xvii, 64. Capt. Cockram, mayor, v, 54, 73. Royal visits, John, i, 135. Edward III., iv, 118. vi, 53. Henry VIII., vi, 53. Charles II., *ibid.* Georges I. and II. *(vide supra.)* Miller of, ix, 40. The Jeakes, various notices of, ix, 45. xiii, 57, 72, 74, 76, 78. Pillory and cucking-stool, ix, 361 *(Lower.)* Tradesmen's tokens, x, 209. Cannon at, xi, 152. Atlas maritimus report, xi, 180. Charters of Cinque-Ports, xii, 159. xiii, 76. Oxenbridge of, xii, 203. Plague at, xiii, 57. Town fortified, xiii, 113. Salt-works, xiii, 138. xvii, 30. Protestant refugees, xiii, 180. Vicars and their patrons, and inscriptions in church and church-yard *(Butler)*, xiii, 270-301. French invasion, xiii, 271. Fletchers of, xiii, 277. Appearance of spirits in 1607 *(Butler)*, xiv, 25. Agincourt, men at, xv, 133. Rye and its inhabitants *(Butler)*, xvii, 123. Church bells, xvi, 222. Harbour, xvii, 134. Passage-book of Rye *(W. D. Cooper)*, xviii, 170. Trial of Breads the murderer of Mr. Grebble, xviii, 188. Whitfeld of, xix, 89. Aliens *temp.* Henry VIII., xix, 149. Public roads, v, 193. xix, 155, 167. Thomas Palmer's journal, xix, 202. Hays, M.P. of, xx, 223. Venetian traffic to Rye, xx, 224.]

SADDLESCOMBE.

Now a farm-house merely, but formerly a Preceptory of Knights-Templars, in the parish of Newtimber. It was a manor at the date of Domesday. In Saxon times, Godwin, a priest, had held it of his namesake, Earl Godwin. The assessment was 17 hides, and there were 24 villeins, and 4 bondmen. Ralph held four hides in the same territory, with three villeins and two bondmen. The total value in Saxon times was fifteen pounds, and after the Conquest eleven pounds. Some of the subsequent lords of the manor were Penfont, Browne, Viscounts Montague Poyntz, and the family of Wyndham, of Petworth (Lord Leconfield). There has been considerable confusion as to the abode of the Knights-Templars, several authorities having fixed it at Sedlescombe, near Battle in East Sussex; but it is quite clear that the place now under consideration was the spot. "Sadlescombe" was an extensive manor extending into the parishes of Newtimber, Bolney, Hurst-Pierpoint, and Twineham, and was held of the De Warennes in the 13th and 14th centuries by the powerful family of De Saye. Among the places to which John, Earl of Warenne, made his memorable claim, by exhibiting the sword with which his ancestor had fought at Hastings, were Newtimber and Sadlescombe. There cannot be much doubt, I think, that the De Sayes founded this establishment for the "half-soldiers, half-monks" of the "Temple of Solomon." Of the history of the Templars here we have few records, but we ascertain from documents that the churches of Southwyke, Woodmancote, and tithes and lands in Kingston-Bowsey, Shoreham, and other places, were held by the Brethren. On the suppression of the Templars in 1309, the Knights-Hospitallers succeeded to their rule and possessions, which they held till the dissolution of the Monasteries. It is interesting to note that among the benefactors to the Templars were members of the families of Scrase and Farncombe, names for centuries identified with Sussex, and still existing in the county. For a full detail of this ancient Preceptory, I must refer to the article by Mr. Blaauw in the ix. volume of the "Sussex Archæological Collections."

SALEHURST.

Domesday, *Salhert;* a parish in the Hundred of Henhurst; Rape of Hastings; distant six miles north from Battle; Post-town, Hawkhurst. Railway-station, Robertsbridge, in this parish. Population in 1811, 1,653; in 1861, 2,014. Benefice, a Vicarage, valued at £625; Patron, Charles Hardy, Esq.; Incumbent, Rev. Alexander Orr, M.A., of Oriel College, Oxford. Date of earliest Parish Register, 1575. Acreage, 6,481. *Seats,* Higham, Iridge, Darvel-bank, and Bernhurst.

The population of this parish is considerably increased in consequence of the town of *Robertsbridge,* and part of the hamlet of *Hurst-Green* lying within its boundaries. Those places are mentioned in separate articles. The parish, like most in this district, is beautifully undulated, and variegated with arable, woodland, pasture, and hop-gardens. There are several eminences of considerable altitude, which command excellent views, especially Silver Hill. Several old families were connected with the parish. That of Wildigos resided at Iridge; Higham gave name to a family; while a branch of the "ubiquitous" Culpepers possessed the old gabled mansion called Wigsell. Boxhulle, now Bugsell, gave name to the family of Sir Alan de Boxhulle, one of the original Knights of the Garter. The family of Dicker were also of some standing in the parish. Fuller particulars of these families and the descent of their estates are given by Horsfield. In more recent days the principal families have been Fowle, Peckham, Micklethwaite, Harcourt, Boys, and Luxford. On the commanding height called Silver-Hill, barracks of great extent were erected during the French war, about the end of the last century.

The church (St. Mary) is of various dates, and is a very picturesque structure. It contains a nave with aisles, and two chancels. The arches are pointed throughout. The tower, which is lofty and embattled, is entered by a porch at the west end, which also has battlements, and a fine pointed arch. The arms of Echingham, Culpeper, and another are carved on this porch. Within a recess in the south aisle is a large altar tomb, but there is no record of its occupant. In the Wigsell chancel there are some old monuments ascribed to the Culpepers of that estate, but here, as in too many other cases, " monuments themselves memorials need." There are tablets and inscriptions with the names of Ashe, Jenkin, Micklethwaite, Peckham, Fowle, Harcourt, Snepp, Stevens, Weller, and other families. There is a peal of eight bells, all of modern date. Altogether this is one of the most interesting churches in the district.

See also the articles ROBERTSBRIDGE and HURST-GREEN.

[Ironworks, ii, 216. iii, 241. xviii, 15. Church of, xiii, 136. Culpeper family, xiii, 254. Boxhulle (Bugsell), xv, 152. xviii, 15. xx, 65. Newingtons of, xvi, 46. Bells, xvii, 223. Cade's insurrection, xviii, 25. Strodes of, xix, 110. Hays of, xx, 65.]

SEAFORD.

Vulgo, *Saifoord;* a parish, extinct Parliamentary Borough, and Corporation, a Member of the Cinque port of Hastings, in the Rape of Pevensey; distant 9½ miles from Lewes, its Post-town. It has a Railway station on the South Coast line. Union, Eastbourne. Population in 1811, 1,001; in 1861, 1,084, though in the "season" the population is much increased; Benefice, a Vicarage, valued at £240; Incumbent, Rev. W. H. Meade Buck. Date of earliest Parish Register, 1558. Acreage, 2,235. *Chief Landowners,* The Earl of Chichester, Mrs Harison, and Dr. Tyler Smith. *Seats,* Sutton Place, Mrs. Harison; Milburgh, J. Purcell Fitz-Gerald, Esq.

This small town is rich in historical interest. In Vol. vii. of "Sussex Archæological Collections" I gave the fullest account of it then practicable, but additions have been made in several subsequent volumes, particularly in Vol. xvii. The locality was early possessed by civilized man. Many traces of Roman occupation occur in the parish. On the cliff, less than a mile eastward of the town, is an earthwork locally called the Roman camp, and a Roman cemetery existed at Green Street, where, about the year 1825, a large number of sepulchral urns were exhumed. Coins of Hadrian and Pius, and of Antonia, daughter of Mark Antony, have been found here. Seaford was one of the claimants of the honour of being the Civitas Anderida, but that claim has been settled in favour of Pevensey. It has been suggested, however, that Seaford is identical with the Mercredesburn of the Saxon chronicle, where, in 485, a great battle between the South Saxons and the Britons took place.

Seaford appears to signify a firth or *fiord* of the sea, and probably received its present designation from a colony of Norsemen, who called it Sae-Fiord, in reference to the bay of the English Channel on which it stands, and to the estuary which formerly extended inland beyond the town. The place is first mentioned, as *Sefordt*, in 1058, in connection with the removal of the remains of St. Lewinna, virgin and martyr, who had long previously died at the hands of the pagan Saxons. The remains had been kept in the odour of sanctity at a religious establishment called St. Andrew's, probably at Alfriston. The story is given at length in " Sussex Archæological Collections " Vol. i, and also in the " Worthies of Sussex."

Soon after the Conquest Seaford became the lordship of William de Warenne, and continued in his descendants down to the reign of Edward III., when the family became extinct in the elder line. Chington, however, an important manor and vill in the parish was held, with Pevensey rape, by the family of De Aquila, lords of Pevensey, one of whom gave it to the priory of Michelham.* King John with his suite passed the night of the 23rd May, 1216, in this town. After the extinction of the De Warennes, Seaford was successively in the hands of the Poynings, Fitz-Alan, Mowbray, and Howard families. When it became a member of the Cinque Ports is not known : it must certainly have been so as early as 1229, when it is mentioned first among the limbs of the port of Hastings. Of all the subordinate ports this is the only one which returned members to Parliament. It is long since that Seaford actually possessed a port; the Ouse debouched there from a very early period until the 16th century when it was straightened and directed to the village of

---

* In 7th Edw. I., Thomas Therel held a certain serjeanty in Chinting, co. Sussex, by finding one serving man as often as the King should go into Wales, " or elsewhere in England," at his own expense for 40 days.—*Blount's Ancient Tenures.*

Meeching, which thence received the name of the "New-Haven."
The course of the old river is still traceable at the back of the
beach, from Newhaven to the Cliff-end at Seaford. The decay
of the harbour was not the only cause of the decline of the
town—it had previously suffered greatly from several incursions
of the French, from fire, and from the great pestilence of 1348,
called the Black Death. Prior to this, as we have seen, Seaford
sent two members to Parliament, viz., from 1298 to 1400. From
that time there was no return until 1640, from which date it
continued to be represented, until the Reform Act of 1832 swept
away the electoral privilege.

During the proprietorship of part of Seaford by the Poynings
family, an attempt was made to found a new town in the eastern part of the parish, on a commanding portion of the South
Downs overlooking the harbour of Cuckmere. There are traces
of buildings extending over many acres, and the site is still
known as Poynings Town. A finer site for a town can scarcely
be imagined.

Henry VIII. gave a new charter to Seaford investing it with
and confirming all Cinque Port privileges, which it still enjoys,
standing eighth in the roll of that ancient league, and being
governed by a recorder, bailiff, jurats, coroner, and the other
officials usual in the larger ports. Not long afterwards, in 1545,
the French made their final descent upon the town, but were
repulsed with disgrace by Sir Nicholas Pelham and an extempo-
rized force of townsmen and neighbours. As Sir Nicholas' epitaph at Lewes informs us, with a quaint pun—

> "What time the French sought to have sackt Sea-Foord,
> This *Pelham* did re-*pel'em* back aboord."

The municipality of Seaford has been duly preserved down to
the present day, and is a jurisdiction independent of the county,
having courts of assembly, quarter and petty sessions, with a
town hall, prison, &c., all, of course, in miniature. The higher
criminal causes are usually transferred to the assizes at the
county town. The town records, from the year 1562, are in excellent preservation. The Parliamentary history of the borough
presents the usual amount of corruption to which such small
constituencies were exposed. One of the latest members, 1827,
was the celebrated statesman, the Right Hon. George Canning. At
an earlier date William Pitt, the great Earl of Chatham, had
represented it.

As to matters ecclesiastical, there is a tradition that Seaford
formerly had five churches, though there is no evidence of its
having ever formed more than one parish, except that it was
early united with the adjoining parish of Sutton, which is now

absorbed by it, the ecclesiastical designation being Sutton-cum-Seaford. There may, however, have been five ecclesiastical establishments, viz.: the parish church of Seaford, that of Sutton, the chapel of Chyngton, dependent upon Michelham Priory, the chapel of St. James, attached to a hospital of lepers which existed so early as the 12th century, in the northern outskirts of the town; and (probably) another chapel attached to a guild within the town, the crypt of which remains in a garden called "The Folly," over which the original town-hall is said to have stood. This crypt has recently been restored in excellent taste by its proprietor, Robertson Griffiths, Esq. Seaford and Sutton are both prebends in Chichester cathedral.

The parish church, dedicated to St. Leonard, until lately, consisted of a western tower, a nave, north and south aisles, and a modern chancel; but, in 1862, the building underwent restorations, and received the addition of two short transepts and a handsome chancel, terminating in a polygonal apse. The original architecture was Norman, with insertions of later date, principally of the Transition period. One of the capitals of the columns, between the nave and the south aisle, is curiously sculptured with the Crucifixion and other subjects, and there is also a slab with an early representation of St. Michael and the Dragon. There are no monuments of early date. Of Sutton church some remains are still traceable in a close near Sutton Place. Sutton and Chyngton (or Chinting) were formerly regarded as vills of Seaford, and the Corporation seal contains the legend "Sigillvm. Burgensium. de Saffordia—with Suttonii, et Chyngton." The devices are (obv.) an Eagle for De Aquila, and (rev.) a three-masted ship.

Seaford is agreeably situated on the bay to which it gives name, and of which, from the chalk cliffs to the eastward, a beautiful prospect is obtained, including views of the town and surrounding country, Newhaven harbour, Lewes, &c. The cliffs between the town and Cuckmere are bold and romantic, and on the verge, near the junction of the Chyngton and Sutton farms, is a ledge called "Puck-church parlour," no longer the abode of fairies, but the resort of foxes, ravens, sea-gulls, and peregrine falcons. A hermitage existed on these cliffs in 1372.

For many years the town has been resorted to as a quiet retreat for sea-bathers, and recently an impulse has been given to building. Could proper sea-defences be made, and the common lands in front of the town brought into proper order, Seaford would offer one of the best sites imaginable for a watering-place. Were the scheme for a breakwater and harbour of refuge in connection with Newhaven carried into effect, this would become the most important point between Dover and Portsmouth.

The families of Gratwicke, Elphick, Harison of Sutton, Hurdis, Bill, &c., have been influential here at various periods. The name of Simmons, formerly Seman, can also be traced for nearly six centuries. For shipwrecks, smuggling, and electioneering manœuvres, for all which Seaford had a bad reputation, see Horsfield's Sussex, Vol. i, and the articles in S. A. C.

[S. A. C. Seal i, 19. Lewinna St., i, 46. King' John at, i, 136. *Lower's* memorials of, vii, 73. Lower and Cooper's ditto, xvii, 141. Elphick of Sutton, pedigree, vii, 131. xvi, 47. xvii, 159, 259. Harison pedigree, vii, 132. Hurdis pedigree, vii, 134. Sutton, viii, 155. Roman urns, ix, 368. xvii, 141. Cuckmere, smugglers at, x, 81. Medieval pottery, x, 193. Fort, xi, 151. xvii, 147. Cuckmere haven artillery, xi, 151. Hospital of Lepers at, xii, 112, 269. xvii, 162. Churchyard inscriptions, xii, 242. Old family names, xii, 251. Salts and Beamlands, xiii, 47. xvii, 147. Sutton annexation of, xiii, 315. Ancient mouth of the Ouse, xv, 164. Cinque-Port privileges, xv, 164. Church bells, xvi, 141, 223. Peter, the Hermit of Seaford, xvii, 143. Chyngton, Phil. of, xvii, 144. Sutton prebendal house burnt by the French, xvii, 147. Wreckers of, xvii, 149. Michelham Priory possessions, &c., xvii, 152. Gratwickes of vii, 129. xvii, 158. Browne, Sir Anthony, xvii, 163. Cade's rising, xviii, 18. Civil marriages, xix, 202. Hay, M.P., xx, 65. Human remains found at; *(Capt. Turner)*, xx, 180. Venetian ships' charts, xx, 225.]

ST. LEONARDS (sometimes called St. Leonards-on-Sea).

In the Rape of Hastings ; a suburb of Hastings ; it has a Station on the South-Coast Railway.

The town of St. Leonards, formerly a small village (if village it could be called), sprang into importance when Mr. Burton erected a new and fashionable town. This grand undertaking resulted in additional popularity to Hastings proper. St. Leonards is situated partly in a valley, which has some pretty scenery inland. The principal range of buildings, called the Marina, extends along the sea front, and there are many agreeable residences around, as also every appliance of a modern watering-place.

Theodore Hook, in " Jack Bragg," thus alludes to St. Leonards :—

" From the meditation in which he was absorbed, Jack was aroused upon his arrival at that splendid creation of modern art and industry, ST. LEONARDS, which perhaps affords one of the most beautiful and wonderful proofs of individual taste, judgment, and perseverance that our nation exhibits. Under the superintendence of Mr. Burton a desert has become a thickly-peopled town. Buildings of an extensive nature and most elegant character rear their heads where but lately the barren cliffs presented their sandy fronts to the storm and wave, and rippling stream s and hanging groves adorn the valley which a few years since was a sterile and shrubless ravine."

Dr. Granville, in his " Spas of England," says: " The whole of this varied region must be a little paradise to invalids; and the houses, whether those detached as Italian or Lombard villas with gardens, or those placed in rows like a series of Gothic cottages, all equally desirable, are much sought after. . . . . The Victoria Hotel has the appearance of a nobleman's mansion. A wide street runs up on each side of it, leading to other and less regular series of buildings, constituting the town of St. Leonards, and also to that paradise of detached villas to which I have already alluded."

St. Leonards has really no history until 1828, when Mr. Burton commenced his buildings. It lies partly in the formerly almost extinct parish of St. Leonards, and partly in that of St. Mary Magdalen. Previously to Mr. Burton's purchase, it had belonged to the families of Lewis and Eversfield.

The parish extends beyond the limits of the Corporation of Hastings. The church was built at private expense in 1831, and the Princess Sophia of Gloucester laid the first stone.

SEDLESCOMBE.

Domesday, *Selescome;* vulgo, *Selzcum;* a parish in the Hundreds of Staple and Battle; Rape of Hastings; distant three miles north-east from Battle, its Post-town and Railway station. Union, Battle. Population in 1811, 506 ; in 1861, 703. Benefice, a Rectory, valued at £320; Patron, the Lord Chancellor; Incumbent, Rev. Edward Owen, M.A., of Sidney-Sussex College, Cambridge. Date of earliest Parish Register, 1558. Acreage, 2,049.

Like most of the neighbouring parishes, this has an undulating and well-wooded surface. The broad village street, which has some antique houses, is highly picturesque. On the little river Brede there are traces of the iron-works formerly carried on here. Roman remains have been discovered in connection with these works, proving that that enterprising people availed themselves of our mineral treasures. Powder mills have long existed in the parish.

Sir William Burrell, who has been followed by Horsfield and others, confounds this parish with Saddlescombe, in the parish of Newtimber, on the South Downs, which had a Preceptory of Knights Templars. The manor passed from Earl Godwin to his son Harold, and after the Conquest it was held of the Earl of Eu by Walter Fitz-Lambert. In 23rd Edward I. William de Echingham was lord. Henry Hallé, John Wybarne, Sir Anthony Browne, the Sidneys, and the Sackvilles were successively owners. It now belongs to the Earl de la Warr. Hancox, in this parish, was some time the seat of a junior branch of the Sackvilles; Great Sanders has for more than three centuries been the estate of the Bishop family; and Brickwall was, in the seventeenth century, the seat of the Farendens, wealthy landowners and iron-masters. This must not be confounded with Brickwall in Northiam.

The church (St. John the Baptist) occupies a commanding site. It consists of a chancel, nave with aisles, and west tower, surmounted by a low spire. The chancel arch is semi-circular. In a window over the Hancox pew are the arms of Downton, predecessors of the Sackvilles: *Arg, on a chief dancetté Sa. three goats' heads erased of the First, attired Or.* The building, which in 1866 underwent sound restoration, at a cost of £2,000, contains memorials of the Sackville, Bishop, and other families.

[S. A. C. Iron-works, ii, 216. Account books of the Everendens and Frewens, iv, 22. xiv, 90. Oxenbridge family, viii, 215. An Agincourt man, xv, 137. Manor of Morley, xiv, 112. Sackvilles, xiv, 229. xvi, 27. Brede river, xv, 154. Bells, xvi, 223. Tithes to Battle Abbey, xvii, 55. Cade's insurrection, xviii, 25.]

SELSCOMBE.   (See Sedlescombe.)

SEDGWICK.

An outlying portion of the parish of Broadwater, in the Forest district between Horsham and Nuthurst. It contains about 150 acres. For two centuries after the Conquest the manor, which extends into the two parishes above mentioned, belonged to the family of Le Sauvage, lords of Broadwater, who, in 1272, exchanged it with William de Braose for other lands. It passed with Bramber until 1572, and since, by purchase and descent, it has been vested in Caryll, Bennet, Lennox, Tudor, and Nelthorpe.

The ancient castle, or hunting seat, which formerly existed here belonged in succession to the Le Sauvages and De Braoses. The park, which surrounded it so lately as 1608, consisted of 624 acres. The building, as appears from the existing remains, was about 200 yards in circuit, and had a double moat. Until within the memory of man much more of the outer walls remained than can now be traced. The vestiges lie within the grounds of Mr. Nelthorpe, of Nuthurst Lodge, who takes due care of them. About 30 yards beyond the outer moat is a supply of water called St. Mary's, or more commonly the Nun's, well.

[S. A. C. Sedgwick Castle (*Turner*), viii, 31, 40.]

SELHAM.

Domesday, *Seleham;* a parish on the Western Rother, in the Hundred of Easebourne ; Rape of Chichester ; distant four miles east from Midhurst. Post-town, Petworth. Union, Midhurst. Population in 1811, 71; in 1861, 123. Benefice, a Rectory valued at £150 ; Patron, Brasenose College, Oxford; Incumbent, Rev. Robert Blackburn, M.A. of that College. Date of earliest Parish Register, 1565. Acreage, 1,042.

The Saxon elements of this name *Sél,* a hall, and *hám,* a home, seem to indicate a place of importance. Before the Conquest the manor was held by Codulf of Earl Godwin—afterwards of Earl Roger, by Robert, and his sub-tenant Fulco. In the reign of Henry II., William de Perci held it of the Honour of Arundel. Much later it became the property of the Montagues, from whom it descended to the late W. S. Poyntz, Esq. It now belongs, with the Cowdray estate, to the Earl of Egmont.

The church (St. James) consists of chancel, nave, and south aisle. The chancel arch is good Norman. The building has lately been restored and enriched with painted glass.

[S. A. C. Domesday watermill, v, 271. xvi, 260. Priory of Calceto had lands in, xi, 104. Bell, xvi, 223. Rents to Battle Abbey, xvii, 55.]

SELMESTON.

Domesday, *Selmestone;* vulgo, *Simpson;* a parish in the Hundred of Danehill Horsted ; Rape of Pevensey ; distant seven miles south-east from Lewes, its Post-town, and on the Eastbourne road. Railway station, Berwick, distant about one mile. Union, West Firle. Population in 1811, 149 ; in 1861, 197. Benefice, a Vicarage, united with Alciston, valued at £208 ; Patrons, the Bishop, and Dean and Chapter of Chichester, *alternis vicis;* Incumbent, Rev. W. Douglas Parish, B.C.L., of Trinity College, Oxford. Date of earliest Parish Register, 1677. Acreage, 1,590. *Chief Landowners,* Viscount Gage, and James Skinner, Esq., M.D.

Sel-meston seems in some way antithetical to West-meston in Lewes rape (see Westmeston), and *Sél* (Anglo-Saxon) may have some reference to an ante-Domesday hall here. At the time of the great Survey, William held it of the Earl of Moreton, Alfer, a Saxon, having previously been possessor. A church, a priest, and five ministri are mentioned. In 25th Edward I., Roger Lewknor held the manor of the king by Knights' service, and it remained with his descendants until 44th Elizabeth, when John Wood was lord. More recently it belonged to the family of Rochester, of Ludlay in this parish, and passed with Wannock

in Jevington. Mays belonged in the 17th century to the family
of Nutt, and is now part of Lord Gage's estate. Sherrington,
the property of James Skinner, Esq., belonged in early times
to the Peverells, and afterwards to John, son of Oliver Brocas,
one of the prisoners taken by the French at the battle of Rottingdean, 1377. It afterwards had a family of its own name, and
the heiress of Simon Sherrington married John Selwyn, whose
descendants removed about *temp.* Henry VII. to Friston. In the
17th century the family of Caldecott possessed it, and from them
it passed to the family of the present owner. Tilton (in Domesday, Telletone) is in this parish, and is now a farm belonging to
Lord Gage.

In 1403 a party of French marauders came to Selmeston and
carried off John Iford, servant of Robert Profoot.

The church (St. Mary), which has just undergone repairs,
previously consisted of nave, south aisle and chancel, with a dovecot turret and tapering spire. The style is Early English, and
the notion that certain unsightly posts pointed to a pre-Norman
wooden church is altogether erroneous. The church has, however, one rare peculiarity, the Altar slab of marble with five
crosses, which remains in situ, and is still used as a communion
table. In the north wall of the chancel is a recessed altar-tomb
for Dame Betris Braye, daughter of Ralph Sherley of Wiston,
1532. There are other memorials to the names of Rochester and
Caldecott. When smuggling was carried on in these parts, the
" free-traders " had a rendezvous in the churchyard. An old
altar-tomb served as their temporary storehouse. By lifting the
incumbent stone they could safely deposit their goods, and it is
said that they never failed to leave a " tub " or two for the use of
the parson ! I have this anecdote on good clerical authority.

[S. A. C. Tilton to the Abbey of Otteham, v. 157. Sherrington family,
v, 160. xv, 210. Manumission of Serfs, ix, 162. Fuller of Mays, xii, 255.
Nutts of Mays, xiii, 98. Manor rents, xiv, 263. Selwyn family, xv, 211.
xviii, 18, 40. Brocas, Peverell, and Fitzherbert, xv, 210. Southall
manor, xv, 210. French incursion, xv, 213. Bell, xvi, 223. Dame Braye's
tomb, xvii, 96. Lewknor family, xvii, 97.]

SELSEY.*

Domesday *Seleisie;* a parish in the Hundred of Manhood ; Rape of Chi-
    chester ; distant about nine miles south from Chichester, its Post-town
    and Railway station. Union, West Hampnett. Population in 1811,

* The etymology of Selsey, as given by Bede, namely, " Insula Vituli Marini,"
"the island of seals," is simply fanciful, there being no record of a seal having been
observed near the place. I should say that an Anglo-Saxon derivation from *Sel* and
ea, the water near the Hall (*i.e.* of the Bishops), is more reasonable.

648; in 1861, 900. Benefice, a united Rectory and Vicarage, valued at £750; Patron, the Bishop of Chichester; Incumbent, Rev. Henry Foster, Prebendary of Chichester, of St. John's College, Cambridge. Date of earliest Parish Register, 1662. Acreage, 3,494. *Chief Landowner*, The Hon. Mrs. Vernon Harcourt.

This peninsula is in many respects, geographical and historical, one of the most interesting parishes in the county. The indent or the land into the channel called Selsey Bill is the most southerly land in Sussex, and is bounded on the west by Bracklesham Bay. It possesses little variety of contour, being generally of flat surface and liable to incursions of the sea, from which it has suffered severely. The earliest monastery founded in the county was that established by Saint Wilfred, bishop of York, who having been tyrannically driven out of his diocese, settled down here for some time, in order to Christianize the South-Saxon pagans. King Edilwalch, and Ali, his queen (new converts), and Ceadwalla, king of Wessex, also a convert of the Saint, became benefactors to the monastery, and an Episcopal See was founded here by Wilfred, whose successors for 400 years were known as bishops of the South Saxons. Here the see remained under a long line of prelates until the year 1070, when it was deemed expedient to remove such establishments from villages into cities and towns. Of the Saxon cathedral and its demesnes no traces remain—on shore, that is—because the sea has so encroached that "the Park" has long been under water. The trees, the deer, and all the etcætera of palatial grandeur have utterly disappeared. Still it appears that, so lately as the time of Bishop Rede of Chichester, about the middle of the 14th century, Selsey Park was in existence, and poachers stole deer therefrom. The prelate excommunicated the offenders, by "bell, book, and candle," and styled them "sons of damnation." The site of the palace is supposed to have been nearly a mile from the present shore, and that of a submerged forest is still traceable at low water, in the shape of stumps of trees. So lately as November, 1824, nearly half the parish was temporarily under salt water. There are fine firm sands on the shore, and a considerable fishery for oysters, lobsters, crabs, &c., is carried on. A place near the shore called the "Hushing* Pool" presents a singular phenomenon. About midway between the churches of Pagham and Selsey the water at certain times of the tide appears to be in a state of ebullition, as if from the rushing of immense volumes of air to the surface. The space so occupied measures about 130 feet by 30. The sound of the bursting of the bubbles is said to resemble the simmering of a large cauldron, and may be heard on shore to the distance of a quarter of a mile. The

* Query: If this word be not a corruption of "hissing"?

cause is conjectured to be a large cavity from which the air is expelled by the in-rush of the water.

The village consists principally of a long street. The old parish church (Our Lady) stood almost two miles from the street, but it has recently been removed, except the chancel, which is retained for burial services. A new church (St. Peter) has recently been erected close to the village. The old fabric originally contained shrines for St. Katherine, St. James, St. Mary, St. Margaret, and St. Nicholas. The building is supposed to have been constructed by Bishop William Rede, between 1369 and 1385. On the south side of the church-yard is a large earthwork with a deep ditch, and other parts of what may have been a British fort were no doubt obliterated by the erection of the church. Some early tombs remained in the nave when I last visited the building, including several coffin-stones with crosses in relief, probably for ancient rectors. Against the north wall of the chancel there is a monument pleasingly designed, for "Jhon Lews, Sqwyr, and Agas his wife," who died in 1537, "on whose soul Ih'u have marce." Their effigies are represented on a small scale, and behind them are their patron saints, St. George and St. Agatha.

The peninsula which formerly became insulated at high water had to be reached by a ferry, but a raised causeway has been constructed, and by means of this it is at all times accessible.

According to Domesday, Selesie was held by the Bishop in domain. In the time of the Confessor it was rated at ten hides, and valued at £12; after the Conquest at £10. There were 14 villeins and 11 bondmen. In 1561 the manor was dismembered from the see of Chichester, and vested in the Crown. In 1635 it was purchased by Sir William Morley. On a subsequent purchase (1736) by Sir Henry Peachey, Bart., it passed to his family, whose nephew, Sir James Peachey, Bart., was created Baron Selsey in 1794, and in his descendant, the Hon. Mrs. Vernon Harcourt, it now vests. Medmeney and Berkleys are reputed manors in the parish. The prebend of Selsey was transferred to Chichester, and Bartleys and East Thorney are prebendal manors.

Among the curious local manufactures of Sussex may be mentioned that carried on in this parish by Mr. Pullinger. He is the inventor and patentee of what is called "the automaton and perpetual mousetrap," and employs a large staff of workmen in this muricidal occupation.

[S. A. C. Morley of, v, 46. St. Wilfred, v, 219. xv, 85. xvi, 261. Oslac at, viii, 183. Eadwulf grants to, ibid. Church, xii, 76. Rede of, xii, 77. Merchant guild at, xv, 176. Bell, xvi, 223. Submerged park, xvi, 261. Lewknor of, xvii, 81. Water-poet at, xviii, 139. Manor, xix, 22. Bishopric of, xix, 22.]

SHERMANBURY.

Domesday, *Salmondesberie;* a parish in the Hundred of Windham and Ewhurst; Rape of Bramber; distant three miles north from Henfield; Post-town, Hurst-Pierpoint, Railway station, Partridge Green, distant about 2½ miles. Union, Steyning. Population in 1811, 270; in 1861, 464. Benefice, a Rectory valued at £387; Patroness, Mrs. Hunt; Incumbent, Rev. John Matthew Glubb, M.A., of Exeter College, Oxford. Date of earliest Parish Register, 1653. Acreage, 1,911. *Chief Landowners,* Mrs. Henry Hunt, Rev. J. Goring, and Henry Rideout, Esq. *Seats,* Shermanbury Park, Mrs. Hunt; The Grange, Mrs. Hoper.

Our ancestors frequently indicated their land boundaries by trees, and this was the case at Shermanbury. A tree at the north east corner of the parish shows its junction with Bolney, Twineham, and Cowfold. At the time of the Domesday Survey the place was held by Ralph, of William de Braose. The ubiquitous Azor had been the previous tenant under Harold, and was rated for two hides. There were a small church, four *ministri,* and three bondmen; and the manor was estimated at 24 shillings. From the date of the Conquest to 1349 the manor belonged to the family of De Buci, or Bowsey, lords of Kingston-Buci, near Shoreham. The De Buci family, as under-tenants of the De Braoses, lords of Bramber, paid murage* to them, but they were exempted in 1267, on payment of 48 marks. Sybil de Buci, co-heiress of the last male heir of that ancient Norman race, married Sir John de Islebon, and they assigned Shermanbury to the other co-heiress, Joan, wife of Sir William de Fyfhide. John de Islebon, and Sybil, renounced, in favour of Sir William and Joan, their claim to the right of " *the coat of arms, crest, and helmet,*" belonging to the late Hugh de Buci—a singular, though not unique instance of this practice in heraldry during the middle ages. After the extinction of the male line of Fyfhide in 1387, the manor belonged for a time to their heritors, the family of Sandys. William, Lord Sandys, in 1542 sold it to William Comber, Esq., whose great-grand-daughter, Elizabeth, married Thomas Gratwicke, Esq., and *his* great-grand-daughter, Anne, wife of Thomas Lintot, Esq., had an only daughter Cassandra, who married Henry Farncombe, Esq., and their only daughter and heiress Cassandra, was wife of John Challen, Esq., father of the late Rev. J. Gratwicke Challen, D.D. The old manor house, which was pulled down about the year 1780, was of quadrangular arrangement, and was replaced by a convenient mansion, which stands in a small deer-park. The Comber family, who possessed the estate for several generations, produced two well-known

---

* For the reparations of Bramber Castle.

personages. Thomas, Dean of Carlisle, and John, Dean of Durham, who both flourished in the 17th century. It was traditional in the family that the first of the Combers killed a Saxon nobleman at the battle of Hastings, and was rewarded by the Conqueror with the manor of Barkham, in Fletching, but the pedigree recorded by the Heralds goes no further back than the reign of Henry VI., and their residence was then at Balcombe, where the name still survives.

Shermanbury contains several other manors :—1. *Morley,* whence, perhaps, our ancient family of that name; 2. *Sakeham,* which in the 13th century gave name to the family of De Sakeham; 3. *Ewhurst,* which extends over a considerable portion of this parish and into Cowfold and Henfield. It was the ancient residence of the Norman family of Peverel, and passed in the same line of descent as Offington to the Lords La Warr. Before thē year 1600 it was acquired by the Pelhams, and passed successively into the ownership of the families of Byne, Heath, and Challen. The old manor-house is destroyed, but the moat, and a most picturesque gateway, said to be of the time of Edward I. (Cartwright), though probably considerably later, still exist. In the reign of Philip and Mary, Thomas West, the opulent Lord La Warr, occasionally resided here, and a document of that period mentions "my Lord's great chamber," a nursery, buttery, kitchen and other apartments. "Abbey Lands" in this parish form the *corpus* of the Prebend of Wyndham in Chichester cathedral.

The church (St. Giles) is a small building, originally in the Early English style, but it has been modernized. It contains tombstones and tablets to the names of Gratwicke, Farncombe, Dr. Bear (rector for more than 50 years), Challen, Lintot, &c. The font, which has been mutilated, is probably of the 13th century. Dr. John Burton, the eminent scholar, and author of the whimisical tour in this county called "Iter Sussexiense," mentions Shermanbury, which he visited in 1751, where his stepfather, Dr. Bear, was rector, and describes it in classical Greek.

[S. A. C. Dr. Burton's visit in Iter Sussexiense, viii, 256. Tithes to Sele Priory, x, 115, 116. Peverel of Ewhurst, x, 125. xvi, 261. Fifhide of, xii, 31. Lillebone, xii, 33. Wood of, xvi, 49. River Adur, xvi, 251. Ewhurst and La Warr *ibid.* Cheale family, xviii, 157. Gratwicke, xviii, 157. Donstall family, xix, 94.]

SHIPLEY.

A large parish of 7,698 acres, six miles south from Horsham; Hundred of West Grinstead; Rape of Bramber. Union, Horsham. Benefice, a perpetual curacy, in the gift of the Hon. Mrs. Vernon Harcourt; Incumbent, Rev. Henry Law Cooper, M.A., of St. John's College,

Cambridge. Population in 1811, 1,011; in 1861, 1,212. *Chief Land-owner*, Sir Percy Burrell, Bart. *Seat*, Knepp Castle, the property of Sir P. Burrell, and occupied by Major John Aldridge. Date of earliest Parish Register, 1609.

This parish consists principally of arable, but there are pasture, woodlands, shaws and furze. The gault produces very fine oak timber, and the wheat is of excellent quality. The principal estate in the parish is Knepp, on which formerly stood Knepp Castle, a fortress of Norman date. In a grant from William the Conqueror to William de Braose, it is styled the " manor and park of *Cnap.*" Of the baronial fortress nothing now remains except a part of the keep. The castle was origi-nally surrounded by a moat. A considerable portion of the out-works remained until the beginning of the present century, when the surveyors of highways demolished it for the mending of parish roads !

The De Braoses, Lords of Bramber, who built the castle, were occasionally resident in it. King John visited it twice on his hurried and hasty journeys through Sussex. The families of Mowbray and Howard were afterwards in possession, but, hav-ing better houses elsewhere, the castle was suffered to go to decay. The estate followed the same line of descent as Bramber.

On the attainder of Thomas, Duke of Norfolk, 38th Henry VIII., the manor and demesne devolved to the Crown, and they were conferred, 1st Edward VI., on Sir Thomas Seymour, on whose attainder, two years later, they were restored to the Duke of Norfolk. In 15th Elizabeth they were again vested in the Crown, and descended by successive purchases to the families of Nye, Caryll, Belchier, Wicker, Ryder and Raymond. On the death of Sir Charles Raymond, Bart., in 1789, they descended to his two coheiresses, one of whom married Sir William Burrell, Bart., whose grandson, Sir Percy Burrell, is now proprietor.

On the estate, half a mile north-west of the ruins of the castle, the late Sir Charles Merrik Burrell built a large mansion in the castellated style, which now forms one of the most convenient residences in Sussex. It contains a very valuable gallery of pictures. Close to it is the largest piece of water in Sussex— Knepp pond, measuring more than 100 acres. It forms a beau-tiful adjunct to the scenery.

Knepp gave name to a family. Paganus de la Knappe ap-pears as a benefactor to Sele or Beeding Priory.

In the southern part of the parish is an estate called Hook-land Park, which belonged to the great estate of the De Braoses. William de Braose obtained a charter of free-warren for it, when it was called Hoke la Stoke. *Temp.* Charles I., it belonged to the Henshaws, from whom it descended to Bartholomew

Tipping, Esq. By Mary-Anne, his niece, wife of the Rev. Philip Wroughton, it was sold to Philip Rickman, Esq. It is an extinct manor. Garingle, or Goringlythe, belonged successively to Le Sauvage, Nevill, Lucy, Caryll, and Peachey. Bentons, formerly called Tavernershall, belonged in 1359 to Thomas de Bayntune, whence the modern name. From the Bayntons, or Bentons, it passed in the lapse of time to the Carylls. In the early part of the eighteenth century, it was purchased by Edward Tredcroft, Esq., of Horsham. The manor of Pinkhurst extends into the parishes of Slinfold and Billingshurst. The Earls of Arundel were possessors in the fourteenth century, and it was granted in 1399 to John, Duke of Exeter, but in 1400 was restored to the Earl of Arundel, and continued with his descendants until 1576, when it was aliened to John Apsley of Thakeham. It now belongs to the Norfolk family.

During the time that the principal part of the parish was in the hands of the Carylls, Philip Caryll, Esq., built on an elevated site a house called "New Building." It consisted of many rooms, and in a closet belonging to the garret there was a cupboard with two shelves, which served for steps. This was one of the many "hiding places" for Romish priests. This functionary could ascend through a false top of the cupboard to a place of concealment. A chapel attached to the building was commenced, but never finished. The Carylls were the leading Roman Catholics in Sussex at the time. Durrants is another extinct manor, which was long the property of the Michell family. There is a tradition that, during the civil wars, some members of this family headed an attack on Knepp Castle, then garrisoned by the Parliamentary forces, but there are no documents relating to this siege.

The church (probably St. Mary), which was formerly served by a "conductitius" or removeable curate, consists of a single pace or nave with a tower, surmounted by a pyramidal shingled spire, between the nave and chancel. The length is 114 feet. The tower arches are semi-circular. The one opening into the nave is elaborately ornamented. The edifice dates from the beginning of the twelfth century, when it was appropriated to the Knights-Templars; but many later insertions have been made. The ceiling is of oak, flat, and divided into compartments, which have been painted alternately azure and gules with gilt knots and mouldings. On the former there were, in 1830, some armorial bearings including the Maltravers fret and the coat of Lucy. On the south side of the chancel is a splendid but dilapidated monument of marble, representing a recumbent knight in armour, and, below, the kneeling effigies of his children. This is for Sir Thomas Caryll, of Bentons, who died in 1616. There are other old memorials for the names of Michell, Hindley, Harmes, &c. In the church chest is a wooden reliquary of great interest and value. It is seven inches long and six high, and is gilt and enamelled on the sides and ends, with the subject of the Crucifixion and with angels. It is probably of Byzantine workmanship, and apparently of the 12th or 13th century.

On the north side of the church there was formerly an echo, which, in a still night, repeated the 21 syllables :—

> " Os homini sublime dedit cœlumque tueri,
> Jussit et erectos."

But, alas! as at Bodiam, the responsive nymph has become shy, and no longer favours us by flinging back our words into our teeth.

[S. A. C. Ironworks, ii, 217. Knepp Castle, iii, 1. v, 143. xvi, 245. xviii, 146. Visit of King John, i, 134, and Edward II., vi, 48. Knights Templars, ix, 246. Reliquary, ix, 264. Papal arrests, ix, 265. Godfrey de Strete given to Sele, x, 118. Church, xii, 108. Wellers of, xii, 108. xiii, 124. Bells, xvi, 223. Mowbrays of, xvi, 245. River Adur, xvi, 249. Knepp Pond, xvi, 249. Cade's insurrection, xviii, 24. British gold coin, xviii, 69.]

SHULBRED PRIORY.

This small monastic foundation was in the parish of Linchmere, on the north-west confines of the county, near Midhurst. It was founded by Sir Ralph de Arderne, before the reign of Henry III. for five Augustinian canons. Its history possesses little of interest. At the dissolution of the monasteries it was granted first to Sir William FitzWilliam, and afterwards to Sir Anthony Browne. Some remains of the Priory still exist in a farm house, with medieval features. There is a room of considerable size, known as the Prior's chamber, which is reached by a stone staircase. This apartment retains some mural paintings, about which a great deal has been said in topographical works, as if they belonged to pre-Reformation times. This, however, I am sure is not the case. They clearly belong to about the beginning of the 17th century, and are quite in the taste of that quaint period. They are nearly obliterated, but still possess considerable interest. The principal painting has reference to the birth of Jesus Christ, and certain animals converse on that great event. The interlocutors are first a cock, which has a label issuing from his mouth, and the words *Christus natus est.* Then a duck says, *Quando, quando?* A raven replies, *In hac nocte.* A cow bellows out, *Ubi, ubi,* and a lamb answers *Bethlam.* The arms and motto of James I. sufficiently fix the date of this curious paint-work. The living of Linchmere was formerly in the patronage of this small priory, the remains of which occupy a low and sequestered dell, and are only approached with difficulty, especially, *me teste*, during the mud of winter.

OLD SHOREHAM.

Domesday, *Soresham;* a parish in the Hundred of Fishersgate; Rape of Bramber, adjacent to New Shoreham, its Post-town and Railway station. Population in 1811, 210; in 1861, 282. Date of earliest Parish Register, 1566. It is a vicarage valued at £458, in the gift of Magdalen College, Oxford; Incumbent, Rev. Jas. Bowling Mozley, B.D.

The parish consists partly of low meadow or brook-land on the left bank of the Adur, and partly of arable and down. Before the Conquest it was held by the great proprietor, Azor, of the King. It was then rated at 12 hides. After that time it was assessed at 5¾ hides only, and had a church, 26 villeins, 49 bondmen, and a wood yielding sustenance for 40 hogs. At a later date it became parcel of the Duchy of Cornwall, and was purchased of the Crown by Charles, Duke of Norfolk. Another manor of Old Shoreham, *alias* Ruspar, belonged successively to the families of Arundel (Fitz-Alan), Cobham, Bowyer, Boorde, Gage, Blaker, Monk, Elliston, Elliot, and Bridger, the last-named family being possessors of the estate of Buckingham, with its handsome mansion. This estate gave name to the family of De Bokyngham. The manors of Erringham-Walsted and Erringham-Braose are now united. The latter belonged in early times successively to the families of De Wistoneston, De Harcourt, Bavent, Braose, Shirley, Bellingham, Juxon, and Tufton. In 1774 it passed to the Bridger family, now proprietors of almost the whole parish. The Bellinghams were an old Northumberland family (whose descendants are still resident in Sussex), and were proprietors till 1650. An ancient ferry over the Adur belonged to the Priory of Hardham. This was superseded in the last century by a wooden bridge, 500 feet long, and since then the Norfolk bridge, and the railway bridge, lower down the Adur, have altogether outdone the once-famed Shoreham bridge.

The cruciform church (St. Nicholas) is in the Norman style, and has within the last few years been repaired and refitted. Mr. Hussey says of it: " It is remarkable for the small number of windows, and the consequent darkness of the nave; as also for possessing on the tie-beams of the chancel the tooth-moulding, which is rarely found carved in wood." The interior arches are highly ornamented. Among the memorials of the dead we find the names of Monk, Poole, Fowler, Elgar, O'Hara, &c.

[S. A. C. Pensions to Beeding Priory, x, 115. Calceto had lands in, xi, 102. Church, xii, 109; xvi, 236. Bell, xvi, 224. Adur at, xvi, 254. Avery of, xix, 201.]

NEW SHOREHAM.

A borough, town, and parish in the Rape of Bramber; distant about six miles west from Brighton. It is a Post-town, and has a Railway station. Union, Steyning. Population in 1811, 770; in 1861, 3,351, and now upwards of 4,000. Benefice, a Vicarage, in the gift of Magdalen College, Oxford. Incumbent, Rev. Harris Smith, D.D., of Oriel College, Oxford. Date of earliest Parish Register, 1568.

This parish of 170 acres is the smallest in the Rape of Bramber, though both its present population and its former historical importance place it in a good rank among Sussex towns. Shoreham has undergone the vicissitudes common to every seaport on our southern coast. On the decay of Old Shoreham, consequent on the decline of the port which once existed there, this town sprang into existence, and was dismembered from its mother parish. It was the port of the river Adur, and had more maritime commerce than any town in Sussex. The river now debouches at Kingston-Bowsey, a considerable distance eastward of the town. The harbour is convenient, and much trade is carried on. But by the encroachments of the sea in and before the year 1432 its population was reduced to 500, and the inhabitants were in a state of great poverty. The manor, which is coextensive with the parish, belonged to the De Braoses, lords of Bramber, and followed the same line of descent as that barony. In 1326 a house of Carmelite Friars was founded here by John de Mowbray. There is little history connected with this establishment, and it shared the common fate under Henry VIII. There were also two hospitals dedicated respectively to St. James, and Our Saviour Jesus Christ.

The borough of New Shoreham returned two members to Parliament from 23rd Edward I.; but in the year 1770, a circumstance occurred which changed the character of the borough. A society calling themselves the Christian Club, nominally formed for charitable purposes, but actually for the sale of the representation, became the subject of Parliamentary investigation. The result was that in 11th George III. the borough was disfranchised, and the right of election was extended to all 40s. freeholders in the Rape of Bramber. Eighty-one of the club were ousted, but the rest and their successors retained their votes. In the reign of Edward III. the port of Shoreham furnished forth towards the royal fleet before Calais 26 ships and 329 mariners.

The church (St. Mary) was, as originally built, a fine cruciform structure, 210 feet in length; but nearly the whole of the nave fell to decay. An effort, however, has been made to restore it, and the rest of the edifice, at a cost of £10,000. The nave, tower, and transepts are Norman, but the capitals on the north and south sides of the tower indicate a difference of date. The rich choir end is later, and disproportionately long with reference to the west limb of the cross (Hussey). The church is one of the most beautiful and interesting in the county, as well as one of the largest. It is externally and internally most grand and picturesque. For architectural details I must refer the reader to Cartwright's "Rape of Bramber," p. 57. The tower contains five bells. The monumental remains are of little interest. The only medieval one is a brass representing a civilian and his wife in the costume of the time of Henry VI., without any inscription. The names commemorated by the others are West, Shirley, Aldersey, Forth, Bulford, Smith, Chapman, Rudhall, Hooper, Kilvington, Reynolds, &c. The election of members for the borough was formerly held in the north transept of the church!

Both this church of St. Mary and that of St. Nicholas, Old Shoreham, were given by William de Braose, the first Lord of Bramber, to the French Abbey of Saumur. They were both probably built by the great baronial family of Braose, assisted by the opulent merchants of the port.*

Shoreham in early times received several royal visits. In 1199 King John, immediately after the death of Cœur-de-Lion, landed at this port, which was then a great *entrepôt* of continental corn and wine. He was accompanied by a considerable army. In the same year he embarked here for the purpose of holding a conference with the King of France. The place then possessed an arsenal, and was equally important as to shipping with the port of Plymouth, and superior to those of Bristol, Dover, and London. In 1305 Edward I. was here on one of his southern journeys. In the reign of Henry VIII. the town suffered much from the predatory inroads of the French. In the great storm of 1703, Shoreham was severely visited. The market-house, a strong and ancient building, was blown down, and all the town shattered.

---

* It is, perhaps, not correct to say that the churches were given by De Braose to the Abbey of Saumur, because neither of them was erected so early as 1075; but the ecclesiastical rights of Shoreham were certainly granted to that establishment, and afterwards transferred to the Priory of Sele, now Beeding

Shoreham is not prepossessing in appearance. Its chief ornament, besides the church, is the fine suspension bridge crossing the Adur, which was built in 1833 at the expense of the Duke of Norfolk, and has been of material advantage to the town. The principal trade carried on is that of ship-building, and the maritime commerce includes relations with many countries. The movement of what are called "high church principles," has one of its chief centres in the town, and there are two educational establishments known as St. Saviour's and St. Mary's, for the sons of the "lower middle class." A full history of this ancient town is a desideratum in Sussex topography.

The escape of Charles II., after his circuitous route from Worcester fight is said to have been from this place, "sed dubito." I believe that the royal fugitive took flight from a spot between Brighton and Shoreham.

[S. A. C. Embarkation of the Duke of Ormond, v, 89. Dr. Burton on the political bribery here, viii, 264. Wool-smuggling, x, 69. Church, x, 102, 115; xii, 109; xvi, 234. Carmelite Friars, x, 109; xv, 22. Blakers of, x, 109. Battery, xi, 151. "Atlas Maritimus" report, xi, 181. Market house, xii, 55. The two hospitals, xiii, 52. Bells, xvi, 223. Church-notes (*Bloxam*). Royal Arsenal, xvi, 223. River Adur, xvi, 233. Sea-encroachments, xvi, 234. Suspension bridge, xvi, 254. Horse-shoes sent to Newcastle, xvii, 117. Road to London, xix, 155, 163. Mention of, xix, 164. Venetian ships' charts, xx, 225.]

SIDLESHAM.

Domesday, *Silleicham*; a parish in the Hundred of Manhood; Rape of Chichester; distant five miles from Chichester, its Post-town and Railway station. Union, West Hampnett. Population in 1811, 865; in 1861, 960. Benefice, a Vicarage, valued at £182; Patron, the Bishop of Chichester; Incumbent, Rev. William Bruton. B.A., of Exeter College, Oxford. Date of earliest Parish Register, 1566. Acreage, 4,109.

This seaboard parish, chiefly arable, with a little pasture and woodland, has a considerable village near its north-east boundary. The manor was conferred by the Saxon monarch Ceadwalla on Wilfred, as a portion of his gift to the see of Selsey, and this grant was confirmed by William the Conqueror to that see. It was rated at 12 hides, and there were 16 villeins with 14 bondmen. There were under tenants, named Gilbert, Rozelin, and Ulph. The value before and after the Conquest was £10, and the homagers paid 65s. The manor vested in the Bishops of Chichester, till they were deprived by the act of 2nd Elizabeth. Montague, then Bishop, complained loudly, but vainly, of this act of spoliation. George Stoughton, one of the Commissioners under that act, bought, it was averred, for £300 what was worth £300 per annum. The property subsequently passed to the names and families of Compton, Farrington, Bull, Johnson, Price, &c. The prebend of Sidlesham is in Chichester cathedral, and possesses a farm here and in Earnley, and it has undergone many changes of ownership. The prebend of Highley, which belongs to the master of the Prebendal Grammar School at Chichester, founded by Bishop Storey, long possessed a large portion of the great tithes of Sidlesham. Okehurst, an estate in the south part of the parish, formerly gave name to a family, one of whom founded a chantry in Chichester cathedral in the year 1287. There are in the parish two reputed manors, called Hammes and Keynor, of no historical interest so far as I have been able to discover. The Sidlesham tide-mills, the only ones in Sussex, except those at Bishopston, in the eastern division of the county, are supplied by the estuary of Pagham Harbour. They were erected by a merchant of Chichester, Mr. Woodroffe Drinkwater. The estuary affords considerable shipping facilities for vessels of small burden. This parish has suffered greatly (like many neighbour parishes) from the incursions of the sea; as many as 2,700 acres are said to have been "devastated," though probably not permanently submerged, before the year 1341. This we learn from the Nonæ Rolls.

The church (St. Mary) is a very picturesque building in the Early English style, with an embattled tower of later date. In the building is a carved chest of considerable antiquity, which is figured in Horsfield's "Sussex." Near the chancel is a mural monument with two kneeling figures, for George Taylor and his wife Rebecca, daughter of John Bennet, of London, Esq., 1631. There are two bells, one of which is inscribed, in Lombardic characters, to St. James.

There seems to have been a chapel, called Easton or Eston, connected with Sidlesham, but Mr. Gibbon, in his elaborate account of West Sussex churches and chapels, cannot discover its *locus in quo*. In several wills of the sixteenth century *Eston* is called a *parish*, and offerings of sheep and cows were bequeathed. It would be interesting to ascertain the site of this defunct chapel. A parish, I think, could never have existed *eo nomine*.

[S. A. C. Church, xii, 77. Eston chapel, *ibid*. Bonville, lands of, xv, 59. Church bells, xvi, 224. Tide-mills, xvi, 260. Bishop Henshawe, lands in, xix, 107.]

SIDLEY GREEN.   A hamlet of Bexhill.

163

SINGLETON.

Domesday, *Silletone;* a parish in the Hundred of Westbourne ; Rape of Chichester ; distant six miles north-east from Chichester, its Post-town and Railway station. Union, West Hampnett. Population in 1811, 275 ; in 1861, 556. Benefice, a Rectory, valued at £115 ; Patron, Duke of Richmond; Incumbent, Rev. F. A. Bowles, M.A., of Magdalen Hall, Oxford. Date of earliest Parish Register, 1664. Acreage, 5,010. *Chief Landowners,* The Duke of Richmond, Lord Leconfield, and the Hon. Mrs. Vernon Harcourt. *Seat,* Molecombe House, H. S. H. Prince Edward of Saxe Weimar.

This pleasant and picturesque village is situated in a valley of the South Downs, about midway between Chichester and Mid-hurst. *Charlton* (which see) is a hamlet in the parish. The population of Singleton, which is very small, considering the area of the parish, is gradually decreasing. In Domesday Book Silletone is mentioned as having been the property of Earl God-win, and was estimated at £89. Afterwards it passed, with the Rape of Chichester, to the Earl of Montgomeri, and was valued at £93, and a mark of gold. Upon the division of the Fitz-Alan estates, John, Lord Lumley became possessor. By an act 31st George II., Charlton Forest was granted by the Crown to the Duke of Richmond, and in his family it still vests. Drove House, the property of Lord Leconfield, is occupied by the Hon. R. Denman, and Molecombe House, the property of the Duke of Richmond, is the mansion of Prince Edward of Saxe-Weimar. The Goodwood race-stand is in Singleton. During the week of those celebrated races nearly one hundred race-horses are stabled in the parish, and the lovers of the turf get accommodation in the neighbouring cottages. Rooks Hill, which is said to have derived its name from St. Roche, is upwards of 700 feet above the level of the sea. It commands one of the most magnificent views in Sussex, including the coast from Beachy Head to Ports-mouth, and a grand expanse of inland scenery. On this hill are ancient earthworks called the Trundle, probably of early British date. During the civil wars of the 17th century, a thousand men called the club men, from the Parliamentary side, having furnished their friends with clubs, occupied this hill, and are said to have been guilty of " divers outrageous proceedings." Dounley Castle, in this parish, no longer in existence, was a hunting seat belonging to the Earls of Arundel, in the 15th and 16th centuries.

The church (St. John the Evangelist) consists of tower, nave, aisles, and chancel. The tower is early Norman. A portion of the building is said to have been burnt down in the 14th century, and the present architecture is early Perpendicular work. It is very symmetrical, and forms a perfect specimen of a modest village church. There are two bells. Of *Charlton Forest* and hunt, see *Charlton.*

[S. A. C. Rising of clubmen, v, 85. Church of, xii, 77. xix, 103. Bells of, xvi, 224. Curious implement found at, xvi, 300. Drove House, xvi, 300. Downley Castle, xvi, 300. xix, 102. Medal found at, xvi, 301. Lavant river at, xvi, 261. Charles II. flight, xviii, 115. Collicks of, xix, 94. Manor belonged to Lord Lumley, xix, 102. Patronage belonged to Lord Lumley, xix, 103. London road to Chichester, xix, 167.]

SLAUGHAM.

Pronounced *Slaffham*; a parish in the Hundred of Buttinghill; Rape of Lewes; distant five miles from Cuckfield and six from Horsham. Post-town and Union, Cuckfield. Railway stations, Horsham and Haywards Heath. Population in 1811, 759 ; in 1861, 1518. Benefice, a Rectory, valued at £460; Patron in 1866, Warden Sergison, Esq. ; Incumbent, Rev. William Sergison, M.A., of Brazenose College, Oxford. Date of earliest Parish Register, 1655. Acreage, 5,363. *Seats*, Slaugham Park, Dencombe, J. Manship Norman, Esq.; High Beeches, Robert Loder, Esq; Ashfold, William Peters, Esq.; Woodside, Ph. Rawson, Esq.; Colwood, Rev. J. Oliver Haweis ; Hyde, Edward Smith Bigg, Esq.; The Hall, Edward Stanford, Esq., &c., &c. The parish abounds with excellent residences.

This Wealden parish contains the four scattered hamlets of Slaugham proper, Handcross, Warninglid, and Pease-pottage— all names of uncertain etymology, except the second, which shows the former existence of a medieval direction-cross, with a hand affixed to point out the principal road. The parish, though somewhat sterile, is undulating and picturesque, and well suited for country houses and villas. A tributary of the Ouse—or perhaps the Ouse itself—rises at Upper Beeding, close by, and here, at Slaugham mill, expands into a lake of 25 acres. This place is not mentioned *eo nomine* in Domesday, and it was probably at that period unreclaimed from the great forest tract. Early in the reign of Edward III., however, it was useful as hunting-ground, as is proved by the fact that Thomas, Lord Poynings had a charter of free-warren here. At his death, in the memorable sea-fight at Sluys, the manor and advowson descended to his son Michael, who accompanied the king in his Continental wars, and was buried at Poynings, where, and at this place, masses were annually said for his soul, as they also were for his son and successor, Thomas, Lord Poynings. At subsequent dates the noble families of Berkeley and Stanley became in succession lords. In the latter part of the fifteenth century the grand old family of Covert, of Norman descent, became owners, and so continued until 1679, when Sir John Covert, Bart., dying without male issue, the estate became a portion of the inheritance of his elder coheiress Anne, who married Sir James Morton. Subsequently it passed from the Morton family to that of Sergison, in whom it now vests.

The Coverts were among the greatest landed proprietors in the South of England, and tradition says that they might travel over their own manors from Southwark to the English Channel. Before becoming possessed of Slaugham they were lords of Sullington, and previously, *temp.* Henry II., of Chaldon in Surrey. In 1494 William Covert, Esq., probably the original settler here, bequeathed 40s. to the repairs of the church where he desired to be buried, and to have a "vertuous priest" (Dr., M.A., or B.A.) to sing for his soul at the yearly stipend of £8. Several later members of the family were buried in the church. Of the earliest residence of the Coverts and their predecessors nothing is known. The now existing remains of the manor-house are doubtless part of what was originally one of the finest mansions in Sussex. The site is low and damp, and quite unworthy of an almost palatial abode. Sir Walter Covert, of Maidstone, who married his cousin Covert, the heiress of Slaugham, was probably the builder; but, like many other Sussex mansions of that period, it seems to have been erected only to fall to almost immediate neglect and decay. The remains are, however, "sublime in ruin," with lofty arcades and splendid heraldric decorations. Of these Mr. Blaauw has given very accurate descriptions and views in the "Sussex Collections," Vol. x. The dimensions, 175 feet by 133, give an idea of its great size, but its ambit was far larger, with a square stone wall, turrets, and a moat—the latter no longer existing. A large sheet of water, close by, was, however, connected with it. The style of the house was a rich and graceful Palladian. The interior court measured 80 feet; the great hall was 54 feet long, and the kitchen 35 feet, with a great fire-place 13 feet wide. It is sad to look upon the ruins of this fine old mansion, though great pains have been taken to preserve what time and mercenary spoliation have left us. The great staircase, of the Jacobean period, much resembling (though better than) that at the Charterhouse in London, is now to be seen at the Star Hotel at Lewes, the re-builder of which, Mr. Ade, rescued it in the last century from destruction. It is most elaborate in ornamentation, and has several allegorical carvings. The house originally had a private chapel, and was surrounded by a park. According to tradition the domestic establishment numbered 70 persons.

The benefice is styled in the Liber Regis, "Slougham cum Crolé," which would indicate that the neighbouring church of

Crawley was formerly a chapel dependent on it. The church
(St. Mary) is chiefly in the Decorated style, with traces of earlier
work. It consists of an excellent vaulted nave, south aisle,
tower, and two chancels. The northern chancel or chapel was
built by the desire of Michael de Poynings, whose will is dated
1368, at a cost of £40. It had an altar dedicated to St. James.
The tower is low, and contains five bells, dated 1773. There
are several interesting memorials of the Covert and other families. A full length brass commemorates 𝕵𝖔𝖍𝖓 𝕮𝖔𝖇𝖊𝖗𝖙, Esq., son
of William Covert, 1503 ; and another, Jane Covert, who
survived two knightly husbands, and died in 1586. A monument in the chancel is for Richard Covert, Esq., who,
together with his two wives, and a numerous progeny by the
first marriage, are represented in effigy—date 1579. The most
remarkable monument is for Richard Covert, who married four
times, and who is represented with three of his *conjuges*, with
curious allegorical adornments, and labels in brass—date 1547.
There are later memorials for the names of Evans, Matcham,*
Ellison, &c. During the progress of alterations in this church
some years since, several mural paintings were discovered. They
represented the Flagellation, Crucifixion, and the Last Supper of
Our Lord, together with the conveyance of a soul to heaven by
angels.

[S. A. C. Ironworks, ii, 217. iii, 242. Covert family, v, 49. x, 158.
xiii, 310. xvi, 33. xviii, 158. xix, 94. Manor-house, x, 158. Poynings
family, xii, 34. xv, 7. Church, xii, 108. xv, 22. Mural paintings *(Campion)*, xiii, 237. Michell and Burstowe, xvi, 49. Church bells, xvi, 224.]

SLINDON.

Domesday, *Eslindone ;* a parish in the Hundred of Aldwick; Rape of Chichester ; distant three miles north-west from Arundel, its Post-town.
Railway stations, Arundel and Barkham lane. Union, West Hampnett.
Population in 1811, 437; in 1861, 543. Benefice a Rectory, valued at
£219 ; Patron, William Joshua Tilley, Esq.; Incumbent, Rev. William Chantler Izard, M.A., of Christ Church College, Cambridge. Date
of earliest Parish Register, 1558. Acreage, 2,504. *Chief Landowner,*
Colonel Leslie, of Slindon House.

" Eslindone " was held at the date of Domesday by Earl
Roger de Montgomeri. It was granted by Henry I. to Anselm,
Archbishop of Canterbury. In 1543, Henry VIII. exchanged
it with Cranmer. *Temp.* Mary it was granted to Anthony
Kempe, Esq., of the great family of that name at Ollantigh

---

* Francis Griffith Matcham, who died at Ashfold Lodge, 1808, æt. 12, was a nephew
of Admiral Lord Nelson.

in Kent, whose descendant in the fifth generation, Barbara Kempe, became heiress, and married James Bartholomew Radcliffe, Earl of Newburgh. His son, Anthony James, Earl of Newburgh, died without issue in 1814, and Slyndon ultimately passed to his cousin and heiress Dorothy Eyre, Countess Newburgh, who married Colonel Leslie, K.H., and so conveyed it to him, and he now possesses it. Slindon House is presumed by Dallaway to have been originally built by one of the Archbishops, in the thirteenth century, and the celebrated primate Stephen Langton died here in 1228. After its acquisition by the Kempes, Sir Garret Kempe, early in the reign of Elizabeth, rebuilt the mansion, which has been altered and added to at various periods. It is delightfully situated on an elevation in a richly wooded park, and commands a sea-view from Worthing to the Isle of Wight. The Slindon beeches have a wide renown. The great hall is rich in the armorial ensigns of the Kempes and their family connections. The Roman Catholic chapel has a good picture of the Taking-down from the Cross, and among the fine works of art with which the house is adorned, is the celebrated painting of the Beggar of Antwerp. This is one of the few places in Sussex in which the cultus of the Roman church has been preserved with little interruption from the days of the Reformation. A new Roman Catholic church was erected in 1865, the Rev. John Sheehan being priest.

The parish church (Our Lady) is small, consisting of nave, north and south aisles and chancel, in the Early English style. In a recessed tomb in the chancel is a knightly effigy in wood, supposed to be for Sir Anthony Kempe, the grantee of Slindon in the sixteenth century, but quite as likely to be that of Anthony St. Leger, whose will, dated 1539, directs burial here. There are other memorials of the Kempes, &c.* (Horsfield). At the entrance to the church-yard there stood, within memory, a chapel of St. Mary, with one lancet window. The parish and its associations deserve far more notice than they have received from local historians.

[S. A. C. Palace of the Archbishops, v. 138. xvii, 121. King Edward I. visits Slindon, ii, 153 (swans and peacocks were part of the royal bill of fare). Families of Hyllys, Pynham, Wyatt, St. Leger, Kempe, with notes on Church, xii, 98, 99. Wyatt, xiii, 303. Allen's charity, xvi, 41. Bells, xvi, 224. Boniface de Slyndon, xvii, 144. Slindon, xviii, 95. Newlands of, xix, 116. Cox, minister of, and Whittingtons of, xix, 120. Canterbury, Archbishops of, xix, 126. Pagham, xix, 126. Newburghs and Leslies, xix, 126. Thomas à Becket at, xix, 128.

* During a recent restoration, the foundations of the church as built by Archbishop Anselm were discovered. It appears originally to have had transepts. Traces of very early Norman work were discovered.

SLINFOLD.

A parish in the Hundred of West Easwrith; Rape of Arundel; distant four miles west from Horsham, its Post-town. Railway station, Horsham ; distant about four miles. Union, Horsham. Population in 1811, 549; in 1861, 755. Benefice, a Rectory and Vicarage united, valued at £472. Patron, the Bishop of Chichester; Incumbent, Rev. Robert Sutton, M.A., of Exeter College, Oxford. Date of earliest Parish Register, 1558. Acreage, 4,330. *Chief Landowners*, The Duke of Norfolk, Captain Bunny, N. P. Simes, Esq., Sir P. F. Shelley, Bart., and Thomas Child, Esq. *Seats*, Strood Park, N. P. Simes, Esq.; the Lodge, Captain Bunny; Windalls, Thomas Child, Esq., &c.

This Wealden parish lies on the Roman road called Stane street, which, passing from Chichester to London, intersects it for the space of more than two miles. The material called Horsham-stone abounds in the north-east part of the parish. The principal manor, Dedisham, is divided between Slinfold and Rudgwick. It belonged to the family of Tregoz from 1271 to the extinction of that family, and in 1530 it was in the hands of their heirs-general, the Lewknors. In 1547, Edward VI. granted it to Sir Richard Blount, Lieutenant of the Tower, from whose descendants it passed about 1630 to the family of Onslow. In 1786, J. Williams Onslow, Esq., sold it to Charles, Duke of Norfolk, and it now forms parcel of the hereditary estates. The great park has been converted into farms, and the ancient manor house, after having been ransacked by Sir William Waller's soldiers in 1643, fell to decay, though a few of the offices remain as a farm-house. The manor of Drungewick lies partly in this parish, and is called Bradbridge. The family of De Bradbridge held it hereditarily from the Bishops of Chichester from 1355 to 1517, when Sir Henry Hussey obtained it by marriage with Eleanor, sole daughter and heiress. The seat was called Town House. George Hussey of this family is supposed to have aliened his right about 1666, and the lands form part of the settled estates of the Duke of Norfolk. Strood belonged in succesion to Atte Strode and Stanbridge. In 1466, John Cowper, Esq., lineal ancestor of the Earl Cowper, and of the poet, acquired it in marriage with the heiress of Stanbridge. The representative of the Slinfold Cowpers sold the estate to John William Commerell, Esq., who was sheriff of Sussex in 1803. "A great part of the ancient residence of the Cowpers still remains, to which considerable additions have been made by the present proprietor." Dallaway (1832). It is now the elegant mansion of Nathaniel P. Simes, Esq.

Hill, so called from its situation on an insulated mount in the centre of the parish, belonged to the Husseys, by whom it was aliened, *temp.* James I., to Thomas Churchar, whose father was of Chiddingly, in 1570.

The church (St. Peter) was built by Bishop Ralph II., of Chichester, about 1230. It had until recently a nave and north aisle, with a small sepulchral chapel belonging to the manor of Dedisham, and a massive tower with shingled spire. The last "was supported by four upright beams, of a length and diameter very seldom seen." (Dallaway.) In 1779, repairs were made which concealed the ancient features. In 1861, the church was rebuilt in the Early Decorated style from designs by Mr. B. Ferrey, at a cost of nearly £4,000. Dallaway mentions among the memorials a slab for Richard Bradbryge, gent. and his family, 1533; another supposed for Ralph Cowper, of Strood; the helmet and crest of Sir Henry Hussey, 1557; two mural monuments of alabaster, with painted figures for Mary, wife of Richard Blount, and daughter of Sir William West, Lord La Warr, and her daughter, Katherine, 1617, and Jane Blount, another daughter, 1621; Edward Cowper, of Strood, 1678; and his son Henry Cowper, 1706; and grandson Edward Cowper, 1725; with other memorials for Leland, Lowe, Jones, &c. In the Dedisham chapel is the carved figure of a lady, supposed of the Tregoz family. Matthew Woodman, grandson of Richard Woodman, the Protestant martyr burnt at Lewes in 1557, was ejected from this rectory in 1662 for nonconformity.

[S. A. C. Ironworks, ii, 217. King Edward II. visits the Lelands, vi, 47. Roman remains, road, &c., xi, 145. Church, xii, 108. Mose of, xii, 108. Churchar family, xiv, 233. Cowper or Cooper, xii, 109; xvi, 35, 50. Parish charity lost, xvi, 37. Theoneden and Hill, xvi, 50. Bells, xvi, 224. Adur, xvi, 249. Arun, xvi, 256. Evershed family, xvii, 247. Slinfold, xviii, 107. Dedisham, xviii, 173. xix, 158. Blounts of, *ibid.* Mone (Moon) of, xviii, 173. Warton, poet and historian, xix, 162.]

SOMPTING.

Domesday, *Sultinges;* vulgo, *Sounting;* a parish in the Hundred of Brightford; Rape of Bramber; distant three miles north-east from Worthing, its Post-town. Railway station, Lancing, distant about one mile. Union, Steyning. Population in 1811, 441; in 1861, 682. Benefice, a Vicarage, valued at £199; Patron, Henry Crofts, Esq.; Incumbent, Rev. John Blake Honnywill, B.A., of St. John's College, Cambridge. Date of earliest Parish Register, 1546. Acreage, 2,930. *Seat,* Sompting Abbots, Henry Crofts, Esq.

This parish contains about 1,000 acres of down, the rest being fertile arable land, sloping towards the south. At the date of the Domesday survey there were 19 villeins, and 16 bondmen, a church, 5 servi, a mill, and 8 salt-pans. A knight held one hide, two villeins, four bondmen, and a salt-pan. In the time of the Confessor it was estimated at £8, and afterwards at £7 8s. Lewin held lands of King Edward. The particulars of this manor are circumstantially given in the record. At present the principal manors are Sompting-Peverell *alias* Welda, Sompting-Abbots, and Lechepool. The manor of Sompting-Peverell extends into the parishes of West Grinstead, Horsham, and Rusper, in the weald, whence the *alias* Welda. It continued in the family of Peverell for several generations until about the end of the 14th century, when it was carried by co-heiresses to the families of West and Brocas. From the Wests, Lords De la Warr, it passed by subsequent purchases to the families of Pelham, Langworth, Morley, and Peachey. Sompting-Abbots belonged in early times to the Abbey of Fécamp, in Normandy, whose monks held a capital messuage and revenues; hence the name Sompting-Abbots. The house has been rebuilt within the last few years in the medieval style, and is now one of the most elegant mansions of the district. On the dissolution of the alien priories it was conferred on the Abbey of Sion in Middlesex, and on the surrender of that religious house it was valued at £17 6s. 9d. Soon after this surrender it was granted to Thomas, Duke of Norfolk; but on his attainder in 1547 it reverted to the Crown. It afterwards returned to the Howard family. Thomas, Earl of Arundel, sold it, in 1641, to Sir Edmund Pye, and afterwards, by successive alienations, it passed to the family of Alderton, and then to that of Crofts, the present possessors. The manors of Sompting-Peverell and Sompting-Abbots are much mixed up together.

Lechepool gave name to a family in the 14th century. The lands were acquired by Richard, Earl of Arundel, who conferred them on his alms-house at Arundel. At the Dissolution the estate was granted to Sir Richard Lee, and we afterwards find it in the hands of the families of Cooper, Moore, and Stanyoake. It is now the property of the family of Crofts, and passes with Sompting-Abbots.

Cokeham is a hamlet in this parish (See that article).

The impropriation of Sompting was granted between the years 1146 and 1173 to the brethren of the Temple of Solomon. On the suppression of the Knights Templars, in 1306, Sir Andrew Peverell resumed it, and conferred it on the Knights of St. John of Jerusalem, who held it until the Dissolution. At an earlier period the ecclesiastical property was known as "The Temple," and gave the name of "At Temple" to its tenants.

The church of this parish is decidedly the most interesting village church in the diocese. It has many peculiar features,

which have been so repeatedly figured and described that no detailed account is necessary here; suffice it to say that it was built
about the year 1150. The nave, chancel, and transepts remain,
though some parts of the whole building as constructed in the
pre-Norman times are in ruins. There are several rude sculptures of very early date in the chancel; but perhaps the most
curious relic in the building is an arched tomb, of which I gave
an account, originally in the "Herald and Genealogist," and
more recently in the "Sussex Archæological Collections." The
particulars are so curious that I venture on some self-quotation:—

"My first visit to this church took place under the guidance of Dr.
Davey, of Worthing, whose researches into the monastic history of the
county of Suffolk are well known. After inspecting the tower and other
remarkable features, I observed in the north wall of the chancel a monument in the style of the so-called "Easter Sepulchre," or "Founders'
Tomb," but apparently not earlier in date than the former part of the
16th century. There was no inscription to guide me to the knowledge
of the person interred beneath, and on interrogating my friend and
cicerone upon this point, I received the curt and unsatisfactory reply,
'Nobody knows!' This I afterwards found to be the case, for the his-
tories of Cartwright and Horsfield and the Handbook of Murray, all
yielded a response equally unsatisfactory. 'Well,' said I, 'there are
some shields upon the tomb; let us see whether Heraldry will not help
us to an identification.' Accordingly I took out my note-book and made
some memoranda, which I subjoin . . . . The workmanship of the
tomb is very poor, the stone bad, and the heraldric sculpture evidently the
work of an unskilled artisan, probably the village mason; added to which
it has until recently been coated with profuse layers of whitewash, in the
removal of which the work may have suffered accidental mutilation. The
armorial coats appear to be as follows:—
"Under the canopy an Angel supporting a shield impaled . . . . the
dexter coat three pairs of keys in saltire, on a chief three dolphins; the
sinister two bars, in chief a lion passant. On the face of the tomb 3
shields, 1, quarterly: 1 and 4, 3 bucks trippant; 2 and 3, 2 bars and a
lion-passant as above; 2, quarterly: 1 and 4, a covered cup with two objects
not very intelligible; 2 and 3, a leopard's head; 3, very much defaced,
though three dolphins may be made out at the upper part of the shield.
The arms are, therefore, probably identical with those first above described.
"The coat with the bars and the lion passant, a Sussex antiquary had
little difficulty in assigning to the well-known family of Tregoz, persons
of leading importance not far from Sompting.
"But alas! what of the cross-keys and dolphins, the bucks trippant,
the covered cups and leopards' heads? Clearly they did not belong to
Sussex heraldry, and I was on the point of giving them up, when a vague
recollection of a paper, written by Mr. J. G. Nichols, in vol. xxx. of the
Archæologia, which I thought might assist my inquiry, occurred to me.
On turning to page 506 of that volume I found the first coat to be that

of the Fishmongers' Company, as anciently borne. The same paper also enabled me to identify the shield with the leopards' heads and covered cups as that of the Goldsmiths' Company; and from another source I discovered that the 3 bucks trippant (with which Tregoz is quartered) were the arms of the Leathersellers' Company. Thus I was able to identify the whole of the bearings."

Not to enter further into the arguments which I have adduced, there is no doubt that this tomb covers the remains of Richard Burré or Burry, whose will was made 19th Henry VIII., and still exists at Chichester. His descendants are yet residing in this parish. The will is very curious, and contains among other bequests the great tithes and glebe of Sowntyng, called the Temple, "that I hold of the house of Saynt Jonys." He also directs an obit for his soul and his wife's, eleven years in the church of Sowntyng. He makes bequests to the friars of Chichester, Arundel, and Beeding. That he was a man of considerable position is shown by the fact that he kept a chaplain, Sir Robert Bechton, who was to sing for his soul.

[S. A. C. Templars at, ix, 257. Serf given to, *ib*. Cokeham chapel, ix, 259. xii, 109. Cokeham hospital of St. Anthony, xi, 114. xii, 109. Lands, &c., belonging to Hardham Priory, xiii, 46. Peverells of, xv, 96. Bell of. xvi, 224. Sompting church, xix, 180. Tomb of Richard Burré, *ib*. Temple farm in, xix, 184. House of St. John's, *ib*. East Ham in, *ib*. Prior of Hardham land, *ib*.]

SOUTHEASE.

Domesday, *Suesse;* a parish on the Ouse, in the Hundred of Holmstrow, Rape of Lewes; distant four miles south from Lewes, its Post-town and Railway station. Union, Newhaven. Population in 1811, 105. in 1861, 84. Benefice, a Rectory, valued at £210; Patron and Incumbent, Rev. Samuel Webb Thomas, M.A., of Worcester College, Oxford. Date of earliest Parish Register, 1536. Acreage, 900.

The Celtic *Ese* or *Ise* seems to have some relation to the position of this place near the estuary of the Ouse. *North*ease is in the adjoining parish of Rodmell. In the year 966 King Edgar gave Southease and other lands in the neighbourhood to the monastery of St. Peter at Winchester, and in Domesday the abbots still continued to hold it, as also in 52nd Henry III., and probably down to the period of the Dissolution. *Temp*. Elizabeth it was in the Crown. In the 17th century the Springetts, and in the 18th, the Dickensons were seised of it.

The church is small and ancient, with Norman features, and consists of a nave, chancel, and a round tower of flint, crowned with a low shingled spire. There are traces of additions on both sides of the chancel. The font is rude and ancient. The only other round-towered churches in Sussex are those of Pidding-hoe and St. Michael, Lewes. There are quaint inscriptions for two rectors, Edmund Rose, 1594, and John Willard, 16 . .

[S. A. C. Manorial customs, iii, 249. " Drinker acre" custom, iv, 305. Ancient interments, v, 204. Bells, xvi, 224. Cade's insurrection, xviii, 24.]

SOUTHOVER. (See Lewes, of which it is a suburb.)

SOUTH MALLING. (The same.)

SOUTHWATER.

A small hamlet and railway station in the parish of Hor-sham, about three miles from the town, on the Horsham and Shoreham branch of the Brighton Railway. The ecclesiastical district includes a small part of Shipley parish. The church (the Holy Innocents), built about 1850, though small, is a handsome edifice, in the Flamboyant style, and much ornamented. There is a memorial window to Sir Henry Fletcher, Bart., the donor of the site and a contributor to the erection. The Benefice, in the gift of the Vicar of Horsham, is held by the Rev. Alexander Henry Bridges, M.A., whose stipend is valued at £45.

SOUTHERHAM.

Formerly a chapelry of South Malling. The chapel, which had long been occupied as a cottage, was destroyed upwards of 30 years since. In the north wall a skeleton was found imbedded —probably that of the founder. The chapel stood on the right side of the turnpike road, about three-quarters of a mile south of Cliffe church; and on the opposite side of the road there is an old building of no architectural pretensions, which bears the name of "the schoolmaster's house;" but nothing is known of its history.

SOUTHWICK.

A parish in the Hundred of Fishersgate; Rape of Bramber; distant 1½ mile east from Shoreham, its Post-town. It has a Railway station on the South Coast line. Union, Steyning. Population in 1811, 321 ; in 1861, 1,358. Benefice, a Rectory, valued at £207 ; Patron, The Lord Chancellor;. Incumbent, Rev. F. Barney Parkes, of Christ Church, Oxford. Date of earliest Parish Register, 1654.

This small parish, the southern *wic* or village (though

there is no correlative *North*wick), is supposed to be included in
the Domesday survey with Kingston-Buci, which it adjoins on
the east. Unlike most of our coast parishes, trees thrive well
here, and there is the pleasing adjunct of a village green.
Lands in Southwick which belonged to Reigate Priory, and
were granted at the Dissolution to William, Lord Howard, were
purchased, 20th Elizabeth, by Henry Smith, Esq., and have ever
since belonged to the well-known " Dog Smith's Charity." The
family of Hall have possessed an estate here for several generations. Remains, conjectured to be those of a Roman villa, have
been found. A ship-canal passing by Southwick to Aldrington
connects Kingston Harbour with the traffic of Brighton.
    The church, popularly called St. Michael's, is given by Mr.
Gibbon to St. Margaret. It has an interesting Norman tower,
with shingled spire; but the body of the edifice has been rebuilt in a style difficult to characterize. The memorials include
the names of Gray, Norton, Bridger, Hall, &c. The church was
given in the 13th century by Simon le Counte to the Knights
Templars at Saddlescombe, in Newtimber. John Pell, F.R.S.,
the skilful, but unfortunate mathematician, son of John Pell,
rector of Southwick, was born here in 1610. (" Worthies of
Sussex, p. 177.)
    FISHERSGATE, which gives name to the Hundred, is a hamlet
in this parish, and has a recently-erected district church.

[S. A. C. Tithes to Sele Priory, x, 115. Church, ix, 235. xii, 109.
xviii, 106. Benefactions of Goodmerich and Michelborne, xiii, 47. Bell,
xvi, 224. Lands to Shoreham chantry, xvi, 235. Roman remains, xvi, 255.
Thomas, xix, 101. Midhurst Chantry had lands here, xx, 24. Baggele,
ibid.]

STANMER.

Vulgo, *Stammer;* a parish in the Hundred of Ringmer, Rape of Pevensey,
    (though *locally* in that of Lewes); distant four miles north-west of
    Brighton; Post-town, Lewes. It has a Railway station close by at
    Falmer. Union, Newhaven. Population in 1811, 105; in 1861, 147.
    Benefice, a Rectory, united with Falmer, valued at £140; Patrons,
    alternately the Earl of Chichester and the Archbishop of Canter-
    bury; Incumbent, Rev. Charles G. T. Barlow, of Balliol College,
    Oxford. Date of earliest Parish Register, 1558. Acreage, 1,346. *Chief
    Landowner*, the Earl of Chichester, of Stanmer Park, Lord Lieutenant
    of Sussex.

As one of the Peculiars of Canterbury, this parish belonged
to Archbishop Lanfranc, and was held of him by the Canons of
Malling. In subsequent times it has been the property of the
Michelbornes, Gotts, and Pelhams. Stanmer Place was built on
an older site, about the year 1724, by Thomas Pelham, Esq.,

ancestor of the present noble owner. The surrounding park is beautifully undulated, and well planted, and has its principal entrance nearly midway on the road from Lewes to Brighton. The village lies within the boundaries of the park. The church, which has been rebuilt by the present Earl of Chichester, is plain and neat, and contains memorials for the families of Scrase, Goffe, Michelborne, and Martin. Stephen Goffe, incumbent here at the beginning of the 17th century, was father of Stephen, John, and William Goffe, all remarkable persons during the Commonwealth—the last being Colonel Goffe, the celebrated republican and puritan, whose constancy marks him a true hero to the cause of civil and religious liberty. In this parish, and in many of the adjoining ones in the South Down district, the geological observer will notice many of those large boulders of stone which do not belong to any local stratum, but which are supposed to have been brought hither at some remote era, from the polar regions, in icebergs.

[S. A. C. Cromwell's Bible, ii, 78. Pelham buckle, iii, 211. Goffe family, in Civil War, v, 83. Pelhams, x, 211. Michelbornes, xiii, 257. xvi, 30. Bell, xvi, 224.]

STAPLECROSS.

A hamlet of Ewhurst, giving name to a Hundred.

STAPLEFIELD.

A scattered hamlet of Cuckfield, 2¼ miles north-west from that town, and 5½ south of Crawley, its Post-town. A district church (St. Mark) was erected in 1847. The living is a Perpetual Curacy ; Patron, the Vicar of Cuckfield ; Incumbent, Rev. J. H. Appleton, M.A.

STEDHAM.

Domesday, *Stedeham ;* a long narrow parish on the Western Rother, in the Hundred of Easebourne ; Rape of Chichester; distant two miles west from Midhurst, its Post-town and nearest Railway station. Union, Midhurst. Population in 1811, 353 ; in 1861, 530. Benefice, a Rectory, united with Heyshott, and in the same patronage. Date of earliest Parish Register, 1538. Acreage, 2,249. *Seats,* Stedham, Sir Charles Taylor, Bart ; Stedham Hall, John Stoveld, Esq. ; Ash, J. B. Smart, Esq. ; Tentworth, Miss Wyndham.

In Saxon times the manor was held by Eddiva of Earl Godwin; at the Conquest William gave it to Earl Roger de

Montgomeri. In later times William de Perci held it of William de Albini. On its seizure by the Crown, Henry VIII. granted it to William, Earl of Southampton. Subsequently it vested in Bulstrode Peachey Knight, Esq., and it was sold by Lord Selsey within the present century to Sir Charles William Taylor, Bart., whose son, Sir Charles Taylor, is now lord, and resides in the parish.

The village is seated in a pleasant rising ground above the Rother. The church of St. James, which represents one mentioned in Domesday, was partly taken down, rebuilt, and " restored" in 1850. It consisted of chancel, nave, and central tower, which bears the date of 1670. During the progress of pulling down, some mural paintings of interest were discovered. The subjects were St. George and the Dragon, St. Ursula, St. Christopher, and the Final Judgment. These have been fully described in the " Sussex Collections," vol. iv. Mr. Butler, the architect, from the rude vestigia in the nave, considers the building to be identical with the Domesday church. Many stones, with crosses in relief, and four stone coffins, were found in the walls, having evidently been placed there as material in some comparatively recent repair of the building. The chancel has Early English features, and the font is ancient.

[S. A. C. Church, mural paintings, iv, 1. Architecture, &c., iv, 19 (*Vernon-Harcourt and Butler*). Three watermills in Domesday, v, 272. Church, xii, 78. Bells, xvi, 225. River Rother, xvi, 259. Stedham manor, &c., xviii, 95. Midhurst brotherhood, xx, 25. Knights-Hospitallers' lands, xx, 28. Legate's lands in, and Sir William Goring, xx, 28.]

STEYNING.

Domesday, *Staninges;* a parish and market-town in the Hundred and Union to which it gives name ; Rape of Bramber ; distant about five miles north from Shoreham ; Post-town, Hurst-Pierpoint ; it has a Railway station on the Shoreham and Horsham branch of the South Coast railway. Population in 1811, 1,210 ; in 1861, 1,620. Benefice, a Vicarage, valued at £400 ; Patron, the Duke of Norfolk ; Incumbent, Rev. Thomas Medland, B.D., of Corpus Christi College, Oxford. Date of earliest Parish Register, 1565. Acreage, 3,383.

Steyning, like many other parishes in Sussex, finds an able exponent in its own incumbent, the Rev. Thomas Medland, whose paper appears in Vol. v. of the " Sussex Collections." The parish lies on the north side of the South Downs, near the point where the hills slope on both sides to the Adur. It is partly on the Downs, and extends northward to the Weald clay, the intermediate space being sand and fertile loam. The chief part of the population is found in the picturesque little town, situated on the malm rock. The name appears to be derived, not from the Anglo-Saxon *stone*, but from one of the Saxon *mearcs*, and meaning the abode of the children of one Staen, the patriarch of a noble family, who probably lived towards the end of the fifth century. (See Kemble.) It was then a place of little importance, and it was reserved for St. Cuthman, the titular patron of the parish, whose life by the Bollandists I have abstracted from the Acta Sanctorum in "Worthies of Sussex," p. 23, to raise it to some renown. It is pretty certain that that personage erected the first church (a wooden one), doubtless on the site of the present noble edifice. Both the saint himself and Ethelwulf, father of Alfred the Great, are believed to have been buried here. Other claims have been set up as to the burial-place of this unfortunate abdicated King of Wessex, but Asser Menevensis, Alfred's preceptor and secretary, says distinctly "Athelwolphus rex sepultus Steninge." King Alfred bequeathed his estates here, with others in Surrey, to his nephew Ethelwold, but they afterwards reverted to the Crown, and Edward the Confessor granted them, subject to a life interest of Bishop Ælfwine, to the Abbey of Fécamp, in Normandy, but afterwards revoked the grant, at the instance of Earl Godwin, whose son Harold held Steyning until his fall at Hastings. After the Conquest, William restored it to the monks of Fécamp, who thereupon sent over six of their number to form a priory, or cell, at Steyning. These Benedictines founded their house on the site afterwards occupied by the parsonage-house. From Domesday we learn that the lands belonged principally to the foreign abbey, though William de Braose, Lord of Bramber, had a portion of them. He, not content with his share, made encroachments on the possessions of the brethren, which resulted in an appeal to Henry I., who confirmed all the rights which Fécamp claimed.

Steyning was in those days a thriving and well-frequented place. According to Domesday there were no less than 223 villeins and 106 bordars, while in the town itself there were 123 dwellings. The Abbot of Fécamp proceeded to erect a church suitable to this increased population. Two churches are mentioned in the record, one being on the foundation of the original establishment of St. Cuthman, and the other probably a *succursale*, or chapel of ease. The principal part of Steyning was known as the parish of Cuthman, while the other church or chapel appears to have been situated on the south side of High Street. It was dedicated to St. Mary, and near it was a well, sacred to the same saint, but now covered over.

The church (St. Andrew), as just remarked, doubtless occupies the site of the humble wooden edifice of Cuthman. When the

brethren of Fécamp built their church they seem to have taken
the church of Graville, in Normandy, dependent on their abbey,
as their model. The greater part of what now remains of this
noble church is apparently of the time of Henry I., though the
capitals of some of the pillars and a rude bas relief are supposed
to be of the time of the Confessor. The original plan was never
completed. The building, as it stands, consists of a west tower,
nave, north and south aisles, and a chancel. The nave and aisles
are somewhat narrow. The former is very lofty, with round-
headed clerestory windows. Between the nave and chancel are
four very high substantial arches, apparently intended to support a central tower. The present tower was added at a later
period, when all idea of extending the church westward had
been abandoned. Mr. Medland thinks that a south transept
was built, but this has long disappeared. The more modern
parts of the structure, particularly the tower and porch, have
worked stones from a more ancient and ornamental structure.
The nave, with its round pillars, carved capitals, and circular
arches with zigzag mouldings, is particularly grand and imposing. The church anciently possessed a chantry of the Virgin,
and chapels or altars for St. Peter, St. Christopher, and the Sa-
lutation. The chancel was reconstructed some years since, not
in accordance with the rest of the building. There are no monuments of greater antiquity than one dated 1508, for Mighill Farn-
field (or Farnfold) and Joane his wife; but there are mural
tablets and slabs for the names of Michell, Prowd, Gratwicke, Coventry, White, Stalman, Ingram, Leeves, Mille, Smith, Lucke,
Hooper, and many others. The bells are six in number. In
the thirteenth century Ralph de Neville, Bishop of Chichester,
claimed obedience from the Canons of Steyning. The Abbot of
Fécamp resisted, and it was decided that Steyning church should
be free of all episcopal jurisdiction.

In 1278 the town was of sufficient political importance to
return two members to Parliament, and, though much dimi-
nished in population, it continued to do so down to the period of
the Reform Act in 1832. Up to the early part of the fourteenth
century it was of some commercial consequence. In Saxon and
Norman times, when the estuary of the Adur flowed up thus
far from Shoreham, it had a port known as the Harbour of
Steyning, or St. Cuthman's Port, where the small vessels of the
period could ride in safety. Like many other places on the
South coast, however, the river having narrowed, Steyning lost
its maritime importance, as shipmen could no longer reach it.
It was further unfortunate when, at the suppression of its priory
as a cell of Fécamp, *temp.* Henry V., the fostering care of the
foreign abbey was withdrawn, and a transfer was made to Syon

Abbey, in Middlesex, the brethren of which cared less for it. Thus Steyning gradually dwindled down to the proportions of a mere village, and only rose to what it now is by the independent exertions of its inhabitants.

The manor of Charlton Court, which had formed the principal part of the monastic possessions, was annexed to the Honour of Petworth, and after the Dissolution was sold, with the advowson of Steyning, to William Pellatt, Esq., from whose family it has passed by transfer to those of Lewknor, Shirley, Tufton, Eversfield, and Goring. Wickham, another ancient manor, has been associated, since 1307, with the names of Graundyn, de Lychepole, de Ifield, de Wickham, de Cobham, Percy of Petworth, Hystede, Farnfold, and Trevor. Wappingthorne is a Domesday manor. "William Fitzmanne holds Wopingthorne. Carle held it of King Edward." It was then assessed at six hides, now at two only. There were seven villeins and 15 bondmen. In the reign of the Confessor it was worth 100s., and afterwards £4. In 1268 Haymen Boynet paid to William de Braose 18 silver marks for Wowend and Wappingthorne, to exonerate him from the latter's claim of murage, a tax due to the Lord of Bramber for the reparation of the walls of his castle. In his family it remained till 1351. It afterwards became the property of the Dukes of Norfolk. In 1607 John Leedes, Esq. left it to his son and heir, Sir Thomas Leedes, K.B., who held it of the Castle of Bramber by knight's service. Edward Goring, of the Burton family, held it *temp.* Charles I., and resided here. Of the house, now a farm-house, there are considerable remains. It is a brick building, with large windows divided by stone mullions. Over the portico is a shield of 12 quarterings, entirely defaced. It still belongs to the Goring family. (Cartwright, 1830.) Gatwick, near the church, was another ancient residence, which gave name to a family. The vicarage-house is a good specimen of a parochial manse, with some curious carved wainscot, having the arms of St. Richard of Chichester, Fitz-James, Bishop of London, and the arms and cognizances of Henry VIII. and Queen Catherine. The gardens are well kept, and a clear stream of water runs through them. Among the rockwork have been placed two ancient stones with crosses, brought from the foundation of the western extension of the church, and evidently of Saxon date.

There was an ancient guild or fraternity in Steyning. The old "Brotherhood hall" formed part of the endowment of the Grammar School, founded in 1614 by William Holland, alderman of Chichester, and the school is still carried on under the gables of that ancient hall, standing on the right hand of the street leading down to the church.

In Saxon times Steyning had a royal mint, and among the pennies brought to light at the now celebrated "Chancton find," were 11 coined here. They are of the reigns of Edward the Confessor and Harold; but an earlier coinage doubtless existed. Of the various types, Mr. J. C. Lucas, F.S.A., has given an account in the " Sussex Collections," Vol. xx. Roman antiquities have been found here. In 1826 a barrow on the Down overlooking the town was removed for the sake of the flints. On its summit, about a foot from the surface, were found three entire skeletons, and in the surrounding fosse upwards of 40 more. An urn, with burnt bones and 50 coins, chiefly of the Lower Empire, were also discovered.

[S. A. C. Town and church (*Medland*), v, 111. xvi, 236. St. Cuthman, v, 112. xx, 214. Four watermills in Domesday, v, 272. Church books extracts, viii, 132. Royal mint, ix, 369. xix, 189. xx, 214. (*Lucas*). Tithes to Beeding Priory, x, 115. Fécamp Abbey, x, 123. xx, 214. Bennets of, xi, 61. Bonet of Wappingthorne, xii, 30. Wappingthorne and Wickham, xiii, 48. xvi, 35. Eversfields of Charlton Court, xiv, 123. Pellatts of ditto, xiv, 150. xvi, 75. Palmer at Agincourt, xv, 135. Leeds of Wappingthorne, xvi, 35. Cooke of, and Parson of, xvi, 49. George Fox, Quaker, at, xvi, 72. Bells, xvi, 225. Cuthman's Port, xvi, 233. Churches, xvi, 236. Ethelwulf, father of King Alfred, xvi, 237, xx, 214. Jarvis of, xvi, 239. Grammar School, xvi, 241. Adur River, and King's Barns, xvi, 253. Cade's insurrection, xviii, 24. Smith of, xix, 95. Goring of Danny, lands, xix, 100. Stalman of, xix, 108.]

NORTH STOKE.

Domesday, *Stoches ;* a parish in the Hundred of Poling; Rape of Arundel; distant 2½ miles from Arundel Railway station. Population, in 1811, 62 ; in 1861, 87. Benefice, a Perpetual Curacy, valued at £57. Patron, Lord Leconfield ; Incumbent, Rev. Edward B. Foreman, M.A. Date of earliest Parish Register, 1678. Area, 860 acres.

This small parish, which is separated from South Stoke by the river Arun, is of some archæological importance. Its area has been so variously stated that it is somewhat difficult to know its real extent. Dallaway states it at 930 acres; a late statistical publication says 160; but the Population Tables of 1852 say 860, which I presume is correct. The manor descended with the castle and barony of Arundel till about 1600, when on the attainder of Philip, Earl of Arundel, it was some time afterwards granted to Thomas, Lord Howard de Walden. In 1611 it belonged to Richard, Earl of Dorset, who sold it to John Stansfield, Esq., the founder of South Malling church in East Sussex. From him it descended to his grandson, John Evelyn, Esq., the author of "Sylva" and "Memoirs." At later periods it passed through the families of Mitchell and Joliffe to the late Earl of Egremont.

To the east of the village is Camp-field, once a strong earthwork, upon a steep acclivity, much worn by ploughing. Many ancient coins and other relics have been found here.

The church is cruciform, with a low tower and a spire. There are three sedilia in the chancel. The building, which was dependent on Tortington Priory from 1337 until the Reformation, is large in proportion to the parish. The dedication is unknown.

In 1834 an ancient British canoe or boat was discovered about 150 yards from the river Arun. It was formed from a single oak tree hollowed out, and was more than 34 feet long. The late Earl of Egremont presented it to the British Museum. Singularly enough another similar boat of smaller dimensions was found near the same spot, at Burpham in a creek of the same river, and is now in the museum at Lewes Castle, together with its wooden anchor—perhaps one of the greatest archæological curiosities in the county. It was presented to the Society by Thos. Spencer, Esq., of Warningcamp.

[S. A. C. Ancient British boat or canoe, xii, 261. Church bell, xvi, 225. River Arun, xvi, 258. Manor of, xviii, 78. Rymans of, xviii, 78. Pellet of, xix, 201.]

SOUTH STOKE.

Domesday, *Stoches;* a parish in the Hundred of Avisford; Rape of Arundel; distant 2½ miles north-north-east from Arundel, its Railway-station and Post-town. Population in 1811, 99; in 1861, 99. Benefice a Rectory, valued at £223; Patron, the Duke of Norfolk; Incumbent, Rev. Richmond Powell, M.A., of Trinity College, Cambridge. Date of earliest Parish Register, 1558. Acreage, 1,294.

This parish (Anglo-Saxon *Stóc*, a place) lies in the valley of the Arun, where that river is remarkably tortuous, and, as Dallaway observes, "refluis sibimet sæpe obvius undis." Nearly 700 acres of the parish are within the new pale of Arundel Park. There are two manors, which have remained distinct since the time of Domesday. In that record it is extremely difficult to define the limits of this parish, and that of the adjacent one of North Stoke, but a church is mentioned in both places. Of the two manors, one is described as having been held in Saxon times of King Edward by Brixi, and afterwards of Earl Roger (de Montgomeri) by Rainald. It was rated at eight hides. There were seven plough-lands cultivated by sixteen villeins and sixteen cottars, and two fisheries rendering 10d. The other manor was held by Ulnod, a free tenant, *temp.* Confessoris, and afterwards of Earl Roger by Ernald, probably the same person as Rainald above-mentioned. It was rated at four hides, and sustained ten villeins and four cottars. Its value was £4.

OFFHAM (Anglo-Saxon, the *hám* or settlement of Offa*) was held of King Edward by a freeman named Alwin; after the Conquest Azo held it of Earl Roger. ·It contained four hides, and there were eight villeins and five cottars, a fishery of 2s., and a wood of three hogs. It was valued at different periods at £7, £6, and £4. According to the Testa de Nevill, John de Nevill held lands here, which were transferred to the Fitz-Alans, Earls of Arundel.

In the *compotus* of Richard, Earl of Arundel, 1380, the manor was valued at the large sum of £20 6s., with a *grange*. It passed through the families of Dixsè, Sackville, and Kempe, and the late Earl of Newburgh by exchange to the Dukes of Norfolk, and is part of the settled estate of that great family, who also possess a farm in Offham, formerly the property of the Dean and Chapter of Chichester. William de Albini, Earl of Arundel, granted about 1,172 lands in Offham to Hugh Esturmie, and a copy of the charter is printed by Dallaway, p. 222. Upon the chalk downs in this parish there are many earthworks and trenches. "The most remarkable trench," says Dallaway, "is that which leads from the summit to the river at its base—the probable remains of a road by which the camp was supplied with water. . . . The general opinion is that they are Danish.

> ' Danorum veteres fossas—immania castra,
> Et circumducti servat vestigia valli.' "

In 1796 a considerable number of Saxon pennies was exhumed near Offham, and this *find* resembled that of 1866 at Washington as being mostly of the reigns of Edward the Confessor and Harold, and fresh from the mint.

The church (St. Leonard) is small, but of high antiquity. It consists of a single pace or nave only, with a corbel table ornamented with the heads of animals and birds at the east end.

The "high-stream" of the river Arun was formerly important in regard to the fisheries and the swans, which latter were duly marked in old times, and there were rules and regulations for the fishermen, beadles, and under-bailiffs to superintend these matters, and the practice of "swan-hopping" was kept up. The

---

* We have in our Anglo-Saxon annals more than one historical Offa ; but the name, judging from the local nomenclature of England, must have been a very common one ; thus we have in Sussex two Offhams, and one Offington, besides several minor places with the initial syllable *Off*.

following regulations respecting swan-marks on the high-stream are worthy of record :—

" Swan-marks, 1624. ·

" Earl of Arundel butted on the right wing, and their heels both cut off; Bishop of Chichester on the left wing, and three notches on the right side of the beak; Sir W. Goring, in right of the Priory of Hardham; Sir John Shelley, of Mitchelgrove ; Sir Edward Bisshopp, of Parham ; Sir Garrett Kempe, of South Stoke ; John Alford, Walter Barttelot, of Stopham ; William Palmer, son of Sir T. Palmer, of Angmering, deceased; William Oneley, of Pulborough ; Anthony Sutton, John Caryl, and Thomas Mille, Esqrs., were severally entitled, in right of their lands, to keep swans upon the High Stream. The fine paid by the heir upon coming to the estate, to the water-bailiff, was 6s., and 8d. for every renewal of the swan-mark."

In the parish register is the entry in 1738 of the baptism of Anne, daughter of Daniel Gittins, L.L.B., rector of this parish. This lady became the wife of R. Bransby Francis, rector of Edgefield, co. Norfolk. Her father gave her a classical education, and she especially excelled in the knowledge of Hebrew, and published several works, including a poetical " Translation of the Song of Solomon," " A Poetical Epistle from Charlotte to Werter," " Miscellaneous Poems," &c. She died in 1800.

[S. A. C. Two watermills in Domesday at Offham, v, 271. Church, xii, 102. Souton, buried at, *ibid.* Bonville, Lords of, xv, 59. D'Albini's grant of Offham, xv, 95. Bell, xvi, 225. River Arun, xvi, 258. Aylwin of Offham, xvii, 254. Kempes, Lords of, xix, 119.]

WEST LAVANT. (See East Lavant.)

WEST STOKE.

Domesday, *Stoches ;* a parish in the Hundred of Bosham; Rape of Chichester. Post-town, Chichester. Union, West Hampnett. Population in 1811, 64; in 1861, 94. Benefice, a Rectory, valued at £170; Patron, the Lord Chancellor; Incumbent, Rev. Charles Buckner, B.D., of Wadham College, Oxford. Date of earliest Parish Register, 1564. Acreage, 880. *Sole Landowner,* the Duke of Richmond. *Seat,* Stoke House, Lieut.-Colonel Frederick Cavendish.

This agreeable little parish consists chiefly of down land, with a small secluded village. On the southern escarpment of the Downs are two large tumuli, " supposed," says Horsfield, " to have been *erected* over the bodies of the marauding sea-kings whom the men of Chichester encountered and slew in the year 900." In the valley below, called Kingley Bottom, the favourite resort of the inhabitants of Chichester for pleasure parties, is a very fine group of yew trees, and the whole scene is remarkably picturesque. Bow Hill stands to the north.

In the time of the Confessor, the freeman Ulnod, held the manor of Stoches. It was assessed at four hides, and had a church. It has subsequently passed through the families of Bigod, Mowbray, Howard, and Compton. In 1764 it was added to the Goodwood estate.

The church (St. Andrew) has on the north wall of the chancel a memorial to Adrian Stoughton, Esq., his wife, and two sons and five daughters, with effigies in a kneeling attitude—date 1635.

[S. A. C. Roman earthworks, x, 171. Church, xii, 78. Bell, xvi, 225.]

STOPHAM.

Domesday, *Stopeham ;* a parish in the Hundred of Rotherbridge; Rape of Arundel, distant four miles south-east from Petworth, its Post-town; one mile south-west from the Railway station of Pulborough. Union, Thakeham. Population in 1811, 163; in 1861, 130. Benefice, a Rectory, valued at £150 ; Patron, George Barttelot, Esq. ; Incumbent, Rev. Felix Brown, M.A., of Trinity College, Cambridge. Date of earliest Parish Register, 1544. Acreage, 876. *Seat*, Stopham House, George Barttelot, Esq., J.P., and Lieut.-Colonel Walter Barttelot, M.P., J.P.

This is, in several respects, one of the most interesting parishes in Sussex. Small in area, it is picturesque, and possesses features which interest every archæologist who visits the locality. It lies on the banks of the most pleasant of Sussex rivers, the Western Rother.

In the reign of Edward the Confessor, five free tenants were possessed of Stopeham. As part of the rape of Arundel, it belonged to Earl Roger de Montgomeri. One Robert held it of him, and sub-let it to Ralph (whoever they may have been). It was rated at five hides. There were four villeins and four cottagers, one serf, three fisheries, and a wood of 10 hogs. "The family of Barttelot are said to have come from Normandy with William the Conqueror, and to have fixed their residence at a place called La Ford in this parish. In the 14th century John Barttelot de la Ford, married the daughter and coheiress of William de Stopham, descended probably from the Saxon proprietor, and thus acquired the whole of the parish." (Dallaway).*
From a MS. at Arundel Castle, it appears that " Estover Ferry, belonging to John Stopham, descended to Walter Barttelot de la Ford, over which ferry there is now a stone bridge that ought

* See also " The Topographer," iv, 346, and Shirley's " Noble and Gentle Men."

to be repaired by the three Western Rapes, which was built 2nd Edward II., 1329." Stopham bridge is a structure of seven arches, the greatest number in any pontine erection in the county. Stopham House, a handsome and spacious residence, was built on an older site during the Tudor period, and rebuilt in 1787.

The church (supposed to be dedicated to St. Mary) is small, and "built upon the Norman plan, with a pace or nave only, and a square tower at the west end. Upon the ancient door is a cross fleury, in iron. The windows are ornamented with stained glass, which is said to have been taken out of the old hall." These decorations consist of armorial bearings and imaginary portraits executed at the expense of Walter Barttelot, Esq., in 1638, by Roelandt, a Dutch artist. There is this inscription in a window :—

AD FORMAM HÆC RENOVATA FENESTRA PRIOREM, 1638.

There are coloured drawings of these embellishments in the Burrell MSS., British Museum. But the most remarkable feature in this little edifice are the memorials of the Barttelot family, including a most interesting series of brasses, &c., for many generations, and almost covering the whole of the pavement. The first is to 𝔍𝔬𝔥𝔞𝔫𝔫𝔢𝔰 𝔅𝔞𝔯𝔱𝔢𝔩𝔬𝔱𝔱, treasurer of the household to Thomas, Earl of Arundel, and his wife, Johanna, daughter of William de Stopeham, 1428. The next is to 𝔍𝔬𝔥𝔞𝔫𝔫𝔢𝔰 𝔅𝔞𝔯𝔱𝔢𝔩𝔬𝔱𝔱, "Consul prudens" to Thomas, John, and William, Earls of Arundel, and Joan his wife, daughter and heiress of John Lewknor, Esq. This tomb has the figure of a man in the armour of the period—date 1453. The third has two brass effigies, to the memory of 𝔎𝔦𝔠. 𝔅𝔞𝔯𝔱𝔢𝔩𝔬𝔱𝔱, Esq., marshall to the Earl of Arundel, 1489. The next in the series is to 𝔍𝔬𝔥𝔞𝔫𝔫𝔢𝔰 𝔅𝔞𝔯𝔱𝔢𝔩𝔬𝔱𝔱, 1493. Then follows a long series of memorials to the same ancient family, down to much more recent times. One of these records William Bartelott, Esq., who died in 1601, aged 97 years. Instead of the ancient formula, "Orate pro anima," we are informed that his " soul restethe with God." There are two bells, one of which is inscribed to St. Augustine.

Thomas Newcombe, M.A., incumbent of Stopham, who died in 1766, in his 91st year, was descended in the female line from the poet Spenser. He wrote many poems in English and Latin, and was a friend of Dr. Young. His principal work on the "Last Judgment," in 12 books, after the manner of Milton, was printed in folio in 1723.

[S. A. C. Domesday watermill, v, 272. Stopham family, arms of, &c., vi, 87. xvi, 257. Ralph de Stopham, a Crusader, ix, 365. Church, xii, 102. Female recluse, xii, 134. Barttelot family (the most ancient commoners in West Sussex), xv, 62, 127. xvi, 35, 50, 257. xviii, 80. Church bells, xvi, 225. River Arun, xvi, 257.]

STORRINGTON.

Domesday, *Estorchetone;* a parish and market-town in the Hundred of West Easwrith ; Rape of Arundel; distant four miles south-east from Pulborough station, and eight north-east from Arundel. Post-town, Hurst-Pierpoint. Union, Thakeham. Population in 1811, 792 ; in 1861, 1,104. Benetice, a Rectory, valued at £600; Patron, the Duke of Norfolk; Incumbent, Rev. John Scott Whiting, B.A., of Worcester College, Oxford. Date of earliest Parish Register, 1590. Acreage, 3,264. *Chief Landowners,* the Duke of Norfolk, Lord Leconfield, and Frederick King, Esq. *Seat,* Fryern House, Frederick King, Esq.

Stór is the Anglo-Saxon for great, vast, and also a personal name, still retained as a surname. Of the initial syllable, " Utrum mavisque accipe " for the derivation. The parish is of irregular shape, and the soil varies from the chalk of the South Downs, to sand and loam on a substratum of sand rock. The town-village consists of two streets intersecting at right angles. Domesday mentions Estorchetone as held by Robert, of the Earl, but previously by Durand. A church is mentioned, and there were six hides, six villeins, seven cottars, and two mills. *Temp.* King Edward its value was £4, and afterwards 40s. Another Storcheton, apparently a separate manor, was held of Earl Roger de Montgomeri, by Robert, and Alwin was the sub-tenant. Alwin was a freeman under the Confessor, and could go where-soever he pleased, and dispose of his land at pleasure, according to the ancient expression, " Potuit ire, cum terra, quo volebat." This estate had one villein, five cottars, two serfs, and a mill. The value was 30s. The manor of Storrington is valued in the computus of Richard, Earl of Arundel, at 60 marks per annum. On his attainder, in 1388, it was granted to John Holland, Duke of Exeter. It was afterwards restored to the Earls of Arundel, and remained with them till Henry Fitz-Alan, Earl of Arundel, conjointly with his son-in-law, John, Lord Lumley, conveyed it to William Apsley, Esq., of Thakeham, whose second daughter, Jane, carried it by marriage to the family of Newton, of South-over, near Lewes. It was afterwards possessed by Wheler, Butler, and Batcock. In 1806 it was transferred to Charles, Duke of Norfolk, and still remains with that noble family. Hurston comprises the demesnes of the manor of Wiggonholt, originally part of the barony of Bramber. Its value, at the time of the Survey, was 10s., and it was held by Aluiet, of William de Braose. A mill is mentioned. Of its descent, nothing appears until 1634, when John Monk, Esq., who had married a daughter of Edward Covert of Slaugham, was pos-sessor. It has since belonged to Elliston, Eliot, Swayne, Ashburnham, and Wyndham, Earl of Egremont. Fryern, or Frier's-land was the original endowment of a chantry in Thakeham church, founded by Stephen le Power, the patronage of which descended to the Apsleys. Subsequent proprietors have been Barttelot, Duppa, Banks, Moulding, and Postlethwaite. It was re-sold to Charlotte, Baroness Dowager King, and her son, the Hon. Geo. King, enlarged the house and resided in it. It is now the seat of Fredk. King, Esq. Chantry farm, part of the Apsley estate, passed to the Shelleys, of Lewes. COOTHAM, or Coudham, is a hamlet about a mile west of the town. It was manorial at the time of Domesday. In the reign of the Confessor, two freemen held it; afterwards Robert, of Earl Roger, and Alberic of him. It was valued at £3, and there were four villeins, and five cottars. Robert also held of the Earl two hides, which had one villein and a cottar; value, 20s. Upon the great partition of the earldom of Arundel, a knight's fee was assigned to Roger de Someri. It is now divided into many small freeholds. The market charter was granted by Thomas, Earl of Arundel, in 1399. The Bynes were ' of Storrington for many years. James Byne is mentioned so early as 3rd Edward III., and Thomas Byne in 23rd Henry VIII.

The church (St. Mary) has been much altered from its original form. On May 20th, 1731, the shingled steeple was struck by lightning and fell upon the nave. In 1746 the tower fell, and the damage was estimated at £1,625. The church, except the chancel, was rebuilt, and it has now a nave, north aisle, and west tower. On the floor of the chancel is a brass, in ecclesiastical costume, for Henry Wilsha, B.D., chaplain of Henry, Earl of Arundel, 1591—a rare instance of so recent a brass. There are two monuments by Westmacott, one for Sir H. Hollis Bradford, K.C.B., 1816, erected by his companions in arms, in recognition of his great military services at Copenhagen, Corunna, Flushing, Salamanca, Vittoria, and Waterloo, where he received a wound, which resulted, after 18 months, in his death. The second has a female figure in relief, bending over a pedestal, and commemorates Major Hugh Falconer, 1827. The rectory house, built soon after 1621, has been much improved by more recent incumbents, and is now one of the best in the county.

Several antiquities have been found in the parish, including a Celtic urn, 21 inches high, and one of the finest specimens of its kind; many Roman coins, &c.

[S. A. C. British urn, i, 55. Domesday watermills, v, 272. Roman coins, viii, 277. ix, 116. xi, 140. Church, xii, 102. xiv, 154. xix, 103. Cootham and Bynes, xii, 111. Parish charity, xvi, 37. Bells, xvi, 225. Millstream to the Arun, xvi, 257. Alwin, xvii, 254. Patronage of benefice to Lord Lumley, xix, 103.]

STOUGHTON.

A parish in the Hundred of Westbourne: Rape of Chichester; distant seven miles north-west from Chichester. Post-town, Emsworth. Railway station, Emsworth, distant about five miles. Union, Westbourne. Population in 1811, 489; in 1861, 633. Benefice, a Vicarage, valued at £270; Patron, the Bishop of London; Incumbent, Rev. Francis H. Vivian, M.A., of Trinity College, Cambridge. Date of earliest Parish Register, 1675. Acreage, 5,422. *Seats*, Stanstead House, Mrs Dixon; Watergate House, A. H. Hall, Esq.

This is a border parish adjoining Warblington, in Hampshire. The soil is chiefly chalk. The lofty range of the South Downs, called Bowhill, extends along the south-east boundary. Stoughton is not mentioned, *eo nomine*, in Domesday. In 1207, Roger Bigod, the last earl of Norfolk of that family, died seised. In 1557, it was purchased by Henry Fitz-Alan, and it became a favourite hunting resort of the Earls of Arundel. About 1480, Thomas, Lord Maltravers, rebuilt the manor-house. Afterwards it belonged to Lord Lumley, and subsequently to the Lewknors and Peacheys, Lords Selsey. It now belongs to the Hon. Mrs. Vernon Harcourt. The principal feature is Stanstead Park, which, with its forest, contains 1,666 acres, about 1,000 of which are in the parish, while other portions extend into Racton and Warblington. The present house succeeds the earlier edifice, which was the seat of Lord Lumley, and in 1644, during the siege of Arundel, Sir William Waller sent 2,000 horse and foot, and two drakes (small guns) to besiege it. The particulars of this attack are not known. It was probably much shattered, as about 1687, the mansion was again rebuilt by the Earl of Scarborough. It has since been much altered. It contains some good wood carving by Grinling Gibbons, and a suit of arras tapestry, representing the Battle of Wynendaal, brought from Flanders by the first Lord Scarborough. The forest lies west of the house, and is divided by three wide avenues, of which the central one is two miles long. De Foe, in his " Tour " (1724), speaks thus of the place :—" From Chichester the road lying still west passes in view of the Earl of Scarborough's fine seat at Stanstead—a house seeming to be a retreat, being surrounded with thick woods, through which there are the most pleasant, agreeable vistas cut, that are to be seen anywhere in England—particularly because through the west opening, in front of the house, they sit in the dining-room, and see the town and harbour of Portsmouth, and the ships at Spithead and St. Helens, which, during war, is a most glorious sight." At a later period Stanstead was the seat of George Montague Dunk, Earl of Halifax, who left it to his illegitimate daughter, Anna Maria, who married Richard Archdall, Esq. By his lordship's trustees, the estate, with its demesnes and extensive manors, was sold for £102,500, to Richard Barwell, Esq., after whose death it was sold to Lewis Way, Esq. Mr. Way, who resided here, took great interest in the conversion of the Jews to Christianity, and, in 1812, fitted up the north-west side of the old mansion as a chapel in the "Gothic" of the period, and had an ordained priest, a converted Jew, for religious ministrations on the episcopal system. This was succeeded by a new church (Christ Church), built and endowed by the late Charles Dixon, Esq., and consecrated in 1855. The living is a Perpetual Curacy, value £210, in the gift of Mrs. Dixon, and held by the Rev. Nicholas Grattan Whitestone, B.A. Stanstead received royal visits from King John, Queen Elizabeth, and the 1st and 2nd Georges.

WALDERTON, or Waldington, and NORTHWOOD, are hamlets of this parish.

The church (St. Mary) is in the Early English style, with nave, chancel, and aisles; but contains nothing of great importance. It had a chancel called St. Catherine's, and lights for the Holy Sepulchre and All Souls. There are three bells, one ancient, inscribed *Ave gracia plena*.

On the Downs there are several tumuli and earthworks, and tradition asserts that Ædelwalch, King of Sussex, and the exiled Cædwalla of Wessex, met here in battle, and further that the vanquished South-Saxon King lies buried in the southern barrow with his arms and his chieftains around him. (Longcroft.)

[S. A. C. Lumley Lords, of Stanstead, v, 49, 65. xvi, 266. xix, 92, 101. Fitz-Alans of ditto, v, 66. xvi, 266. Lewknor of, v, 66. Royal visits: King John, i, 136; Queen Elizabeth, v, 197. xvi, 266; George I. and II., xvi. xix, 147, 8. Mathews of Stansted, xi, 69. xviii, 13. Church and new district church, xii, 78. Bells of these churches, xvi, 225, 232. River Ems or Racon at, xvi, 264, 266. xviii, 185. Earthworks and tumuli, xvi, 264. Walderton bridge, and Pitt the gunman, xvi, 264. Maltravers, xvi, 266. Stanstead besieged, xvi, 266. The Rector to arm, xvii, 198. Flight of Charles II., xviii, 115. Scarborough, Earls of, xix, 147.]

STREET or STREAT.

Domesday, *Estrat;* a parish in the Hundred of the same name; Rape of Lewes; distant 6½ miles from Lewes. Post-town, Hurst-Pierpoint. Railway stations, Burgess Hill, and Hassock's Gate. Union, Chailey. Population in 1811, 133; in 1861, 190. Benefice, a Rectory, valued at £172; Patron, H. C. Lane, Esq.; Incumbent, Rev. William

Anthony Fitzhugh, M.A., of Trinity College, Cambridge. Date of earliest Parish Register, 1561. Acreage, 1,270. *Chief Landowner*, H. C. Lane, Esq.

Street is a name given by our Saxon ancestors to the old Roman roads (*viæ stratæ*) which traversed England, and it has been conjectured that such a road passed through this parish; but this is uncertain. The parish, like most of those in the Weald of Sussex, is long and narrow, its length from north to south being between four and five miles, while its breadth does not exceed half a mile. It extends from the chalk of the South Downs to the Wealden clay, and has a soil which is mostly fertile. There are many coppices and several woods. Near the church are two fine specimens of the quercus ilex, which is a rather rare tree in these parts.

The manor of Street, which includes the greater part of the parish, is mentioned in Domesday as Estrat, and part of the possessions of William de Warenne. Both before and after the Conquest it was valued at 100s. In 1192, it belonged to Geoffrey de Saye, in whose descendants it remained till 1383, when it passed by marriage to the family of Fynes, subsequently Lords Dacre. *Temp.* Elizabeth it belonged to the Goring family, and later it was possessed by the family of Dobell, from whom it passed by marriage to the Lanes, the present owners. Street Place is a large handsome house, of the latter part of the reign of Elizabeth, and commands extensive views of the adjacent picturesque country. The principal front facing the east is 86 feet long, and has two projecting wings. The room on the first floor in the south wing of the front is paneled in oak, and has remains of numerous Latin mottoes. Mr. Blaauw supposes it to have been the study of Walter Dobell, who died in 1625. One of his descendants, who joined the Cavalier party during the Civil Wars, is said to have contrived a place of concealment in the house, the entrance to which was up the great hall chimney. There are several curious legends and traditions respecting this old mansion, which ceased to be the residence of the Dobells on their acquisition of Folkington Place, and early in the eighteenth century Street Place became a farmhouse.

Two "small churches" are mentioned in Domesday, but where the second stood is unknown. Street church consists of chancel, nave, north porch, north chancel, and a recently added south transept. The building, though much patched in later times, has doors and other features of Norman date. A turret over the west end contains one bell. There are memorials to the families and names of Dobell, Vinal, Gott, Lane, &c. Before the Reformation, an acre of land, called East-town, was held by this church for the support of a light.

[S. A. C. Street Place, iv, 93 *(Blaauw)*. viii, 269. xvi, 292. William Dobell's accounts, iv, 98. East-town, xiii, 47. Black-brook, xv, 162. Bell, xvi, 225.]

SULLINGTON.

Domesday, *Sillintone;* a parish in the Hundred of East Easwrith; Rape of Bramber, distant five miles north-west from Steyning Railway station. Post-town, Hurst-Pierpoint. Union, Thakeham. Population in 1811, 234; in 1861, 241. Benefice, a Rectory, valued at £400; Patroness, Mrs. Palmer; Incumbent, Rev. Henry Palmer, M.A., of Trinity College, Cambridge. Date of earliest Parish Register, 1555. Acreage, 2,340. *Seat,* Sandgate Lodge, George Carew Gibson, Esq.

Sullington lies partly on the South Downs, but the greater portion consists of arable land. Its length from north to south is 3¼ miles, and its breadth ¾ of a mile. The soil varies from chalk to sandy loam. Like Beeding, it has a detached portion in the forest district near Horsham, called BROADBRIDGE HEATH, about twelve miles to the north, with a population, in 1861, of 86. From Domesday, Sillintone appears to have been among the smallest of manors, possessing only one villein with half a plough, and valued at 2s.! Ulward held it of the Confessor, and Robert of Earl Roger de Montgomeri. Soon after the Conquest the family of Aguillon, or De Aquila, held it, and Richard de Aguillon's only daughter carried it by marriage to William de Covert, who had two knights' fees in Sullington and Broadbridge. Several disputes respecting game in this manor are recorded. In 1275, Hugh, son of Otho, brought an action against Roger de Covert, for unlawfully detaining a falcon valued at £10, an immense price in those days; and in 1288, William de Braose prosecuted him for killing two hares in his free-warren in Washington and Findon. Roger pleaded that he had always hunted there for hares and foxes, and cut sticks in the woods to carry hares on. The manor house of this ancient sporting squire was valued at 3s. 4d. per annum. He had a park, two watermills, one windmill, and the advowson of the church. His descendants continued in possession for several generations, till Baldwin de Covert,* in 1379, granted the reversion of the manor, after his death, to Richard, Earl of Arundel, who gave it to his Hospital of the Holy Trinity at Arundel.

---

* A very curious will of Margaret, wife of John de Covert, and mother of Baldwin, 1366, is in the possession of W. Smith Ellis Esq., of Hydecroft: it has been translated and printed in Cartwright's Rape of Bramber.

After the dissolution of that house, it passed through the families of Lee, Shelley of Warminghurst, Apsley, and Shelley of Lewes. The manor-house close to the church has some traces of antiquity. The name of the Park is still retained by a portion of the estate, and two watermills now exist, probably on the Domesday sites. (Cartwright, p. 122.) On the north-west side of the parish are two farms called Wantleys, which took their name from the family of De Wantele, before 1296, one of whom, John de Wantele, has a brass in Amberley church, dated 1424. In later times the families of Michell, Bennet, Standen, and Shelley have owned these lands. At Sandgate, near the centre of the parish, Sir George Warren, K.B., erected a cottage *orné*. After his death, Henry Shelley, Esq., enlarged it and made it his residence. It afterwards passed to the names of Anderson, Hill, and Bosanquet. In 1825, it was purchased by George John Gibson, Esq., who further enlarged it, and by subsequent alterations, made it one of the most agreeable residences in Sussex. It is now the property and seat of George Carew C. Gibson, Esq., who in 1869 made additions which place it among the finest of Sussex mansions in Elizabethan architecture. The gentle family of Wase resided at Sullington in the sixteenth and seventeenth centuries.

The rectory and vicarage were formerly distinct, but they were united by Bishop Praty in 1441, on account of the poverty of the vicarage, which had prevented any priest from accepting it, and the service of the church had been neglected for twenty-six years. The church (St. Mary) consists of a nave, chancel, north aisle, and low west tower, with a pyramidal cap. The nave has traces of Early English date, but the chancel is Decorated. In the north aisle, Richard, Earl of Arundel, in 1389, founded a chantry, and gave the chapel of St. Martin in Arundel Castle for its support. In 37th Henry VIII. the incumbent, Thomas Sackville, " a student at the gramer scole of thage of 13," had the endowment towards his exhibition £3 16s.—a very young incumbent. Under the tower is a recumbent cross-legged effigy of a knight in armour, which was removed thither from the north aisle. Though much mutilated, it retains traces of excellent workmanship. It is of the time of Henry III., and is believed to represent William de Covert, lord of the manor. In 1825, a stone with a cross fleury was dug up in the church-yard, and placed within the building. There are other memorials for the names of Goring, Dixon, Williams, &c. There is one bell dated 1522, and dedicated to the Trinity.

In 1809, some tumuli were opened on Sullington Warren. They contained imperfect parts of urns and charcoal of the Celtic period. One perfect urn was exhumed. In 1812, several

Roman warlike implements (spear-heads, swords, &c.) were found north of Sandgate.

[S. A. C. Domesday mills, v, 272. De Covert a Crusader, ix, 365; xv, 95. Tithes to Beeding Priory, x, 115. Church, xii, 108. Goring, xvi, 49, xix, 94, Bell, xvi, 225. Mill-stream to the Arun, xvi, 257.]

SUTTON.

Domesday, *Sudtone* (" the southern enclosure "); a parish in the Hundred of Rotherbridge ; Rape of Arundel ; distant five miles south from Petworth, its Post-town. Railway stations, Petworth and Amberley. Union, Sutton. Population in 1811, 342; in 1861, 364. Benefice, a Rectory, valued at £256 ; Patron, Lord Leconfield ; Incumbent, Rev. Henry Lockett, M.A., of Exeter College, Oxford. Date of earliest Parish Register, 1656. Acreage, 2,061. *Chief Landowner*, Lord Leconfield.

The village is situated on a pleasant elevation at the foot of a high range of the South Downs. In Saxon times five Thanes (they must have been very small ones) held it as a free manor. At the Conquest Robert held it of Earl Roger, and when the Earldom of Arundel came into possession of Queen Adeliza, it became as a part of her gift to her brother, Josceline of Louvaine, an appendage to the Honour of Petworth, and still so remains. By a roll of 26th Edward I., it appears that Peter de Sutton held ten librates here by the service of furnishing a sparrow-hawk to the king, and Fulco Basset other lands by that of certain furred gloves (quasdem cirothecas griseo-furratas). The church (St. John) has a nave and chancel, north transept, south aisle, and porch, with Transition or Early English features, and a fine western tower. The chancel, which is Decorated, has been restored. In the east window are the arms of Percy, Louvaine, and De Albini. The learned Hebraist, Julius Bate, was rector of this church in 1742 (" Worthies of Sussex," p. 336). Roman pottery has been found in this parish, and even within the church.

[S. A. C. Three watermills in Domesday, v, 272. Church, xii, 102. Roman pottery, xv, 242. Bell, xvi, 225.]

SUTTON,

In East Sussex, is now parochially united with Seaford. The foundations of the church are traceable near Sutton Place. It is a prebend in Chichester Cathedral. See Seaford.

SWANBOROUGH.

An ancient *grange* of Lewes Priory in the parish of Iford.
Remains of a chapel still exist, with other ancient features.

TANGMERE.

Domesday, *Tangmere;* a parish in the Hundred of Aldwick; Rape of
Chichester; distant three miles north-north-east from Chichester,
its Post-town. Railway station, Drayton, distant about 1½ mile.
Union, West Hampnett. Population in 1811, 157; in 1861, 201.
Benefice, a Rectory, valued at £280; Patron, the Duke of Richmond;
Incumbent, Rev. George Gaisford, M.A., of Christ Church, Oxford.
Date of earliest Parish Register, 1539. Acreage, 774. *Chief Land-
owner,* the Duke of Richmond.

A level and fertile parish well adapted for cereals. Domesday places it in the Hundred of Pagham. It was then a rather
important manor, held of the Archbishop by clerks, with a bailiff,
15 villeins, and 15 bondmen, who were provided with a church.
Temp. Henry VIII. it passed from the see of Canterbury, through
Archbishop Cranmer, to the King. Ultimately it was attached
to the Halnaker estate, and has thus passed to its present lord,
the Duke of Richmond.

The church (St. Andrew) is a Peculiar of the Archbishop. It
consists of nave and chancel; the former is early English, the
latter less ancient. It has lately been thoroughly repaired and
decorated with painted windows. In the church-yard stands a
hollow yew, more than eight feet in diameter.

[S. A. C. Church xii, 78. Bells, xvi, 225. Worth in, Kempes, xix,
119. Road through, xix, 159.]

· TARRING NEVILLE, or EAST TARRING.

A parish in the Hundred of Danehill-Horsted; Rape of Pevensey; on
the Ouse, 2½ miles north from Newhaven. Post-town, Lewes. Railway station, Newhaven. Union, Newhaven. Population in 1811, 80;
in 1861, 84. Benefice, a Rectory united with South Heighton,
valued at £406; Patroness, Mrs. Cornelia Fothergill. Incumbent,
Rev. M. Wyell Mayow, M.A. Date of earliest Parish Register, 1569.
Acreage, 938. *Chief Landowner,* the Rev. F. W. Gray.

Of the history of this parish little is known, except that
at an early period it belonged to the family of Neville, whence
the suffix to distinguish it from Tarring Peverell, in the western
division of the county. About the year 1640 it was ecclesias-

tically united to Heighton, whose parishioners, since the destruction of their church, have worshipped here. The church (St. Mary) consists of a chancel, nave with south aisle, and a small west tower with pyramidal cap. The outside is entirely covered with plaster, but the interior has some Early English features, and a few interesting points. The one bell is ancient and inscribed to St. John. There are several memorials for the family of Geere, who were formerly incumbents of this benefice and of Heighton. On a part of the South Downs, called Tarring Lowe, are several fine and apparently unexplored tumuli.

[S. A. C. Laurence Waterhouse, priest, xiii, 56. Bell, xvi, 141, 225.]

TARRING, WEST, or TARRING PEVEREL.

A parish conterminous with the Hundred to which it gives name;* Rape of Bramber; distant one mile north-west from Worthing Railway station. Post-town Worthing. Union, East Preston. Population in 1811, 568; in 1861, 606. Benefice, a Rectory, a Peculiar of Canterbury, with Heene annexed, valued at £474; Patron, the Archbishop of Canterbury; Incumbent, Rev. John Wood Warter, B.D., of Christ Church, Oxford. Date of earliest Parish Register, 1559.

This parish, on the South Coast, possesses much local and historical interest, and it is fortunate in its learned Rector, the son-in-law of the immortal Southey, whose "Seaboard and the Down," and "Parochial Fragments" contain a good deal of information relating to it, with more than has any immediate connection with this brief notice. The soil is a rich wheat-producing loam, with a substratum of marl, except towards the north, where it is more chalky. Ecclesiastically it has some peculiarities. Cartwright sums up the curious divisions which it possesses. The number of acres, he tells us, is 2,054, of which Tarring proper contains 624; Salvington, 390; Durrington and Coate, 641; Heene, 397, exclusive of 20 acres of Down adjoining Findon, called "No-man's-land." The chapelries of Heene and Durrington maintain their own poor, and are for civil purposes in the Hundred of Brightford. Salvington is a hamlet.— The earliest account we have of the manor of Tarring is that King Athelstan gave it to the Church of Canterbury before the year 944, and the Domesday survey states that it had been immemorially subject to that see. In the reign of the Confessor, it was rated at 18 hides, nearly corresponding with present dimensions. There were 27 villeins, 14 cottars, two churches, and a wood of 6 hogs. It fluctuated in value between the Saxon and the

* Except a few outlying lands in Horsham, Rusper, and Shipley.

Norman rule from £14 4s. to £15. At the date of Domesday
William de Braose held four hides of the manor, and had three
in demesne. According to the Hundred Rolls, 1274, the tenants
of the Archbishop in Tarring and Salvington performed suits to
the hundred of Brightford. In 1227 we have a curious list of
the necessaries of life as assessed under a distraint of the Primate. A quarter of wheat was worth 18d.; of oats, 8d; a
yearling hog, 8d.; a carcase of mutton, 4d.; two good hens a
penny, a good goose a penny; and four gallons of good beer
also a penny! How the manor passed from the Archbishop to
the Crown is not known. In 6th James I. it was chiefly held
under a Crown lease for 70 years by Jane Dering. From 1620
to 1710 the family of Garway held it. It subsequently passed to
the families of Travies and Barker. In 1796 the demesne lands,
281 acres, which are very fertile, were purchased by Thomas
Henty, Esq. Mr. Henty brought the breed of Merino sheep to
great perfection, and exported many of them to New South
Wales. The inhabitants of Tarring were by ancient right
excused from serving on juries on account of the service due to
the Archbishop. In 24th Henry VI. "the men of Terryng in
the shyre of Sussex, upon the se banks dwelling," complained to
the Lords in Council that their people had frequently been injured in life and property by the incursions of the King's ene-
mies from France, Brittany and Spain. Two years afterwards
the inhabitants obtained a charter for a weekly market on
Saturdays, but this was of no long continuance. The original
petition and charter are in the hands of the parish officers.
(Cartwright.) The family of Hamper, which afterwards produced the late well-known antiquary William Hamper, Esq.,
F.S.A., of Birmingham, were long resident in Tarring. In 1582
George Hamper married Alice Selden, aunt to the illustrious
John Selden, "the glory of the English nation," as Grotius calls
him.

John Selden was born at Salvington in this parish in 1584, and
the parish register records his baptism on the 20th of December,
as "John the sonne of John Selden the minstrell." The father,
however, is described by Aubrey ("Letters," Vol.ii.,p. 530) as "a
yeomanly man of about £40 a year, who played well on the
violin." Hence his description as a "minstrel." This acquire-
ment brought him the favour and love of a gentlewoman, Margaret, daughter of Thomas Baker, of Rustington, of the knightly
family of that name in Kent. For a copious account of the
eminent jurist, antiquary, and patriot, John Selden, see "Johnson's Life of Selden," and "Worthies of Sussex," p. 1—11. His
birth-place is a small timbered house formerly called Lacies,
probably a fragment of a larger one. It bears the date 1601, to

indicate some repairs then made, for the original house must have been of earlier date. On the lintel of the low door inside is the following distich, said to have been carved by Selden himself when a boy of ten :—

"GRATUS. HONESTE. MIHI. NON CLAUDAR. INITO. SEDEQUE.
FUR. ABEAS : NON SUM FACTA SOLUTA, TIBI."

Which Mr. J. G. Nichols happily paraphrases—

"Welcome if honest ! Glad such men to greet,
I will not close—walk in and take thy seat.
Thief, get thee gone ! 'gainst thee a stout defence,
I open not, but boldly bid thee hence."*

I strongly doubt the fact of Selden's having either composed or cut this inscription, as the letters are much too archaic for the assumed date. The Rectory-house, of which some remains exist, is supposed to stand on the site of the Archbishop's palace. This is doubted, but I believe the statement to be correct, as the chapel, 38 feet by 25, and the hall 40 feet by 20, remain, together with a range of buildings called Parsonage-row. "They are of the time of Henry VI. or Edward IV., and are among the most perfect specimens of ancient architecture in the Rape of Bramber." (Cartwright). Hither Thomas-à-Becket is said frequently to have resorted, and to have planted figs near the house. The fig orchard adjoining it was raised from some old stocks in the rectory garden. It was planted in 1745, and contains 100 trees, which produce about 2,000 dozen of the fruit annually. This is probably the largest plantation of figs in England. It is a curious fact that a bird resembling the Beccafico or fig-eater of Italy migrates hither during the fig season. The flocks remain five or six weeks, and then disappear as they came, seaward.

The church (St. Andrew) is large and handsome, with chancel, nave with aisles, north porch, and west tower, supporting a lofty octangular shingled spire. The nave and aisles are Early English, the former very lofty with narrow clerestory windows. The chancel and tower are Perpendicular, the former having a large east window, a piscina, six oak stalls, some panneling and benches. (Hussey.) The building was thoroughly restored some years since at an expense of nearly £3,000. The window under the tower is a memorial to Robert Southey, set up at the expense of his eldest daughter, the wife of the present vicar. In this church was formerly a chantry, dedicated to the Virgin, probably founded by one of the family of Atte Felde (who were very ancient in this and the neighbouring parishes) before the

* "Gentleman's Magazine," September, 1834.

year 1282. There are memorials in this fine church for the names of Negus, Coopper, Whitpaine, Brookbanks, Cooke, Stiles, Mitford, Whitebread, Jordan, Campion, Green, Haines, &c. There are six modern bells. The church chest contains the churchwardens' accounts from 1515 till 1579, and are full of curious entries. The Tarringites must have led a merry life occasionally, especially at their "church-ales," when they feasted and drank right heartily. The bill of fare for 1562 contains among other items, "5 calvys, 8 lams, 4 sheype xxjs. iiijd., 5 bushels of malt, to cawfys hedes, ijd., a lygke of motton iiijd.," with pepper, saffron and other spices. Their "mynsterylles" had 6s. 8d., exclusive of the "Drowme pleyr," who had 12d.

For DURRINGTON and HEENE, now ecclesiastically united with Tarring, see those articles.

[S. A. C. John Selden, v, 79. viii, 271. xv, 170. xviii, 163. xix, 190. Ancient house, vii, 47. Durrington tithes to Sele Priory, x, 115, 121. Durrington church, x, 115. xii, 110. Stephen de Offington, land in Durrington, xi, 100. Heene, Tortington Priory had lands, xi, 110. Parish church, xii, 110. xv, 41. Heene, chapel of St. Botolph, xii, 110. Lucas at Agincourt, xv, 137. Archbishop's manor, xv, 153. Bells, xvi, 225. Hampers of, xix, 190.]

TELSCOMBE.

A parish in the Hundred of Holmstrow; Rape of Lewes; distant six miles south-south-west from Lewes, its Post-town. Railway station, Newhaven. Union, Newhaven. Population in 1811, 95; in 1861, 156. Benefice, a Rectory, valued at £286; Incumbent, Rev. James Hutchins, M.A., of Christ Church, Oxford, who is also Patron. Date of earliest Parish Register, 1684. Acreage, 1,349. *Chief Landowners*, the Beard family, the Earl of Abergavenny, and the Earl De la Warr.

A very secluded South Down village, seldom visited except by huntsmen and lovers of racehorses. It is in a deep *combe* or valley, whence the termination. It is thought to be the "Laneswice" of Domesday, but it certainly bore the name of Titelescumbe in Saxon times. At the end of the reign of Elizabeth the manor belonged to Thomas, Lord Buckhurst, and after several changes it passed, in 1690, to Henry Shelley, Esq., of Lewes, to whose descendants, Henry and William D'Albiac, Esquires, it lately belonged. Robert Plumer, Esq., who held the manor farm of Courthouse in 1657, aliened it to Henry Smith, Esq., the founder of the well-known "charity," and its proceeds are devoted to six parishes in Surrey. The Hoddern or Hothdown, farm, in this parish was, until the last century, a rabbit warren. Near the village is one of the "Tyes," of frequent occurrence on and near the Downs.

The church (St. Lawrence) was given with Southease, to the abbey of Hyde near Winchester, in the 10th century. It is a very small building, of chancel, nave, with north aisle and west tower, with a pyramidal cap. A north chancel, long since destroyed, was rebuilt a few years since, during the renovation of the church, towards which the late William Cotton, Esq., was a great benefactor. The date is Transition-Norman. There are memorials for the names of Colley, Higgins, Crew, Povey, &c.

Portobello, a coast-guard station, is a kind of hamlet of Telscombe, and possesses nearly one-half of the population of the parish.

[S. A. C. Bell, xvi, 226. Alcock of Tetelescombe, a partizan of Jack Cade, xviii, 24.]

THAKEHAM.

Domesday, *Taceham;* a parish in the Hundred of East Easwrith; Rape of Bramber; distant four miles south-east from Pulborough station. Post-town, Hurst-Pierpoint. Union, Thakeham. Population in 1811, 522; in 1861, 559. Benefice, a Rectory, valued at £710; Patron and Incumbent, Rev. John Hurst, M.A., of Trinity College, Cambridge. Date of earliest Parish Register, 1628. Acreage, 2,980.

It is a parish of the very usual Sussex shape, much longer than it is broad. It is about five miles from south to north, and about three-quarters of a mile from west to east. There are two small detached portions of this parish, one called Muttons or Childe's farm, adjacent to Washington, and the other West Caltons, which is entirely surrounded by West Chiltington. In Domesday, Morice held the manor of William de Braose, Brixi having before held it of King Edward, as 20 hides, three roods. Afterwards it was reduced to five hides. There were 14 ploughlands, besides two in the demesne, 30 villeins, and 12 cottagers, with eight ploughs. There were a church, a mill, and a wood of 60 hogs. "A knight holds one hide of land, where he has five oxen with a bondman." *Temp.* Edward I., the manor was valued at £14. It was held in 1270 by the ancient family of Le Poer or Power, when Stephen Poer died seised. "His son or grandson," says Cartwright, "died in 1352, leaving two daughters and coheirs, between whom the manor became divided. It is a singular circumstance that the lineal descendants of these two daughters are, at present (1830),

joint proprietors of the manor which has descended in two un-
interrupted lines, without any alienation, during the long period
of 474 years." One moiety descended through the families of
Apsley and Caldecot, to that of Shelley, of Lewes, now extinct; the
other came through the Clothalls, Wilsheres, Bellinghams, Boys,
and Lambs, to the Rev. Thomas Ferris. Thakeham Place, formerly the residence of the Apsleys, was acquired by the marriage
of Stephen Apsley with Margaret, daughter of Stephen le Poer,
in the 14th century. A modern house marks the site of the
ancient mansion, which, about a century since, enclosed a
quadrangle, with an entrance gateway, a chapel, and a great
hall. A spring of clear water, known as St. Mary's well, exists
near the site. From the two coheirs of Richard Caldecot, one
portion of this property passed through several generations of
the family of Butler, and it is now part of the settled estate of
the Duke of Norfolk. The other moiety of the estate passed to
the family of Newton of Southover, and was, a few years since,
vested in their descendant, the late Mrs. W. Courthope Mabbott.
Abingsworth, in the south part of the parish, formerly gave name
to a now extinct family. It was for two centuries in the family
of Mellersh, and has descended through two heiresses to Edward
Fuller Upperton, Esq. *Campions* was formerly a place of some
importance, though now only a farm, and belonged to a branch
of the Shelleys. *Apsley* or *Apslee*, on the north-east side of the
parish, now also a farm, gave name to an influential family, who,
as we have seen, inherited a moiety of the Le Poer estate in this
parish. Sir Allen Apsley, Lieutenant of the Tower, was descended from a younger branch of this race, and was father of
Lucy, wife of Colonel Hutchinson, and authoress of the well-
known " Memoirs " of her husband, who occupied a considerable position in the reigns of James I. and Charles I. (" Worthies of Sussex," p. 156.)

The church (according to Cartwright dedicated to St. Mary,
but, as Mr. Gibbon says, St. Peter and St. Paul) is a picturesque
building, of nave, chancel, and two transepts, with lancet windows. The tower appears to be of the time of Henry VII. I
have not visited this church, but a few years since it had screens
dividing the chancel and the north transept, and benches indicating that date. In the tower are five bells, the fourth of which
has this distich :—

" I will be glad, and much reioyce on the, o God most hie,
And make my songs extol thy name above the starrie skie, 1748."

There are many monumental inscriptions. On the floor there
are brasses for 𝔗𝔥𝔬𝔪𝔞𝔰 𝔄𝔭𝔰𝔩𝔢𝔶, son of William Apsley, Armiger,
1517, and for 𝔅𝔢𝔱𝔯𝔦𝔵 𝔄𝔭𝔰𝔩𝔢𝔶, mother of William Apsley, Armiger,

1515. On an altar-tomb of Alabaster, is another brass for 𝕸𝖎𝖑𝖑𝖘. 𝕬𝖕𝖘𝖑𝖊𝖞, Armiger, 1527. Another altar-tomb, without inscription, commemorates John Apsley, and Mary Lewknor his wife, the former of whom died in 1587. An altar-tomb of Sussex marble, despoiled of its brasses, is for William, son and heir of John Apsley, Esquier, 1583. A much-defaced mural tablet of Caen stone bears the arms of the same family, but no inscription, according to Cartwright's account. Still another mural tablet remains for Edward, only son of Sir Edward Apsley, of Apsley, 1651. Altogether the mortuary memorials of this ancient family are most interesting. There are also tablets for the names and families of Butler, Shelley, Mellersh, Butcher, Fuller, Lear, Banks, Hill, Williamson, Milner, &c., &c.

In 1351 King Edward III. confirmed to Stephen le Poer or Power, the grant of a messuage and 42 acres of arable, and pasture for two oxen in Thakeham, for the maintenance of a chantry in the chapel of the Blessed Virgin, in the churchyard of Thakeham.* In 1512 a dispute arose between William Apsley and Ralph Bellingham as to the right of patronage to this chantry, who both claimed to be equally descended from Stephen le Power, the founder. The Vicar-General declared that the gift should be alternate, and the chantry is described as " Cantaria perpetua in capella Beatæ Mariæ Virginis in cemeterio ecclesiæ de Thacham." In the pleas of the Crown, 7th Edward I., it is averred that John le Suche (Zouche) rector of Chiltington, came armed with his neighbours and dependents into a certain field called Rushfield in this parish, where Martin, rector of Thakeham, came with his men and a cart to collect the tithes of the same field, and when Suche saw the aforesaid Martin, he assaulted him with an iron fork, and a tenant of his shot the said Martin in the right breast with an arrow. Another tenant attempted to kill the poor rector as he lay upon the ground, with a hatchet; whereupon the latter's servant struck the assailant with a bundle of wood and slew him. A coroner's inquest followed, but with no result. Such battles of the " church militant " were not unfrequent in the middle ages. The names of the combatants and the witnesses are given by Cartwright, p. 251.

[S. A. C. Apsley MSS. iv, 219. xii, 109. xiv, 224. Apsley pedigree, iv, 220. Domesday watermill, v, 272. Tithes to Sele Priory, x, 115. Church of, xii, 109. Weller of, xvi, 49. Church bells, xvi, 226. Lancet Brook, xvi, 250. Butler family, xvii, 222.]

* The existence of chantry chapels in church-yards, unattached to the main building, was not unusual at this date, and much later.

THORNEY ISLAND (or West Thorney).

Domesday, *Tornei;* a parish in the Hundred of Bosham; Rape of Chichester, distant about seven miles south-west from that city; Posttown, Emsworth; Railway station, Bosham. Union, Westbourne. Population in 1811, 62; in 1861, 93. Benefice, a Rectory, valued at £320; Patron, Philip Lyne, Esq.; Incumbent, Rev. Chas. Philip Lyne, M.A., of Queen's College, Oxford. Acreage, 3,005. *Chief Landowners,* Frederick Padwick, Esq., and the Lyne family.

This little insulated parish lies near the centre of the estuary called Chichester Harbour, and owing to the shallowness of the sea, either gains or loses area by the reflux or influx of every tide. It is within the peculiar jurisdiction of Bosham, and the descent of the manor has been the same. After the Conquest it was held of the church of Bosham by one Malger. A priest is specially mentioned in Domesday.

The church is a plain ancient building of rubble and stone, dedicated to St. Nicholas, the mariner's saint, and there is one medieval bell, inscribed " JHESUS." Dallaway ascribes the edifice to the time of Warlewast, Bishop of Exeter, founder of the College of Bosham, about 1120. It has zigzag and other ornaments of the Norman period.

[S. A. C. Church, xii, 79. Bell, xvi, 226. Chichester Harbour, xvi, 262. References to " Gentleman's Magazine," xviii, 95.]

THREE BRIDGES.

An important station of the London and Brighton Railway, from whence diverge lines to Tunbridge Wells and Midhurst. It is situated in the parish of Worth, on a branch of the river Mole, which formerly had three streamlets, crossed by as many bridges, *unde nomen.*

TILGATE FOREST. (See Worth.)

TICEHURST.

Vulgo, *Tisus;* a parish in the Hundred of Shoyswell; Rape of Hastings; distant eight miles south-west from Cranbrook; Post-town, Hawkhurst; Railway station, Ticehurst Road, distant about 3½ miles. Union, Ticehurst. Population in 1811, 1,593; in 1861, 2,758. Benefice, a Vicarage, valued at £700 ; Patron, the Dean and Chapter of Canterbury; Incumbent, Rev. Arthur Eden, M.A., of Queen's College, Oxford. Date of earliest Parish Register, 1559. Acreage,

8,202. *Chief Landowners*, George Campion Courthope, Esq., and Nathan Wetherell, Esq. *Seats*, Whiligh, C. Courthope, Esq.; Ridgeway, Samuel Newington, Esq., M.D.; Pashley House, Nathan Wetherell, Esq.; Pickford, E. Curry, Esq.

Ticehurst is "the wood on the Tees," a little tributary of the Medway, which flows through part of the parish. The manor of Ticehurst does not appear in Domesday. In 23rd Edward I. William de Echingham held it, and in 35th of the same reign Edmund de Passeley, or Passeleu (Pashley) held lands here, and in 10th Edward II. Edmund de Passele, the same, or a descendant, is described as lord. Two years earlier Alan de Buxhull is said to have held Tychehurst. The descent of the manor is very obscure. The names of Wanton, Ore, and others occur as proprietors of lands. In 1600 Thomas Pelham obtained a grant of two fairs to be held here. In 16th George III. James Dalrymple, Esq., married the daughter and heiress of John Apsley, Esq., whose son, John Apsley Dalrymple, Esq., was lord of the manor under his grandfather's will. The true descent of the manor awaits investigation.

This large parish possesses many points of interest. The village is remarkably neat, and occupies a gentle eminence. It is surrounded by a pleasing undulated country. Hops are grown to a considerable extent.

Pashley, a manor and estate in Ticehurst, gave name to the ancient family of Pashley, or Passeleu, which produced the well-known Edmund de Passeleu, Baron of the Exchequer *temp.* Edward I. In the reign of Elizabeth it became the property of the family of May, from whom descended the Mays of Burwash (the poet's branch), and of Rawmere in West Sussex. The heiress of Thomas May, Esq., married the Rev. Richard Wetherell, and died in 1833. The mansion was built *temp.* James I. It has the date of 1612, and contains some excellent oak carving of that date. It was formerly moated. Borezell is a moated manor house of considerable antiquity, and was for many descents the estate of the family of Roberts, descended from the ancient house of that name, at Glassenbury, in Kent. It is now the property of George Burrow Gregory, Esq., M.P. The family of Newington are of long standing in Ticehurst. They are descended from Sir Adam Newington, of Withernden in this parish, Knight, who was living in 1481, and the estate, until lately, remained in their possession. They have still excellent property in the parish. The family have been for several generations famed for their medical skill, and the late Mr. Newington, sen., of Vineyards, founded an establishment for the reception of lunatics of the higher class. His son, Mr. Charles Newington, much enlarged the original plan, and at Highlands erected a splendid series of ornamental buildings on a commanding and beautiful site, about half a mile from the village. The Chinese Gallery is a large building for indoor promenades, and there are spacious grounds, occupying 200 acres, with carriage-drives, walks, plantations, cricket and archery grounds, billiard-rooms, a museum, fountains, aviaries, conservatories, and a handsome chapel. This is one of the finest establishments in the kingdom for the nervous and insane, and the kind and humane treatment which the unfortunate inmates receive tends much to relieve their sufferings. (See memoir of Charles Newington in the "Worthies of Sussex," 254). The establishment is now the property and under the care of his son, Dr. Samuel Newington.—Whiligh, an ancient manor, formerly held by the families of Pashley, Warde, Shoyswell, and Sanders, came into the possession of John Courthope, Esq., in 1512, from whom it has descended to George Campion Courthope, Esq., the present proprietor. Whiligh is a large structure of brick, surrounded by fine trees in the centre of an extensive park, and lies about three miles from the village. There are several other excellent residences, villas, &c., in the parish. Ticehurst gave name to a family now widely spread in the middle and lower classes of society.

The church (St. Mary) consists of a nave, with aisles, a chancel, flanked with two chantry or manorial chapels, each having a piscina, and a tower with shingled spire. There are six bells, dated 1771, with doggerel verses on each. On the north side of the porch are the arms of Echingham. In the windows are some remains of ancient painted glass. There is a brass for 𝕵𝕠𝕙𝕟 𝖂𝖆𝖞𝖇𝖆𝖗𝖓𝖊, Esq., and his two wives, Edith and Agnes, date 1490; and there are interesting memorials for the Courthopes of Whiligh, the Mays of Pashley, the Robertses of Borezell, and the Newingtons of Withernden, and references to the names of Rivers, Elliot, Hollist, Scafe, Busbridge, Apsley, and many others. Over the porch is a parvise, or upper chamber, with a grated window, supposed to have been a manorial prison.

Ticehurst has two district churches:—

STONEGATE, 2¼ miles south-west of the parish church, is a Perpetual Curacy; Patron, G. C. Courthope, Esq.; Incumbent, Rev. J. D'Arcy W. Preston. Population in 1861, 525. Dedication, St. Peter.

FLIMWELL, 2½ miles east, is also a Perpetual Curacy, value £100, in the gift of the Bishop of Chichester, and held by the Rev. Chas. James Eagleton, B.A. Population in 1861, 804. Dedication, St. Augustine.

[S. A. C. Iron-works, ii, 217. Wybarne brass and family, viii, 17. Passeley and La Leake Chapels, &c., xiii, 47. xix, 88. Grant of lands by

Queen Elizabeth, xiii, 110. Rectory belonged to Hastings Priory, xiii, 156. Hamerden manor, xiv, 112. Apsley family, xiv, 114. Courthope family, xvi, 46. Whiligh, xvi, 46. Church bells, xvi, 226. xvi, 231. xvi, 232. Borezell and Roberts family, xvi, 292. Pashley, *ibid.* May family, xvi, 292. xix, 88. Tyse, or Tees, river, xvi, 272. Manor to Battle Abbey, xvii, 54. Cade's insurrection, xviii, 24.]

TIDEBROOK. (See Wadhurst.)

TILLINGTON.

Domesday, *Tolintune;* a parish in the Hundred of Rotherbridge; Rape of Arundel; distant one mile west from Petworth, its Post-town and Railway station. Union, Midhurst. Population in 1811, 650; in 1861, 908. Benefice, a Rectory, valued at £740; Patron, Lord Leconfield; Incumbent, Rev. Robert Ridsdale, M.A., of Clare College, Cambridge. Date of earliest Parish Register, 1572. Acreage, 3,766. *Chief Landowners,* Lord Leconfield and William Townley Mitford, Esq., M.P., of Pitts Hill.

In the reign of Edward the Confessor the Countess Eddeva held under that monarch, and *temp.* Domesday Robert was tenant of Earl Roger. At the creation of the Honour of Petworth for Josceline of Louvaine, Tillington became a constituent part, and has so continued, Lord Leconfield holding in demesne and free land 1,957 acres, part of which is in the great park of Petworth. In 1760, William Mitford, Esq., descended from the great northern family of Mitford Castle, co. Northumberland, began the erection of the mansion called Pitts Hill, which was completed by his son in 1794. The site is remarkable for great natural beauty, and the appliances of art have rendered it a charming residence.

The church of Allhallows has portions in the Decorated style. It consists of a chancel, and a nave and south aisle, separated by a low arcade, the capitals of which are of the early part of the 14th century. The light and lofty tower finished with flying arches, crossed in the centre, was erected in 1807 at the expense of the late Earl of Egremont (Dallaway). The inscriptions in the church are interesting, and comprise the names of Spencer (1593), Milward, Rowe, Mitford, and Capron, and of Dr. William Cox, a controversial rector, 1658 (see " Worthies of Sussex," p. 340). At River in this parish there seems to have been a chapel; there are enclosures known as Chapel Field, Lady Field, Soul Field, and Chantry Field. A stone coffin was dug up here. (Arnold's Petworth). The rectory house is substantial and handsome.

At or near Tillington was born, in 1753, John Keyse Sherwin, the talented but unfortunate engraver. (" Worthies of Sussex," p. 37.)

[S. A. C. Clock of Charles I., iii, 103. Domesday watermill, v, 272. Church, xii, 103. xvi, 226.]

TORTINGTON.

A parish in the Hundred of Avisford; Rape of Arundel; distant 1½ mile south-west from Arundel, its Post-town. Railway stations, Arundel and Ford. Union, East Preston. Population in 1811, 78; in 1861, 112. Benefice, a Vicarage, valued at £175; Patron, the Duke of Norfolk; Incumbent, Rev. R. F. Tompkins, B.A., of St. John's College, Cambridge. Date of earliest Parish Register, 1560. Acreage, 1,131. *Chief Landowners*, the Duke of Norfolk and J. Montefiore, Esq.

Tortington lies partly on the alluvium of the Arun, which river forms its eastern boundary. On the north, towards Arundel Park, there is considerable woodland. The manor was held in Saxon times by one Lewin, a free man, and was assessed at 4 hides. After the Conquest, Ernucion held it of Earl Roger de Montgomeri at 3 hides. There were 6 villeins, 2 cottars, and a wood of 6 hogs. In 1210 the Prior of Tortington was rated at 2 knights' fees, which he held by the service of defending Arundel Castle for forty days, during the time of siege. In 1244 John Fitz-Alan obtained it, and annexed it to his demesne of Arundel. A subsequent member of the Arundel family, in 9th Elizabeth, sold it to John Apsley, Esq., who transferred it to Roger Gratwicke, Esq., who built the manor-house called Tortington Place. It afterwards passed through the families of Weekes and Leeves into the hands of Charles, Duke of Norfolk, in whose noble descendant it still vests. Pedigrees of the Gratwicke and Leeves families are given by Dallaway (" Rape of Arundel," page 83).

The Priory of Tortington stood on the banks of the river, about 1½ mile below Arundel, and its existing remains are confined to some walls in a barn near the farm-house of Tortington. This Priory of Augustinian canons, which was dedicated to St. Mary Magdalen, was founded by the Lady Hadvisia Corbet, who is conjectured to have been of the D'Albini family; but of this lady's history and the exact date of the foundation little is known. The Priory was in existence *temp.* King John, and it was probably dependent upon the Abbey of Seez in Normandy. Its revenues were mainly derived from lands in West Sussex, and the Prior had an " inn " or town house in the parish of St.

Swithin, in London. Few and simple are the annals of this small establishment, and, like others of its class, it was in a state of poverty down to the date of the Dissolution, when the revenues were valued at only £101 4s. 1d. The establishment was evidently badly conducted, for in 1478 the Prior was accused of idolatry by adoring the bread and wine, and by placing relics of the saints on the altar, wherefrom arose unseemly strife.

The church is very small, and has only chancel and nave, with a wooden bell-cot over the west end, and south porch. It was formerly larger, and probably cruciform in arrangement. It has Norman features, and some which are probably Early English. There is some early painted glass. The building has been much patched. There is a brass plate for **Roger Gratwik**, lord of the manor of Tortington-Cheneys, 1596, and another inscription for the names of Lister, &c. There is one bell.

[S. A. C. Priory had lands in Lyminster, xi, 106. xiii, 46. Notes on the Priory (*Turner*), xi, 109. xviii, 55. Leeves family, xii, 102. Boxgrove Priory lands here, xv, 90. Bell, xvi, 226. River Arun, xvi, 258. Gratwick family, xvii, 159.]

TREYFORD.

Domesday, *Treverde;* a parish in the Hundred of Dumpford; Rape of Chichester; distant five miles south-west from Midhurst; Post-town, Petersfield. Union, Midhurst. Population in 1811, 114; in 1861, 123. Benefice, a Rectory, with the Vicarages of Elsted and Didling annexed; Patroness, Hon. Mrs. Vernon Harcourt; Incumbent, Rev. William Downes Willis, M.A., of Sidney Sussex-College, Cambridge. Date of earliest Parish Register, 1728. The whole parish, consisting of 1,260 acres, belongs to the Hon. Mrs. Vernon Harcourt.

It is a long and narrow parish, and the village stands on a slope of the South Downs. On the top of Treyford hill is a line of five lofty barrows, called "Devil's Jumps." The manor was held, before the Conquest, by Alard, of Earl Godwin; afterwards of Earl Roger, by Robert Fitz-Tebald. In the 16th century, and probably earlier, it was held by the Aylwins, a family of great antiquity in this district. They continued in possession until 1772, when Robert Aylwin, the last male of the elder line, died, leaving two daughters and co-heiresses, Mary, married to Charles Talbot, second son of George, Earl of Shrewsbury, and Elizabeth, wife of Sir William Mannock, Bart. They sold it to Sir James Peachey, Bart., whose descendant, Henry John, third Lord Selsey, dying without issue in 1838, the property passed to his only sister, the Hon. Mrs. Vernon Harcourt. The name of Aylwin is still subsisting in younger branches, chiefly farmers, in this and the adjacent parishes. The ancient manor-house of the Aylwins, which has some remarkably fine brickwork, still remains.

The old church (St. Mary) was superseded by a new one, dedicated to St. Peter, which was consecrated in 1849, having been built at the charge of the patrons, the Rev. L. Vernon Harcourt, and the Hon. Mrs. Vernon Harcourt. It is from designs by Ferry, and consists of a chancel, nave, north and south aisles, with a tower and spire at the north-west angle. The style is Decorated, and the workmanship excellent. The spire, reaching the height of 120 feet, is a conspicuous ornament to the landscape. This church affords accommodation to the two affiliated parishes of Elstead and Didling.

[S. A. C. Domesday watermill, v, 272. Church, xii, 79. Bell, xvi, 226. River Rother, xvii, 259.]

TROTTON.

Domesday, *Traitune;* a parish in the Hundred of Dumpford; Rape of Chichester; distant four miles west from Midhurst; Post-town, Petersfield, which is also its Railway station, distant about six miles. Union, Midhurst. Population in 1811, 370; in 1861, 452. Benefice, a Rectory, valued at £296; Patron and Incumbent, Rev. Edward William Batchellor, B.A., of Christ Church, Oxford. Date of earliest Parish Register, 1581. Acreage, 3,877.

Like many parishes in this district, Trotton is much disproportioned in its length and breadth, the former being from south to north nearly seven miles, while the latter averages but ¾ of a mile. The village is situated on a fertile soil, near the north bank of the Western Rother. The scenery in many parts is rich and picturesque. The manor was held in Saxon times by the Countess Goda of the King. At the date of Domesday it had a church and a mill, and formed part of the vast estate of Earl Roger de Montgomeri. In the reign of Edward I. it was held by military tenure by Sir Ralph Camoys, who gave it the name of Camoys Court. His distinguished descendants, the Barons Camoys, became extinct in the male line in the 15th century, when Trotton passed, by a co-heiress, to the Lewknor family. The male issue of this branch failed in 1520, and a co-heiress conveyed it to the family of Mille, at a later period Baronets, who held it for several generations. In 1723 it belonged to Alcocke, in 1834 to Twyford, afterwards to Mowatt, and it is now in the possession of Reginald Henry Nevill, Esq. DUMPFORD, in this parish, gives name to the Hundred; and the chapelry of MILLAND, in a remote part of the parish, has a chapel (St. Luke) called, in the 16th century, " the chappill of Tuck's-hythe." *

The church (St. George) was re-built towards the year 1400, by Thomas, Lord Camoys, K.G., who also erected the bridge over the Rother. It consists of a nave and chancel, under one roof, and tower, with shingled spire. It contains an interesting brass, unfortunately much mutilated, for the Lady 𝔐argaret 𝔠amoys, 1310 (perhaps the earliest for a lady in England), and a magnificent table-tomb with canopied brasses for 𝔗homas, 𝔅aron 𝔠amoys, and Elizabeth, his wife, the widow of Henry (Hotspur) Percy, and the " Gentle Kate " of Shakspeare (1419). There are likewise three table-tombs, of which the inscriptions are almost erased, but one of then seems to commemorate the family of Forster. There are later memorials for the families of Alcocke, Aylwin, Twyford, &c.

At the rectory-house in this parish, was born, in 1651, Thomas Otway, the greatest tragic poet, next to Shakspeare, whom the English tongue has known. At the time of his birth, his father, Humphrey Otway, was curate of Trotton, and afterwards rector of Woolbeding. For memoirs of this man of genius, whose rugged and troublous life and wretched death were in themselves a tragedy, see "Worthies of Sussex," p. 203. William Joliffe, Esq., a short time since resident at Trotton, has paid a tribute to the poet's memory by a Latin inscription on a brass plate in the church.

Trotton Bridge of five arches spans the Rother, and is unquestionably the finest bridge in Sussex. The arches are supported by ribs, and the whole structure, which is of the stone of the country, is eminently picturesque. A local tradition asserts that it cost Lord Camoys only a few pence less than the church, which is extremely probable.

At Trotton Place, close to the church-yard, a mansion of the time of Queen Anne, with recent additions, resides Arthur Edward Knox, Esq. (lessee) the accomplished author of " Ornithological Rambles in Sussex," and other works on similar subjects. The house, doubtless, represents the site of the manorhouse, though the old Camoys Court, or Castle, I think, from inspection, must have stood on a hillock to the south-east of the church, near which traces of old foundations are frequently turned up.

[S. A. C. Domesday watermill, v, 272. Milland chapel, and Cobden, xii, 75. Church, xii, 79. Forster, xvi, 50. Bells, xvi, 218, 226. Otway, xvi, 257, 259. River Rother and Bridge, xvi, 259. Lewknor,. xvii, 97. Milles, of Camois Court, xvii, 112. Trotton topography, xviii, 95.]

---

* Milland is now dismembered from Trotton, and forms a separate parish.

TUNBRIDGE WELLS.

This beautiful and elegant resort of fashion lies partly in the parishes of Tunbridge and Speldhurst, in Kent, and partly in Frant, in Sussex. The population now probably exceeds 12,000. It has a railway station on a branch of the South-Eastern line, and lies about 32 miles from London and five miles south of " Tunbridge town." This now well-known place was, two centuries and a half since, for the most part a heathy plain, interspersed with rocks, till, in 1606, Dudley, Lord North, then on a visit at Eridge, the seat of Lord Abergavenny, discovered the valuable chalybeate spring emanating from a bed of secondary iron ore, and having drunk the waters of it found great benefit from them. The Earl of Abergavenny enclosed the spring, and made improvements for the attraction of visitors. The scheme was successful, and in 1630 Queen Henrietta came hither with a large retinue, but was obliged to encamp on the down for want of house accommodation. For many years after this the visitors, during the summer season, were literally "dwellers in tents," or had to resort for lodging to Southborough and other places. Catharine of Braganza, Queen of Charles II., admired the spot, which soon became a fashionable watering-place, but it was not until such men as Cibber, Dr. Johnson, Garrick, Richardson, &c., a century later, patronized the place that it acquired a wide renown. The original spring still remains open, and is surrounded by modern erections. The articles of inlaid wood for boxes, toys, &c., known as " Tunbridge ware," have long been manufactured here.

The scenery is everywhere pleasing and romantic, and one hardly knows whether to call Tunbridge Wells an *urbs in rure* or a *rus in urbe*, so delightfully mixed up are its houses, commons, green glades, and sandstone rocks. The " high rocks" are most interesting. In a valley close to Rusthall Common, about a mile distant, is another group of rocks very remarkably shaped, and one of them, the most singular in the group, is known as the " Toad Rock." The living is a perpetual curacy, and the old chapel of ease, originally built in the seventeenth century, is dedicated to St. Charles the Martyr ! Christ Church and Trinity are modern *succursales*, and there are other places of worship for nearly every denomination. Public institutions of many kinds are abundant. The undulating character of the country gives rise to several rather curious designations, as Mount Ephraim, Mount Sion, Mount Pleasant, and Bishop's Down. Calverley Park is another pleasant spot. New mansions are springing up in every direction, and *me judice*, there is no more delightful retreat in England than Tunbridge Wells.

· TURNER'S HILL.

A considerable hamlet in the parish of Worth.

TURWICK or TERWICK.

A parish in the Hundred of Dumpford, Rape of Chichester; distant about six miles west from Midhurst; Post-town, Petersfield. Union, Midhurst. Population in 1811, 109; in 1861, 106. Benefice, a Rectory, valued at £173; Patron, T. A. Richards, Esq.; Incumbent, Rev. William Steward Richards, M.A., of Jesus College, Oxford. Date of earliest Parish Register, 1577. Acreage, 718. *Chief Landowners*, Thomas Ridge, Esq., and Reginald H. Nevill, Esq.

From Norman times the descent of Turwick has been associated with that of Rogate, which see.

Dangstein House in this parish is a large mansion, built within the last 40 years, in the Grecian style, and occupying a commanding site, with a genuine West Sussex landscape. It is the seat of Reginald H. Nevill, Esq., and the Hon. Lady Nevill. The gardens attached to this house are very large and beautiful, and the numerous conservatories contain an extensive collection of all that is botanically rare and choice. The fernery is, perhaps, under the skill and taste of the honourable lady of the house, the finest in England.

The church, dedicated to St. Peter, is a small plain structure, and was restored in 1847.

[S. A. C. Church, xii, 79. Bells, xvi, 226. River Rother, xvi, 259.]

TWINEHAM.

A parish in the Half-Hundred of Wyndham; Rape of Lewes; distant 5½ miles south-west from Cuckfield, its Post-town. Railway station, Burgess Hill, distant about five miles. Union, Cuckfield. Population in 1811, 234; in 1861, 339. Benefice, a Rectory, valued at £400; Patron, Sir Charles Goring, Bart; Incumbent, Rev. William Molyneux, M.A., of Christ Church, Oxford. Date of earliest Parish Register, 1716. Acreage, 1,908. *Chief Landowner*, John Wood, Esq., of Hickstead.

Twineham is described in Domesday as Benefelle. Its principal manor is now called Twineham Benfeld, and had formerly owners of its own name. In the 17th century it belonged to the Coverts, and passed from them by marriage to the Gorings of Highden, who still hold it. The manor of Twineham proper belonged to the Lords la Warr, who were resident there; but in the reign of Elizabeth it became the property of the family of Stapley, who dwelt at their manor house of Hickstead until 1762, when, on the death of Richard Stapley, Esq., it devolved on Martha, his eldest daughter and co-heiress, who married John Wood, Esq. His son, J. Wood, Esq., who died in 1831, bequeathed it to his nephew, the present possessor. It was anciently held of the barony of Lewes by the service of a pair of gilt spurs and 6d. Hickstead Place, which has traces of the architecture of *temp.* Henry VII., including carved work with the badges of the Lords la Warr, has been fitted up most tastefully in medieval fashion by the present proprietor. Near the house is a building fancifully called the Castle, which is evidently only a portion of the original mansion.

The church (St. Peter) consists of chancel, nave, south porch, and western tower, the whole, except a low shingled spire, built of *brick*, a material very unusual in this district. It is probably of the last half of the 16th century. It contains many inscriptions for the Stapleys, and one or two for the Woods. There are three bells, two of which are ancient and inscribed to St. John Baptist, and Simon Peter. In the south window of the chancel are the arms of La Warr, probably removed from an earlier church.

[S. A. C. Interesting Diaries of the Stapleys, ii, 102—128 *(Turner)*. xviii, 151—162 *(Turner)*. Pedigree of, ii, 117. Coverts of, x, 160. Bynes of, xii, 111. Poynings of, xv, 16. Killingbeck of, and Quakers, xvi, 71. Bells, xvi, 226. River Adur, xvi, 251. Edward Hinde, rector, xviii, 152. Church, xviii, 154. Westlands in, xviii, 159. Earthquake, record of, xviii, 161. Wapses, Colwells, Wyndhams, Cripps, Wood, xviii, 153. Morley manor, church repaired, Streatfeild, xviii, 154. Lintott, "the largest man that ever was seen," died 1732, Benefields, Goring, xviii, 158. Roman remains, xix, 195.]

UCKFIELD.

Vulgo, *Uckful;* a parish in the Hundred of Loxfield-Dorset; Rape of Pevensey; distant eight miles north-east of Lewes. It is a Post-town, and has a Railway station on the Brighton and Tunbridge Wells line. It is the centre of a Poor-Law Union. Population in 1811, 916; in 1861, 1,740. Benefice, a Perpetual Curacy, valued at £335 2s. 6d.; Patron, the Archbishop of Canterbury, one of whose Peculiars it is; Incumbent, Rev. Edward Thomas Cardale, M.A. Date of earliest Parish Register, 1538. Acreage, 1,717. *Seats,* The Rocks, Richard James Streatfeild, Esq.; Uckfield House, John Day, Esq.; Molesey Gore, Fred. Brodie, Esq., &c.

This interesting little town is delightfully situated on the sand formation forming the Forest Ridge of Sussex, and is remarkable for its healthful climate and picturesque scenery. It was anciently a portion of the great parish of Buxted, but it has been dismembered for civil and ecclesiastical purposes for a considerable length of time. The Rev. Edward Turner's account of the parish is full of interest as to its ancient history. ("Sussex Collections," vol. xii.) That gentleman justly observes that "this place has become singularly modern—almost everything of antiquarian value about it having of late years fast disappeared." The church (formerly *chapel*) of Uckfield is a recent building for the most part, though a few ancient features have been retained. The Tudoresque old bridge of three arches, which spanned the Uckfield branch of the Ouse, has given way to a railway bridge of no picturesque interest. Madame d'Arblay, so long ago as 1779, could not discover anything of interest in Uckfield, when she visited it with Mrs. Thrale, *en route* from Tunbridge Wells to Brighton.

The name of the parish is probably derived from the oak tree, though this etymology has been doubted, as this is not an oak-growing district. Perhaps some remarkable oak stood here. Ashcombe is not celebrated for its ash trees, nor Thornhill for its thorns, nor Appledore for its apple-trees; but among our Saxon ancestors it was quite customary to name a place from some individual tree, and, upon the *lucus a non lucendo* principle, the rarer a particular tree was, the more likely it was to confer its name on the locality. The medieval spelling of the name is Okenfeld or Okyngfeld. The parish, or rather chapelry, does not appear in Domesday, and the earliest record we have of it is, according to Mr. Turner, 1291 ("Pope Nicholas's Taxation"), though he thinks a church existed here nearly a century earlier than that date. In 1299 King Edward I., on a "progress" from Canterbury to Chichester, staid at Uckfield for one night. His retinue must have been large, for he had to purchase a great deal of beer. The entry in the record is: "To the clerk of the pantry for 82 gallons of beer, bought from Arnald de Uckfield, at Uckfield, 23rd June, 10s." The roads were no doubt dusty, and the suite thirsty after their ride.

The old church, dedicated to the Holy Cross, had features of Perpendicular, Decorated, and probably earlier styles. It being in a state of dilapidation, and inadequate to the population, it was taken down in 1839. There are memorials for the families and names of Wilson, Courthope, Egles, Goring, Streatfeild, Ogle, Ellis, and Fuller. The last mentioned has a brass of a male figure, and bears the date of 1610, and a record of his benefaction to several parishes, of which Uckfield is one. The gift consisted of 10s. per annum, and the following doggerel stanza is placed on the tomb:—

> "Now I am dead and layd in grave,
> And that my bones are rotten,
> By this shall I remember'd be,
> Or else I am forgotten."

A gentleman having read this epitaph gave the following impromptu:—

> "O, traveller, stop! for tho' his bones be rotten,
> Fuller rests here, and must not be forgotten:
> For lo, he gave ten shillings that his name
> Might live for ever on the scroll of fame!"

This John Fuller, gentleman, whose family were settled here for three generations, was ancestor of the Fullers, a family of great importance, who settled at Waldron, at Lewes, and several other places in East Sussex, and ultimately at Rose Hill, in Brightling, and were amongst the chief iron-masters of the county. The tower contains eight bells of no great antiquity, but with quaint inscriptions.

Opposite the King's Head Inn is an apartment of stone with several recessed arches in the wall. It is now occupied by a baker. There is a tradition that this was formerly a prison cell, and that Richard Woodman, the well-known Protestant Martyr, was once confined in it during the Marian persecution; which is quite probable, as that brave man was born at Buxted, close by, and he speaks of one Goodman Day, of Uckfield, in his examination.

A free school was founded in or about 1690 by Dr. Anthony Saunders, rector of Buxted. By his will, dated 1718, he provided for the education of twelve boys, six belonging to the parish of Buxted and six to Uckfield. He left his library, which consists of several hundred volumes of theology and classics, to this charity, which has been extended to twenty-four boys. The school-house stands in Church Street. Here in former years several well-known Sussex men, among whom was Dr. Edward Daniel Clarke, the celebrated traveller, received their preliminary education. It may be mentioned that another learned English writer, Jeremiah Markland, resided at Uckfield in the middle of the last century.

The town is, as I have said, delightfully situated. The High Street is particularly neat, and is flanked by several excellent residences; but the great picturesque beauty of the place is the Lake close to the mansion called the Rocks. It is nearly surrounded by sandstone cliffs overhanging the water, from twenty to thirty feet high. Among their crevices trees grow luxuriantly, and in the lake there is an island covered with shrubs and trees.

Uckfield may be regarded as a kind of head quarters for astronomical science in the county. C. Leeson Prince, Esq., F.R.A.S., and Frederick Brodie, Esq., F.R.A.S., having observatories in the town, while Captain Noble, of Forest Lodge, in the adjacent parish of Maresfield, possesses another. The purity of the local atmosphere has probably led these gentlemen in some measure to this branch of scientific enquiry.

[S. A. C. Ironworks, iii, 243. xix, 206. King Edward I. at, ii, 143. xii, 6. Wilson, family of, x, 38. xii, 20. Hutchinsons of, xi, 45. Woodwards of, xii, 10. Church, xii, 1. xx, 230. Ancient stone apartment—Woodman's prison, xii, 9. Dr. Saunders' school, xii, 12. xiv, 165. John Fuller, gentleman, xii, 18. Fuller family, xiii, 97. Egles family, xii, 19. xix, 206. Jeremiah Markland, xii, 21. Dr. E. D. Clarke, *ibid.* Eversfield of, xiv, 111. River, xv, 161. Centre of Wildish parts, xvi, 30. Hart family, xvii, 257. Baker of, and Jack Cade, xviii, 23, 38. Lindfield accounts passed at, xix, 47. The Bitorne's clee, xx, 226. Chapel of Uckfeld, xx, 230.

UDIMORE.

Domesday, *Dodimore;* vulgo, *Uddymer;* a parish in the Hundred of Gostrow; Rape of Hastings; distant 3½ miles from Winchelsea. Post-town, Rye. Railway station, Winchelsea. Union, Rye. Population in 1811, 375; in 1861, 444. Benefice, a Vicarage, valued at £100, with several benefactions. Patron, Frederick Langford, Esq.; Incumbent, Rev. Thos. Lewis, M.A. Date of earliest Parish Register, 1558. Acreage, 2,221.

This parish, which lies chiefly on upland ground, is bounded on the south by the Brede channel. In the fourteenth century it suffered much from inundations on its lower side. Dodimore is described in Domesday as in the hundred of *Babinreode* which most probably corresponds, or nearly so, with the modern hundred of Gostrow. Reinbert held it of the Earl of Eu. Before the Conquest, Algar (a name still existing in East Sussex) held it of Godwin, father of Harold. It was always held as six hides. There was a church, and the manor was valued at eight pounds. In 23rd Edward I. William, Lord Echingham, obtained free-warren for his manor of Odymere. In his descendants it vested until *temp.* Henry VI. In 1478, John Elrington obtained another grant of free-warren, for Udimere, and to enclose a park and fortify his mansion. *Temp.* Elizabeth, Henry, Lord Windsor, was lord. Later still, it passed to the Burdets and Bromfields, who held it of the family of Pelham, as of their castle and honour of Hastings. In 1717, Spencer Compton was lord, and it descended to the Cavendish family. Among the principal old houses in the parish were or are—Parsonage Place, once the abode of a branch of the Coopers of Icklesham; Knellstone, the residence of the family of Frebody, who were here for many generations; Hammonds (the Woodhams family); and Jordans, which was the home of a gentle family bearing that name. The old manor-house of the Bromfields stood to the south of the church-yard. Thomas Bromfield, Esq., who died in 1690, is supposed to have been the last of that family resident in Udimore. A detached portion of the parish known as *Little* Udimore is surrounded by Sedlescombe and Brede. By the Reform Act of 1832, the whole parish was annexed for electoral purposes to the borough of Rye.

The church (St. Mary), though small, is ancient (Horsfield says Early English), and has a chancel, nave, and a tower containing three bells. There was formerly a south aisle. The chancel contained, in 1835, no less than nine lancet windows. (Horsfield.) There are monuments or inscriptions for the families of Jordan, Frebody, Burdet, Cooper, Woodhams, &c. This church was anciently appropriated to the Abbey of Robertsbridge.

A curious legend to the effect that Udimore derives its name from a circumstance connected with the building of this edifice is remembered by old inhabitants. The parishioners began to build themselves a church on the opposite side of the little river Ree, to that on which it was eventually reared. Night after night, however, witnessed the dislocation of huge stones from the walls built on the preceding day, and the pious work bade fair to be interminable. Grave suspicions arose among the parishioners that they had selected an unholy, and consequently, an improper, site for the building, and these were eventually confirmed. Unseen hands hurled the stones to the opposite side of the stream, and an awful supernatural voice in the air uttered, in warning and reproachful tones, the words " *O'er the mere; o'er the mere*;" thus at once indicating a more appropriate situation for the sacred edifice, and by anticipation conferring a name upon it, for the transformation of the phrase " O'er the mere," into Udimore, was no great difficulty.*

The following hexameters are inscribed in the parish register :—

> " Udimer infelix ! nimis est cui Presbyter unus ;
> Presbyter infelix ! cui non satis Udimer una ;
> Impropriator habet Clero quæ propria durus,
> Atque alter proprios Clerus peregrinus et hospes ;
> Ex decimis decimis fruitur lege sacerdos.
> Alter Evangelio reliquis prohibente potitur
> Eheu ! quam pingui macer est mihi passer in arvo
> Idem est exitium fidei fideique ministro."
>
> *Ita queritur Step. Parr, Vic.*

[S. A. C. King Edward I. visit, ii, 140. Smugglers, x, 92. Manor house

* I must beg the reader's pardon for this piece of self-quotation. It originally appeared in my " Contributions to Literature."

fortified, xiii, 117. Elryngtons of, xiii, 116. Church, xiii, 136. Grant of Ranulph to the Canons of Hastings, xiii, 138. Legend respecting the church, xiii, 226. Burdett family, xiv, 30. Bromfield, xiv, 115, 229. Church bells, xvi, 227. Tithes to Battle Abbey, xvii, 55. Cade's insurrection, xviii, 25.]

UPPER BEEDING, See BEEDING UPPER.

UPMARDEN.

Domesday, *Merdon;* vulgo, *Marn;* a parish in the Hundred of Westbourne; Rape of Chichester; distant nine miles north-west from Chichester. Post-town, Emsworth. Union, Westbourne. Population in 1811, 246; in 1861, 366. Benefice, a Vicarage, united with Compton. Date of earliest Parish Register, 1748. Acreage, 2,928. *Chief Landowners,* Admiral Sir Phipps Hornby, and Alexander H. Hall, Esq., of Watergate House.

The group of villages called "the Mardens" lies on the Downs, and its derivation from the Saxon *mor,* a waste heathy land, and *dún,* a hill, answers to the geographical position and ancient state. Domesday mentions four Merduns, and although four still exist, it would be difficult in each instance to appropriate description to locality. One was held in Saxon times by Aldwin, and Alaric; another by Lepsi, of Gida, the countess of Earl Godwin; the third by Alwin, of the Confessor; and the fourth by Earl Godwin. After the Conquest, Earl Roger held them all. Upmarden has belonged at different periods to the Fitz-Alan family, to John, Lord Lumley, the Pages, and the Peckhams, and has from the last-named passed as Compton.

WEST MARDEN is a hamlet in this parish: its chapel was destroyed long since. The mansion of Watergate was built by William Drury (who was afterwards a gentleman of the privy chamber to Charles I.) before the year 1609, and continued in his descendants for several generations. It is now the property of Alexander H. Hall, Esq.

The Church (St. Michael) is small and ancient. Rickman (1848) considers the wall-plate of the building to represent an example of the Early English style, with the tooth moulding. There are memorials for the names of Thomas, Phipps, Peckham, &c.

[S. A. C. Church, xii, 79. Bells, xvi, 218. Green of West Marden, xvi, 50. Oxford road to Chichester, xix, 169. Knights Hospitallers of Midhurst had lands in, xx, 27.]

UP-WALTHAM, or UPPER WALTHAM.

Domesday, *Waltham*; a parish in the Hundred of Box and Stockbridge; Rape of Chichester; distant six miles south-west from Petworth, its Post-town. Union, West Hampnett. Population in 1811, 49; in 1861, 71. Benefice, a Rectory, valued at £128; Patron, Lord Leconfield; Incumbent, Rev. Henry Cogan, M.A., of St. John's College, Cambridge. Date of earliest Parish Register, 1790. Acreage, 1,245. *Chief Landowner*, Lord Leconfield.

It is Up or Upper Waltham (sometimes West Waltham) in contradistinction from Cold Waltham, near the Arun. It occupies a hilly site on the Downs, whence the prefix. Two Walthams are mentioned in Domesday. At an early period the family of De Alta Ripa, or Dawtrey, held the manor, and continued in possession for many generations. In 1776 it was purchased of the family of Luther (who inherited from that ancient race) by the late Lord Egremont, and added to the Petworth estate.

The church is a small building of nave and chancel, with a dovecot spire. A late description calls it Early English, but as the diminutive chancel terminates with a semi-circular apse, it must be at least on Norman foundations. A rude engraving in the "Gentleman's Magazine" for 1793, misnames it *Much-*Waltham.

[S. A. C. Lands to Tortington Priory, xi, 110. Parish, &c., xviii, 96. Reede of, xix, 201.]

VERDLEY.

A manor in Farnhurst, which formerly had a small fortified building known as Verdley Castle, the ruins of which existed within the memory of persons still living. The manor is not mentioned in Domesday, but it has long been held of the Honour of Petworth. Of the history of this "Castle," little or nothing is known. Several traditional stories as to its original use have been current, without the slightest foundation. I believe, with the Rev. Edward Turner, that it was simply a hunting-tower, attached to some lordship, probably that of the De Bohuns. Some fragments of the walls were standing in Sir William Burrell's time, and a drawing of them with a ground plan (1770) is preserved among his MSS. Two or three of the window openings were in the Early English style. There was formerly a wood called Verdley Park, which contained 250 acres, and the early maps of Sussex represent the tower as surrounded by a park pale. The dimensions of the castle were 68 by 33 feet, and the walls were nearly six feet in thickness. These remains were destroyed for the sake of the stone, which the steward of the late Mr. Poyntz employed to mend the roads in the neighbourhood! There are faint traces of a moat. See Rev. Edward Turner in " Sussex Collections," Vol. xii.

WADHURST.

A parish in the Hundred of Loxfield-Pelham; Rape of Pevensey; distant six miles south-east from Tunbridge Wells. It has a Railway station. Union, Ticehurst. Population in 1811, 1,815; in 1861, 2,470. Benefice, a Vicarage, formerly a peculiar of the Archbishop, valued at £659, in the gift of Wadham College, Oxford; Incumbent, Rev. John Foley, B.D., of the same College. Date of earliest Parish Register, 1604. Acreage, 10,147. *Chief Landowners*, E. W. Smyth, G. C. Courthope, J. J. Newington, Esqrs., and the Marquis Camden. *Seat*, Wadhurst Castle is the residence of Edward Watson Smyth, Esq.

The name of this parish seems to be derived from the Anglo-Saxon *wâd*, a ford, and *hurst*, a wood—" the ford by the wood." The parish is divided into six " quarters," viz.: Town-quarter, Cousey-Wood-quarter, Bivelham-quarter, Faircrouch-quarter, Reseden-quarter, and Weeke-quarter. The surface is hilly, and the soil varies considerably. The scenery is pleasingly diversified with woodland and hop-gardens. The soil is ferruginous, and hence the iron manufacture was largely carried on here. It may be mentioned that the iron-masters of this and the neighbouring parishes, and their connections were interred beneath cast-iron slabs. The passages of the nave and aisles of the church are almost covered with these slabs, with rude inscriptions and armorial bearings. They are no less than 30 in number, ranging between the years 1625 and 1799.

High-Town belonged, in or before the reign of Henry VIII., to the family of Maunser, and so continued for many generations. It then passed to the Newingtons, and subsequently to the Bakers of Mayfield. Faircrouch was an ancient stone mansion, but fell to dilapidation nearly two centuries since. The family of Whitfeld, formerly of Alstonmoor, in Cumberland, were once considerable proprietors here, and their descendants still survive in Sussex and Kent. A coheiress conveyed the estate to the family of Ballard. The Dunmolls also had good lands in the parish, which descended, through female lines, to the families of Mercer and Durrant. The family of Fowle, who built in 1591, the fine mansion of Riverhall, were great iron-masters. The house still retains traces of its original grandeur, but the family has fallen to decay. The family of Barham, also iron-founders, are said to have been descended from Robert de Berham, son of Richard Fitz-Urse, and brother of the assassin of Thomas à Becket. They lived at Great Butts, and about 1630 John Barham, Esq., erected or re-built the spacious mansion of Shoesmiths. David Barham built the greater portion of the present house of Snape about 1617. The family fell into decay, and their present representative is a wheelwright at Wadhurst. Of this family was the celebrated lawyer, Nicholas Barham, Queen's Sergeant, *temp.* Elizabeth.

The church (St. Peter and St. Paul) is partly in the Early English and partly in later styles of architecture. It consists of a chancel, nave, with aisles, and tower with a lofty shingled spire, and a musical peal of six bells. There are inscriptions and mural tablets to the memory of the families and names of Whitfeld,* Barham, Dunmoll, Tapsell, Legas, Comber, Porter, Colepeper, Alcorn, Aynscombe, Newington, Willett, Davison, Burgis, Courthope, Salmon, &c.

TIDEBROOK is a hamlet 2½ miles south-west from Wadhurst. In 1856 a district church (St. John the Baptist) was erected here. It is a perpetual curacy, value £53 per annum. It is in the alternate gift of the vicars of Wadhurst and Mayfield; the present incumbent is the Rev. Albert J. Roberts, M.A., of St. John's College, Oxford. My late friend, William Courthope, Esq., Somerset Herald, made extensive collections respecting this and some neighbouring parishes, which he left in MS. Of their present ownership I know nothing.

[S. A. C. Iron-works, ii, 217. iii, 241. xviii, 15. xix, 84. Extracts from parish register, iv, 269. Riverhall, xi, 12. xviii, 15. ii, 188, 218. Fowles of, xi, 12. ii, 54. Courthopes of, xi, 45, 68. vi, 87. Weekes of, xi, 82. Whitfeld family, xiv, 222. xix, 83. Lucks of, xvi, 48. Ballards of, xvi, 48. xix, 87. Benge of, xvi, 48. Humphreys of, and Sanders of, xvi, 48. Church bells, xvi, 227, Streams at, xvi, 272. Battle Abbey lands, xvii, 55. Cade's insurrection, xviii, 25. Snape iron-works, xviii, 15. Maynard's Gate iron-works, xviii, 15. Nicholas Barham, xix, 33. Hightown and Maunser family, xix, 179.]

WALBERTON.

Domesday, *Walburgetone;* a parish in the Hundred of Avisford; Rape of Arundel; distant 3½ miles south-west from Arundel, its Post-town. Union, West Hampnett. Population in 1811, 612; in 1861, 588. Benefice, a Vicarage, with Yapton annexed, valued at £557;

* Thomas Whitfeld, of Worth, Esq., a native of Wadhurst, founded three alms-houses here, and an annual charity of £10, besides 12 cords of wood for six poor families. In recognition of this liberality the parishioners placed a monument to his memory in 1631.

Patron, the Bishop of Chichester; Incumbent Rev. Thos. S. Lyle,
Vogan, M.A., of St. Edmund Hall, Oxford. Date of earliest Parish
Register, 1556. Acreage, 1,722. *Chief Landowner*, Richard Prime,
Esq. *Seats*, Walberton House, Richard Prime, Esq. Avisford House,
Mrs. Reynell Pack, &c.

Dallaway derives the name of this parish from the Anglo-
Saxon *wæl-burg-tun*, " demonstrative of a military station." The
manor appears to have been connected with the lordship of Halnaker. In the time of the Confessor it was held by three freemen, and was rated at 11 hides and two virgates. There were,
at the making of Domesday, a church, six serfs, and a wood of
four hogs. The manor, when detached from the earldom of
Arundel, passed through the families of St. John, Poynings,
Bonville, and Paulet. It belonged subsequently to those of
Racton and Bennet. Before 1687 Thomas Nash, gentleman,
purchased the manorial estate, and his descendants enjoyed it
for several generations. In 1800 Gawen Richard Nash, Esq.,
sold it to General John Whyte, whose son, in 1817, sold it to
Richard Prime, Esq. The mansion was pulled down and re-built
on a larger scale by Mr. Prime. Walberton House has been
characterized as " a handsome mansion, with a beautiful and
costly hall, staircase, and library." The architect was Sir Robert
Smirke. Avisford Place, associated with the name of the hundred in which Walberton lies, is an elegant residence. The site
is elevated, and commands an interesting sea view. This estate
belonged some years since to Admiral Sir George Montagu,
G.C.B., who sold it to General Sir Wm.Houston, G.C.B. A remarkable archæological discovery was made on this estate in 1817.
There were many fictile and glass vessels of the Roman period,
most of which had been deposited in a stone cist or coffer, four
feet in length. The Romans, no doubt, occupied the whole of the
Sussex coast, and left many of their *vestigia*, but, alas, where
shall we find from inscription or votive altar what particular
Roman colonist it was who lived at Walberton!
     The church (Our Lady) has a large chancel, a nave, and two
aisles, with a shingled turret containing three bells. Many
coarse patchings appear to have been made since the period of
the Reformation. Sir George West of Halnaker was buried
here in 1538, but no memorial remains. There are inscriptions
for the names of Nash (Gawen Nash, merchant, is described as
" a great benefactor to this church and parish," ob. 1749),
Rowe, Pette, Dorset, Whyte, &c. The Bishop's Register (R. f.
43) has an entry of the excommunication of John Hore, vicar
of this parish, dated 1441, for maiming William Skyrre, chaplain
of Slyndon. " His crime was the effect of jealousy, and the
catastrophe similar to that in which originated the most beau-

tiful and pathetic poem which has immortalized the genius of
Pope." The same crime and punishment occur in the Archbishop's Register at Lambeth—" Castratio Edm. Roger, Prioris
de Bilsington, per R. Poundcheat."

[S. A. C. Roman remains at Avisford, viii, 290. xi, 130. Fowler of,
xii, 102. Church, xii, 103. xv, 90. Manor, xv, 59. Lands to Boxgrove,
xv, 87. *ibid*, 90. Church bells, xvi, 227. Lord Lumley's lands, xix, 102.
Avisford Hill and Mackrel's Bridge, xix, 159.]

WALDRON.

Domesday, *Waldrene;* vulgo, *Waldon;* a parish in the Hundreds of Shiplake and Dill; Rape of Pevensey; distant six miles south-east from
Uckfield, its Railway station; Post-town, Hawkhurst; Union, Uckfield. Population in 1811, 840; in 1861, 1,132. Benefice, a Rectory,
valued at £455; in the gift of Exeter College, Oxford; Incumbent
Rev. John Ley, B.D., formerly Fellow of that College. Date of
earliest Parish Register, 1564. Acreage, 6,218. *Chief Landowners,*
Louis Huth, Esq., and Fuller-Meyrick, Esq.

This is a beautifully undulated parish, in a picturesque
part of the Weald, whence its name, Anglo-Saxon *wald*, a wood,
and the views from various parts are very striking, especially
that from the church-yard. In the last generation Waldron
was almost a by-word for rusticity and lack of civilization. Now
it is favoured with the presence of several persons of influence
and wealth, who have entirely changed its character. Several
excellent residences have sprung up, and among these may be
named those of J. G. Boucher, Esq., R. H. Stainbank, Esq., and
especially Possingworth (vulgo, Possingfoord), the magnificent
seat of Louis Huth, Esq. It is one of the grandest mansions in
the South of England, and cost more than £60,000. It is from
designs by Mr. Digby Wyatt, and contains every appliance of
luxury and taste, including a fine picture gallery and noble conservatories. Seams of coal, or fibrous lignite, with the appearance of jet, and with a velvet-like smoothness, occur in the geological strata of the parish.

In the time of Edward the Confessor, Ælveva held a part of
Waldrene, as allodial or free land. At the date of Domesday,
Ansfrid held it of the Earl of Moreton. The principal manor in
the parish, in later times, was that of Herringdales, *alias* Waldron. The manors of Laughton, Chiddingly, and Isenhurst also
extend into it, and other manors, existing or reputed, are Foxhunt (formerly belonging to Robertsbridge Abbey), Possingworth, Tanners, and Horeham.

In vol. xiii. of " Sussex Archæological Collections," the Rev.

John Ley, Rector, has printed an excellent paper on the church, the manors, and the old mansions of the parish, a very brief *précis* of which is here given.

To begin with the church of All Saints, sometimes written All Hallows, it consists of chancel, nave, north aisle with porch, and a low battlemented western tower, in the Perpendicular style, containing eight musical bells. The nave has Decorated insertions, and the chancel is Early English. A marble slab on the floor, incised with five crosses, was doubtless the original altarstone. The east window is peculiar, and of the period from the Transition to the Perpendicular style. It formerly had, in painted glass, a man in armour kneeling, with the legend, 𝔓𝔯𝔞𝔶 𝔣𝔬𝔯 𝔱𝔥𝔢 𝔰𝔬𝔲𝔩 𝔬𝔣 𝔍𝔬𝔥𝔫 𝔓𝔢𝔩𝔥𝔞𝔪, who probably built the tower of this church as well as those of many others in the neighbourhood.

About *temp.* Henry II. Robert de Dene gave the tithes of this rectory to the Priory of Lewes, and his descendant, Sybilla de Icklesham, by license of the date of 1233, built a chapel for her own use in her manor-house of Walderne. Her husband was Nicholas Harengod, or Heringaud, from whom, doubtless, the manor received its now corrupted name of Herringdales. The church contains many memorials to the names of Courthope, Fuller, Dalrymple, Dyke, Offley, Lewis, &c., with many hatchments of some or other of these families. In one of the windows are the arms of Pelham.

In times soon after the Conquest, Waldron was almost in a state of forest, and so continued for some centuries. So lately as 1842, when the tithes were commuted, 2,000 acres, or nearly a third of the whole parish, were regarded as tithe-free, as being woodland, or yet uncultivated, though this was not literally the case. The names Walderne, Foxhunt, the Dern, &c., all refer to a period when the place formed a portion of the Forest of Anderida, the great Weald of Sussex. Foxhunt belonged, in 1327, to Sir Ralph de Camoys. In the next century it vested in the Brownes of Betchworth Castle, ancestors of the Viscounts Montague; afterwards in the families of Threele, Pelham, Smith, and Gilliat. Heringauds, or Herringdales manor-house, where Sybilla's chapel existed, stood a little westward of the church, within a circular moat of 150 feet diameter, with embankments around it. From this family it passed to those of De Poynings, Browne (Viscount Montague), Fawkenor, Middleton, Pelham, and Smith. Possingworth manor was owned by a family who derived their name from it. John, son of Lawrence de Possyngewerse, demised it in the fourteenth century to the Heringauds, and after many changes of proprietorship, it became vested in the Abbot and Convent of Robertsbridge, who held it until the Dissolution. At later dates it passed, through the Sidneys and Pelhams, to the great London-merchant family of Offley, one of

whom, a Lord Mayor, Sir Thomas Offley, *temp*. Elizabeth, left
half his estate (£5000) to the poor, and was thence called the
London Zacchæus.   He was remarkable for his abstemiousness,
and it was said of him (as mentioned in Fuller's " Worthies")—

> " Offley three dishes had of daily roast,
> An egg, an apple, and, the third, a toast."

It is worthy of remark, that a much earlier Lord Mayor had been
associated with this parish, namely, Sir William, son of Geoffrey
de Walderne, of Walderne, who held the chief magistracy of the
city in 1412 and 1422.   The first of the Offleys who possessed
Possingworth was probably Humphrey Offley, who died in 1643.
His son Thomas built, or rebuilt, Possingworth House, which
bears date 1657, and the initials T. O.   Subsequently the estate
passed through Fuller, Apsley, Dalrymple, and Thomas (or Treherne) to the present owner.   A considerable portion of the
mansion still remains, and is figured in vol. xiii. of " Sussex Archæological Collections," p. 80.   Tanners, or Tanhouse, was
another mansion in the parish, which passed through the Sydneys and Sackvilles to the family of Fuller, ancestors of the
Fullers of Rosehill, in Brightling, great Sussex iron-masters.
The present house was built by Samuel Fuller, in the first half
of the seventeenth century.   It was originally a mansion of considerable dimensions, but now exists as a farm-house.   The
Fullers appear to have been a London family who settled in
Sussex in the sixteenth century, and are now represented by
Fuller-Meyrick, Esq.   They were successively of Uckfield, Waldron, and Brightling.   Horeham gave name to the family of De
Horeham, in or before the fourteenth century. Later it belonged
to the Walshes, whose heiress married Thomas Dyke, Esq., in
the early part of the seventeenth century.   Mr. Dyke probably
built Horeham, a great mansion on an older site, and his descendant was created a baronet in 1676, as Sir Thomas Dyke, of
Horeham.   The greater part of the mansion has been pulled
down, and the remains are now a farm-house.   A level tract of
land where the parishes of Waldron, Chiddingly, and Hellingly
meet, is called Horeham Flat.

[S. A. C.   Coal found here, ii, 211. Ironworks, ii, 219. iii, 241, 245.
xviii, 15.   Possingworth, viii, 152. xiii, 92. xvi, 292. xix, 53.   Bronze
Celts, ix, 366.   Church, mansions, and manors (*Ley*), xiii, 80. xx, 233.
Pelham, xiii, 82.   Ralph and Sybilla de Icklesham, Haringots, Denes,
Sackvilles, xiii, 84. Offley family, xiii, 93. xvi, 292. De Waldern, xiii, 92.
Fullers of Tanners, xiii, 94. xiv, 237.   Selwyn of, xiii, 96.   Bonnicks of,
xiii, 98.   De Horeham and Walsh, xiii, 100.   Dyke family, xiii, 101. xvi,
292. xviii, 197.   Legend of church, xiii, 226.   Tooths of, xiv, 254.   Dur-
rants of, xvi, 48.   Bells, xvi, 227.   Horeham Place, xvi, 292. xviii, 197.
Nuremburg tokens, xvii, 253. Cade's insurrection, xviii, 25.   Worked flints,
xix, 53.   Bad roads, xix, 162.   Civil marriages at Glynde, xix, 202.]

225

WARBLETON.

Domesday, *Warborgetone*; a parish in the Hundred of Hawkesborough; Rape of Hastings; distant about seven miles north from Hailsham; Post-town, Hawkhurst. Union, Hailsham. Population in 1811, 966; in 1861, 1,431. Benefice, a Rectory, valued at £663; Patron and Incumbent, Rev. George Edward Haviland, M.A., of St. John's College, Cambridge. Date of earliest Parish Register, 1558. Acreage, 5,763. *Seats*, Stonehouse, J. Roberts Dunn, Esq.; Markly, George Darby, Esq.

This is in many respects an interesting parish. Its surface is agreeably undulated with well-wooded slopes, while the sheltered portions possess many hop-gardens. There are several rivulets tributary to the Cuckmere, and some ferruginous springs. In the days of the Sussex ironworks there were several establishments in this parish for that manufacture. Among the iron-masters was Richard Woodman, a native of Buxted, but a resident at Warbleton, where he carried on extensive works; he was burnt, together with nine other Protestants, at Lewes, in 1557. (See " Worthies of Sussex," p. 138.) His house on the south side of the church still exists, as also the lane down which he ran when pursued by his persecutors. The church tower is said to have been the place of his temporary incarceration.

Warbleton was rather remarkable before the Reformation for its religious establishments, for besides the church there were a chantry and a deanery (probably connected with the College of Hastings), and a priory.

The Priory of Warbleton, originally established at Hastings by Sir Walter Bricet, having been destroyed by the inroads of the sea, Sir John Pelham refounded the establishment in this parish in the time of Henry IV., and it was called the New Priory of the Blessed Trinity of Hastings, though Warbleton is upwards of ten miles from that town. It was a small establishment, and its revenues arose from several parishes in East Sussex, and its present relics are limited to the foundations of its church, and an antique farm-house, the property of George Darby, Esq., of Markly. There is also a stable with the remains of a pointed arched doorway. Of the history of this new and short-lived establishment very little is known; but at the dissolution of the smaller priories it shared the fate of all such houses.* In 1537 the premises were granted to John Baker, Esq., and in 37th Henry VIII. to John Caryll, Esq. Subsequently the estate became the property of the family of Roberts, from whom it descended to that of Lade, Baronets, who resided

---

* The establishment appears to have consisted of three canons and one novice.
VOL. II. Q

here, and whose descendant, the late Mr Thomas Lade, sold it to John Darby, Esq. In one of the apartments of the old house are preserved two ancient skulls, which are connected with a superstitious legend, and in another room there are stains, said to be of human blood, which cannot be effaced. According to the popular belief it is unlucky to remove the skulls from the habitation, though a profane hand not many years ago placed one of them in a neighbouring tree, where it remained a whole summer, and a bird's nest was built in it. The awful sounds which are heard at night time proceed from a colony of owls which have established themselves in the old building. For historical and archæological notes respecting this priory I must refer the reader to the paper of the Rev. E. Turner, in the " Sussex Collections," Vol. xiii. At Bucksteep, formerly a mansion, but now a farm-house, there was a chapel supposed to have been attached to Battle Abbey.

RUSHLAKE GREEN is a pleasant hamlet in this parish, and contains the principal part of the population. Close by are Stone House, the seat of J. R. Dunn, Esq., a fabric of considerable antiquity, once the abode of the Roberts family; also Markly, the seat of George Darby, Esq., formerly M.P. for Sussex. Cralle, another house in the parish, anciently belonged to a family of the same name, whose heiress in the 14th century conveyed it to the ancient family of Cheney. Iwood was once the principal mansion of the family of De Warbleton. It belonged in 1st Richard III. to Margery Warbilton, and subsequently passed to the family of Fynes, Lords Dacre, then to the Piers, Pelham, and Stollyon families. The house, which commands most picturesque scenery, was formerly very large, but in 1722, being in a ruinous condition, it was partly pulled down and reduced to the state of a farm-house. The old gateway was built in 1591.

In 1795 the old house was taken down and replaced by a commodious farm-house. One of the family of Stollyon sold the estate before 1616 to Henry Smith, Esq. (" Dog Smith "), to whose benevolent charity it now belongs. According to tradition Iwood was once occupied by a notorious robber, who constructed a secret chamber, to which the only ingress was the chimney. Stollyons, another ancient property in this parish, and Heathfield derived its name from the family just mentioned. In the 17th century it belonged to the ancient Kent and Sussex family of Haffenden, many of whom lie buried in Heathfield church. About 1624, John Markwick, who was a family connection of the Haffendens, was attainted of felony, and so lost the estate. On this property grows the rare plant *Phyteuma spicatum*, supposed to be unique in England in its wild state.

Concerning the manor of Warbleton we have very few particulars; it is mentioned in Domesday as having been held of the Earl of Moreton by the Countess Goda. In Saxon times it was worth 40s., and after the Conquest 20s. How it came into the hands of the De Warbletons is unknown. The village near the church contains a few houses of antique appearance. The way-side inn has for its sign a halbert thrust into a tun of ale, and bears the punning name of the "War Bill in Ton."

The church, which stands on a pleasing elevation, is dedicated to St. Mary, and consists of chancel, nave, north aisle, and west tower. There are traces of Early English, Decorated, and Perpendicular work. At the east end of the aisle is a chantry chapel. In the windows there are or have been arms of the families of Pelham, Lewknor, De Warbleton, De Iwood, Cralle, and Cheney. In the north aisle is a very elaborate monument of various-coloured marbles and a finely executed bust to the memory of Sir John Lade, five times M.P. for Southwark, a native of this parish, who died in 1740. On a slab of marble is a brass commemorating 𝔚illiam ℭrestwick, Dean of the College of Hastings, of the date of 1436. It exhibits a full length portrait of the Dean, on the edges of whose robes is an extract from the book of Job, "Credo quod Redemptor meus vivit," and the beautiful crocketed canopy is surmounted by a finial composed of a pelican feeding her young with her blood, and a scroll with the words "Sic Christus dilexit nos." The surrounding legend (now partially destroyed) I have thus rendered:—

> " Leaving the fleeting honours of this world to die,
> Beneath this marble hard doth William Prestwick lie;
> A constant, patient, humble man, devout, urbane,
> And just to all. The poor a mighty loss sustain.
> Clergy will weep, and common people deeply mourn,
> So great a father from his much-loved College torn ;
> This rule of holy life, the weakest men's defence,
> This man of counsels wise, alas! is hurried hence;
> His outstretched corse lies buried here; his vital breath
> November's earliest-coming morn exchanged for death,
> When fourteen hundred years their course had gone about,
> And three times twelve. May Christ his every sin blot out.—Amen."

The father and mother of the Dean (John and Joan Prestwick) are commemorated by a small brass plate, which I discovered in a heap of rubbish many years since. There are other monuments and inscriptions for the families of Roberts of Warbleton Priory, Harcourt, Beeston, &c. Outside of the south wall is a rounded arch, which doubtless covers a tomb, an object of rare occurrence. The tower contains five bells. The church stands partly within a Roman earthwork, the outlines of which are clearly traceable.

[S. A. C.   Ironworks, ii, 219. iii. 241, 245. xviii, 15.   Prestwick's brass, ii, 307. xiii, 153. xvii, 167.   Pelham family, xiii, 156.   Re-founders of Hastings Priory at Warbleton, xiii, 157. xv, 155. xvi, 295. xvii, 55. Roberts family, xvi, 46. xx, 60.   Quakers at, xvi, 73, 118.   Jack Cade's insurrection, xviii, 25, 27.   Woodman's door, xvii, 164.   Ancient chest in church, xvii, 167.   Roman earthwork, xvii, 168.   Cralle of Cralle, xix, 179.   Cheney family, *ibid.*]

WARMINGHURST.

A parish in the Hundred of East Easwrith; Rape of Bramber; distant five miles north-east of Steyning, its Railway station; Posttown, Hurst-Pierpoint.   Union, Thakeham.   Population in 1811, 91; in 1861, 106.   Benefice, a Donative, valued at £50; Patron, the Duke of Norfolk; Incumbent, Rev. Robert Blakiston, M.A., of Queen's College, Oxford.   Date of earliest Parish Register, 1714. Acreage, 1,051.

This small parish, occasionally written Worminghurst, pertains principally to the settled estate of the Duke of Norfolk. In early times the manor belonged to the Abbey of Fécamp in Normandy, and the abbot had free-warren for his reeve, who resided here, and had a park in 39th Henry III., as also a chaplain, whose fee was 100s. in the reign of Edward II.   On the dissolution of the alien priories, the property was conferred on the recently-founded monastery of Sion, in Middlesex.   In 1448 it was valued at £15 12s. 10d. per annum, and a roll of that date gives minute details of the conveyance of timber and Horsham stone used in the building of Sion monastery.   It required two wagons, sixteen oxen, and six men to convey eight oak trees from Warminghurst to Kingston in eight days!   In 1540 the lands were transferred to Edward Shelley, Esq., for £391 10s.   In the conveyance there is mention of vineyards. Mr. Shelley died in October, 1554.   He had bequeathed the "remainder" to the heirs male of John Shelley, of Michelgrove, but other claimants coming forward a great law-suit, called the "Shelley case" followed.   In that case Queen Elizabeth took great personal interest.   It was ultimately decided in favour of Henry Shelley, Esq., the grandson, who held it till 1618, when a part of it was aliened to the Apsleys.   Subsequently it belonged to Sir Thomas Haselrige and Sir Thomas Williamson, whose wives were daughters of Sir John Butler, who sold it to Henry Bigland, Esq., by whom it was re-sold in 1676 to William Penn, Esq., the celebrated Quaker and founder of Pennsylvania.

That eminent man resided here for some years. In 1702 Penn sold the estate to James Butler, Esq., and it vested in his descendants till 1789, when it was conveyed by marriage to the family of Clough. In vol. xiv. of the " Sussex Collections" there is a remarkable story of an apparition of John Butler, Esq., in 1766, when he was M.P. for Sussex. His shade appeared to Miss Frances Browne, his sister-in-law, and to his steward. He was absent from Warminghurst at the time, but he died at the very moment at which these manifestations occurred.

There is a small manor or farm, called Bowfolds, which belonged in 1622 to the Shelleys; subsequently to several other families. The estate is of little importance. At the beginning of the eighteenth century James Butler, Esq., built a large brick mansion, and converted a great portion of the parish into a deer park. Since the property has come into the hands of the Duke of Norfolk, the house has been pulled down, the lake dried up, the timber felled, and the park converted into a farm. Among the timber was a magnificent chesnut tree, which was reckoned, from the rings of its wood, to be 270 years old.

The church (Holy Sepulchre?) consists of a single pace or nave. It has Early English features, but the east window is of the Decorated style, and the building has been much patched. There is a brass to the memory of 𝔈𝔡𝔴𝔞𝔯𝔡 𝔖𝔥𝔢𝔩𝔩𝔢𝔶, Esq., sometime one of the Masters of the Household to Henry VIII., Edward VI., and Queen Mary, and Joan his wife, who, with their seven sons and three daughters, are duly represented. The date is 1554. Other monumental records comprise the names of Benet, Cæsar, Butler, Blount, Morgan, Clough, Dolben, Riches, Devall, Bovey, Leeves, Oldham, Fenwicke, &c. The church contains only one bell.

[S. A. C. Apsley family, v, 54, 56, in Civil Wars, 1643. William Penn, v, 67. xx, 36. Possessions of Fécamp Abbey, x, 122. Shelley family, x, 127. xvi, 49. Butler family, xiv, 133. xvii, 222. Battle Abbey, lands in, and exchange of 400 bushels of salt and 10 casks of wine with De Braose, xvii, 29. Bridger family, xvii, 89. Imprisonment of a bondwoman, xvii, 120. Park, xvii, 121. Cade's adherents, xviii, 24.]

WARNHAM.

A parish in the Hundred of Singlecross; Rape of Bramber; distant three miles north from Horsham, its Post-town; it has a Railway-station on the Mid-Sussex line. Union, Horsham. Population in 1811; 774; in 1861, 1,006. Benefice, a Vicarage, valued at £314 18s. 5d., Patrons, Dean and Chapter of Canterbury; Incumbent, Rev. James Wood, M.A., of Christ Church, Oxford. Date of earliest Parish Register, 1558. Acreage, 4,920. *Chief Landowners*, Rev. J. Broadwood, Mrs. Barnett, Sir Percy F. Shelley, — Henderson, Esq., D.

T. Lucas, Esq., and Mrs. Wood. *Seats*, Warnham Court, C. T.
Lucas, Esq.; Field Place, William Innes, Esq.; Warnham Lodge,
W. N. Franklyn, Esq.

This parish, which extends to the frontiers of Surrey, has
long been of considerable importance. There appears to be no
mention of it in Domesday. The manor was sometimes called
Denne. It was held in 1272 by William de Saye. In 1319 it
belonged to Sir John Doyley, and in 1375 to Sir Thomas Lewknor, whose grand-daughter carried it by marriage to John Barttelot, of Stopham, Esq., who died in 1473. Subsequently it passed
to the families of Cooper, Upton, Leland, and Commerell. Denne,
with its demesnes, was severed from the manor in 1650, and devised to Christopher Coles, of Pulborough, who had married one
of the daughters of Walter Barttelot, of Stopham. They were,
in 1695, the property of John Evershed, Esq., of Eversheds in
Surrey, and subsequently passed into the hands of Young, Luxford, Collier, Murray, Milward, Lanham, Charles, Duke of
Norfolk, and Broadwood. Field Place, in the southern part
of the parish, was the estate, for several centuries, of the
family of Michell, who originated at Horsham, and possessed
Stammerham, in that parish. The last of the family resident
here left a daughter and heiress, who was wife of Sir Bysshe
Shelley, Bart. Warnham Pond is an extensive sheet of water,
and here it was that Percy Bysshe Shelley, our great Sussex
poet, used to amuse himself, in his childhood, with his diminutive boat. Near it stood a mansion of the Caryll family, who
resided here in the sixteenth and seventeenth centuries. Warnham Court, a handsome structure in the Elizabethan style, commanding very extensive views, and forming a very ornamental
feature in the landscape, was built some years since by Henry
Tredcroft, Esq. In 1331 John de Upperton settled on Stephen
de Slaughterford a parcel of land at the rent of a barbed arrow.
This shows the antiquity of the name of Upperton in Sussex.

The impropriation was granted to the neighbouring nunnery
of Rusper by William de Braose. On the dissolution of that
convent it was granted to the Dean and Chapter of Canterbury,
who leased it for a certain term, and it is now held by the
Shelley family. " The church," says Cartwright, " exhibits a
variety of style. It consists of a nave and south aisle under a
sloping roof. There are three chancels. That on the north,
enclosed by a Gothic screen, formerly belonged to the Carylls;
that on the south to the Michells, of Field Place;* and that in

* Of the family of Mychell or Michell, Mr. Gibbon, Richmond Herald, observes in
Vol. xii. of the " Sussex Collections," that those of Stammerham, Horsham, and Amberley, were " all branches of one stem." The name still prevails in these localities,
and Mr. Gibbon adds : " I have not any hesitation in saying that I could, with very
little trouble, show the descent from our Visitation of Sussex in 1634, of a vast
number of the name who at present have little idea of their claims to coat armour."

the middle to the impropriation." They all belong at present, I believe, to the Shelley family. The building is dedicated to St. Mary. There is a well-preserved monument to Sir John Caryll, knight, who died in 1613, and his wife Maria. It has effigies of the knight and his lady, and of their four sons and five daughters. Among other names and families commemorated are those of Amherst, Yates, Shelley, Michell, Shuckford, Napper, Bax, and Rapley. " In the pavement of the south aisle is the site of an altar-tomb, with three shields with quatrefoils, of the time of Edward I." (Cartwright.) In 1518, there was a chantry in this church, dedicated to St. Margaret. In the last century Warnham was celebrated for its cricketers, and a leader in that sport, who kept an inn, had painted on his sign:—

> " I, John Charman,
> Can beat half an 'em,
> With e'er a long-legged man in Warnham."

[S. A. C. Borer family, xi, 81. Church of, xii, 110. Michell family, xii, 110. Caryll, xiii, 126. xix, 19. Weston, xvi, 49. Rapley, *ibid*, 50. Bells, xvi, 228. Kingsfold, xvi, 256. Middleton family, xix, 108. Ironworks, xviii, 15.]

WARTLING.

Domesday, *Wirlinges;* vulgo, *Watlin;* a parish in the Hundred of Foxearle; Rape of Hastings; distant five miles from Pevensey station. Post-town, Hawkhurst. Union, Hailsham. Population in 1811, 874 ; in 1861, 914. Benefice, a Vicarage, valued at £441 ; Patron, John Graham, Esq.; Incumbent, Rev. Edward Curteis Graham, B.A. Date of earliest Parish Register, 1539. Acreage, 4,736. *Chief Landowner,* Herbert Mascall Curteis, Esq., of Windmill Hill.

This parish, with its hamlet of BOREHAM, possesses an agreeable variety of surface, rising from the level of Pevensey marsh to the pleasant eminence of Windmill Hill. In Domesday, the manor is said to be held by William, of the Earl of Eu. *Temp.* Henry III., it belonged to William de St. Leger. In 1327, Sir Thomas Hoo, then lord, obtained for it a weekly market on Tuesday, and a fair at Magdalen-tide. In 33rd Henry VI., Thomas Lord Hoo was lord, and in his family it remained until their extinction. In later times, it was vested successively in Gage, Sydney, Montague, Sackville, and Craven. Lord Craven, who built a house at Boreham, sold the manor, in 1766, to John, Earl of Ashburnham.

Windmill Hill, on which formerly stood a beacon, was long the residence of the family of Luxford. It afterwards belonged to Comyns and Pigou. William Pigou, Esq., erected the pre-

sent mansion on the old site. It was purchased of him by
Edward Jeremiah Curteis, long M.P. for the county ("Worthies
of Sussex," p. 233), to whose grandson it now belongs. Old Court,
the moat of which remains, was the estate of the family of
Fynes, before their removal to the adjacent parish of Hurst-
Monceux, where afterwards they built their stately castle. It
was near the church. At Foul-mile, in this parish, Speed's map
of Sussex indicates a chapel, of the history of which nothing is
known. For Boreham, see that article.

The church (St. Mary Magdalen) was formerly prebendal, and
attached to the college of St. Mary-in-the-Castle, of Hastings.
The building, which stands at Wartling Hill, rather remote
from the general population of the parish, consists of a nave
with aisles and a chancel. The south aisle, or rather chapel,
has on the outside a Pelham Buckle, and a Catherine wheel,
implying, perhaps, its erection by Catherine, daughter of Sir
John Pelham, Constable of Pevensey, *temp.* Henry VI. There
are inscriptions for the families of Luxford, Curteis, and Inglis.
The mural monument by Bacon to Caroline, wife of Herbert
Barrett Curteis, Esq., mother of the present Herbert Mascall
Curteis, Esq., is a fine work of art.

[S. A. C. Salt-pans, v, 159. xiii, 135. Pelham Buckle, &c., iii, 227.
Will. "called of the water" a serf, given to Otham Abbey, v, 160. Luxford,
arms of, vi, 77. Chapel and prebend to Hastings College, xiii, 134, 144.
Porters of, xiii, 308. Bell, xvi, 228. Tithes to Battle Abbey, xvii, 55. Jack
Cade's insurrection, xviii, 25 (mis-spelt Worthyng), 27, 28. Manor, xix,
111. Lords of, xix, 111. Carew, Gage, Craven, Ashburnham, xix, 110, 111.
Colbrond, xviii, 27 and 40. Proof of age of William Fiennes, 1378 (mis-
placed under Worthing), xii, 38.]

WASHINGTON.

Domesday, *Wasingetune ;* a parish in the Hundred of Steyning; Rape of
Bramber ; distant five miles north-west from Steyning station. Post-
town, Hurst-Pierpoint. Union, Thakeham. Population in 1811, 619;
in 1861, 908. Benefice, a Vicarage, valued at £200, in the patronage
of Magdalen College, Oxford; Incumbent, Rev. John Walker
Knight, M.A., of that College. Date of earliest Parish Register,
1558. Acreage, 3,162, though estimated by Cartwright at only 1,889.
Chief Landowners, Major C. F. Sandham, the Duke of Norfolk, Sir
Charles Goring, Bart., and the Rev. John Goring. *Seats*, Rowdell,
Major Sandham ; and Highden, Sir Charles Goring, Bart.

Washington is Saxon—Wasa-inga-tún, " the settlement of
the sons of Wasa." (See "Patronymica Britannica.") The manor
at the time of Domesday was more extensive than at present,
and included the hide of land on which stood Bramber Castle.

It was, therefore, part of the barony of Bramber, held by William de Braose. Before the Conquest, Earl Guerd (Gurth, the brother of Harold) was owner of the principal part, but there were several other proprietors; and at the time of the great Survey, the whole manor was farmed for the large sum of £100. The five salt-pans mentioned in the record must have been in the detached portion of the manor, on the Adur. From the De Braoses it passed to the Mowbrays, and continued, with some interruptions, in the Dukes of Norfolk. Early in the reign of Elizabeth, it belonged to the Carylls, and was by them held until 1765, since which time it has passed, like Muntham, through the Franklands, to the present owner. Chancton manor gave name to a family in the thirteenth century; and, after many changes, associated with the names of De Guildeford, Le Mareschal, Arundel, Browne, Shirley, Edsaw, Butler, and Clough, it became, in 1805, part of the settled estate of the Dukedom of Norfolk. In December, 1866, a remarkable discovery of Saxon coins took place on Chancton farm. It consisted of about 3,000 pennies of the reigns of Edward the Confessor and Harold II., which must have been deposited immediately before the Battle of Hastings, probably by a tenant of Guerd, who fell in that dire conflict. The vessel which had contained them was turned up by the plough, and they were so scattered broadcast, that they were regarded by the peasantry as pieces of old tin, and sold, principally to the village innkeeper, for the purchase of ale. In one instance half a pint of them was offered for a quart of "double X!" At length, public attention was called to the "find," and various claims were put in. Ultimately the greater portion of them was delivered over to the Solicitor of the Treasury. The coins were of upwards of fifty mints, including Chichester, Hastings, Lewes, and Steyning. A long-enduring tradition of treasure concealed in the place existed, and the spot had always been haunted by a Ghost, in the form of an ancient white-bearded man, who appeared to be in search of something. This is remarkable, and proves that the "uncertain voice of tradition" is not always to be disregarded. It is quite within the regions of probability that the depositor of this hoard was one of the victims of the Norman invasion.

Near the church is Rowdell, which from 10th Henry VIII. belonged to the old Sussex family of Byne, and remained in it for five generations. The fine old Jacobean mansion has been replaced, within the present century, by a much less picturesque building. The proprietors since the Bynes have been Caryll, Butler, Goring, and Burrell. In 1825, it was purchased by Major Sandham. On the south side of the parish is Highden, owned in the fourteenth century by the family of De Hiden. Henry Goring, Esq., purchased it in 1647. His son, Sir Henry Goring, Bart., built the present house, and his descendant, Sir Charles Goring, Bart., is now possessor.

The church (St. Mary) had Norman features, but falling to decay, it was rebuilt in 1866, at the cost of about £2,000. The tower, of the time of Henry VII., has been retained. The inscriptions commemorate members of the families of Byne, Fortrie, Butler, Waldegrave, Hammond, Goring, &c.

On an elevated point of the South Downs, in this parish, is a well-known circular earthwork of Celtic origin, now planted round with trees, and known as Chanctonbury Ring. It is one of the most commanding heights in the county, and said to be 814 feet above the level of the sea. It is visible from the east, west, and north, at great distances. Over this part of the Downs, and in this parish, runs one of the numerous steep roads known as " Bostalls," a word scarcely heard out of Sussex, but of good Saxon meaning, for a hill path.

[S. A. C. Domesday watermills, v, 272. Tithes to Sele Priory, x, 115. Chanctonbury, a monk murdered at, xii, 28. Church, xii, 111. Byne family, *ibid.* Lands to Shulbred Priory, xiii, 46. Family of Edsaw, xvi, 49. Goring of, xvi, 49. xvii, 82. Bells, xvi, 141, 228. Adur River, xvi, 251. Highden, xvii, 82. Jack Cade's adherents, xiii, 24. Rowdell, xviii, 107. Flight of Charles II., xviii, 121. Saxon coins found here, xix, 189. xx, 288. The Washington Ghost, xx, 213.]

WESTBOURNE.

Domesday, *Borne;* a parish in the Hundred of its own name; Rape of Chichester; distant seven miles from Chichester; Post-town, Emsworth; Railway station, Emsworth, distant about one mile. Union, Westbourne. Population in 1811, 1,702; in 1861, 2,165. Benefice, a Rectory and Vicarage, valued at £450; Patron and Incumbent, Rev. J. Hanson Sperling, M.A., of Trinity College, Cambridge. Date of earliest Parish Register, 1550. Acreage, 6,000. *Chief Landowners,* Earl of Dartmouth, Mrs. Dixon, Lord Leconfield, C. Dorrien, Esq., and Messrs. Hopkin, Wyatt, Quick, Osmond, &c.

This important parish comprises the hamlets or villages of Aldsworth, Nutbourne, Prinsted, Woodmancote, The Hermitage, and several other minor places. The soil varies from chalk on the north to loam and alluvium on the south. The land is generally highly cultivated and very productive. The main village was formerly a trading town of some importance. It is pleasantly situated near the little river Ems, and lies near Emsworth, which takes its name from that river. The parish is beautifully wooded, and the sea separates it from Thorney Island.

The manor of Borne is described in Domesday as lying in the hundred of " Ghidenetroi," a designation now obsolete. It had belonged to Earl Godwin, but was now a part of the territory of the Earl Roger de Montgomeri. It had been rated at 30 hides, but was now assessed at only 12. There were seven ministri, four mills, a fishery, and a wood. Henry Fitz-Alan, the last Earl of Arundel of that name, died seised of it, and it then devolved on Jane, one of his co-heiresses, who married John, Lord Lumley. In subsequent years it passed with the Stansted estate to the Rev. Lewis Way, and later to C. Scrase Dickins, Esq.

The church (St. John the Baptist), which is altogether one of the most interesting ecclesiastical buildings in West Sussex, is approached from the north by a venerable avenue of yew trees, said to have been planted in 1530 by Lord Maltravers. The edifice was twice altered by two of the Earls of Arundel and formerly contained a chapel dedicated to All Souls. There are vestiges of Norman architecture, and Transitional work, but the church has been much altered and patched by the introduction of the Perpendicular style. In the chancel is a beautiful piscina, probably of the fifteenth century, which is engraved in " Hussey's Churches." In 1770, George, Earl of Halifax, lord of the manor, made some benefactions to the building, including a spire, which Horsfield characterizes as of Chinese architecture! This, however, has been altered, and it is now a great ornament to the landscape. In 1782 the church consisted of nave, chancel, and two aisles. In the years 1863 and 1865 much true restoration was effected. There are six bells, and some painted glass, chiefly modern. Besides one or two ancient monumental slabs, there are many monuments and inscriptions to the families of Barwell, D'Oyley, Bensley, Montague, Eliot, Tatersall, Farley, Needham, Campbell, Oldfield, Lumley, Ward, Roberts, Browne, Pryme, Sedgwick, Cathcart, Walleston, Newland, Mundy, Wallis, Williams, Lyne, Ashburnham, Peake, Allen, &c.

The hamlets of PRINSTED, NUTBOURNE, and THE HERMITAGE each anciently possessed a chapel; but few remains of them now exist. The origin of the last-named building was due to " Simon Cotes of Westborne, Ermyt," who in his will, dated 1527, tells us that he had built upon his own land a house and a chapel, which he dedicated to St. Anthony. These, with other buildings, bridges, and highways, he bequeathed to William, Earl of Arundel, K.G., with a view to the maintenance of a Hermit for ever. This, I think, is among the latest of Hermitages in England. Simon was perhaps not a hermit at all, except that he lived a religious life, in his simple habitation, and worshipped

in his little sacellum. Mr. Longcroft, in his "Valley of the
Ems," thinks he was simply one of those benevolent persons
who in earlier times made it a duty and a pleasure to provide
for the safety of wayfarers at dangerous fords, such as that of
the Ems must then have been.

[S. A. C. Domesday watermills, v, 272. Calceto had lands in, xi, 103.
Dutelor, John of, *ibid.* Wodemancote, xi, 104. Nutbourne chapel, xii,
69. Matthew de Mount Martin, xiii, 108. Bells of, xvi, 228. River Ems,
xvi, 266. Lord Lumley, xix, 102, 103. Since this volume was in the
hands of the Printer, the learned and excellent rector, has published in
vol. xxii. of the "Sussex Collections" a "Parochial History of Westbourne."]

WEST BURTON.

A hamlet of Bury, which see.

WESTFIELD.

Domesday, *Westewelle;* vulgo, *Wessvull;* a well-wooded and beautifully
undulated parish in the Hundred of Baldslow; Rape of Hastings;
distant five miles east from Battle, its Post-town and Railway station. Union, Battle. Population in 1811, 707; in 1861, 900. Benefice, a Vicarage, valued at £372; Patron, the Bishop of Chichester;
Incumbent, Rev. Mark Henry Vernon, M.A., of Trinity College,
Cambridge. Date of earliest Parish Register, 1552. Acreage, 4,272.
Chief Landowners, Charles Hay Frewen, Esq., R. B. and B. S. Follett, Esqrs., and B. H. Brabazon, Esq. *Seats,* Oaklands, B. Hercules
Brabazon, Esq., and Major B. Harvey Combe; and Westfield House,
— Follett, Esq.

Before the Conquest the manor was held by Wenestan of
Edward the Confessor; afterwards one Wibert held it of the Earl
of Eu. It is a sub-infeudation of Warbleton. Westfield manor-
house, now a farm-house, near the church, was for several generations the property and seat of the family of Peirs, who had
been seated at Goteley in Northiam, as Perez or Perys, from
16th Henry VI., and afterwards at Ewhurst, Warbleton, Cowfold, &c. Thomas Peirs of this family resided at Stonepits, in
Seale, co. Kent, and was created a Baronet in 1663. His descendant, Sir George Peirs, sold Westfield, and it has since
passed by successive transfers to the families of Allen, Craggs,
Lade, Lutman, and Lamb, of Rye. Sir Richard Sackville
possessed a manor in this parish in 1565. On the north side of
the parish is Crowham, presumed to be identical with the Cro-
teslei of Domesday, and the largest manor in the parish. Robert

Crowham, the last Prior of Lewes, 1537, is supposed to have taken his name from this place. In the earlier part of the seventeenth century it belonged to the Cheyneys; afterwards to the Farndens of Sedlescombe; and subsequently by various modes of transfer to the Snow, Mosley, and Smith families. Lankhurst manor, in the south-east part of Westfield, belonged to the Dynes in the seventeenth and eighteenth centuries, when it passed by an heiress to the family of Brisco, and is now held *jure uxoris* by C. H. Frewen, Esq., M.P. Spray's Bridge, an estate near the northern boundary of the parish, belonged to a family of that name, the last of whom, Adrian Spray, died early in the eighteenth century. This is altogether an interesting parish, and deserves more attention than it has hitherto received. Ironworks were formerly carried on here.

The church (St. John the Baptist), which was restored in 1862, consists of nave, aisle, and chancel. Its original style was Early English, with little admixture of other styles. (Rickman.) At the west end is a shingled spire with three bells, one of which has an inscription in Lombardic characters, " Sit nomen Domini benedictum." There are monumental records for the names of Peirce, Weekes, Davis, &c.

[S. A. C. Ironworks, ii, 219. xviii, 16. Weekes family, xi, 82. xiv, 115, 116, 229. Piers family, xiv, 102. Brede river, xv, 155. Bells, xvi, 228. Tithes to Battle Abbey and ordeal by water, xvii, 24. William Westfield, abbot of Battle, xvii, 46. Cade's insurrection, xviii, 25.]

WEST-GRINSTEAD.

A parish in the Hundred of its own name; Rape of Bramber; distant eight miles north from Steyning, and seven south from Horsham. Post-town, Horsham. Railway stations, Westgrinstead and Partridge Green. Union, Horsham. Population in 1811, 998; in 1861, 1,403. Benefice, a Rectory, valued at £1,120; Patron, Lord Leconfield; Incumbent, Rev. Thomas Wall Langshaw, B.A., of St. John's College, Cambridge. Date of earliest Parish Register, 1556. Acreage, 6,658. *Chief Landowners*, Sir Percy Burrell, Bart., and Rev. John Goring. *Seat*, West-Grinstead Park.

This parish consists chiefly of arable land, though there is a good proportion of meadow and wood. No less than 400 acres are occupied by thick hedgerows and copses, which add much beauty to the scenery. There is no specific mention of this place in Domesday. It was part of the large possessions of the De Braoses, Lords of Bramber, but seems to have been aliened in the middle of the 14th century. In 1417, John Halsham, and Philippa, his wife, held it by a feoffment of Richard Waneling, clerk, and others. The Halsham family, who originated at Hailsham, in Pevensey Rape, became of much importance here, and acquired the manors of Applesham, Notcham, and West Grinstead. At the death of John Halsham, in 1417, his eldest son, Richard,. was owner. His brother, Sir Hugh Halsham, succeeded, and made his will in 1441. John, the first-mentioned, appears to have married, first Philippa Michel, and, secondly, another Philippa, daughter of David Strabolgy, Earl of Athol. The latter had previously married Sir Ralph Percy, son of Henry, Earl of Northumberland, by whom she had no children; by Sir John Halsham she had two sons, who died without issue, and a daughter, Joan, who married John Lewknor, Esq. Later, the manor fell to the Crown, and in 1st Edward VI., Thomas Seymour held it in fee-farm. On his attainder, it was granted to Thomas Shirley, a younger son of Ralph Shirley, of Wiston, from whom it descended to Thomas Shirley Esq. This gentleman was an ultra-Calvinist, and in his will, made in 1606, he informs us that he has full assurance of resting "both soul and body in the highest comfortable heaven of heavens," among the elect saints of God, of which number "I assuredly account myself to be one." On his death the manor and estate were sold to Sir Edward Caryll, whose grand-daughter, Philippa, wife of Henry, Lord Morley and Monteagle, was seised of them for life, with remainder to her son Thomas, Lord Morley. He joined with his mother in settling the property on Richard Caryll, who died in 1701, when it descended to his grandson, John. This gentleman being a staunch Roman Catholic, and an adherent of James II., accompanied the fallen monarch to France, where he assumed, by grant of the Pretender, the title of Lord Caryll. By him the estate was sold in 1750 to Sir Merrik Burrell, Bart., who having added to it several farms, left it to Mrs. Isabella Wyatt, with remainder to Walter Burrell, Esq., second surviving son of his nephew, Sir William Burrell, Bart., and it is now the property of Sir Percy Burrell, Bart. The present mansion is on a rising ground, north-east of the old house. It was built in 1806 in a semi-castellated Gothic, from designs by Nash, and has many fine apartments. A good deer-park, with excellent timber, surrounds the house. There are some good pictures by Vandyke, Lely, Jansen, Reinagle, Lawrence, Opie, and by some of the best foreign masters. The house has an historical interest from the fact that Pope was a frequent visitor to the Carylls, and his "Rape of the Lock" had its origin from an incident which occurred here. On the east side of the Park is a Roman Catholic chapel, endowed by the Caryll family. Clothalls, near the church, as a manor, derived its name from the family of De Clothall, who resided here in the 15th century. From them it descended by heirship and marriage through the names of Wilt-shire, Bellingham, Boys, Lamb, and Ferris. Champions, on the north side of the parish, was the possession for nearly 200 years of the family of Ward. The manor of Bidlington belonged, as part of the Wiston state, to Sir Robert Fagge, from whom it has descended to the Goring family.

The fact of the benefice of West Grinstead being so well en-dowed, is attributable to the circumstance that very little of the land in the parish was granted away to monastic institutions. The parsonage house, of the date of James I., was added to by the late rector, Rev. W. Peckham Woodward, and with modern additions, now ranks amongst the highest order of parochial residences. Among the rectors no less than five of the Woodward family held the living in succession from 1695 until a recent period. The people of West Grinstead seem to have been a rather law-less race, and Mr. Cartwright, from ancient records, mentions several murders in the parish. The church (St. George) consists of two aisles of equal length, divided by an arcade. The original edifice was Early English, but later insertions have been made. The end of the north aisle is the chancel, and that of the south aisle was the chapel of St. Mary, the burial place of the lords of the manor. The tower stands in the middle of the south aisle, and has a shingled spire. There are six modern bells. In the manorial burying-place are two brasses. The first is to a lady, and much mutilated, and commemorates Philippa, wife of John Halsham, one of the daughters of David de Strabolgie, Earl of Athol, 1385. The other brass is now placed on a low altar tomb, and has canopied figures of an armed knight and lady. The surrounding riband has been torn off by sacrilegious hands; but a record of it shows that it was for Sir Hugh Halsham, Knight, and Joyce (Jocosa) his wife, 1421 and 1420. A banner above the canopy bears the quartered arms of Halsham and Strabolgie. This is a very interesting brass. There are tablets commemorating the families and names of Caryll, Beding-feld, Harrington, Burrell, and Raymond; but the principal monument is by Rysbrach, which cost £2,000, to the memory of Captain William Powlett, of St. Leonard's Forest, who married Elizabeth, 4th daughter of John Ward, of Champions, in West-Grinstead, and his wife. This gallant captain is associated with the superstitious legend of the " headless ghost of St. Leonards." There is also a flat gravestone with a brass plate for Robert Ravenscroft, and Joan, his wife, 1520, and 1522. Other inscrip-tions commemorate the names of Woodward, Pellatt, Gale, White, Nash, Morgan, Gratwicke, &c. Altogether this is a most picturesque and interesting church.

For KNEPP CASTLE, see Shipley.

[S. A. C. Bynes of, x, 118. Shirley of, xi, 49. Champions of, xi, 69.

Tregoz, xii, 39. Church, xii, 92, 106. Gratwicke of, xii, 106. St. Leonard's Forest legend and Pawletts, xiii, 222. Ward of, and Godsmark of, xvi, 49. Bells, xvi, 210. Park, xvi, 250. Cade's insurrection, xviii, 24. Shirley of, xix, 68. Marle in, *ibid.* Ashurst in, and Bridgers of, xix, 94. Carylls of, xix, 112, 191. Parker and Young of, xix, 112, 113. Adlington, Protestant martyr, xx, 153.]

WESTHAM.

A Parish in the Hundred and Rape of Pevensey. It is the western hamlet of the ancient town of Pevensey, whence its name. It has a Railway station on the South Coast line. Union, Eastbourne. Population in 1811, 584; in 1861, 850. Benefice, a Vicarage, valued at £550; Patron, the Duke of Devonshire ; Incumbent, Rev. Henry Thomas Grace, M.A., of Pembroke College. Date of earliest Parish Register, 1571. Acreage, 4,718. *Chief Landowners,* the Duke of Devonshire, and Sir James Duke, Bart.

That this parish was an ancient hamlet of the parish of Pevensey is the accepted tradition of the district, and, in fact, in ecclesiastical records, the church of St. Mary is described as a dependent benefice. The village consists chiefly of a main street, separated from the little town of Pevensey by the Roman castle. It contains two very picturesque little houses, with timbered fronts, one of which has, over the doorway, the Pelham badge of the Buckle. The church is large and handsome, consisting of a nave, a north aisle, a south chancel, and a massive west tower, formerly much higher than at present. There is a considerable mixture of styles from Norman to Perpendicular. The south wall has very small windows of the earlier date, very high up, and with glazing nearly flush with the external surface. The north aisle and the chancel are both Perpendicular, of about the time of Edward IV. In the large eastern windows still remain portions of well-executed painted glass, which would appear to have formerly represented Christ and the twelve apostles. In the building are memorials to the families of Fagge of Glynley, Thatcher of Priesthawes, Hammond and Meeres, besides traces of much older ones now partly destroyed.

Priesthawes is popularly supposed to have been a religious foundation, though no documentary or architectural evidence can be adduced on the subject. It was long the seat of the ancient family of Thatcher, and there is an absurd tradition of a subterraneous connection between it and Pevensey Castle (two miles distant), such as we find all over England, in Normandy, and many other parts of the Continent, when a "religious" site is not far remote from a fortress. Glynley—vulgo, "Greenlee"—was originally an Elizabethan mansion of considerable pretensions, which belonged successively to the Meeres, Fagges, and

Peacheys. It had excellent grounds, fish-ponds, and groves, in the last century. Both these mansions exist simply as farm-houses. Near the village is an ancient almshouse of four tenements, known as the Hospital of St. John the Baptist, alias "Gorogltown," of uncertain foundation, and of equally uncertain etymology. Peeling is another house of considerable antiquity; as likewise is Hankham, now corrupted to Handcombe, which is frequently mentioned in the archives of Battle Abbey, though misprinted in Thorpe's Catalogue as Ha*u*kham. For LANGNEY, see that article. A very small hamlet in the parish bears the singular name of Friday-street.

[S. A. C. Marshall's benefaction to church, xviii, 51. Church, xiv, 99, 265. Thatcher family of Priesthawes, xiv, 265. xviii, 38. xix, 194. Church bells, xvi, 228. Iron fire-back, xviii, 13. John Morley, gentilman, and two yeomen, adherents of Jack Cade, xviii, 27. Ordinances made at, xviii, 43. Richard Borde, brother of "Merry Andrew" Borde, vi, 213. xix. 7. Mr. Bristowe's Visitation-book, 1634, xix, 194.]

WESTHAMPNETT.

Domesday, *Antone (?)*; a parish in the Hundred of Box and Stockbridge; Rape of Chichester; distant 1½ mile from Chichester, its Post-town and Railway station. Union, Westhampnett. Population in 1811, 444; in 1861, 502. Benefice, a Vicarage, valued at £52; Patron, the Duke of Richmond, who is also chief landowner. Date of earliest Parish Register, 1734. Acreage, 1,899.

West Hampnett, so called in distinction from East Hampnett, a tithing in Boxgrove, is not mentioned in Domesday, but it was an early appendage to the lordship of Halnaker. *Temp.* Henry VI. Robert Tawke had good lands here. Joan, daughter and co-heiress of William Tawke, married in the sixteenth century, first, Richard Ryman, of Appledram; and secondly, Edward Barttelot, of Stopham. Anne, the other co-heiress, married Thomas Devenish, of Hellingly, who was partially resident here. The families of Chapman and Rose were afterwards influential. The large mansion, West Hampnett Place, now used as a union workhouse, was the seat of the Sackville family, and is supposed to have been built by Richard Sackville, uncle of the Lord Treasurer Buckhurst. The back part of the house is Elizabethan; the brick front towards the road is modern, having been rebuilt in the last century by Sir Hutchins Williams, Bart., husband of Judith Booth, celebrated for her talents and beauty. Their son, Sir W. Peere Williams, sold it to Charles, third Duke of Richmond, who converted it to its present use. The parish contains the vills of Woodcote, Westerton, Waterbeech, and Maudlin.

The church (St. Mary or St. Peter) consists of chancel, nave, and south aisle, in the Early English and later styles. In the aisle under the belfry is a small chantry chapel. In the mouldings of the north door, both inside and out, are three shields of arms including Tawke; three mullets in chief (Benion?); and three hammers. In the chancel is a monument to the memory of Richard Sackville, Esq., and Elizabeth Thatcher, his wife, with kneeling figures of both; and of a son and daughter, together with the arms of Sackville and Thatcher, and a mutilated representation of the Trinity. During some restorations in 1867, some very interesting, and much more ancient, features, which had been concealed by lath and plaster, were brought to light. The chancel arch was found to have been constructed of brick of Roman make, which had doubtless been brought hither from the ancient station of Regnum (Chichester). Mr. Gordon Hills, the architect employed, believes that the chancel, at least, was constructed in Saxon times, and probably in the time of St. Wilfred, the founder of the South Saxon bishopric of Selsey. ("Journal of British Archæological Association," 1867, p. 1.) In the churchyard is a tombstone to the memory of the late Mr. W. H. Brooke, artist and F.S.A., well-known for his etchings in several volumes of the "Sussex Archæological Collections," who was interred here by his friend, Mr. Robert Elliot, F.S.A., of Chichester.

The union of West Hampnett is the largest in the county, and comprises nearly forty parishes.

[S. A. C. Two watermills in Domesday, v, 272. Roman road at, xi, 128. Church, xii, 73. xviii, 96. Bonvilles, lords of, xv, 59. Church to Boxgrove Priory, xv, 86, 89. Bells, xvi, 210. Arms of Tawke, xviii, 81.]

WEST HOTHLY.

Vulgo, *West Hoâdlye;* a parish in the Hundred of Buttinghill; Rape of Lewes; distant five miles south-west from East Grinstead, its Post-town. Railway station, Balcombe, distant about four miles. Union, East Grinstead. Population in 1811, 840; in 1861, 1,120. Benefice, a Vicarage, valued at £150; Patron, the Lord Chancellor; Incumbent, Rev. Francis Kirkpatrick, M.A., of Trinity College, Dublin. Date of earliest Parish Register, 1645. Acreage, 4,863. *Seats,* Gravetye, F. Cayley, Esq.; Selsfield Lodge, J. C. Powell, Esq., Calcott, J. Chatterton, Esq.; Courtlands, R. Sharpe, Esq., and several others.

A considerable and picturesque parish on the Forest Ridge,

commanding enchanting views. The manor descended as Worth. In this parish is the denuded range of sandstone called the Chiddingly Rocks, one of which, known as *Great-upon-Little*, is "a parallelopipedon, about 20 feet high," whose four sides measure more than 63 feet. This immense mass, weighing 500 tons, is poised upon a little point of another rock, which just protrudes from the soil—whence the appellation. It has been supposed to be of Druidic origin, and Governor Pownall communicated a learned disquisition respecting it to the "Archæologia;" but the slightest view of it, with an examination of the adjacent rocks, will show that it is the result of geological denudation. It has long been an object of curiosity, and names and dates from the early part of the 17th century downwards, are cut upon it.

The Elizabethan mansion of Gravetye was once the seat of the Infield family, who carried on iron-works here; and there are two other houses of considerable importance, one at Stoneland, and the other near the church, the supposed residence of the Feldwickes. On Selsfield Common, a commanding height, there was formerly a beacon. The church consists of a nave, chancel, south aisle, and a handsome tower and shingled spire, which is a great ornament to the landscape. There are five bells, one of which is inscribed to St. Mary. The building has Transition-Norman, and Early English and later features. There are memorials to the names of Infield, Sawyer, Nairn, Wood, Griffiths, and Wetherell. In the chancel are a piscina and three sedilia.

[S. A. C. Ironworks at, ii, 220. iii, 242. Gravetye, x, 166. Infield family, *ibid*. Philpott's and Barley's (lands), xiii, 48. Church to Lewes Priory, xiii, 244. Turner of, xiii, 253. Feldwicke, xvi, 49. Church bells, xvi, 112.]

WESTMESTON.

A parish in the Hundred of Street; Rape of Lewes; distant six miles north-west from Lewes. Post-town, Hurst-Pierpoint. Railway station, Hassock's Gate, distant about three miles. Union, Chailey. Population in 1811, 189; in 1861, 288. Benefice, a Rectory, valued at £536; Patron, William H. Campion, Esq.; Incumbent, Rev. C. Heathcote Campion, B.A., of Christ Church, Oxford. Date of earliest Parish Register, 1587. Acreage, 2,260. *Chief Landowners*, Rush Cripps, Esq., of Stantons, and Henry Charles Lane, Esq., of Middleton House, both in this parish.

The etymon seems to be the *tún* or enclosure where *mæste*, mast, or food for swine, &c., abounded. The epithet West was to distinguish it from similar localities, *e.g.*, from Sel-meston, in Pevensey rape. Before the Conquest the manor

belonged to the Countess Gueda. It came with Lewes Rape to
the De Warennes. In 6th Edward II., John, Earl of Warenne,
procured a charter for a fair, on the feast of St. Martin, the
patron saint of the parish. In later times it has been possessed
by the noble families of Poynings, and Fynes, Lords Dacre. In
the sixteenth century, the Michelbornes were of Westmeston
manor, and probably built the "Place" house. To them succeeded the Dobells, whose successors have held the manor in
the same line as Streat.

In or near this parish is Chatfield, which gave name to a
widely-spread Sussex family. So early as 1287 the names of
Robert and Reginald de Chattefeld occur in a transfer of land
here. The estate of Hayley anciently had a park, some vestiges
of which are still existing. In the sixteenth century the Earl
of Derby had a moiety of it, which, *temp.* Philip and Mary, his
son and heir granted to John Carril, of Warnham, for twenty-
one years. John Carril, his son, demised the same for his term
to John Shelley. EAST CHILTINGTON is an outlying chapelry of
this parish.

The church (St. Martin) consists of a nave, chancel, south
aisle, and a shingled dovecote steeple at the west end. It has
Norman features. The chancel, Mr. Hussey thinks, is Early
English, though the chancel arch is semicircular. The west
end has Perpendicular insertions. In 1862, the Rector, in the
course of some restorations, discovered a series of mural paintings of Norman date, covering the north and east walls of the
nave, together with part of the south wall. The subjects consisted of the Scourging, the Crucifixion, the Taking down from
the Cross, the Adoration of the Magi, the legend of St. Vin-
cent's martyrdom by Datian, Dioclesian's pro-consul in Spain,
&c. A fully illustrated account of these early works of art is
given in the "Sussex Archæological Collections," by the Rev.
C. H. Campion. The church has memorials for the names of
Chaloner, of Chiltington, Martin, Rideout, Campion, Wilson,
Peckham, Hampton, &c.

[S. A. C. Wilson, xiii, 253. Michelborne pedigree, xiii, 257. Mural
paintings in church, xiv, x. xvi, 1—19 *(Campion)*. Bells, xvi, 228. Springett family, xx, 46.]

WHATLINGTON.

Domesday, *Watlingetone;* a parish on the small river Brede, in the Hun-
    dreds of Battle, Staple, and Netherfield, but principally in the first-
    named; Rape of Hastings; distant two miles north from Battle, which
    is the Post-town and Railway station. Union, Battle. Population in
    1811, 242; in 1861, 343. Benefice, a Rectory, valued at £160; Pa-

tron and Incumbent, Rev. William Margesson, M.A. Date of earliest Parish Register, 1558. Acreage, 1,255. *Seat*, Rushton Park (olim Vinehall), W. Rushton Adamson, Esq.

Harold was lord of this manor at the time of his unfortunate downfall, after which Reinbert held it of the Earl of Eu. In later times, it belonged to the powerful family of De Echingham, and subsequently to the Finches, ancestors of the Earls of Winchelsea. In still later times, the Pelhams possessed it, and it now belongs to the Earl of Ashburnham. The parish gave name to an ancient family called De Watlyngton, and in 1307, John de Watlyngton was elected abbot of Battle. The manor of Farne or Vinehall, anciently, Fynhawe, gave name to the family of De Fynhawe, who ultimately wrote themselves Vinall, settled at Kingston, near Lewes, and became extinct about the end of the seventeenth century. It afterwards belonged to the Dunks and Davises. Until recently, it was possessed by Tilden Smith, Esq., and it is now the property and seat of W. Rushton Adamson, Esq., by whom it has been re-named Rushton Park. The mansion possesses every appliance of luxury, including gas made on the spot, and commands a fine view.

The church (St. Mary Magdalen), as described by Hussey in 1852, comprised only chancel, nave, porch, and western wooden bell-turret. There were Decorated and Perpendicular features, a square piscina, a plain sedile, and a closed low-side window. In Sir W. Burrell's time, some shattered painted glass in one of the north windows contained portions of the arms of Battle Abbey, from which Sir William infers that the building was erected by one of the abbots. Within the last few years it has been thoroughly repaired.· There are memorials for the names of Dunk, Seare, Theobald, &c.

[S. A. C. Brede river, xv, 154. Bells, xvi, 229. Abbot John de W., xvii, 46. Church, xvii, 53. Tithes to Battle Abbey, xvii, 55. xviii, 39. Vinehall family of, xviii, 39.]

WIGGONHOLT.

Anciently, *Wynkenholte;* a parish in the Hundred of West Easewrith; Rape of Arundel ; distant three miles south-west from Pulborough station, and 7½ south-east of Petworth, its Post-town. Union, East Preston. Population in 1811, 43 ; in 1861, 34. Benefice, a Rectory, united with Greatham, valued at £205 ; Patron, Lord De la Zouch ; Incumbent, Rev. Thomas Bacon, M.A., of Merton College, Oxford. Date of earliest Parish Register, 1597. Acreage, 841.

Of the history of this small parish nothing of value is

known until the 13th century. When Henry Tregoz held it,
temp. Henry III., it was erected into a manor, the lands of which
extended into many of the neighbouring parishes. In 1550 the
greater part of the estate was granted, with Parham, to Sir
Thomas Palmer, who, or his representatives, transferred it to
the family of Bisshopp, whose descendant, the Baroness De la
Zouch, brought it to the family of Curzon, its present possessors.
(See PARHAM.) The church, which I have not seen, is described
by Dallaway as " very small, and without any vestige of architectural ornament." The font is early Norman, large, square,
and of Sussex marble.

In 1827 some curious Roman remains were found in the parish.
They consisted of sepulchral urns and other vessels, some of
which were Samian, with good ornamentation. Coins of Nero,
Vespasian, Claudius, Hadrian, and M. Antoninus were also found.

[S. A. C. Roman remains, ix, 112. xi, 139. xiv, 37. Lands of Torting-
ton Priory, xi, 110. Roman road, xi, 139. Manor granted by Queen
Elizabeth, xiii, 48. Coins found at Redford, xiv, 37. Rectory, xiv, 166.
Monke of, xvi, 50. Church bell, xvi, 229. London road to Arundel, xix, 158.]

WITHDEAN, *vulgo*, Wighting.   See Patcham

WILLINGDON.

Domesday, *Willendone*; vulgo, *Wilndon*; a parish in the Hundred of its
own name; Rape of Pevensey; distant two miles north-west from
Eastbourne. Post-town, Hawkhurst. Railway station, Polegate, distant about one mile. Union, Eastbourne. Population in 1811, 445;
in 1861, 709. Benefice, a Vicarage, valued at £150. *Patrons,* Dean
and Chapter of Chichester ; Incumbent, Rev. Thomas Lowe, M.A.,
of Oriel College, Oxford. Date of earliest Parish Register, 1560.
Acreage, 4,217. *Chief Landowners,* Representatives of the late F.
Freeman Thomas, Esq., of Ratton,* the only *seat* in the parish,
though there are several other excellent residences.

The village is seated on an eminence near the base of the
South Downs, and commands a fine view of Pevensey Bay. A
lofty height of the Downs, which run directly southward to
Beachy Head through this parish, is called Crow-crouch, from a
cross which formerly stood there. The modern mansion of
Ratton occupies an elevated spot on a declivity of the Downs.
Of the ancient manor-house nothing but the old gatehouse
remains, though, towards the end of the last century, it was

* Ratton anciently had a park, the remembrance of which is perpetuated in " Park
Farm," a portion of the estate, and formerly celebrated for its decoy of ducks, the
ponds of which remain.

entire, and had its venerable hall decorated with halberts, partisans, cross-bows, and other warlike implements. It was deserted, as the residence of the proprietors of the estate, on the erection of the new Ratton-place by Sir George Thomas, Bart.; Governor of Antigua, who had acquired the property by purchase of Samuel Durrant, of Lewes, Esq. The earlier history of Ratton (coinciding with the manor of Willingdon) is interesting. It extends into the parishes of Willingdon and Eastbourne, and proceeds by a narrow slip of land into the distant parishes of Hellingly, Chiddingly, and Heathfield. In one part of Hellingly the connection is formed only by a thick hedge, as I have heard my late father say. In the time of the Confessor it was held by Godwin, Earl of Kent, and was valued at sixty pounds. After the Conquest the Earl of Moreton obtained the manor, when it was valued at forty pounds. Richard de Aquila, a subsequent lord of the great barony of Pevensey, gave a portion of it to the abbey of Grestein in Normandy. Henry III., in the 44th year of his reign, granted the manor to his kinsman, Peter of Savoy. Edward IV. settled it in dower on his consort, Queen Elizabeth. Queen Elizabeth (Tudor) granted it about 1568 to Thomas, Lord Buckhurst, for the annual rent of £73 10s., and a pound of pepper. It would appear that the manor was formerly held by sub-feudatories, as there is a tolerably clear history of Ratton, unconnected with the noble and royal personages above enumerated. Indeed a separate manor of *Radetone* is mentioned in Domesday. Ratton gave name to a family at an early period, and their ultimate heiress married Walter de Rackele, whose last descendant espoused John Parker, who was living in 18th Henry VI. The Parkers became one of the most eminent families of the county, and held this estate for upwards of three centuries. They had previously been resident at Bexhill (then called Bexley) in East Sussex, for several generations, and before and after their acquisition of Ratton they were allied with the best families in this and other counties, namely, Halle of Ore, Levet of Hollington, Bate of Lydd, Thatcher of Ringmer, Pelham, Farnfold, Gage, Sackville, Waller of Groombridge, Selwyn of Friston, Courtney of Powderham, co. Devon, Temple of Stowe, co. Buckingham, Dacre of Hurst-Monceux, Newdigate of Warwickshire, Campion of Combwell, Shurley of Isfield, &c. In fact, the genealogical rolls of our county scarcely exhibit a greater number of splendid alliances. In 1674, Sir Robert Parker was created a baronet, but the title became extinct with his grandson, Sir Walter, in 1750. Of this family were John Parker, deputy of George Boleyn, Lord Rocheford, Lord Warden of the Cinque-Ports, who rebuilt Ratton and died in 1558, and Sir Nicholas and Sir John Parker, both captains of

the important fortress of Pendennis Castle, in Cornwall; but
the most noticeable member of the family was Henry, son of Sir
Nicholas Parker, who was born at Ratton about the beginning
of the 17th century. After his university career at Oxford, he
became a member of Lincoln's Inn ; and at the commencement
of the Civil War, he took the Parliamentary side, and was secretary of war under the Earl of Essex. On the Earl's death he
retired to Hamburg, from whence he was recalled by Cromwell
to be his secretary, or, as Anthony-a-Wood calls him, *" a brewer's
clerk ! "* He was an industrious author, and published several
theological and political works, which acquired considerable
popularity in their day. He died in 1657. His grandmother,
Hester, wife of Sir Thomas Temple, of Stowe, Bart., survived
him and lived to see the astonishing number of upwards of
seven hundred descendants from her own body. This fact is
vouched for by Fuller in his " Worthies of England," that
" worthy " having lost a wager on the subject. (Vol. i, p. 210,
edit. 1840.) The estate of Ratton passed through the Parkers
to the family of Trayton, and the last male heir of that family
devised it to Samuel Durrant, Esq., of Lewes, to whom he was
under heavy pecuniary engagements. It may be remarked here
that the name of Trayton, so common as a Christian name in
this part of Sussex, is owing to the fact that Mr. Edward Trayton,
a rather " fast man " of his time, and highly popular among
the farmers and tradesmen, became godfather to many children ;
and to this day hundreds of Sussex people bear the prænomen
of Trayton, believing it to be as orthodox and regular as John or
William.

The church consists of nave, chancel, north aisle, and south
porch, with a tower at the west end of the aisle. Mr. Hussey
considers the tower to have been partially or wholly rebuilt,
though the arch is of Norman date. There are Early English
features, but the windows are chiefly Perpendicular. " The
nave is remarkably spacious. The aisle was evidently once more
considerable than at present, and might have originally been
the nave." (Hussey's " Churches," p. 378.) This arrangement,
however abnormal, produces a pleasing and picturesque effect,
and the commanding site of the building renders it one of the
most interesting churches in this part of the county. There
are five bells. In the Parker chapel are several interesting monuments to that family. There is a brass of a man in armour
with the coat of Parker quartering Rakeley and Ratton, and
impaling Sackville, to 𝔍𝔬𝔥𝔫 𝔓𝔞𝔯𝔨𝔢𝔯, Esq., and Johan, his wife,
1543 ; as also another with the arms of Parker, and its quarterings impaled with Waller of Groombridge, to Thomas Parker,
Esq., of the date of 1580. But the monumental glory of the

church is a marble tomb to Sir Nicholas Parker, representing the effigies of the knight in armour under a canopy, with kneeling figures of his three wives, and the arms and quarterings of his several alliances. Beneath the arch is a metrical epitaph, concluding thus :—

" Then blame not aged Britain's feeble womb,
For in her Parker's birth she did consume
Her utmost strength. The world will scarce be strong
For such another brave conception."

There are numerous other memorials in the building.

Roman and other coins have been found at Willingdon. HIDNEY, formerly a member of the Cinque Ports, in this parish, is mentioned in a separate article. Far out at sea, on the south boundary, is a shoal called the "Horse of Willingdon."

[S. A. C. Leaden coffer, i, 160. xviii, 63. Domesday mill, v, 271. Parkers of Ratton, xiii, 54. xiv, 122. xviii, 40. Possessions of Gilbert de Aquila, xiv, 41. Picknoll, a Quaker, fined, xvi, 88. Bells, xvi, 229. Rakle family, xviii, 28, 40. Hydneye (see Hidney), xix, 27 and 28. Hydoneye, *ibid.* Ratton, xix, 32. Interments in church, and stone coffin-lid, xx, 233.]

WILMINGTON.

Domesday, *Wineltone;* a parish in the Hundred of Longbridge; Rape of Pevensey; distant six miles from Eastbourne. Post-town, Hawkhurst. Railway station, Berwick, distant about two miles. Union, Eastbourne. Population in 1811, 270; in 1861, 251. Benefice, a Vicarage, valued at £111; Patron, the Duke of Devonshire; Incumbent, Rev. George Miles Cooper, M.A., of St. John's College, Cambridge. Date of earliest Parish Register, 1538. Acreage, 1,744. *Chief Landowner*, The Duke of Devonshire.

This agreeable village, standing on a declivity of the South Downs, commands a view of those undulating hills, and from the heights above it the great Weald is seen to much advantage. The manor of Wineltone belonged in Ante-Norman times to Earl Godwin, father of Harold. After the Conquest it fell, with the Rape of Pevensey, into the hands of Robert, Earl of Moreton, who gave it to the great Benedictine Abbey of Grestein, near Honfleur, in Normandy, which had been founded by his father. The Domesday record states that the manor consisted of eight hides, with an arable of nine ploughlands, one of which was detached, in the Rape of Hastings. Alnod had held it of Earl Godwin, and besides this there appears to have been another manor of four hides, which the Norman abbot also held; but the account is much confused. There were 16 villeins, 10 bondsmen, and 9 ploughs. The total value was thirteen pounds. In the reign of William Rufus the Norman monks sent over some of their brethren to take care of their lands, and a small cell to the mother abbey was founded here, and was known as Wilmington Priory. It subsisted till 1414, when Henry V., during his wars with France, suppressed the "Alien" priories. The Rev. G. M. Cooper has brought together all the known facts connected with this small ecclesiastical establishment, in Vol. iv. of the "Sussex Archæological Collections." These are not numerous, but we learn that the principal possessions of the house were, besides the demesne at Wilmington, Frogfirle in Alfriston, property at Pevensey, and certain rights in Ashdown Forest for pannage (pig-feeding), and for wood, fuel, and church-building. Other possessions are mentioned in Waldron, Laughton, East Hothly, Hellingly, Tilton, in Selmeston, Heighton, Langney, and also the advowsons of Eastdean, Westdean, and West-Firle. There were smaller benefactions from others, as Charlston in Westdean, Milton in Arlington, Sutton-juxta-Seaford, Berwick, Exceit, Sherrington, in Selmeston, Westham, and many other neighbouring places. Edward II., seized the property of all the alien priories in this county, and Wilmington was of course included in the number. Edward III. also confiscated the priory estate, but restored it after his war with France had terminated. The subsequent history of Wilmington Priory consists of a series of squabbles between this establishment and the Crown, until its final disestablishment by Henry V. Mr. Cooper has stated all these matters with minute detail in his elaborate paper. The families of Sackville and Compton became in turn lords of the manor, and Sir Spencer Compton, the eminent statesman, was created, in 1730, Earl of Wilmington. By an heiress of the Compton family it was conveyed to Lord G. A. H. Cavendish, whose descendant, the Duke of Devonshire, is the present lord.

Of the priory there are but slight remains, consisting chiefly of an entrance gate, flanked with two towers of the 15th century; an apartment with a vaulted roof, now used as a parlour; and a crypt or vaulted cellar of considerable architectural interest. The remains of the building have long been occupied as a farm house. To the south-east of the monastery, on the escarpment of the South Downs, is a gigantic figure of a man, which was formerly laid bare to the chalk, after the manner of the "white horse" in Wiltshire. It can only be seen when the sun's rays strike the spot at a particular angle, or when there is some snow on the ground. The figure is 240 feet in length, and holds a staff in each hand parallel to the body. Some antiquaries assign these hill-side figures to a very remote antiquity, but I think there is little doubt that this was an idle freak of the monks of Wilmington, especially as an analogous giant, 180 feet high, armed with a club, is found opposite the abbey of Cerne in Dorsetshire, on the face of a chalk hill. Our figure is locally known as the "Long Man."

The church (St. Mary and St. Peter) is a small building close to the priory, and principally of late Norman and Early English work, with admixtures of later styles. "The form of the church," as Mr. Cooper observes, "is singular, the north and south transepts in no way corresponding; the former bears the appearance of a side chapel." In the church-yard is a noble yew-tree, probably older than the church itself. There are memorials for the names of Hay, Edwards, Hodsden, Hubersty, Sunderland, Ade, &c. A branch of the "ubiquitous Culpepers" resided sometime at Wilmington Priory, and their arms appear on a mutilated monument in the south chapel.

A considerable number of the bronze implements, called Celts, was found in this parish in 1861. They are preserved at Lewes Castle. In this parish is a place called Mountain Pin, corrupted from Monken-Pyn, or the Monk's Pine, probably from its having been connected with Wilmington Priory.

[S. A. C. Priory and church *(Cooper)*, iv, 37. xvii, 145. xviii, 69. The Giant on the hill, iv, 63. Grange tithes granted by Queen Elizabeth, xiii, 46. Henry Marshall, priest, his will, xiii, 49. Honey, Scrase, and Jordan families, xiii, 52—54. Roman way called *Green Street*, xiii, 55. Celts and British antiquities *(Cooper)*, xiv, 171. Endlewick bailiwick, xiv, 263. Church bells, xvi, 229. Fotur in Cade's insurrection, xviii, 27. Priory keys at Lewes, xviii, 69. Compton family, xx, 138.]

WINCHELSEA.

A parish and "Ancient Town" in the Rape of Hastings; distant three miles south-west from Rye, its Post-town and Union. It has its own Railway station on the South Eastern Railway. Population in 1811, 652; in 1861, 719. Benefice, a Rectory, valued at £278; Incumbent, Rev. James John West, M.A. Date of earliest Parish Register, 1538. Acreage, 1,120. *Seats*, The Friars, Captain Stileman; Mariteau-house, R. Buchanan Dunlop, Esq.

Few small local towns have been favoured with so competent an historian as W. Durrant Cooper, Esq., F.S.A., whose "History of Winchelsea," 1850, is replete with interest and careful record. The site of the original Winchelsea was a low flat island at the south-east extremity of the county, two miles south-south-east of the rock upon which the town of Rye now stands. It was then bare and insulated. There is no evidence

of this place having been known to the Romans, though two or
three authorities have made the assertion. To the Saxons it
was known, and from them derived its name—*Wincel*, a corner,
and *ea*, water, which well describes the original situation. A
ridiculous verse quoted by Jeake, alluding to the eastern members of the Cinque Ports, runs—

" Dovor, Sandivicus, Ry, Rum, Frig-mare-ventus,"

and the last name has been rendered " Wind-chills-sea !"—not a
phenomenon quite peculiar to this place. The Saxon Chronicle
and Domesday book are both silent, yet it is stated by Ruding
that King Edgar had a mint here in 959. A charter of Henry
III. mentions that Edward the Confessor granted this town with
Rye to the monks of Fécamp, in Normandy. Mr. Cooper
thinks he traces Winchelsea, though not actually mentioned, *eo
nomine*, in the record ; but this point requires further research.
The importance of Winchelsea at the time of the Conquest and
in succeeding reigns is shown by several facts. Here, on December 7th, 1067, the Conqueror landed, and by his sudden arrival
defeated the plans of the Saxons for shaking off the Norman
yoke. In 1138, King Henry II., having been over sea respecting State affairs, landed here. Norden states that when it was
in its most flourishing condition it contained 700 householders,
but quotes no authority. Kilburne, the Kentish historian, says
it was anciently " a pretty town and much resorted to ;" and a
M S. in the Dering collection says it had once in it 50 inns and
taverns. The towns of Winchelsea and Rye were probably
added to the Cinque Ports by the Conqueror. They were certainly brought into that ancient league before the time of
John, since in the first year of his reign (1200) both rendered
service in the navy as members of Hastings. The style of these
towns was " nobiliora membra Quinque Portuum." They are
now called " the Ancient Towns." In the early part of the
thirteenth century, Old Winchelsea was in its greatest prosperity : it had a large commerce, and its bay was the rendezvous
for the English fleet. More than once it was menaced by the
French, and a descent was expected in 1216, when King John
wrote to the Barons of Winchelsea to order them that if his
enemy Louis (son of Philip of France, an aspirant to the
monarchy of England) should land there, that rather than his
town should be burnt or greatly damaged, they should offer
him 200 marks as a ransom. In 1217, the men of Winchelsea
took an active part in the naval engagement between the Ports'
fleet, under Hubert de Burgh, against the French, under De
Courtney. During the first half of the thirteenth century,
tremendous storms took place on the English coast. Up to

the year 1250, Winchelsea had escaped tolerably well. But then some churches, several bridges, mills, banks, &c., and 300 houses were destroyed by the rising of the waters. The sea is said to have flowed twice without ebb, making a horrible noise, and at night it seemed to be " light-a-fire ;" three noble ships and smaller craft, at a place called Hucheburn, were cast away, and foundered. Four years later, the crops could not be gathered in as usual, the ground being covered with salt.

The old town had several religious establishments, consisting of the churches of St. Thomas and St. Giles, a House of Grey Friars, founded soon after the introduction of that order in 1224, and a hospital of St. Bartholomew. In the Barons' War, the Cinque Ports sided with De Montfort. King Henry reached Winchelsea on the 8th of May, 1264, and remained till the 10th, when he marched towards Lewes to meet the baronial army, and on the 14th of the same month the tremendous battle of Lewes took place. When Eleanor, countess of the successful De Montfort, made her journey with the Earl from Porchester to Dover in the following year, they passed with their suite through Winchelsea, where they spent a day and feasted the burghers. For two years after the Barons' success at Lewes the men of Winchelsea devoted their energies to piracy, in which Simon de Montfort, son of the baronial leader, took an active part. In 1266, a terrible retribution occurred. Prince Edward took the town by assault, and much bloodshed ensued. The bulk of the population, however, were spared, and commanded to forsake their piratical practices. In 1276, the King himself arrived at Winchelsea, no longer to chastise, but to arrange for the transfer of a new and more favourable site. At length, in 1287, the great inundation happened, which submerged all the marshy ground between Clivesden, near Fairlight, and Hythe. This was on February 4th, 1287, and this place was no longer habitable.

In the Old town of Winchelsea was born, in the thirteenth century, Robert of Winchelsey, the celebrated Archbishop of Canterbury.

Following Mr. Cooper, we find that after Henry's visit to the threatened town, he sent thither John Kirkeby, Bishop of Ely, and Treasurer of England, to fix upon a site for a new town. The site adopted was a hill in the adjoining parish of Icklesham, then called Iham. The spot was principally a sandstone rock, used as a rabbit-warren. The base of this rock was washed by the waters on the east and north sides. The whole land assigned for the town was 150 acres, and the work of rebuilding was proceeded with. In the quaint words of Leland, " The King set to his helpe in beginning and wauling New Winchel-

sey; and the inhabitants of Old Winchelsey tooke by a litle
and litle, and buildid at the new toune. So that wythyn the vi
or vii yere afore expressid the new toune was metely welle furnished, and dayly after for a fewe yeres encreasid." Thomas,
of Walsingham, calls the new town a Port upon a hill, very
steep on the side looking towards the sea, or where it overlooks
the road where the ships lie at anchor. He adds that on this
precipitous side there is only a rampart of earth, while on the
other sides there was a wall of stone. An accident happened
to the King who had gone down to view the progress of the
works. His horse, frightened by the rattling of a windmill,
plunged, and threw the rider; but the townsmen took him
up almost unharmed. Besides the wall, there was a castle
which commanded the inner harbour, and until 1828 there
stood a round watch-tower, called the Roundle. Of the ancient
gateways three are still standing, namely, Strand-gate, New-gate,
and Pipewell-gate, and form very picturesque objects. Besides the
two churches of St. Thomas and St. Giles within, and that of
St. Leonard without, the walls, the house of Grey-friars and the
hospital of St. Bartholomew, which had existed in the old town,
were represented in the new. There were also hospitals of St.
John and the Holy-Rood; and afterwards, in the reign of Edward
II., a house of Black-Friars was founded. Water supplies were
easily obtained from six open wells, known as Pipe well, St.
Catherine's, Strand, New, Friars', and Vale wells. The town
abounds with crypts and vaults, some of which have handsome groinings. It was among these, probably, that Grose
found what he considers 14 or 15 chapels which traditionally existed; but they were doubtless nothing more than stores
for wine and other merchandise. The town was laid out
in 39 quarters or squares of varying shapes and dimensions, the
streets enclosing them generally running at right angles. Some
of the quarters had singular names, as Cook's Garden, Ballad-
singer's Plat, Trojan's-hall, and Tinker's-garden. The exact
sites of the squares and places are given as they existed 20th
Edward I., in a record remaining among the national records,
together with the names of each proprietor in the 39 quarters,
several hundreds in number. Many of the names are those of
families still extant in East Sussex, such as Milward (le Meleward)
Coleman, Petit, Dawe, Crouche, Pollard, Broker (Brooker), Lamb,
Frost, Deryng, Pilcher, Terry, Pace, Seman, now Simmons, &c.
The name of Alard is the most conspicuous. Mr. Cooper mentions the comparative importance of the naval resources of the
town among its sister Cinque Ports in 1294, when Edmund, the
king's brother, was about to sail for Gascony. Out of the 50
ships supplied by the ports, Winchelsea furnished 13, the names

of which, with their masters and constables, are given by Mr. Cooper. As the king's foreign affairs became more urgent, the town walls were strengthened, and as the sea began to make encroachments, it was necessary to add to and strengthen the embankments. It would be impossible in this limited space to mention in detail the royal orders, charters, &c., which followed these events; Mr. Cooper, however, gives most of them. For warlike affairs the town had its governor, and for internal matters its bailiff and corporate officers. The French made frequent attacks, and in 1350 a naval engagement took place off Winchelsea, between the English fleet, commanded by King Edward III., assisted by the Black Prince, and the Spanish armament, which consisted of 10,000 men. The struggle was tremendous, and lasted many hours, ending in the discomfiture of the Spaniards, who lost 14 out of 40 ships, while the rest fled in disorder. The King and his nobles anchored in the evening at Rye and Winchelsea, and taking horse rode two leagues to the mansion where the Queen was—probably at Echingham. The Queen was overjoyed to meet her husband, her sons, and the other great lords, for she had received a full account of the conflict which her attendants had viewed from a height which commanded the scene of action. A graphic account of the battle is given by Froissart and other chroniclers. In 1359 the French attacked Winchelsea, entered it, to the number of 3,000, and partly burnt it down. The atrocities they committed are almost too horrid for recital. They entered the church during divine service, and carried off the most beautiful of the women, and took 13 ships, well freighted with wine and victuals. The English had their reprisals, for in the following year the Cinque Ports navy, with their allies, numbering 80 ships, assembled at Winchelsea, and, setting sail for France, burnt the town of Luce, in the isle of Sans, and afterwards entered the isle of Caux. In fact, throughout the reign of Edward III., Winchelsea was the scene of war and naval preparations, which proves that the town was then regarded in the same light as Portsmouth and Plymouth became in later ages. The most memorable attack of the French was in 1376, when the valiant Hamo of Offington, Abbot of Battle, with an improvised army, routed their forces. Two years later he was less successful. An attack was made, and the Abbot put to flight, after great damage had been done to the town. In later times Winchelsea became the port of embarcation for pilgrims to St. James of Compostella. The last attack of the French was in 1448 or 1449, when no great damage was done. From that date Winchelsea gradually decreased in trade and importance, and the sea having receded, Rye became the port for this part of the coast. The dissolution of the religious houses, as Mr. Cooper observes, completed the ruin of the town. Although when Queen Elizabeth in 1573 visited the place, and was met in procession by the mayor and jurats in scarlet gowns, she named it "Little London," its day was gone by, and its subsequent history is one of decline and decay. Since Elizabeth's time the sea has receded a mile or more. The merchants retired to more profitable resorts. From time to time this once important town dwindled down to the proportions of an inconsiderable village, and still so continues, though it possesses numerous remains of its ancient importance. Among the oldest is the Court-hall, or Water-bailiff's prison, which seems to have been built on an older site in the Tudor period. But by far the most interesting relic is the church of St. Thomas, now a mere fragment of the original building, yet still forming one of the most interesting and picturesque ecclesiastical edifices in the diocese. The choir and chancel, with fragments of the transepts, now only remain of this large cruciform church. The south aisle was formerly the chapel of St. Nicholas, in which was the chantry of the Alard family, while the north aisle (St. Mary) contained the Farncombe chantry. During repairs of modern date, mutilated remains of a piscina and three highly ornamented sedilia were brought to light. The architectural details of the whole building are of most interesting character. Near the south-west side of the church-yard stood, until 1790, a campanile or bell-tower. " In the aisles of the choir are five fine monuments ; three are canopied tombs of cross-legged secular warriors (probably Crusaders) one of a young man who had not been knighted, and the fifth of a lady in the dress of Edward III.'s time." (Cooper.) The monumental glory of the building is the richly canopied tomb ascribed to Gervase Alard, Admiral of the Cinque Ports, with a recumbent effigy. This magnificent memorial, which has been figured by Blore and Cooper, is without doubt the finest in Sussex, and belongs to the later part of the 13th century. In the choir is a slab, the brass of which has disappeared, for 𝕽𝖊𝖕𝖓𝖆𝖚𝖉 𝕬𝖑𝖆𝖗𝖉, 1354. There is also a small brass for a priest, without name or date. There are more modern memorials to the names of Jorden, Lambard, Godfrey, Dawes, Stuart, Dyne, Hollingberry, Denne, Newman, Maliphant, Baldwin, Stileman, Richards, Terry, Ade, &c. The church of St. Giles stood on the west side of the town, and consisted of a nave, chancel, one aisle, and a small tower with one bell. The walls were in a ruinous state in 1608, and were in course of time removed.

The monastery of Grey Friars, originally established at Old Winchelsea, had one of the best sites in the new town allotted to it. It was built on the east side of the town. It was a large building, and had a chapel dedicated to the Virgin Mary. The choir is still standing as a picturesque ruin in the grounds of Mr. Stileman. There is little history attached to this foundation, and at the Reformation it shared the common fate. After having passed through several proprietorships, it came into the possession of the late Richard Stileman, Esq., and still remains in his family. The house of Black Friars was founded by Edward II., in 1318. The prior and his brethren built a commodious house with an oratory. The establishment was dissolved in 1535, and no remains of it exist except a few walls and five large crypts in what is called Chesnut field. The site now belongs to the Dawes family. There was in the town a Preceptory dedicated to St. Anthony, but except a brass seal of the time of Henry VI., no record of the foundation exists. The hospitals of St. John, the Holy Cross, and St. Bartholomew, fell, of course, with the rest of the religious houses of the town.

The Wesleyan chapel of this town was built in 1786. Mr. Wesley once officiated in it, and in 1790 he preached his last open-air sermon beneath a large tree near the church-yard, to a numerous auditory. "I went," he says, "over that poor skeleton of ancient Winchelsea "—a felicitous expression. The tree is still standing.

Among the ancient families of Winchelsea were those of Alard, of Saxon origin, and still existing in Kent; Finch, great merchants here, and ancestors of the Earls of Winchelsea; Oxenbridge, ancestors of the family of that name at Brede Place; Londenays; Godfrey, M.P.'s for this and other towns, and founders of the chantry in St. Thomas's church; and Farncombe, originally "of that ilk" in Patcham, from whom descended Ald. Thomas Farncombe, Lord Mayor of London in 1850.

The manor of Yham, Iham, or Higham, lies in this and several adjoining parishes. It belonged to the Kentish family of Guldeford, originally of East Guldeford, near Rye, and passed through the families of Caryll, Wyndham, and Ashburnham, to the present possessor, H. Mascall Curteis, Esq. Within this manor in 1849 was built a new church. It lies on the west side of the mouth of Rye harbour, and is popularly known as Rye-harbour church. In this manor lies the Camber, meaning on this coast a haven, part of which is east of the Rother, and was doubtless part of Old Winchelsea. Winchelsea, or Camber Castle, is actually in the parish of Icklesham. It is one of the numerous coast defences built by Henry VIII. about 1539. It stands on a marshy plain, two miles north-east of the town. Many of the main walls, built of brick, cased with squared stones, are still standing. The plan is a large circular tower or keep, surrounded by smaller ones connected by short curtain walls.

There is but little of interest now in these crumbling remains, though the castle must have been considered in its time an important fortress, having a governor and a suitable staff of officers. At length it was dismantled, and the sea having deserted the site, it has gradually fallen into the ruinous condition in which we see it at this day. The decay of Camber haven has gone *pari passu* with that of the castle. Norden tells us, however, that so lately as 1624, the old men remembered having seen 400 tall ships of all nations anchored in the Camber, "where now sheep and cattle feed."

At the north-west corner of the town lie the small Parish and Liberty of St. Leonard. It belongs to the port of Hastings. The church formerly contained an image of St. Leonard holding a vane in his hand, to which the women of Winchelsea used to resort, and turned the vane in the direction "towards such coasts as they desired the wind to serve for the speedy return of their friends or husbands." The last rector instituted was in 1484, and after that the building fell to decay.

The town is governed by a mayor and jurats, and enjoys all Cinque-Port privileges. The common seal is very elaborate, and belongs to the reign of Edward I. Winchelsea sent two members to Parliament from 42nd Edward III., till 1832, and by the Boundary Act of that year it was thrown into the electoral district of Rye.

This article is an imperfect abridgment of Mr. Cooper's work, and that gentleman has supplemented his valuable volume by a paper in Vol. viii. of the "Sussex Collections," chiefly relating to corporation and maritime affairs, with an elaborate account of the great East Sussex family of Oxenbridge.

[S. A. C. Town seal, i, 21. Samuel Gott, v, 96. Royal visits, William I., v, 282. John, i, 135. Henry III., i, 137. Edward I., i, 138. Edward III., iv, 113. vi, 53. Elizabeth, v, 190. vi, 63. Alards of, viii, 154, 212. Notices of town *(Cooper)* after 15th century, viii, 201. Oxenbridges of, viii, 213. Westons of, *ibid*, 233. Royal mint, ix, 369. Smugglers, x, 93. Tradesmen's tokens, x, 209. Atlas maritimus, xi, 181. Pilgrims to Compostella, xii, 27. Charters of Cinque ports, xii, 159. Image of St. Leonard, xiii, 70. The town fortified, xiii, 115. Refugees, xiii, 180. Strowings at weddings, xiii, 231. Champayne, &c., at Agincourt, xv, 125. Bell, xvi, 229. Abbot Offington's defence against the French, xvii, 46. Pipewellgate, xviii, 61. Venetian ships' charts, xx, 225.]

WISBOROUGH GREEN.

Vulgo, *Green;* a parish in the Hundreds of Bury, Rotherbridge, and West Easwrith ; Rape of Arundel; distant three miles west from Billingshurst Railway station, and six miles east of Petworth. Post-town,

Horsham. Union, Petworth. Population in 1811, 1,421; in 1861, 1,682. Benefice, a Vicarage, with the Curacy of Loxwood, valued at £440; Patron, the Bishop of London; Incumbent, Rev. M. W. Gregory, M.A., of Wadham College, Oxford. Date of earliest Parish Register, 1560. Acreage, 8,484.

This Wealden parish lies upon a clayey soil, and a considerable portion of it is occupied by woodland and waste. It is divided into the several districts of Palingham, Drungewick, Loxwood, Hasfold, &c. Palingham was anciently one of the tithings of West Easwrith, and it extends into Petworth and Kirdford. The manor was held of the Honour of Arundel, and was annexed to those of Shillinglee and Hibernow, with the parks of Medhone and Bignor. It passed by a forced exchange between Henry VIII. and the Earl of Arundel, for the site and lands of Michelham in Pevensey Rape. Afterwards it returned to the Earls of Arundel, and in 1790 came to Sir Edward Onslow, of Drungewick, whose descendants sold it to the late Earl of Egremont. In the reign of Elizabeth the river Arun was made navigable to Palingham, for the purpose of bringing down timber from the Weald, and a large iron furnace was established here. The canal connecting the Arun with the Wey at Shalford, in Surrey, runs through this parish. It was opened for general traffic in 1816. Drungewick, including the manor of Bradbridge in Slynfold, originally belonged to the Abbey of Seez, in Normandy, and their cell at Arundel. In 1256 it was transferred to Climping, Bishop of Chichester, who established there a *staurum*, or store of cattle, which consisted of 250 oxen, 100 cows, 10 bulls, 3,100 sheep, 120 she-goats, 10 he-goats, and 10 horses, and this stock was kept up from 1256 to 1560. Thus the episcopal *ménage* must have provided well for its kitchen. Of course there were a grange and a chapel, but of these we know but little. The bishops, however, frequently visited their property here, and held ordinations in the chapel. At a later date the knightly family of Onslow, from whom sprang Sir Richard Onslow, Bart., Speaker of the House of Commons, 1708, and his brother, Foot Onslow, Esq., became respectively progenitors of the Barons and Earls of Onslow. Loxwood, formerly Lokyswood, was parcel of the manor of Bury, and was held of the Honour of Arundel by the family of Threele for several generations. The families of King and Onslow were afterwards proprietors. The chapel of Loxwood was built by license of Bishop Praty, in 1414. About the year 1540, three maiden sisters are said to have repaired and endowed the chapel. The building, which consists of nave and chancel, was repaired by an injunction from the Bishop about the year 1828. Hasfold, or Haresfold, belonged, *temp.* Edward I., to Richard, Earl of Arundel, and in the reign of Henry VI. to Mary, wife of Sir Rowland Lenthal. Subsequent owners have been Apsley, Threele, Cowper, Osborne, and Peachey, of Lord Selsey's family.

The benefice is a prebendal rectory, with the impropriate tithes and the advowson of the vicarage. The church (St. Peter and St. Paul) and the village stand upon a hill. The former consists of a nave with two aisles, and a tower with a lofty shingled spire. There are memorials for the names of Threele, Dalgress, Mille, King, Yates, Laker, &c., and three bells.

[S. A. C. Ironworks, ii, 220. xviii, 15. Philip at Aldre, xi, 105. Church, xii, 91. Loxwood chapel, xii, 91. Cooks and Baldwins, xii, 92. Threeles, xiii, 89. King family, xvi, 50. Church bells, xvi, 207, 229. River Arun, xvi, 256. Drungewick, xvii, 248. Palling (Palingham), xx, 27. Knights-hospitallers had lands here, xx, 27.]

WISTON.

Domesday, *Wistoneston*; vulgo, *Wissun;* a parish in the Hundred of Steyning; Rape of Bramber; distant 1½ mile north-west from Steyning. Post-town, Hurst-Pierpoint. Railway station, Steyning. Union, Thakeham. Population in 1811, 289; in 1861, 311. Benefice, a Rectory, valued at £430; Patron, Rev. John Goring, M.A.; Incumbent, Rev. C. W. A. Napier, M.A., of Christchurch, Oxford. Date of earliest Parish Register, 1638. Acreage, 2,865. *Chief Landowner*, the Rev. John Goring, of Wiston House.

This parish, formerly called Wistoneston, is a very picturesque one. At the time of the Domesday Survey, William de Braose let it to Ralph; Azor had previously held it of Earl Godwin. It had 10 hides, and there were 10 villagers and 24 bondmen. A church, 5 ministri, and a wood, producing pannage for 30 hogs, are also mentioned. It would seem that the manor underwent a considerable depreciation in consequence of the Conquest, as before that event it was valued at £12, but was afterwards reduced to £4. Soon after the Conquest the manor was in the possession of a family called De Wistoneston, whose ancestor Mr. Cartwright considers to have been the Ralph of Domesday. About the end of the reign of Henry III. Alicia, sole heiress of William de Wistoneston, married Adam de Bavent. His son was father of another Adam who was at the celebrated siege of Carlaverock. His son Roger was summoned to Parliament in 1313. The ultimate heiress married William de Braose. From the period of the extinction of that family the Shirleys, descendants of the very ancient family of Shirley, of Eatington in Warwickshire, held the estate for many generations down to the time of Thomas Shirley, M.D., who was born in 1634. This family, which sent off branches to West Grinstead, Preston, Chiddingly, &c., was remarkable for historical characters, especially the "Three Brothers," Sir Anthony, Sir Robert, and Sir Thomas, whose exploits during the time of Elizabeth form an interesting episode in our local history, and indeed in our national annals. Their lives have been written in several forms, particularly in a monograph, by E. P. Shirley, Esq., M.A., M.P., etc., of Eatington; in a small separate publication; in the " History of Western Sussex ;" and in my own " Sussex Worthies." The Sussex branch of the family changed the orthography of the name to Sherley. The " Brothers " were sons of Sir Thomas Shirley, Knight. It would be beyond the scope of this work to enter into the romance of their proceedings, except in a simple outline :—

Thomas Sherley was born in 1564, and Anthony in 1565; Robert was some years younger. In 1584 Anthony went with his father into the Low Countries, and was at the battle of Zutphen in 1586. Next we find him in Brittany, as one of Essex's Colonels against the Spaniards. His gallant service won for him the order of St. Michael from Henry IV. of France, but he thereby incurred the displeasure of Queen Elizabeth, and returned to England a poor man. He was in the expedition against the Portuguese, on the African coast, and assisted in the capture of Jamaica in 1596. Soon after this he accompanied his patron Essex to Ireland. He was again in the wars in Spain, returning to England in 1597. The following year he was in the singular mission to Persia, his object being partly religious and partly commercial. He wished the King of Persia to join the Christian powers against their common enemy the Turks, as well as to promote trading relations between the East and West. Many were his perils on the way home. He was treated with great indignity by the Turks, and on the route fell into the hands of a horde of Arabs, who robbed him, but at the end of his journey the king received him as a dignified ambassador. He taught the king the English mode of casting artillery, so that ere long he had five hundred pieces of brass cannon in his army. For this service Shah Abbas created him a Mirza, or Prince. He returned to Europe in 1599, and visited the courts of Russia, Germany, Bohemia, and finally that of Rome, where he declared himself a Roman Catholic ; but from some cause or other he left the Pontifical Court in disgrace, and retired to Venice. In subsequent days he underwent many other perils and adventures, but with little success in any enterprise. He was the means of introducing through Count Gondomar, the Spanish ambassador, our English artillery into the Peninsular army, for which he again incurred the jealousy and displeasure of Government. He died in abject poverty, bordering sometimes on starvation.

So much for the vicissitudes of this gallant knight, who had been in all the wars of his time, and had been sent diplomatically to nearly every court in Europe. His brother, Sir Robert, at the early age of 18, was with Anthony in the wars in the Netherlands, and afterwards at Venice, in favour of Don

Cesare d'Este, against the Pope　　In 1598 he shared in the enterprises and honours of his brother in Persia, and remained there after his brother had returned to Europe.　Shirley went by way of Poland, and was entertained at Cracow by Sigismund III.　He married Teresia, daughter of Ismael Khan, a Circassian lady.　He received the honour of knighthood from the Emperor Rodolph, and was created a Count-palatine of the Empire.　He next proceeded to Rome with a suite of eighteen persons, eight of whom were Persians.　He wore Persian costume, distinguishing his turban with a crucifix.　Pope Paul V. received him with great state.　From Rome he proceeded to Spain, and at the Spanish Court was joined by his wife, the Princess Teresia.　In 1611 he came with his eastern bride to Wiston.　His father, Sir Thomas Shirley, had for some time been in disfavour at Court, and to meet his liabilities to the Crown had sold the ancient family properties of West Chiltington, Erringham, and other estates, reserving only Wiston, which he had settled on his wife.　After a long series of further troubles he died in 1612, and was buried in the church of Wiston, where there is a black marble tablet surmounted by figures of himself and his wife.　To return to Sir Robert Shirley, he had, with his Asiatic wife, a favourable reception at the court of King James.　In 1613 he again set out for Persia, taking India in his route, and paying a visit to the great Mogul.　Then, after many wanderings, we find him successively at Goa, at Lisbon, and at Madrid.　In 1622 he again visited Rome, and there it was that Vandyke painted the fine portraits of Sir Robert and the Princess Teresia, now preserved in the Petworth collection.　After many struggles he returned to Persia, and there died at the age of about 50.　The Princess Teresia ended her strange, eventful history by becoming a nun.

The life of Sir Thomas Shirley, the eldest of this remarkable triad, was less romantic than that of his two brothers.　He received his military education under his father in the Netherlands.　Subsequently he served in Ireland, where he was knighted in 1589.　He next became a courtier, and contracted a clandestine marriage with Frances, daughter of Sir Thomas Vavasour, and for this offence Queen Elizabeth put him into prison for 14 weeks.　At a later period he purchased two ships as privateers against the Spaniards, and captured four vessels, besides making an attack upon several villages.　In 1602 he set sail from Leghorn, and was taken captive by the Turks, who carried him in chains to Constantinople.　After two years' captivity, he wandered about in Italy and Germany, and arrived in England in 1606 in a state of poverty.　After many other misfortunes, including imprisonment in the Tower, overwhelmed with debt, and broken in spirit, he sold Wiston and retired to the Isle of Wight, where he died.

Another distinguished member of this family was Dr. Thomas Sherley, physician to Charles II., born in 1638.　He was a medical writer of some repute.　He underwent, like so many of his ancestors, great trials and misfortunes.　With him ended the ancient and honourable line of Sherley of Wiston—" a family not needing hyperboles."　To the family of Sherley succeeded that of Fagg, Baronets, who held Wiston for several generations, and in 1743, Elizabeth, the ultimate heiress, carried

it by marriage to Admiral Sir Charles Matthews Goring, grandfather of the Rev. John Goring, the present lord of Wiston.
Wiston House, standing in its own deer park, was built, *temp.*
Elizabeth, by Sir Thomas Sherley, and was a grand specimen of the style of that period, and though it has been considerably reduced in size it is still among the principal of Sussex mansions.
The hall, with a very fine timber roof, is a cube of 40 feet, and the dining-room, of the date of 1576, retains much oak carving.
Cartwright gives a series of inscriptions in this room, containing a pedigree of the family of Brewse, or Braose, for many generations.

The church (St. Michael) stands near the mansion, and consists of a nave, south aisle, and chancel. Some parts of the building are in the Decorated style, but there are traces of a much earlier date. At the east end of the aisle is a sepulchral chapel. Here is a fine brass to Sir 𝔍𝔬𝔥𝔫 𝔡𝔢 𝔅𝔯𝔞𝔬𝔰𝔢, 1426, " powdered with the words " Jesu," " mercy," with a Latin inscription, which may be thus rendered :—

> " Be witness, Christ! this stone is placed,
> Not that my body may be graced,
> But that my soul remembered be ;
> Then, passer-by, whate'er thy time—
> Old age, or youth, or manhood's prime—
> Devoutly offer prayers for me. . . ."

Under an arch in this chapel is a stone effigy of a child, which is supposed to be for the son of this Sir John, on whose premature death the estate passed to the Sherleys. The next monument in succession is that of Sir William Sherley, who is represented in armour, standing on a rock, with a dove sculptured above, and figures of his two wives (1551). Against the wall are the effigies of a knight in armour and his lady in a kneeling posture. This monument is to Sir Thomas Sherley, who lived in wedlock 53 years and had 12 children, of whom nine lived to be married. There are memorials to the names of Beard, Luxford, Goring, Fagg, Morley, Shenton, Norcross, Hart, &c.

[S. A. C. Roman buildings, ii, 313. Descent of manor (*Lower*), v, 1.
Pedigree of Wiston, v, 3. Pedigree of Braose, v, 5. xv, 17. Sherley family, notices of, v, 7. xiv, 232. xvi, 253. xvii, 96. xviii, 130. xix, 63. Fagg family, v, 26. xx, 61. Goring family, v, 197. Wiston arms, vi, 80. Tithes to Sele Priory, x, 115. De Braose epitaph, x, 205. Church, xii, 111. A Bavent at Agincourt, xv, 136. Bennet, a Quaker, fined, xvi, 68. Church bell, xvi, 229. Broadbourne stream, xvi, 253. Elringtons of, xix, 64.]

WITHYHAM (or Withiam).

Vulgo, *Widdy-hám;* a parish in the Hundred of Hartfield; Rape of Pevensey ; distant eight miles south-east from East Grinstead and 6½ south-west from Tunbridge Wells; Post-town, Tunbridge Wells. It has a Railway station on the line between East Grinstead and Tunbridge Wells   Union, East Grinstead. Population in 1811, 1,155 ; in 1861, 1,597. Benefice a Rectory, valued at £700; Incumbent, Thomas Frederick Rudston Read, M.A., of University College, Oxford. Date of earliest Parish Register, 1663. Acreage, 8,086.

This extensive parish on the Forest ridge consists of arable, pasture, and woodland, and contains within its limits part of the Forest of Ashdown. It partakes of the undulating and picturesque character of the neighbourhood. The large wood, known as the Five Hundred Acres, south of the village, is remarkably pleasing. The village chiefly consists of scattered houses, and a small tributary of the Medway passes through the parish. Withyham does not appear under any name approaching it in Domesday. A considerable portion of the parish, however, must have been included in the manor of Brochest, a corrupt spelling of the Anglo-Saxon *boc-hyrst,* the beech wood, or perhaps a covert for bucks (now Buckhurst). In the twelfth century this manor was the estate of the great family of De Dene, by whose heiress, Ela, it passed to Jordain de Sackville (see Bayham), and thus it descended through an illustrious line of Sackvilles to the late Duke of Dorset, whose co-heiress, Elizabeth, conveyed it by marriage, in 1813, to the late George John West, Earl De la Warr, who assumed the name of Sackville before West by royal sign-manual in 1843, and in his lordship's son it now vests. Another manor is Monkencourt, of which, in 45th Edward III., Gilbert Atte-Hall was lord. At a later period the Priory of Mortein in Normandy possessed it; but having been deprived of it in the fifteenth century, during our wars with France, it was given to Sir John Pelham, who granted it for a term of years to the New Priory of Warbleton, which he had removed from Hastings, in consequence of the old establishment having been destroyed by the sea. The manor of Bullockstowne belonged to Bayham Abbey. Henry VIII., on the dissolution of that house, granted it to Wolsey, who gave it to his college at Oxford. In the reign of Elizabeth it passed to the noble family of Neville. The manor of Hendall likewise extends into the parish. Gilderedge, an ancient house and estate, gave name to a family of considerable antiquity, who subsequently had their chief residence at Eastbourne, and gave name to the manor of Eastbourne-Gildridge. Gilderegg was originally a vicarage, annexed to Buxted, and had a chapel, but for the convenience of the inhabitants so remote from the parish church, Archbishop Peckham, in 1292, permitted it to be united with Withyham. No traces of this chapel exist. The family of Walwyn resided here, in gentle position, in the sixteenth century, as did also that of Baker (originally for many generations at Battle, and subsequently at Mayfield), who were proprietors of Gilderedge and of Ducking House in Withyham.

The chief mansion and estate in the parish, however, was Buckhurst, where, *temp.* King John, Sir Geoffrey de Sackville was lord, holding it of the Honour of the Eagle (Pevensey). In 21st Edward I. his descendant obtained a charter of free-warren. This great family, originally lords of Sauqueville, near Dieppe in Normandy, came to England at the Conquest, and the records of the race are so generally known as to require little mention here. It produced many eminent personages, the most note-worthy being Thomas Sackville, who was born at Buckhurst in 1536. After a brilliant career as scholar, poet, and statesman, he was created by Queen Elizabeth, Baron of Buckhurst, appointed Lord High Treasurer, and on the accession of James I. he was continued in office, and created Earl of Dorset. He died while sitting at the council-table at Whitehall in 1608, and the obsequies having been performed in Westminster Abbey, his body was brought to Withyham for interment among his ancestors. For a memoir, see " Worthies of Sussex," p. 187. His son Robert, second Earl of Dorset, inherited much of his father's learning, but died shortly after his coming to the title, and was buried at Withyham, beneath a splendid monument. His best monument, however, is " Sackvil College for the Poor," at East Grinstead, founded by his will. (See East Grinstead.) Another descendant was Charles, the sixth Earl of Dorset, K.G., the well-known courtier and man of taste, in literature and art. He went to Holland as a volunteer at the commencement of the Dutch war, in 1665, and the night before his departure, composed the well-known song, " To all you Ladies now on Land." He died in 1706, and also found sepulture at Withyham. (See " Worthies," *ut supra*.) The present Lord Buckhurst (late the Hon. and Rev. Reginald Sackville-West) in his " Parochial History of Withyham," has given an account of the descent of this very ancient line, and of their monuments in the church. Buckhurst House, once a very lordly abode, measuring 260 feet by 200, with a capacious quadrangle, hall, and chapel, and partly surrounded by a moat, having been deserted for the still more majestic residence of Knole, near Sevenoaks, was permitted to fall to ruin, and part of its materials were employed for the erection of Sackville College. The solitary survivor of so much magnificence is the gateway tower. The family, however, did not wholly neglect their ancient abode, but built in the park, on the site of a keeper's lodge, a competent mansion, which was finished by the first Duke of Dorset, and leased to his son, Lord George Germain, afterwards Viscount Sackville. Still later various members of the family, and the late Earl and Countess De la Warr, have made it their occasional residence. It was formerly called Stoneland, but now Buckhurst Park. The grounds are beautifully laid out.

The church (St. Michael) was partially burnt down by lightning 16th June, 1663. The lightning is stated to have entered " at the steeple, melted the bells, and proceeded to the chancel, where it tore the monuments of the Dorset family to pieces." There is some exaggeration here, though the damage done to the fabric alone was estimated at £1,800. Among the memorials destroyed were a brass for 𝕳𝖚𝖒𝖋𝖗𝖞 𝕾𝖆𝖐𝖊𝖇𝖞𝖑𝖊, Esq., 1488, and a monument representing kneeling figures of Richard Sackevile, Esq., Isabel, his wife, with their four sons and six daughters—date 1524. The reparations of the church are said to have been completed about 1680. The building, as it now stands, consists of chancel, nave, with south aisle, and porch, a large chapel on the north side of the chancel, and a massive embattled west tower, with six bells. In the chancel are three sedilia and a piscina. There are features of Early English, Decorated, and Perpendicular. The north aisle was destroyed by the fire. The Buckhurst Chapel is Late Perpendicular. The principal existing monuments are—1, an altar tomb with recumbent effigies of an infant, and standing figures of the father and mother. In relief on the sides of the monument are figures of other children. This is for Richard, Earl of Dorset, 1677, and Frances, his Countess, and their family—2. a monument by Nollekens, for John Frederick, Duke of Dorset, 1799—3. another, by Flaxman, for George John Frederick, last Duke of Dorset, killed by a fall from his horse, just after his majority, in 1815—and 4. a monument, by Chantrey, for Arabella Diana, Duchess of Dorset, 1825. There are also memorials for Charles, Earl of Dorset, K.G., 1705, and for the names of Pennington, Gray, and Alfrey. The last two are iron slabs, 1582 and 1610. The Sackville vault contains numerous coffins inscribed with the names of members of this illustrious race, including that of the great Lord Treasurer.

[S.A.C. Iron-works at, ii, 220. iii, 243. Gilderedge arms, vi, 80. Chapel, xx, 231. Monkencourt manor, xiii, 155. Ashdown Forest, xiv, 35. King Edward II., xiv, 45. Church struck by lightning, xiv, 153. Buckhurst, Sackville family, xiv, 216. xvi, 271. xix, 162. Church bells, xvi, 229. Hammes of, their Oratory, xvii, 249. Bad roads, xix, 162. Comptons, xx, 137.]

EAST WITTERING.

A parish in the Hundred of Manhood; Rape of Chichester; distant 7¾ miles south-west of Chichester, its Post-town and Railway station. Union, West Hampnett. Population in 1811, 214; in 1861, 223. Benefice, a Rectory, valued at £190; Patron, the Bishop of London; Incumbent, Rev. John Cooke, M.A., of Corpus Christi College, Cambridge. Date of earliest Parish Register, 1658. Acreage, 1,260.

This small parish is of very irregular outline. Its southern boundary is Bracklesham Bay, which (owing to the flatness of the country near Wittering, and the nature of the soil) has eaten away a considerable portion of the parish. In fact, the greater part of what was East Wittering is now submerged in the Bay. In compensation of this damage there are fine sands for the pedestrian, and an admirable field of observation for the geologist, as some fossils of great rarity are to be found here. Soon after the Conquest, a family, who were then owners, took their name from this village. In 11th Henry VIII., Sir John Dawtrey was in possession, and his family were succeeded by that of Ernley. There are three prebendal manors either partly or wholly in this parish, viz.: Bracklesham, East Thorney, and Somerley. A farm of 100 acres, called Stubcroft, formerly supported a chantry in St. Michael's chapel at Chichester. There was also a chapel which was annexed to the vicarage in 1518, by Bishop Sherburne.

The church (St. John) is a small building, with Norman features, and consists of a nave and chancel, with a belfry of wood, and one bell.

[S. A. C. Roman road at Bracklesham, xi, 127. Church, xii, 81. Bell, xvi, 229. Bracklesham, Wm. de, xix, 26.]

WEST WITTERING.

Domesday, *Westringes;* a parish in the Hundred of Manhood; Rape of Chichester; distant eight miles from Chichester, its Post-town and Railway station. Union, West Hampnett. Population in 1811, 483; in 1861, 616. Benefice, a Vicarage, valued at £180; Patron, the Bishop of Chichester; Incumbent, Rev. Charles Gaunt, M.A. Date of earliest Parish Register, 1622. Acreage, 3,615.

This parish, which is bounded on the west by Chichester harbour, consists chiefly of productive arable land. The village lies in the south-west part of the parish. The country is flat, but commands very picturesque marine views. Westringes is mentioned in Domesday as being in the obsolete hundred of the same name. It is said to belong to Earl Roger (de Montgomeri), but it is stated in another part of the record that the Bishop held it. Probably there were two manors belonging to these respective proprietors; there is no doubt that West Wittering was an episcopal manor from the time of Edilwalch, King of Sussex, who granted it in 673 to the see of Selsey. Cakeham manor-house, the occasional residence of the Bishops from the 13th to the 16th century, was a spacious mansion with its hall, chapel, and other considerable apartments. It was a favourite abode of Bishop Sherburne, who erected a lofty hexagonal brick tower, early in the 16th century. The family of Atte Fenne or Fenner, of Crawley, held considerable lands in the parish during the Tudor period.

Daniel Whitby, D.D., held the prebend of Wittering in 1660; he was a controversial writer against the Roman Catholics, and died in 1726. The prebendal estate was long held by the trustees of Oliver Whitby, Esq., founder of the free-school at Chichester.

According to Pope Nicholas' taxation, 1290, the vicarage was valued at 20 marks, and in the Nonæ-roll, 1341, at the same sum, though it is declared that so much arable land had been absorbed by the sea that the value was lessened 7 marks. Much grass had also been devoured by the rabbits of the Bishop—no new complaint! The church (St. Peter and St. Paul) is thus described by Horsfield. " It exhibits portions of architecture of the 13th and 14th centuries. The tower stands detached from the nave, and on the north side. Three stalls of oak, with *misereres* ornamented with rosettes, are preserved in the chancel, as also a monument of Caen stone, partly mural and partly projecting. The bas-reliefs represent the Resurrection, and the Annunciation of the Virgin Mary. It has no inscription upon it, but the arms of Ernley appropriate it to William Ernley, Esq., who was resident at Cakeham, 28th Henry VIII., and died in 1545. John Ryman, who is said to have built the great tower near the Cathedral, or contributed towards it by appropriating the stones intended for his castle at Appledram, had an estate in this parish." There are three bells.

[S. A. C. Domesday watermill, v, 272. De Boys of, xi, 81. Cakehamston battery, xi, 150. St. Clere, xii, 26. xv, 122. Church, xii, 80. Saxon invasion, xv, 165. Holden of, xvi, 50. Bells, xvi, 229. Symmes of, xix, 95.]

WHITESMITH.

A hamlet near the junction of the three parishes of Chiddingly, East Hothly, and Laughton.

WIVELSFIELD.

Vulgo, *Willsful;* a parish in the Hundred of Street, and Rape of
Lewes ; distant four miles south-east from Cuckfield; Post-town,
Hurst-Pierpoint. Railway station, Haywards Heath, distant about
2½ miles. Union, Chailey. Population in 1811, 468 ; in 1861, 709.
Benefice, a Perpetual Curacy, valued at £130; Patroness, Miss Jane
Tanner; Incumbent, Rev. John Smith Foster, M.A., of Pembroke
College, Oxford. Date of earliest Parish Register, 1559. Acreage,
3,103. *Chief Landowners,* the Tanner family. *Seat,* The Ferns
(anciently Fanners), Lt.-Col. J. Holden-Rose.

The " field " or " clearing " of Wivel (a Saxon personal
name, still existing as a surname*), is pleasantly situated near
the Forest-ridge, in a picturesque district. The manor of Otehall
gave name to the family of De Otehall, in the 14th century or
earlier. At subsequent dates the owners were Kentish, Atteze,
Michelborne, and Godman. The Godman heiress conveyed it by
marriage to a junior branch of the Shirley family of Wiston,
about the beginning of the 18th century. Of this family was
Lieut.-General William Shirley, Governor of Massachusets Bay
in 1741, and afterwards of the Bahama Islands. His son, Major-
General Thomas Shirley, was created Baronet of Otehall in 1786,
but with his son, Sir William Warden Shirley, who died in 1815,
the title became extinct. Late in the last century it was purchased by William Tanner, Esq., in whose descendants it still
vests. A considerable part of the old mansion built in 1600 by
Thomas Godman still remains. In the windows there were
formerly the arms of its successive possessors. During the
Shirley proprietorship, Selina, Countess of Huntingdon, foundress of the well-known religious " Connexion," resided here
for some time, and the Rev. William Romaine, the celebrated
divine, frequently preached in the house.

Temp. John and Henry III., the Bardolfs had the manor of
Wivelsfield, and *temp.* Henry VI. it belonged to Thomas Beaufort.
Franklands has successively passed in and since the Tudor period
to Mascall, Bray, Pope, Luxford, Woodyer, Warden, Sergison,
and Tanner. More House, which has the remains of a moat,
gave name to the family of At-More or Moore. One of this
family was at Agincourt, and another was Capt. Thomas More,
an eminent loyalist during Cromwell's government. From the
Mores the estate descended through the Middletons and Fullers
to the Tanners. Fanners, an ancient house, has been modernized, and is now called " The Ferns."

The picturesque little church of St. John the Baptist, was
anciently a chapel of Ditchling. " From its peculiar position,

* Wivels*den* is also the name of a farm at no great distance.

it has been sadly patched and neglected, but still retains interesting features. It comprises nave, with south aisle and chancel, south porch, and a square tower with shingled cap at the west end of the aisle. The chancel contains a piscina, which was used as a cupboard! and what appears like a sepulchral arch in the north wall. In the south chancel (or chantry) are a trefoil-headed piscina and aumbry. The walls of the building seem to be Norman and Transition Norman; the north door early Norman, and the south door Perpendicular. At least the lower part of the tower is Decorated, with Perpendicular windows higher up. The church is so mutilated that its character is difficult to decipher; the piers and arches between the nave and aisle, as also the chancel, exhibit some traces of the Early English style." Thus writes Mr. Hussey in 1852, but in 1869, 70, the building underwent judicious restoration and repair, the chancel was lengthened, and a new north aisle added; and now the building may claim to rank among the most picturesque of small churches in East Sussex. There are memorials to the names of Richbell, More, Middleton, Holey, &c. The bells are five in number, one of which is dedicated to St. Augustine. Popular tradition calls this William Rufus's bell!

In this parish stands the Hayward's Heath County Lunatic Asylum. The buildings are very extensive, and occupy a commanding site. The interior arrangements are calculated to promote as far as possible the comfort of the unhappy inmates. There is a chapel, the incumbent of which is the Rev. Thomas Crallan, M.A. The resident master and physician of the establishment is S. W. D. Williams, Esq., M.D. The asylum was erected in 1857-9, and subsequent additions have been made, the cost from first to last having been nearly £70,000. The number of patients is (alas!) upwards of 500.

[S. A. C. Parish register, iv, 259. Church to Lewes Priory, xiii, 244. Ote-Hall (*Turner*) xiii, 247. Families of Godman, Shirley, Tanner, *ibid*. Moore at Agincourt, xv, 136. Cleavewater watershed, xv, 160. Bells, xvi, 230. Podstream, xvi, 251. Cade's insurrection, xviii, 29. De Otehall, xix, 62. Chapelry to Ditchling, xix, 62. Moorhouse, xix, 69. Moores of, xx, 46. Countess of Huntingdon, and Rev. W. Romaine, xix, 69, 70. Spoons found at, xix, 70. Moores of, xx, 46.]

WOODMANCOTE.

Domesday, *Odemancote;* a parish in the Hundred of Tipnoake; Rape of Bramber; distant about two miles south-east from Henfield station. Post-town, Hurst-Pierpoint. Union, Steyning. Population in 1811, 247; in 1861, 331. Benefice, a Rectory, valued at £485. Patron, the Lord Chancellor; Incumbent, Rev. Richard Cox Hales, M.A., of Magdalen Hall, Oxford. Date of earliest Parish Register, 1582. Acreage, 2,236. *Chief Landowners*, J. L. W. Dennett, Esq., Sir Percy Burrell, Rev. John Goring, and Arthur Smith, Esq.

Woodmancote is doubtless neither more nor less than the " Cote, or abode, of the Woodman," who before and long since the Conquest, would have ample scope for his axe in this well-wooded locality. In the time of Edward the Confessor, the Countess Goda held the manor, and Domesday describes it as afterwards held of William de Braose by William Fitzralph. Its subsequent history is very obscure. Early in the seventeenth century it was possessed by the family of West, originally from Berkshire. In 1691, Walter West, the representative, sold it to Thomas Dennett, Esq., of an ancient family in this parish, with whose descendant it still remains, Woodmancote place being the seat of J. L. W. Dennett, Esq. Mr. Cartwright considers the name of Dennett, or Dennatt, an inversion of the ancient At Dene, which existed at Woodmancote in 1341. De la Dene, a still older form of the name, is found there in 1298. The rectory house, with its attached glebe, is superior to most in the district.

The church consists of nave and chancel, and has an east window of *temp*. Henry VI. (Cartwright.); also another window containing two shields of the fourteenth century : 1, Chequy, Arg. and Az. on a canton Gules, a cross moline Or; 2, Azure, six mullets, 3, 2 and 1, Or. The latter is the coat of Graundyn, a family connected in 1330 with Wickham, in Steyning. The font is Norman, and square. There are memorials for the names of Dennett, Blithman, and Shore. A church is mentioned here in Domesday.

In 1555, Thomas Harland, carpenter, and John Oswald, husbandman, both of this village, were burnt at Lewes for Protestantism.

[S. A. C. Amusing disputes between the Rector and Squire, 1679, iv, 281. Sackville gift, xiv, 216. Bells, xvi, 230.]

WOOLAVINGTON.

Vulgo, *Lavinton;* a parish in the Hundred of Rotherbridge; Rape of Arundel; distant 4½ miles south-west from Petworth. Post-towns, Petworth and Midhurst. Union, Midhurst. Population in 1811, 201 ; in 1861, 488. Benefice, a Rectory, united with Graffham, valued at £277 ; Patron, the Right Rev. S. Wilberforce, D.D., Bishop of Winchester. Date of earliest Parish Register, 1668. Acreage, 2,530.

Dallaway says the etymology is obvious, from the Anglo-

Saxon WUL-LAVING-TON, a superior pasture for sheep, with the adjunct of *lavant* a source of water ; *sed dubito*. The parish consists of several *disjecta membra*, which Dallaway distinguishes as Old Lavington, Dangstone, Midhurst division, and Farnhurst division. It is curious how such a distribution of a parish could have occurred. Domesday informs us that Loventone was held of Earl Godwin, by another Godwin, and by Ivo of Earl Roger de Montgomeri. The aggregate was nine hides, the value being £8. There were 10 villeins, and 10 bordars. The manor was afterwards the possession of the great families of D'Albini and Fitz-Alan, and is now considered as part of the Honour of Pet-worth. There was a *staurum* of cattle and sheep belonging to the lord, with a park. At later dates, it belonged to the Lumleys and Gartons, and passed in succession to the Ormes and Sargents. In 31st Elizabeth, the Gartons built a large mansion with towers at the angles. The existing residence on a smaller scale, though still elegant and commodious, was completed in 1794, by John Sargent, Esq. The arms of the successive proprietors are displayed on the front. It is delightfully situated, and has fine grounds, gardens, and a park, with most extensive and agreeable views. Mr. A. E. Knox in his work, " Game-birds," &c., speaks of the " dark hanging woods of Lavington," which clothe the steep South Down hills, and of the accompanying clumps of beech and juniper, and of the picturesque valley of the Rother, and the circumjacent " heathery commons, evergreen woods, brown copses, and cultivated fields."

The church (St. Peter), though of early date, is small and unimportant, and contains little of interest. In the western division of the parish a new church has recently been erected, and is dedicated to St. Mary Magdalen. In the churchyard is the grave of the late Richard Cobden, the eminent politician and statist.

In connection with this parish must be mentioned the names of two possessors of the estate, the late John Sargent, Esq., author of the " Mine," and other poems, and Dr. Wilberforce, long Bishop of Oxford, and now of Winchester.

[S. A. C. Domesday watermills, v, 272. Visit of King John, i, 136. Church, xii, 103. West Lavington church, xii, 103. Gartons of, xiv, 115. Foxhunt, xv, 81. Bell, xvi, 215, 230. Betsworth, xvii, 238. Bohun's lands in, xx, 14.]

WOODMAN'S GREEN.

. A small village in the parish of Linch.

WOOLBEDING.

Domesday, *Welbedlinge;* a parish in the Hundred of Easebourne; Rape of Chichester; distant one mile north-west from Midhurst, its Post-town and Railway station. Union, Midhurst. Population in 1811, 238; in 1861, 338. Benefice a Rectory, valued at £250; Patroness, Hon. Mrs. George Ponsonby; Incumbent, Rev. Francis Bourdillon, M.A., of Emmanuel College, Cambridge. Date of earliest Parish Register, 1581. Acreage, 2,253. *Seat,* Woolbeding House, Hon. Mrs. Ponsonby.

Pleasantly seated on the Western Rother, which is here remarkably sinuous. In Domesday, Odo is said to hold the manor of the King. "A carucate of land in Ulebeding was held by Roger de Ulebeding, by the serjeanty of carrying the gonfanon or square banner before the King at Sparkeforde, in Hampshire." Woolbeding was long possessed by the Earls of Arundel. In 16, Edward I., John de Arundel of Woolbeding, held of the king in chief, by the similar service of carrying the ensign or "foot colours" (*vexillum peditum*) through Mid-Sussex should it happen for the king to pass that way in time of war. (Blount). Later it was held by the family of Mill, Barts. The ancient manor-house for some time the residence of Charlotte Smith, the poetess, was much enlarged and modernized in the last generation by Lord Robert Spencer. It now belongs to the Hon. George and Mrs. Ponsonby.

The church, dedicated to Allhallows, has been much altered and repaired at different periods. The tower and chancel were rebuilt in the last century. Sir Henry Mill, the eighth Baronet, when rector, placed in the chancel window some singular painted glass removed from Mottisfont Priory, in Hampshire. The font is of great antiquity and bell-shaped. One of the three bells is inscribed to St. Margaret. There are memorials for Lord and Lady Robert Spencer, and for various members of the family of Mill, &c.

[S. A. C. Domesday water-mill, v, 272. Church, xii, 81. Bells, xvi, 230. River Rother, xvi, 259.]

WORTH.

A parish in the Hundred of Buttinghill; Rape of Lewes; distant about seven miles south-west from East Grinstead. Post-town, Crawley. There are three Railway stations in the parish, namely, Three Bridges (near which is the village), Rowfant, and Grange Road. Union, East Grinstead. Population in 1811, 1,539; in 1861, 2,988. Benefice, a Rectory, valued at £608; Patron, G. Banks, Esq.; Incumbent, Rev.

G. Wilson Banks, M.A., of Corpus Christi College, Cambridge. Date of earliest Parish Register, 1600. Acreage, 13,400.

This large and interesting parish derives its name from the Anglo-Saxon, and signifies land, farm, street, hall, &c. (Bosworth.) It is a border parish adjoining Surrey on the north. The soil is generally poor and unproductive, yet abounding with birch and other woods, and is full of picturesque undulations. The ancient Forest of Worth, formerly one of the principal woodland districts of the county, extends into several adjacent parishes, and from a survey made in 1583, it contained upwards of 5,000 acres. Tilgate Forest, so famous for its fossil remains, was formerly considered parcel of the Forest of Worth. The parish contains many private residences of importance, but the village is a straggling and inconsiderable place. There are several seats which have belonged to gentle families connected with the county. Crabbet Park was the abode of the Smiths, descended from the Smiths, of Shelford, co. Warwick; and afterwards of the Blunts. Gibsaven was long the estate of a branch of the Thorpes, of Newdigate in Surrey; and Huntland was the property of the Edwards family from 1550, and they held it for more than 150 years. Rowfant, an old stone mansion, after having passed through several families, came into the hands of the Rev. George M. Bethune, LL.D., rector of Worth. Fenn Place, a house of considerable antiquity gave name to the family of Atte Fenne, or Fenner, and came to the Bysshes and Shelleys.

The impulse given to the erection and enlargement of considerable houses in this part of the Weald by the opening of the London and Brighton Railway has conduced to make Worth, with its bracing air and picturesque scenery, a very favourite settling place for gentle families, who have either purchased or leased residences within the last few years. Among these may be mentioned—Rowfant, Sir Curtis M. Lampson, Bart.; Tilgate manor, John Nix, Esq.; Huntsland, J. Russell Reeves, Esq.; Crabbet Park, George Smith, Esq.; Worth Lodge, George Latham, Esq.; The Grange, George Lilley, Esq.; Worth Park, Joseph M. Montefiore, Esq.; Oakfield, Rev. William Henry Hoare; The Grove, Edwin Martin, Esq.; Copthorne, William Fennings, Esq.; The Rectory, Rev. George Wilson Banks, &c. These are all situated in beautiful grounds, mostly with the adjuncts of excellent forest scenery, and pieces of water. There are also several hamlets, including Turner's Hill, Three Bridges, and Copthorne.

Worth is not mentioned in Domesday, and the history of its manor, or rather several manors, is difficult to narrate. For some time after the Conquest the greater portion of what is now the parish was for the most part an unreclaimed forest, including the two districts afterwards known as Worth Forest and Tilgate Forest, which were here and there interspersed with glades and parks, and everywhere well suited for the purposes of the chase. It was in early times part of the great territory of the Earls of Warenne, and in 7th Edward I., John, Earl of Warenne, Lord of Lewes Rape, being questioned by the justices itinerant as to his claim for this and other lands, stated that he and his ancestors had alwas been faithful to the Kings of England; that they had lost their French possessions for their adherence to King John against the King of France, and moreover as his name was *Warenne* he claimed the right of free-*warren* over his English manors, so that he may be said to have held them by *pun*-hold! (See Bosham.) John, the last Earl, died possessed in 1347, and the chief lordship seems to have passed like the barony of Lewes to the noble families of Fitz-Alan and Bergavenny. The principal manor lost its name of Worth, and became known as Heighleigh. After several changes we find it associated with the names of Sherley, Caryll, Covert, Middleton, Fowle, Newnham, and others.

Several families of distinction, besides those already mentioned, have been associated with Worth. Some of the members of these families were iron-masters of considerable importance, especially the Gales, who sprang from a blacksmith at Sevenoaks, and carried on large iron-works in this part of the county. Interesting memoirs of the family have been edited by R. W. Blencowe, Esq., in the "Sussex Collections." In 1698, Leonard Gale, Esq., purchased Crabbet, which had been held by the Norman family of Playz, and afterwards by that of Moore, of Odiham, in Hampshire, and by them by a re-marriage of the widow of the last of their race to the Smiths, of Shelford. The three co-heiresses married Blunt, Clitherowe, and Humphrey. The Whitfelds, of Rowfant, originally from Alston-Moor, in Cumberland, and afterwards of Wadhurst and Worth, were great iron-masters in the sixteenth century.

The church is one of the most remarkable in England, both for the peculiarity of its form and its great antiquity. It stands on elevated ground in a large church-yard, which is entered from the north-west by an ancient lich gate. The building is cruciform, and consists of nave, north and south transepts, and a chancel with a circular apse. Over the north transept is a wooden bell-chamber with a dwarf shingled spire, which rests on four large wooden uprights within, which present a singular appearance. Mr. W. S. Walford, who has given a critical account of the building in "Sussex Collections," admits its Saxon origin, and this is generally thought to be the case. The edifice has been so much patched with insertions of different dates, and the addition of buttresses of extreme ugliness, that no brief description of it would be intelligible. The most remarkable portion of it is the chancel, which is approached by a semi-circular arch of extremely rude work. The font is curious and ancient, and really consists of two fonts placed one upon the other, both being probably of the 13th century. The arms of De Warenne are found in one of the windows. There are monuments and inscriptions for the families of Gale, Smith, Bysshe (of Fenne Place) Shelley, Smith, Whitfeld, Goodwin, Bethune, Towers, and many others.*

[S.A.C. Ironworks, ii, 220. iii, 242. xiii, 128, 129. xviii, 15, 16. xix, 86. The church, viii, 235 (Walford). Gales of Crabbet, xii, 52. xiii, 307. Families of Playz and Moore, xii, 52. xv, 16. Michell, xiii, 130. Blunt, xiii, 311. Bells, xvi, 230. Tributary of the Medway, xvi, 270. Oaks for engines in the Tower, xvii, 116. Whitfeld, xviii, 16. xix, 86. Edwards of Huntland, &c., xix, 88.]

WORTHING.

A hamlet and chapelry of Broadwater, in the Hundred of Brightford and Rape of Bramber, 11 miles west from Brighton, and 61 from London. A recent writer designates it "a pleasant broad-streeted watering-place, 'discovered' some time before Brighton, but not destined to attain the dimensions of that marine London." Although a Domesday manor, and a recognized hamlet of Broadwater from early times, its condition was that of an inconsiderable fishing village, and so continued until the last century. The first "fashionable" impulse was given to it by a visit, shortly before 1800, of the Princess Amelia. Since then it has been the temporary abode of the Princess Charlotte, Queen Caroline, and Queen Adelaide. Its situation on the English Channel, with its pleasant long range of sands, extending four miles to the east and nine to the west, and forming what is called Worthing Point, with the known salubrity of its climate, have rendered the town a favourite resort. The site is, for the most part, flat and monotonous; but as it is sheltered on the north by a delightful strip of South Downs, and is within the reach of much good scenery and many objects of interest, few places on the South Coast are more attractive than Worthing, especially for those who seek a quiet sea-side resort. From the new iron

---

* Since this article was written, great alterations have been made in the building ; whether they are improvements I am unable to say.

pier there is a commanding sea view, extending from the Isle of Wight to Beachy Head. The town is furnished with every appliance for the lounger and the invalid, but for these matters the local "guides" must be consulted. The town is fast increasing in size, and a recent extension of it is called West Worthing. The manor is described in Domesday under the name of *Ordinges*. Seven allodial tenants had held it under Earl Godwin as 11 hides, but, after the Conquest, Robert held it of William de Braose, lord of Bramber. There were six villeins, nine bondmen, and a serf. In the time of the Confessor and afterwards it was rated at 100s. Another manor called Wordinges was held in Saxon times by Leiven and afterwards by Robert. Although it was assessed at only half a hide and valued at 12s., it had a villein and five bondmen. Ralph held half a hide worth 5s. In later times the manor of Worthing was granted to the Priory of Easebourne, and at the Dissolution passed among the possessions of that house to Henry Fitzwilliam, Earl of Southampton, who, in 34th Henry VIII., bequeathed it with his other estates to his half-brother, Sir Anthony Browne, and it passed, like Cowdray, to the Viscounts Montague and their heritrix Elizabeth, wife of William S. Poyntz, Esq. In 1219 William Berneus granted to Dyonisia his mother, for her life, a hide of land at Wyrddingg, at the rent of a horse-load of salt, which shows the existence of salt-pans here. The sea encroached much on the coast, and the hamlet now contains little more than 300 acres. The principal proprietors of it were successively Wade, Booker, Luther, the Earl of Warwick, Commerell, Ogle, Barrington (Bishop of Durham), and Colberg. A chapel existed at Worthing from early times, but of its site nothing is remembered. In 1409 the Bishop of Chichester granted permission for masses, &c., to be performed in this chapel, saving the rights of the mother church of Broadwater. The existing episcopalian places of worship are the chapel of ease, built in 1812, (value £150), and held by the Rev. William Read, M.A., of St. John's College, Cambridge; Christ Church, built in 1843, with a benefice, worth £300, is held by the Rev. F. Cruse, B.A., of St. Edmond Hall, Oxford; and a new church has been quite recently erected at the east end of the town. The patronage of these is vested in the Rector of Broadwater. A new Roman-Catholic church and a nunnery have been founded here; and there are chapels for several dissenting denominations. Roman urns, pottery, and coins of Dioclesian and Constantine have been discovered within the present century.

[S. A. C. Roman coins, i, 26. Smugglers, x, 93. Tortington Priory lands, xi, 110. Churches, xii, 105. Bells, xvi, 232. Shirley's lands in, xix, 68.]

YAPTON (anciently Yabeton).

A parish in the Hundred of Avisford; Rape of Arundel; distant five miles south-west from Arundel, its Post-town. Union, West Hampnett. Population in 1811, 512; in 1861, 589. Benefice, a vicarage united with Walberton. Date of earliest Parish Register, 1548. Acreage, 1,690.

This is a level and almost entirely arable parish, yielding excellent cereal crops. Its manorial history is of no interest. It belonged to the Honour of Arundel, until it was sold in 1571 by Henry Fitz-Alan, to John Edmundes, Esq., whose descendant, Charity in the fifth generation conveyed it in marriage to Lawrence Elliott, of Busbridge in Surrey, and died in 1716, S.P. In 1759 it passed by purchase to George Thomas, Esq., afterwards created a Baronet. His daughter Margery married Arthur Freeman, Esq., whose son Inigo Freeman-Thomas, afterwards of Ratton in Willingdon, inherited. The old mansion house of the family of Edmundes was partly rebuilt and added to in 1800. BALSHAM, the Bilesham of Domesday, in the southern part of the parish, was originally a hamlet and chapelry: the chapel now forms a double cottage for labourers, and has an ancient door and three buttresses. The manor, with that of Yapton and the advowson of the church, was given by Richard, Earl of Arundel, to the foundation of Arundel College. The priories of Shulbrede and Tortington also had good lands here.

The church has a nave and aisles, "of the style prevalent in the reign of Henry III., with a low tower at the west end. The chancel has been rebuilt." (Dallaway.) The font is ancient and curious. Of the four bells one is ancient with the inscription "Ave Maria." The mortuary inscriptions refer to the families of Barnard, Roe, Thomas, Sydserfe, White, Page, &c.—Yapton probably signifies the *tún* or settlement of Eappa, a recognized Saxon personal name.

[S. A. C. Tortington Priory, xi, 110. xiii, 46. Edmondes family, xii, 92. Forster family, xii, 102, 104. Church, xii, 103. xviii, 102. Bilsham chapel, xii, 104. Thomas, Sir George, xiv, 122. Bonville, lands, xv, 59. Nash family, xvi, 50. Bells, xvi, 230. Bronze celts and metal found, xviii, 195. Kempe had lands in, xix, 119.]

APPENDIX.

L.

Laughton Place. *Blaauw.* VII, 64.
Lewinna (St.) of Seaford. *Blaauw.* I, 46.
Lewes Priory, early history. *Blaauw.* II, 7. III, 185.
Landing of William the Conqueror. *Lower.* II, 53.
Lindfield Church, mural painting. *Miss Slater.* II, 129.
Lindfield, parochial documents. *Lower.* XIX, 36.
Lewes rape, subsidy roll, 1296. *Blaauw.* II, 288.
Lewes Priory, relics. *Spurrell.* VI, 253.
Lewes Priory, lantern. *Figg.* VII, 151.
Lewes rape, subsidy roll. *W. S. Ellis.* IX, 71.
Lewes Levels Commission. *Sir H. Ellis.* X, 95.
Lewknor, pedigree. *W. D. Cooper.* III, 89.
Lewes ("Old Lewes"). *Figg.* XIII, 1.
Lewes Castle museum. *Lower* and *Chapman.* XVIII, 60.
Lyminster, dragon-slayer. *Evershed.* XVIII, 180.

M.

Mayfield Palace. *Hoare.* II, 221.
Midhurst free chapel. *Sir H. Ellis.* III. 23.
Michelham Priory. *G. M. Cooper.* VI, 129.
Monasteries of Boxgrove, Shulbred, Bayham, Dureford, and Lewes, their suppression. *Blaauw.* VII, 217.
Miller, family of Burghill and Winkinghurst. *Lower.* IX, 83.
Maresfield and Dudeney chapels. *Turner.* IX, 41.
Maresfield. *Turner.* XIV, 138.
Midhurst. *W. D. Cooper.* XX, 1.
Midhurst, St. Ann's Hill. *Turner.* XX. 175.

N.

Newhaven Church. *Lower.* IX, 89.
Newhaven, Roman remains. *Spurrell.* V, 262.
Nonæ return of Sussex, 1340. *Blaauw.* I, 58.
Newton family. *Noyes.* IX, 312.
Ninfield. *Sharpe.* XVII, 57.
Newhaven, kitchen-midden. *Lower.* XVIII, 165.
Northeye and Hydneye, lost towns. *Turner.* XIX, 1.
Nineveh (old house at Arundel). *Turner.* XX, 184.

O.

Oliver Cromwell's pocket Bible. *Lower.* II, 78.
Otteham Abbey. *G. M. Cooper.* V, 155.
Oxenbridge family. *W. D. Cooper.* XII, 208.
Old Speech and Manners in Sussex. *Lower.* XIII, 209.
Otehall. *Turner.* XIX, 61.

P.

Paxhill, &c. *Blencowe.* XI, 1.
Parish Registers, extracts. *Blencowe.* IV, 243.

T.

U.

W.

———

₊ Under the head of " Notes and Queries" from Vol. VII. to Vol XX. are several minor articles which could not be included in this Index.

LIST OF SUBSCRIBERS.

A.

Adams, G. E., Esq., College of Arms, London

Ade, Geo., Esq., 23, Upper Westbourne Terrace, Hyde Park

Albery, Edwin, Esq., Midhurst, Sussex

Aldridge, Major J. St. Leonard's, Horsham

Anchor, Miss, Wickham, near Chichester

Arnold, Rev. F. H., L.L.B., Ashling, Chichester

Ashby, Mr. George, Eastdean, Eastbourne

Ashby, Mr William P., Willards, Eastdean, near Eastbourne

Aylwin, Mr. Jas., Offham, Lewes

B.

Bacon, G. P., Esq., Lewes

Baker, J. B. Esq., Buxted, Sussex

Banks, Rev. G. W., Worth Rectory, Crawley

Barchard, F., Esq., Little Horsted

Barttelot, Brian B., Esq., Bramblehurst, East Grinstead

Barttelot, George, Esq., Stopham House, Petworth, 2 copies

Barttelot, Colonel W. B., Stopham House, Pulborough

Beard, Thomas Edwd., Esq., High Street, Lewes

Beattie, A., Esq., Summerhill, Chislehurst, Kent

Beck, W. C., Esq., Ore, Hastings

Benge, J., Esq., Royal Masonic Institute, Wood Green, W.

Bennett, T. J., Esq., Chichester

Berry, Brothers, Wine Merchants, Lewes

Biddulph, A. W., Esq., Burton Park, Petworth

Blaauw, W. H., Esq., Beechland, Uckfield

Blagden, J. A., Esq., Petworth

Blencowe, R. W., Esq., The Hook, Chailey, Lewes

Bloxam, Rev. J. R., D.D., Beeding Priory, Hurst-Pierpoint

Blyth, H., Esq., Seaford

Boileau, Sir F. G. M., Bart., Ketteringham Park, Wymondham, Norfolk

Borrer, Linfield, Esq., Henfield, Sussex

Borrer, Rev. C. H., Hurst-Pierpoint Rectory

Bowles, Rev. F. A., Singleton, Chichester

Boxall, W. P., Esq., Belle Vue Hall, Parknowle, Cowfold

Boys, J., Esq., 59, Grand Parade, Brighton

Bramwell, Mrs., 3, Cambridge Road, Brighton

Brown, Alex., Esq., Cottesmore Hall, Oakham

Brown, Rev. Felix, Stopham Rectory, Pulborough

Brown, Richard, Esq., Allington, near Lewes

Brown, The Rev. H., M.A., Pevensey, Eastbourne

Browning, Arthur H., Esq., Lewes

Bruce, J. Collingwood, LL.D., Newcastle-on-Tyne, Northumberland

Burgess, Mr. A., New Inn, Seaford

Burke, Sir Bernard, Ulster King of Arms Castle, Dublin

Burrows, J. C., Esq., 62, Old Steyne, Brighton

Burton, A., Esq., St. Leonards-on-Sea

Butler, G. S., Esq., F.S.A., Rye, Sussex

C.

Campkin, H., Esq., F.S.A., Reform Club, London

Carnegie, The Hon. J. J., Fair Oak, Petersfield

Carpenter, Hen., Esq., 36A, Moorgate Street, City

Cavendish, Lord Edward, Devonshire House, Piccadilly

Catt, A., Esq., School Hill, Lewes

Cattell, Miss Helen, 42, Buckingham Road, Brighton

Caton, R. R., Esq., F.S.A., Union Club, Trafalgar Square

Chadwick, H. S., Esq., Brighton

Cheesman, Mr. James, Wadhurst, Sussex

Chichester, The Very Rev. the Dean of, Deanery, Chichester

Clayton, J. Esq., F.S A., Newcastle-on-Tyne

Colchester, Lord, Kidbrooke

Combe, B. H., Esq., F.S.A., Oaklands, Westfield, Sussex

Coppard, Thos., Esq., Lanehurst Lodge, Albourne
Cooper, Mrs., 44, Sussex Square, Brighton
Cooper, C. A., Esq., 44, Sussex Square, Brighton
Cooper, J., Esq., F.S.A., Lewes
Cooper, W. D., Esq, 81, Guilford Street, London
Cooper, Miss, 44, Sussex Square, Brighton
Cosens, F. W., Esq., Water Lane, London
Cosens, R., Esq., Barnham, Arundel
Courthope, Geo. C., Esq., Whiligh, Hurst Green
Cripps, R. M., Esq., Westmeston, Hurst-Pierpoint
Croix, Rev. W. de St., M.A., Glynde, Lewes
Currey, E. C., Esq., Lewes
Cox, Mr. Alderman, 15, London Road, Brighton
Crofts, Mrs., Malling House, Lewes
Crosskey, R., Esq., Lewes
Cubitt, Geo., Esq., 17, Princess Gate, W.
Curteis, Major E. B., Leasam, Rye
Curteis, H. M., Esq., Windmill Hill, Hailsham

D.

Daintrey, A., Esq., Petworth
Daniell, Rev. Geo. Fred., Aldingbourne Vicarage
Daniell, Rev. G. W., Aldingbourne Vicarage
Day, W. A., Esq., 16, St. Swithin's Lane, London
Davies, Colonel F. J., Danehurst, Uckfield
Dearden, Captain, Nymans, near Crawley
Derby, C. H., Esq., B.A., 53, Thistle Grove, West Brompton
Devonshire, Duke of. K.G., Devonshire House, Piccadilly (2 copies)
Diamond, Dr. H. W., Twickenham House, Middlesex
Dilke, William, Esq., Chichester
Dodson, J. G., M.P., Esq., Coneyboro', Lewes
Drakford, Rev. D. J., Brookside, Crawley
Dunn, J. R., Esq., Stone House, Warbleton, Sussex
Duke, Sir James, Bart., Laughton Lodge

E.

Edwards, T. Dyer, Esq., 5, Hyde Park Gate, Kensington
Ellis, W. S., Esq., Hydecroft, Crawley
Ellman, Rev. E. B., Berwick Rectory
Elsted, W. P., Esq., 13, Snargate Street, Dover
Elwood, Mrs. Colonel, Clayton Priory
Evans Thos., Esq., Lyminster, near Arundel
Evans, R., Esq., Dean's Place, Alfriston
Eyton, J. W. K., Esq., F.S.A., 46, Portsdown Road, Maida Hill, London

F.

Farnes, William, Esq., Lewes
Featherstonehaugh, Lady, Uppark
Ferguson, R., Esq., Morton, Carlisle
Ferrey, B., Esq., F.S.A., 2, Inverness Terrace, Kensington
Fisher, R., Esq., Hill Top, Midhurst
Fisk, Rev. H. J., Hastings
Fletcher, J. C., Esq., Dale Park, Arundel
Flint, Frederick, Esq., 41, High Street, Lewes
Flower, J. W., Esq., Park Hill, Croydon
Foley, Rev. J., B.D., Vicar of Wadhurst, Sussex
Foster, Rev. J. S., Vicarage, Wivelsfield
Foster, Rev. R., Burpham, Arundel
Fowler, J. A., Esq., 1, Westminster Chambers, London, S.W.
Franklyn, W. N., Esq., Warnham Lodge, Horsham
Freund, Mrs., 20, Goldsmith Road, Brighton

G.

Gage, Lord Viscount, Firle
Gatty, C. H., Esq., Felbridge Park, near East Grinstead
Gilbert, the Hon. Mrs., Eastbourne
Godman, Joseph Esq., Sladeland, Petworth
Goodwin, W. H., Esq., Solicitor, Hastings
Godlee, B., Esq., Leighside, Lewes
Goldsmith, Mr H., East street, Lewes
Gorring, Mrs., Seaford, Lewes
Gorringe, P., Esq., Pebsham, Bexhill
Gosden, J., Esq., Eastbourne
Grantham, William, Esq., Sussex Place, South Norwood, Surrey
Griffiths, Rev. J., LL.D., The College, Brighton
Guy, Miss, Hamsey Place, Lewes
Guy, Miss, 20, Goldsmid Road, Brighton

H.

Hales, Rev. R. Cox, M.A., Rectory, Woodmancote, Hurst-Pierpoint
Halliwell, Rev. J., Walpole Villa, Brighton
Hancock, H J. B., Esq., Duke's Hill, Bagshot
Harcourt Colonel, Buxted Park
Harland, J. C., Esq., 4, Lansdown Place, Lewes
Harland, H., Esq., M.D., Mayfield
Harris, J., Esq., Lesney Park, Belvedere, Kent
Harris, W., Esq., 4, Bedford Row, Worthing
Harrison, George, Esq., Brighton
Harwood, H., Esq., Amberley
Harwood, Major, The Elms, Ringmer (2)
Haviland, G. E., Esq., Warbleton, Hurst-Green
Hawkins, E., Esq., London

Haydon, Rev. W., Midhurst

Hazlitt, William, Esq., Registrar, Court of Bankruptcy, London

Hepburn, Col. H. P., 18, Charles street, Berkeley Square

Hill, Charles, Esq., Rockhurst, West Hothly, East Grinstead

Hillman, J., Esq., Stoneham, Lewes

Hillman, R., Esq., Lewes

Hogg, R., Esq., 99, St. George's Road, Pimlico, S.W.

Holland, Rev. T. A., Poynings Rectory, Hurst-Pierpoint

Hollingdale, W., Esq., North Mundham, Chichester

Holmes, E. C., Esq., Brookfields, Arundel

Honywood, Thomas, Esq., Horsham, Sussex

Hope, A. J. Beresford, Esq., M.P., 1, Connaught Terrace, London

Horton, George, Esq., 23, Oxford Terrace, Edgware Road, London

Howell, James, Esq., Brighton

Hubbard, W. E., Esq., Leonardslee, Horsham

Huckstepp, Mr. Joseph, Sheldwick, near Faversham

Hughes, Edward, Esq., 31, Earl street, Maidstone

Husey-Hunt, B., Esq., Lewes

Hussey, Edward, Esq., Scotney Castle, Lamberhurst

I.

Ingram, James, Esq., Ades, Chailey

J.

Jackson, Miss, 11, Pavilion Parade, Brighton

Jeffries, Mrs., 18, Undercliff, St. Leonards-on-Sea

Jenkyn, Rev. D. W., Rye

Johnson, E. W., Esq., The Pallant, Chichester (2 copies)

Jones, Charles G., Gravelye, Lindfield

Jones, H., Esq., Lewes

K.

King, Captain, R.N., Chithurst House, Petersfield

Kirkland, W., Esq., 16, Hyde Gardens, Eastbourne

L.

Lane, H. C., Esq., Middleton, Hurst-Pierpoint

Laurie, P. N., Esq., Paxhill Park, Lindfield

Laurie, R., Esq., Clarenceux King of Arms, College of Arms

Leconfield, Lord, Coates, Petworth

Lee, Rev. F. G., D.C.L., F.S.A., 6, Lambeth Terrace, S.E.

Lemon, Mark, Esq., Crawley

Lewis, Captain, The High Beech, Hollington, Hastings

Lewis, John, Esq., Lewes

Lennox, Lord H. G., 13, Albert Terrace, Knightsbridge

La Trobe, C. J., Esq., Clapham House, Lewes

Lewes Library Society

Lintott, W., Esq., Hill, Slinfold

Lucas, J. C., Esq., F.S.A., Lewes

Lucas, Francis, Esq., Hitchin

Luxford, Rev. G. C., Higham House, Hurstgreen

Lower, W. de W. H., Esq., Angers, France

Lower, Nynian H., Esq., Henbury, near Bristol

Lower, E. H., Esq., 7, Westminster Chambers, Victoria Street, London

Lower, W. Anthony, Seaford, Lewes

Lower, Miss, Henbury

M.

Mackinlay, D., Esq., Pollokshields, Glasgow (2 copies)

Madgwick, Wm., Esq., Alciston Court

Major, Mr. George, Seaford

Malden, H. C., Esq., Windlesham House, Brighton

Manby, Lt.-Col., The Greys, Eastbourne

Marris, Miss, 51, Sydney Street, Brompton

Martin, E., Esq., The Grove, Worth, Crawley

Mann, T., Esq., jun., Tysmanns House, Horsham

Mauleverer, Miss, The Hall, Armagh, Ireland

Mayer, J., Esq., F.S.A., Liverpool

Medland, Rev. Thos., Steyning Vicarage

Meek, Geo., Esq., Brantridge, Balcombe

Milner, Rev. J., Beech Hurst, Haywards Heath

Mitchell, Rev. Henry, F. S A., Bosham

Mitchell, W. W., Esq., Arundel

Molesworth, George, Esq., North Street, Chichester

Mond, Mr. M., Lewes

Montefiore, J. M., Esq., Worth Park, Crawley

Morris, Mr. A., Post Office, Lewes

Mortimer, J., Esq., Pippingford Park, Uckfield

Munn, Rev. J. R., Ashburnham Vicarage, Battle

N.

Napper, H. F., Esq., Laker's Lodge, Wisborough Green, Horsham

Nevill, The Lady Dorothy, Dangstein, Petersfield

Newington, A. T., Esq., The Highlands, Ticehurst

Nichols, J. G., Esq., F.S.A., Holmwood Park, Dorking

Norman, G., Esq., Cooksbridge Brewery, Lewes

Norman, H., Esq., Cooksbridge

O.

Olliver, Thomas S., Esq., Courtlands, near Worthing

Orme, Rev. J. B., Angmering Rectory, Arundel

Otter, The Venerable Archdeacon, Cowfold, Sussex

Ouvry, F., Esq., F.S.A., 12, Queen Anne Street, London

P.

Page, Mr. Thos., Bookseller, Brighton

Paine, Cornelius, Esq., F.S.A., Oak Hill, Surbiton, Surrey

Paine, Lieut.-Col., Patcham Place, Brighton

Paine, W. D., Esq., 22, Mincing Lane, London

Paris, George de, Esq., 13, Denmark Terrace, Brighton

Parsons, J. L., Esq., Lewes

Peat, Rev. J., M.A., Vicarage, East Grinstead

Peckover, W., Esq., Wisbeach

Pelham, Lord, M.P., Stanmer (4 copies)

Penley, Montague, Esq., 3, Montpelier Crescent, Brighton

Peskett, W., Esq., M.D., Ditchling

Phillips, J. Pavin, Esq., F.S.A., 16, High Street, Haverfordwest

Phillips, J., Esq., Hastings

Powell, C., Esq., Speldhurst, Tunbridge Wells

Powell, Rev. R., South Stoke Rectory, Arundel

Pratt, D., Esq., Cuckfield, Sussex.

Prime, A., Esq., Warbleton, Arundel

Pullinger, Mr., Keere Street, Lewes

Purseglove, Mrs., Seaford

Putron, Rev. P. de, Rodmill Rectory

R.

Rees, Mrs., Trowbridge, Wiltshire (4 copies)

Renshaw, Thomas C., Esq., Sandrocks, Haywards Heath

Reynard, E. H., Esq., Sunderlandwick, Driffield

Rhodes, A., Esq., North Hall, Plumpton

Robertson, P. F., Esq., M.P., Halton, Hastings

Rogers, Rev. Henry, Stone House, Petworth

Rook, James, Esq., Domons, Northiam

Rolland, Monsieur P., Angers, France

Roswell, Mr. E. H. W., Market Street, Lewes

Russell, Rev. J. C., Albion Street, Lewes

S.

Sadler, E. A., Esq., Bepton, Midhurst

Sandford, Mr. William T., Storrington

Sanders, Jas., Esq., Hailsham

Saxby, Mr. T, Firle, near Lewes

Sclater, J. H., Esq., Newick Park, Uckfield

Scott, M. D., Esq., Hove Brighton

Selmes, J. Esq. ,jun., Northiam

Shaw, Captain W. E., 16th Lancers, Windsor Castle

Sheffield, Lord, Sheffield Park

Shiffner, Rev. Sir George, Bart., Coombe, Lewes

Shirley, E. P., Esq., Eatington Park, Stratford-on-Avon

Simmons, H., Esq., The Crouch, Seaford

Skinner, R. V., Esq., Winchelsea, Sussex

Smith, George, Esq., Paddockhurst, Crawley

Smith, J. A.., Esq., M.P., 37, Chester square, London (2 copies)

Smith, Rev. H., M.A., F.S.A., Firle Vicarage

Smith, J. M., Esq., Lewes

Smith, Mr. W. J., North Street, Brighton (6 copies)

Somerville, Capt. P., R.N., Gipsy Hill, Upper Norwood

Sperling, Rev. J. H., Westbourne Rectory, Chichester

Stenning, J. C., Esq., Halsford, East Grinstead

T.

Thacker, Mr. W., Poynings, Hurst-Pierpoint

Thomas, Rev. S. W., Southease Rectory, Lewes

Tompsett, James, Esq., Deans, Piddinghoe

Tompsett, Mr. J., Seaford

Tompkins, Rev. R. F., Arundel

Trevor, Rev. G. A., 48, Queen's Gardens, Lancaster Gate, London

Turner, Captain W. W., Chyngton, Sussex

Daniel-Tyssen, J. R., Esq., Brighton

Daniel-Tyssen, Amherst, Esq., Hare Buildings, Lincoln's-Inn

U.

Upton, H., Esq., Meadow Lodge, Petworth

V.

Verrall, J. F., Esq., The Mulberries, Denmark Hill, London

W.

Wace, Rev. R.H., Wadhurst, Hurst Green

Waldegrave, Countess of, Hastings

Warren, R. A., Esq., Preston Place, Arundel

Ward, S. N., Esq., Havelock Lodge, Brighton

Warter, Rev. J. W., B.D., West Tarring Vicarage, Worthing

Watts, Jas., Esq., Battle

Waterman, W., Esq., Piddinghoe

Weeden, W. D., Esq., Hall Court, Rype

Weekes, Geo., Esq., Carey Hall, Hurst-Pierpoint
Weir, J., Esq., F.L.S., 6, Haddo Villas, Blackheath
Webster, F., Esq., Battle
West, F.G., Esq., Horham Hall, Thaxted, Essex
Whitfeld, Thos., Esq., Hamsey House
Whiting, Mr. W., High Street, Uckfield
Wetherell, Capt. R., Tunbridge Wells
Winchester, The Rt. Rev. the Bishop of, Woolavington
Winkley, W., Esq., F.S.A., Harrow-on-the-Hill
Wisden, Captain, Broadwater

Woodhams, T. K., Esq., Seaford
Wood, S. N., Esq., Havelock Lodge, Brighton
Woods, Rev. G. H., Shopwyke House, Chichester
Worcester, The Bishop of, Hartlebury, Kidderminster
Worge, J. A., Esq., Ore, Hastings
Wyatt, H., Esq., LL.D., Cissbury, Worthing

Y.

Young, W. B., Esq., Wellington Square, Hastings

This List will be kept open for a short time for the convenience of persons desirous to subscribe at the original price, Twenty-five Shillings.

GEO. P. BACON, LEWES, SUSSEX.